Volume 3
DAILY STRENGTH 3
DEVOTIONS FOR BIBLE BELIEVING STUDY

Douglas D. Stauffer
Andrew B. Ray

Copyright © 2016
McCowen Mills Publishers & LTB Publications
All rights reserved
Printed in the United States of America
Text Design: Rick Quatro (Carmen Publishing Inc., Hilton, NY)
Jacket Design: Tom Rood (Intelligent Design, Hamburg, NY)

ISBN 978-1-942452-37-9

No part of this book may be reproduced or transmitted in any form or by any means—electronic or mechanical, including photocopying, recording, or by any information storage and retrieval system—without permission in writing from the publisher. However, it is the desire of the authors to disseminate this information so permission is granted to copy several pages for study so long as the copy includes credit.

Scripture quotations from the King James Bible need no permission to quote, print, preach, or teach. For clarity, all scripture is in italics with reference and any emphasis in bold print. Any deviation from the King James Bible is not intentional.

For more information, contact:

McCowen Mills Publishers
Dr. Douglas D. Stauffer, President
6612 Hickory Way Lane
Knoxville, TN 37918
(866)344-1611 (toll free)
Website: *www.BibleDoug.com*
Email: *Doug@BibleDoug.com*

LTB Publications
Dr. Andrew B. Ray, Pastor
5709 North Broadway Street
Knoxville, TN 37918
(865)688-0780
Website: *www.LearntheBible.org*
Email: *pastorray@LearntheBible.org*

Acknowledgements

The authors would like to express their deepest appreciation to the following:

Most preeminently, the precious Lord Jesus Christ for His saving and sustaining grace.

Those who invested the time and effort into our spiritual development, along with the men and women who have been persecuted and sometimes put to death for the faith and their trust in the Saviour and His word.

Our devoted wives for their constant support, encouragement, and understanding through our years of marriage and ministry together. They are truly God's *second* greatest gift to each of us **(Romans 6:23)**.

Mrs. Lois Barnes for her many hours of proofreading and grammatical suggestions.

Mr. Rick Quatro and Mr. Jonathan Judy for their invaluable assistance in formatting the book text.

Mr. Tom Rood for his creativity reflected in an impressive cover design.

Lastly, the members of Antioch Baptist Church, Knoxville, TN for their faithful support and encouragement during this long process of writing our third devotional book.

Recommendation

"Many find the Lord's command *six days shalt thou labour,* combined with *study to shew thyself approved unto God*, a bit overwhelming. In such a busy age, even the most sincere Christians often find it difficult to dig into the Bible as deeply and consistently as they should or would. Just as millions have benefited from pastors' sermons, countless others have been aided by devotional works produced by gospel ministers. This is such a work, and it carries with it the bonus of having been produced by men who love and believe every word of God's holy scripture. These daily readings will provide guidance, instruction, and encouragement to the church of God."

Pastor James Knox
THE BIBLE Baptist Church
DeLand, Florida
www.jamesknox.org

Author Biographies

Dr. Douglas D. Stauffer is an internationally recognized authority in the fields of Bible history, apologetics and prophetic studies. He is a prolific author, having written over a dozen books along with many writings published in Christian periodicals. Because of his biblical expertise, *Oxford University Press* commissioned Dr. Stauffer to work as one of two contributing editors for the notes on the *New Pilgrim* King James study Bible.

Immediately, following high school, Doug served a four year tour of duty in the USAF. Upon discharge, he returned to Pennsylvania to attend *The Pennsylvania State University*, graduating with a BS degree in accounting. A few months later he began attending Bible college.

While attending Bible college, Dr. Stauffer passed the CPA exam. He then worked as controller of several organizations. In 1994, he gave up his work as CFO of a multimillion dollar company along with managing his own accounting and consulting firm when God began dealing with him about dedicating his time more fully to the ministry. Since that time, he has earned his ThM and PhD in Religion from *International Baptist Seminary*.

Along with being a frequent guest speaker on radio and television, he has served ten years in pastoral ministries and logged thousands of hours teaching in churches and at the college level. Dr. Stauffer currently serves as an evangelist and president of *Partners for Truth Ministries*.

Doug and his wife Judy are blessed with two children, Justin and Heather.

Dr. Andrew B. Ray is the pastor of Antioch Baptist Church in Knoxville, Tennessee. He has a heart for the Lord, His word, the church, the family, as well as the next generation. He spends countless hours counseling and obediently declaring *"all the counsel of God."* As a diligent student of the scriptures, he earned his Doctor of Theology degree and faithfully preaches and teaches at the church, as well as the Bible institute.

Before becoming pastor in May 2007, Dr. Ray served as assistant pastor for four years at Antioch Baptist Church under Dr. David F. Reagan. Upon Dr. Reagan's death, Andrew was unanimously voted as pastor of Antioch Baptist Church.

Bro. Ray is the author of *The Fingerprint of God* along with a four year series of devotional books called *Daily Strength: Devotions for Bible-Believing Study*. This is the fourth book co-authored with Dr. Stauffer. He has also written several gospel tracts and is currently serving as an editor for a songbook that incorporates scriptural songs, bringing back original lyrics altered or removed by modern hymnals.

God has blessed Bro. Ray and his wife Lula with five children: Noah, Hannah, Sara, Charity, and Isaac.

How to Use This Book and an Admonition to the Reader

Two vital admonitions for personal use of the scriptures entail reading *(1 Timothy 4:13)* and studying *(2 Timothy 2:15)* the Bible. Yet, far too many Christians allow books and other materials to supersede their personal interactions with God's word. This devotional series should never usurp either of these crucial commands and God-given admonitions. Rather, the role of this volume serves to assist, expand, and help focus personal or group Bible study.

NOTE: The heading at the top of each page has a box to check when you complete any particular study followed by a place for entering the *completion date*. This book is intended to be more like a springboard to launch the student deeper into the most precious book ever written. It is not intended to be an end-all to Bible study. Each devotion consists of five component parts.

I. SCRIPTURE PASSAGE

The first section before the *Introductory Thoughts* presents the relevant scripture. Be sure never to skip over the reading of each *Scripture Passage* in its entirety. If you are using the book to lead others in Bible study, make sure to read and meditate on the passage and its context ahead of time though you may want to break the passage into shorter segments while teaching. The devotion will be completely ineffective when the *Scripture Passage* has been overlooked or discounted in any way.

II. INTRODUCTORY THOUGHTS

The *Introductory Thoughts* immediately follow the *Scripture Passage*. Apart from the scripture, this section communicates the heart of the devotion. Read it carefully and completely, taking time to examine each referenced scripture. If you are leading a study for others, it is not necessary to read this section verbatim to them. Instead, study the contents ahead of time and use it as a guide for your words and thoughts. Doing so will increase the study's effectiveness and add a personal element to the study.

III. DEVOTIONAL THOUGHTS

The *Devotional Thoughts* section serves to make the study more personal by offering some questions to stimulate self-examination. The first section in the series of questions or thoughts is geared toward younger children.

However, older children, teens, and adults may also find these thoughts helpful. Feel free to skip this first portion if there are no young children in the study group. If you are studying alone, be sure to take the time to consider each thought or question to see how it might improve your walk with the Lord. If you are leading or studying with a group, this section should help provoke discussion and prayerful consideration.

IV. Prayer Thoughts

Prayer Thoughts serve to guide the reader to thoughtfully going to the Lord with specific prayer requests. Be sure to pray as God leads. Prayer should always be a matter of the heart so you should never merely repeat the written words. If you are studying as a group or as a family, you could take time for prayer requests followed by one person leading the group in prayer. You could also dedicate some time for each member to pray. Remember that this prayer time can offer a great opportunity for teaching children the importance of prayer.

V. Song

The final section, *Song*, is self-explanatory. Some of the songs will be unfamiliar but each has been prayerfully chosen. Each of these songs will eventually be included in a single songbook. Though some individuals and families might shy away from the thought of singing out loud in a group or alone, it was historically common for people to sing together during times of study. Follow the "song" link at *www.Learnthebible.com* for many of the lyrics and tunes of the recommended songs.

Table of Contents

Week 1	Aging	1
Week 2	Aging (con't)	9
Week 3	Carefulness	17
Week 4	Appetite	25
Week 5	Appetite (con't)	33
Week 6	Appetite (con't)	41
Week 7	Bereavement	49
Week 8	Comfort	59
Week 9	Confusion	67
Week 10	Contention or Strife	75
Week 11	Contention or Strife (con't)	83
Week 12	Contention or Strife (con't)	91
Week 13	Envy	99
Week 14	Envy (con't)	107
Week 15	Heresy	115
Week 16	Heresy (con't)	123
Week 17	Hypocrisy	131
Week 18	Hypocrisy (con't)	139
Week 19	Liberality	147
Week 20	Loyalty	155
Week 21	Loyalty (con't)	163
Week 22	Loyalty (con't)	173
Week 23	Meddling	181
Week 24	The Home	189
Week 25	The Home (con't)	197
Week 26	The Home (con't)	205
Week 27	Resolution	213
Week 28	Resolution (con't)	221
Week 29	Communication	231
Week 30	Chastening or Punishment	239
Week 31	Chastening or Punishment (con't)	247
Week 32	Rebellion	255
Week 33	Rebellion (con't)	263
Week 34	Relationships	271
Week 35	Relationships (con't)	279
Week 36	Relationships (con't)	287
Week 37	Reputation	295

Week 38	Reputation (con't)	303
Week 39	Sacrifices	311
Week 40	Sacrifices (con't)	319
Week 41	Salvation	327
Week 42	Salvation (con't)	335
Week 43	Sobriety	343
Week 44	Sobriety (con't)	351
Week 45	Stewardship	359
Week 46	Stewardship (con't)	367
Week 47	Temptation	375
Week 48	Temptation (con't)	383
Week 49	Tradition	391
Week 50	Tradition (con't)	399
Week 51	Violence	407
Week 52	Violence (con't)	415
Scripture Index		423

1
Aging

Aging—Note: The topical nature of this study makes it difficult to pinpoint a specific word count.

Variations: aged, ancient, ancients, old, elder, elders, eldest; Note: These words are frequently used to express aging but the certainty of the intended usage can only be ascertained by considering the surrounding context.

Defined: the process of growing older

Interesting fact: *Psalm 90:10* says, *"The days of our years are threescore years and ten."* Whether or not this statement was intended to set a hard fast rule for the years of a man's lifetime, it is curiously accurate with the present average life expectancy. Though this number of years seems to be the starting point, men can certainly adjust their life expectancy up or down. In fact, *Psalm 90:10* suggests that *"by reason of strength"* some people may reach *"fourscore years."* Confirming the uniqueness of attaining to such an age, the Bible identified Barzillai at eighty years of age as *"a very aged man" (2 Samuel 19:32).*

Bible study tip: The objective of Bible study ought to be a personal likeness to Jesus Christ. The Bible has something to say that facilitates this purpose regardless of a person's age group. Consider studying the Bible based upon your age bracket (young, aged, very aged) to explore what it says about your personal responsibilities.

Sunday, Day 1—Church Day (no devotional)
Monday, Day 2—*The Cycle of Life*
Tuesday, Day 3—*The Fear of Growing Old*
Wednesday, Day 4—Church Night (no devotional)
Thursday, Day 5—*Glory and Beauty*
Friday, Day 6—*All Have Something to Offer*
Saturday, Day 7—*Sin Cares Not for Your Age*

Day 1: Church Day

Job 32:9 Great men are not always wise: neither do the aged understand judgment.

Day 2: (Monday)
The Cycle of Life

*2 Samuel 19:35 I am this day fourscore years old: and **can I discern** between good and evil? **can thy servant taste** what I eat or what I drink? **can I hear** any more the voice of singing men and singing women? wherefore then should thy servant be yet a burden unto my lord the king?*

INTRODUCTORY THOUGHTS

Life is cyclical. Many of the physical challenges experienced by young children will once again be encountered by those who live long enough. As a person ages, many things taken for granted long ago in the prime of life begin to deteriorate. For instance, the Bible says that Israel's eyes *"were dim for age"* **(Genesis 48:10)**, Barzillai's hearing and taste buds were ill affected **(2 Samuel 19:34-35)**, and David *"gat no heat"* **(1 Kings 1:1)** as he grew old. For these reasons and others, the Bible emphasizes that aged saints are *"old and well stricken in age"* **(Genesis 18:11)**. In other words, the passing of time or the coming of age strikes the physical well-being of the body and its physical and mental functions. This physical and mental degeneration is the fulfillment of the cycle of life as the body prepares to return to the dust from whence it originally came *(Ecclesiastes 12:7).*

Devotional Thoughts

- **(For children):** As our bodies grow older, we may not be able to effectively or efficiently do everything we once did. This includes driving a car, mowing the grass, chopping down trees, climbing steps, cleaning house, standing and cooking, etc, etc. Aging resulted from Adam and Eve's sin *(Genesis 2:17; Genesis 3:19).* For this reason and others, it is important to work while you can. Fortunately, our bodies in heaven will be perfect *(1 Corinthians 15:51-53).*
- **(For everyone):** Why is it so very important that people of all ages consider the implications of old age? How should this knowledge and understanding change the way we live each day of our lives?
- What are some of the things that the youngest children deal with that older individuals may also have to endure? How can this reflect the cycle of life?

Prayer Thoughts

- Ask the Lord to help you use each day to its fullest.
- Thank God for the abilities He has given you today.

SONG: *JUST WHEN I NEED HIM MOST*

Day 3: (Tuesday)
The Fear of Growing Old

Psalm 71:18 Now also when I am old and grayheaded, O God, forsake me not; until I have shewed thy strength unto this generation, and thy power to every one that is to come.

Introductory Thoughts

Many people suffer from *gerascophobia* which is the *fear of growing old*. Perhaps this condition is ultimately the fear of death rather than simply growing old, but other conditions indicative of old age cause people to fret. One of these concerns was expressed by the penman of **Psalm 71**. On two separate occasions, he requested that the Lord would not forsake him when he was old and grayheaded *(Psalm 71:9, 18)*. The Lord knew the fears of man and promised, *"even to your old age ... and even to the hoar hairs will I carry you: I have made, and I will bear; even I will carry, and will deliver you" (Isaiah 46:4)*. The thought of growing old should not bring fear or trepidation to God's people. In fact, the Bible points to it as a blessing and one of the greatest blessings the Jewish people will experience in the kingdom *(Zechariah 8:4)*.

Devotional Thoughts

- **(For children):** God makes it plain that He is in charge of our lives *(Psalm 37:23a)* and He will always be with us *(Hebrews 13:5)*. He also makes it plain that we are not to live anxiously or worry. This truth also applies to agonizing over the thought of one day growing old *(Matthew 6:34; Philippians 4:6, 19)*.
- **(For everyone):** What do you fear about growing older? Are these fears legitimately accurate? How will God's presence and help allow you to overcome your fears?
- What are some of the blessings of growing older? Why will it be such a blessing to the Jewish people to be able to grow older in the kingdom? Why should it be a blessing to those living today?

Prayer Thoughts

- Ask the Lord to help you overcome your fears of growing older.
- Thank God for the blessings you enjoy at each point of your life.

SONG: *GOD WILL TAKE CARE OF YOU*

Day 4: Church Night

Ecclesiastes 12:1 Remember now thy Creator in the days of thy youth, while the evil days come not, nor the years draw nigh, when thou shalt say, I have no pleasure in them;

2 While the sun, or the light, or the moon, or the stars, be not darkened, nor the clouds return after the rain:

3 In the day when the keepers of the house shall tremble, and the strong men shall bow themselves, and the grinders cease because they are few, and those that look out of the windows be darkened,

₄ And the doors shall be shut in the streets, when the sound of the grinding is low, and he shall rise up at the voice of the bird, and all the daughters of musick shall be brought low;

₅ Also when they shall be afraid of that which is high, and fears shall be in the way, and the almond tree shall flourish, and the grasshopper shall be a burden, and desire shall fail: because man goeth to his long home, and the mourners go about the streets:

₆ Or ever the silver cord be loosed, or the golden bowl be broken, or the pitcher be broken at the fountain, or the wheel broken at the cistern.

₇ Then shall the dust return to the earth as it was: and the spirit shall return unto God who gave it.

Day 5: (Thursday)
Glory and Beauty

***Proverbs 20:29** The **glory of young men** is their strength: and the **beauty of old men** is the gray head.*

INTRODUCTORY THOUGHTS

Each phase of life bears the marks of certain strengths and weaknesses. In youth, man has a great amount of zeal. In fact, the Bible points out that *"the glory of young men is their strength."* A young man might have the fortitude, strength, and stamina to accomplish great things, but his limited knowledge hinders his ability to accomplish greatness. As time elapses, man learns from both failure and success. He obtains the knowledge and enjoys the wisdom that often eluded him during his youth. His glory no longer resides in his strength, but his beauty is now *"the gray head."* The very thing that limited his ability to accomplish great things in youth is now a virtue he has achieved. The glory of his youth may have departed, but there remains hope. He has the knowledge but lacks the strength he once possessed. Fortunately, he can invest his knowledge into those who still retain their youthful vitality.

DEVOTIONAL THOUGHTS

- **(For children):** God calls grey hair a crown of glory for those who have trusted in Him *(Proverbs 16:31)*. Even if they are confined to a

bed or wheelchair, they can pray, praise God, and help others to know the Lord *(Hebrews 13:15)*. Consider Anna *(Luke 2:36-38)*.
- **(For everyone)**: Who are the people you know with the greatest strength and zeal? Who are the people you know with the greatest amount of knowledge and wisdom? Are they one and the same?
- What would be the best way for young and old to use their strengths to best serve the Lord? How could they work together to accomplish more for the Lord than they could achieve separately?

Prayer Thoughts
- Ask the Lord to increase your wisdom and strength.
- Ask the Lord to help you serve Him to your fullest capacity.

SONG: *HOW FIRM A FOUNDATION*

Day 6: (Friday)
All Have Something to Offer

Deuteronomy 32:7 Remember the days of old, **consider the years of many generations***: ask thy father, and he will shew thee; thy elders, and they will tell thee.*

Introductory Thoughts

The strength of any people will be determined by how they deal with two people groups: their young and their old. If at any point, either of these two groups becomes viewed as simply burdensome, both will cease to effectively attain God's intended desire for society. The aged members of society are most often its wisest. They have had successes and failures and learned from both *(Deuteronomy 32:7)*. They have witnessed the Lord's provision through difficult times *(Psalm 37:25)*. God purposed for the aged to instruct the young in practical and spiritual matters *(Titus 2:1-11)*. While the young should feed off of the wisdom of the aged, the elderly members of society can be nourished by the joy, strength, and life of younger people *(Ruth 4:15)*.

Devotional Thoughts
- **(For children)**: The Bible testifies of children helping their parents. David made sure his parents were safe when Saul chased him *(1 Samuel 22:3-4)*. Joseph brought his father into Egypt where there was

plenty of food *(Genesis 45:16-18)*. Jesus made sure His mother would be cared for after He returned to heaven *(John 19:26-27)*.
- **(For everyone):** Would you be considered young or old? How could you best benefit those in your family, church, or community? Can you offer wisdom? Can you be a nourisher of someone's old age?
- Around what people (young or aged) do you spend the bulk of your time and expend your energies? How could you benefit from fellowshipping with people who are both older and younger than yourself?

PRAYER THOUGHTS
- Thank the Lord for the godly influences in your life.
- Ask the Lord to help you strengthen others.

SONG: *BLEST BE THE TIE THAT BINDS*

Day 7: (Saturday)
Sin Cares Not for Your Age

*Genesis 8:21 And the LORD smelled a sweet savour; and the LORD said in his heart, I will not again curse the ground any more for man's sake; for **the imagination of man's heart** is **evil from his youth**; neither will I again smite any more every thing living, as I have done.*

INTRODUCTORY THOUGHTS

From youth, man is gripped by sin's attraction. As he ages, the source of temptation may vary, but the fact that he is tempted remains constant. Paul instructed young Timothy to *"flee . . . youthful lusts"* **(2 Timothy 2:22)**, yet Solomon's heart was turned after other gods when he *"was old"* **(1 Kings 11:4)**. Many believers have wasted the precious years of youth by succumbing to the youthful lusts of which Paul warned Timothy. Others have fought the good fight in their youth, only to regretfully compromise in their waning years. There is no time or age for the believer to be at ease concerning sin. Sin can be pleasurable but is always deceptive with uncertain outcomes for those who indulge.

DEVOTIONAL THOUGHTS
- **(For children):** Samuel was willing to learn of and serve God at an early age *(1 Samuel 2:26)*. From childhood to old age, he stayed true to the Lord *(1 Samuel 12:1-4)*. Learn God's word now *(Psalm 119:11)*.

- **(For everyone):** What are some of the temptations young people may face? What are some temptations the aged may face? Are the temptations different? How and why?
- What are some biblical examples of people who gave in to youthful lusts? What are some biblical examples of people who failed the Lord when they were old? How can we guard against both?

PRAYER THOUGHTS

- Ask the Lord to keep you from sin in each stage of life.
- Ask the Lord to give you an understanding of the danger of sin.

SONG: *DAY BY DAY*

Notes: _____

_____

_____

_____

_____

_____

_____

Quotes from the next volume

(VOLUME 4, WEEK 1)

Subject: Amusements or Worldly Pleasures

Pleasure seeking breeds poverty. The more men require amusement and seek pleasure, the more they are willing to spend to have both.

The individual who partakes in worldly pleasures does so only to find a greater need for additional pleasure. He becomes pleasure's servant with no hope of freedom apart from the Lord.

2
Aging (con't)

Aging—Note: The topical nature of this study makes it difficult to pinpoint a specific word count.

Variations: aged, ancient, ancients, old, elder, elders, eldest; Note: These words are frequently used to express aging but the certainty of the intended usage can only be ascertained by considering the surrounding context.

Interesting fact: Time can be viewed like a cup continuously being filled to the brim. This is why the Bible ties events and life spans to time. For example, *"when the **fulness of the time** was come, God sent forth his Son" **(Galatians 4:4)**.* As time pertains to a man's days upon the earth, the Bible often identifies one's end of life as being *"full of days"* **(Genesis 35:29; 1 Chronicles 23:1; 1 Chronicles 29:28; 2 Chronicles 24:15; Job 42:17; Jeremiah 6:11)**.

Bible study tip: The same age can be stated in multiple ways in scripture. For example, *"Cainan lived seventy years"* **(Genesis 5:12)**. In another passage, *"The days of our years"* are said to be *"threescore years and ten"* **(Psalm 90:10)**. The word *score* indicates a measure of twenty years so threescore equals sixty years plus ten more which equals seventy total years.

Sunday, Day 8—Church Day (no devotional)
Monday, Day 9—*Exploits of the Aged*
Tuesday, Day 10—*Let No Man Despise Thy Youth*
Wednesday, Day 11—Church Night (no devotional)
Thursday, Day 12—*Age Does Not Equal Wisdom*
Friday, Day 13—*A Window of Time to Serve*
Saturday, Day 14—*Rejoice in Each Day*

Day 8: Church Day

Psalm 90:12 **So teach us to number our days, that we may apply our hearts unto wisdom.**

Day 9: (Monday)
Exploits of the Aged

Joshua 14:6 Then the children of Judah came unto Joshua in Gilgal: and Caleb the son of Jephunneh the Kenezite said unto him, Thou knowest the thing that the LORD said unto Moses the man of God concerning me and thee in Kadeshbarnea.

7 **Forty years old was I when Moses the servant of the LORD sent me from Kadeshbarnea to espy out the land**; and I brought him word again as it was in mine heart.

8 Nevertheless my brethren that went up with me made the heart of the people melt: but I wholly followed the LORD my God.

9 And Moses sware on that day, saying, Surely the land whereon thy feet have trodden shall be thine inheritance, and thy children's for ever, because thou hast wholly followed the LORD my God.

10 And now, behold, the LORD hath kept me alive, as he said, these forty and five years, even since the LORD spake this word unto Moses, while the children of Israel wandered in the wilderness: and now, lo, I am this day fourscore and five years old.

11 As yet I am as strong this day as I was in the day that Moses sent me: **as my strength was then, even so is my strength now**, for war, both to go out, and to come in.

*12 **Now therefore give me this mountain**, whereof the LORD spake in that day; for thou heardest in that day how the Anakims were there, and that the cities were great and fenced: if so be the LORD will be with me, then I shall be able to drive them out, as the LORD said.*

INTRODUCTORY THOUGHTS

Unfortunately, some Christians have become convinced that old age serves as a sufficient excuse for a lack of service to the Lord's work. Granted, the field of one's service may change, but there should always remain a willingness to serve. For instance, Moses received his initial call to deliver Israel at forty years old *(Acts 7:23)* but did not lead God's people out of Egypt until he was eighty *(Exodus 7:7)*. When he died at 120 years of age, he remarked that *"his eye was not dim, nor his natural force abated" (Deuteronomy 34:7)*. At forty years of age, Caleb received a promise from Moses concerning the possession of land in Canaan *(Joshua 14:7-9)*. Forty-five years later, Caleb took possession by driving out the mighty Anakims *(Joshua 14:10-12)*. Caleb did something in his old age that many of the young men could not or would not attempt *(Joshua 17:13)*.

DEVOTIONAL THOUGHTS

- **(For children):** Zacharias and Elisabeth served God even into their old age *(Luke 1:5-7)*. In fact, while Zacharias was serving in the temple, an angel of the Lord made a great announcement to him *(Luke 1:8-13)*. This elderly couple raised their son to serve God *(Luke 1:80)*, resulting in the Lord speaking well of John *(Luke 7:28a)*.
- **(For everyone):** Even as older men, Paul *(Philemon 9)* and John *(3 John 1)* continued to write epistles encouraging God's people. You will never pen an inspired epistle, but what are some things you might be able to do even when you are older?
- How might history be different if Moses, because of his age, had refused to lead Israel out of Egypt? How might history be different if Paul and John, as they grew older, refused to write as God led them?

PRAYER THOUGHTS

- Ask the Lord to give you a desire to serve Him regardless of your age.
- Ask God to give you strength each day to do His will.

SONG: *I WANT THAT MOUNTAIN*

Day 10: (Tuesday)
Let No Man Despise Thy Youth

1 Timothy 4:12 Let no man despise thy youth; *but be thou an example of the believers, in word, in conversation, in charity, in spirit, in faith, in purity.*

Introductory Thoughts

Respect is not inherited but must be earned. Paul wrote to young Timothy admonishing him to *"let no man despise"* his youth. In other words, Timothy was responsible for how others handled his youthfulness. Paul's advice for Timothy was for him to be an example to other believers in every facet of life. If he did that, no man would despise his youth. They would begin to see Timothy as a man and would have no problem following his leadership. His youth would not be a hindrance. In the beginning, David was disdained because of his youth **(1 Samuel 17:33, 42)**, but when he defeated Goliath and gave Israel the victory, he was given the respect of a war hero. David did not show up demanding or even expecting others to respect him; he earned it through his actions.

Devotional Thoughts

- **(For children):** If you, as a child, want others to know you love the Lord, then you need to consistently act like you truly love Him. How should you behave at home, at church, in Sunday School, and in publick? Consider these verses for some guidance: **Psalm 101:2a; 2 Thessalonians 3:7; Titus 2:7a.**
- **(For everyone):** Why do young people become frustrated when adults fail to respect them? Is it possible they think they are entitled to the respect of others regardless of their actions?
- What are some ways you could keep others from despising your youth? What would you need to change in order to earn more respect from those around you?

Prayer Thoughts

- Ask the Lord to help you earn respect rather than expecting it.
- Ask God to give you wisdom beyond your years.

SONG: *WHILE IN THE DAYS OF YOUTH*

Day 11: Church Night

Proverbs 16:31 The hoary head is a crown of glory, if it be found in the way of righteousness.

Day 12: (Thursday)
Age Does Not Equal Wisdom

Ecclesiastes 4:13 Better is a poor and a wise child than an old and foolish king, who will no more be admonished.

INTRODUCTORY THOUGHTS

Wisdom often results from time and experience. It should not, however, be assumed that old age automatically equals wisdom. For instance, the Bible says, *"Better is . . . a wise child than an old and foolish king."* Wisdom comes from the Lord, and He distributes wisdom irrespective of one's age. Perhaps the wisest statements given by man found within the Book of Job were given by a young man named Elihu *(Job 32:6)*. He listened carefully as Job's older friends spewed forth foolish words. He thought that *"days should speak, and multitude of years should teach wisdom" (Job 32:7)*. Eventually, he came to the conclusion, *"great men are not always wise: neither do the aged understand judgment" (Job 32:9)*.

DEVOTIONAL THOUGHTS

- **(For children):** No matter what your age, if you fear the Lord and do what He says, you attain to wisdom *(Job 28:28)*. However, be admonished that age does not always result in becoming wise. For instance, Eli was old and knew God, but didn't fear Him enough to do what God had said *(1 Samuel 2:22a, 27- 29; 1 Samuel 3:13)*. Thus, Eli was old but not wise.
- **(For everyone):** Why is it important to understand that old age does not automatically suggest wisdom? Is it possible to receive foolish advice from an older person while receiving wise advice from a youth? Understand that when this happens, it is frequently the exception and not the rule.
- What is the source of wisdom? How can you insure that you will grow wiser with age? Why is it important for you to increase in wisdom as you increase in age?

14 • Aging (con't) ☐ Completion Date

PRAYER THOUGHTS
- Ask the Lord to give you the ability to know and recognize wise counsel.
- Thank God for His willingness to give wisdom regardless of age.

SONG: *GIVE OF YOUR BEST TO THE MASTER*

Day 13: (Friday)
A Window of Time to Serve

Acts 13:36 **For David**, *after he had* **served his own generation by the will of God**, *fell on sleep, and was laid unto his fathers, and saw corruption:*

INTRODUCTORY THOUGHTS

This life offers only a window of time and opportunity to work for the Lord. Youthfulness and old age both offer their own hindrances to service. In many ways, though not entirely, youth should be spent in learning, middle age in doing, and old age in teaching those who are learning and doing. Many of the greatest servants of the Lord found in scripture began their journey in youth by learning of the Lord and His ways *(1 Kings 18:12; Psalm 71:5; 2 Chronicles 34:3; Job 29:4; Ecclesiastes 12:1)*. As they approached the prime of life, they invested their learning by serving the Lord *(Numbers 8:24-25)*. As they passed their prime, they would pass their knowledge on to the next generation in hopes of the Lord's work continuing and flourishing *(2 Timothy 4:1-8)*.

DEVOTIONAL THOUGHTS
- **(For children):** What can you do for the Lord? You can be like Timothy and learn your Bible verses *(2 Timothy 3:15)*. It is important to practice what you know to do: obey dad and mom; listen to your teachers in Sunday School and those in church; be helpful. In doing so, you will be equipped, ready, and able to help others *(2 Timothy 2:2)*.
- **(For everyone):** In what age group do you find yourself today? To the best of your abilities, are you serving the Lord? Are you learning of Him, serving Him, and teaching others about Him?

☐ Completion Date

- How is each time of life just as important as every other time? How can one's failure to learn in youth affect his service in his prime? How are others hurt and severely limited when the elderly refuse to teach because they feel they have less to offer?

PRAYER THOUGHTS
- Ask the Lord to help you become faithful in each phase of life.
- Ask God to help you make the best use of your window of time.

SONG: *LITTLE IS MUCH WHEN GOD IS IN IT*

Day 14: (Saturday)
Rejoice in Each Day

Ecclesiastes 11:9 Rejoice, O young man, in thy youth; and let thy heart cheer thee in the days of thy youth, and walk in the ways of thine heart, and in the sight of thine eyes: but know thou, that for all these things God will bring thee into judgment.

10 Therefore **remove sorrow from thy heart, and put away evil from thy flesh***: for childhood and youth are vanity.*

INTRODUCTORY THOUGHTS

Many people fail to enjoy the present blessings by worrying about the inevitability of future difficulties. Though each time of life is certainly filled with its difficulties, it is also filled with tremendous opportunities for blessing. When young, a person ought to rejoice in his youth while keeping in mind that God will bring his deeds into judgment. When growing older, people ought to rejoice in getting married, having children, working, and serving the Lord. As one grows older, he can enjoy the benefits of each phase of life knowing that God has special blessings in store for each day. After all, why be robbed of today's joys by worry concerning troubles and sorrows that may never come to pass? And if they do transpire, effort spent in worrying about them was useless.

DEVOTIONAL THOUGHTS
- **(For children):** Do not forget that God is always present in your life *(Jeremiah 23:23-24)*. He truly wants each and every person to enjoy life *(1 Timothy 6:17b)*. In order to be truly happy and content, be sure

you know that the Lord approves of what you are doing *(Colossians 3:17)*. Never forget that each of us will give an account of our lives to God *(Ecclesiastes 12:14; Romans 14:12)*.
- **(For everyone):** During His earthly ministry, the Lord used each day to its fullest. The Bible says that He increased in wisdom, in stature, and in favour with God and man *(Luke 2:52)*. How could you learn from His example for us?
- What have you failed to enjoy because you were worried about things that never came to pass? What concerns do you have now? What blessings will be missed because of these concerns?

PRAYER THOUGHTS
- Ask the Lord to keep you from worrying about the future.
- Ask the Lord to help you rejoice in each day He gives you.

SONG: *HE GIVETH MORE GRACE*

Notes: _____

_____

_____

_____

_____

Quotes from the next volume

(VOLUME 4, WEEK 2)

Subject: Amusements or Worldly Pleasures (con't)

Not surprisingly, much of the world's amusement centers upon demeaning, mocking, or humiliating others.

Mixing amusement into any true worship always yields varying types of idolatry.

The ways in which any individual seeks and finds pleasure speaks volumes about the condition of his heart.

3
Carefulness

Carefulness—found fifteen times in fifteen verses

Variations: careful, carefully, carefulness; Note: A study of the word *care* would also be helpful in this area.

First usage: *Deuteronomy 15:5* (carefully)

Last usage: *Hebrews 12:17* (carefully)

Defined: the state of being full of care or caution

Interesting fact: Care or carefulness is not a sin. If it were a sin, God would be a sinner *(Deuteronomy 11:12; 1 Peter 5:7)*. The context of the word's usage determines the nature of carefulness, whether it is righteous or unrighteous *(2 Corinthians 7:11; Philippians 4:6)*.

Bible study tip: Martha was *"careful and troubled about many things" (Luke 10:41)*. For this reason, the Saviour addressed her as *"Martha, Martha."* There are other instances in scripture when someone's name is repeated in a single passage. In such cases, there is specific purpose for the repetitious use. It would be helpful to study the context of these occurrences in order to determine the reason for the heightened sense of concern.

Sunday, Day 15—Church Day (no devotional)
Monday, Day 16—*Be Careful for Nothing*
Tuesday, Day 17—*Cast Your Care upon Him*
Wednesday, Day 18—Church Night (no devotional)
Thursday, Day 19—*Worry Is Vain*
Friday, Day 20—*The Goal of the Adversary*
Saturday, Day 21—*Fretting Because of Others*

Day 15: Church Day

***Luke 10:41** And Jesus answered and said unto her, Martha, Martha, thou art careful and troubled about many things*:

Day 16: (Monday)
Be Careful for Nothing

***Philippians 4:6 Be careful for nothing;** but in every thing by prayer and supplication with thanksgiving let your requests be made known unto God.*

INTRODUCTORY THOUGHTS

Believers are commanded to *"Be careful for nothing."* Contextually, the word *careful* means to be *care full* or full of cares. That being said, this is one of the most disobeyed commands in all of scripture. In **Matthew 6:25**, the Lord warned His disciples against dwelling upon or worrying about what they would eat, or drink, or how they would be clothed. The Lord's rebuke implies that not even the necessities of life should serve as a source of worry for God's people. It is important to note that worry and faith are at opposite ends of the spectrum because they do not and cannot coexist within the believer's life and walk. A believer who is *"careful"* for things cannot and will not simultaneously trust God's faithful provision. When a believer worries rather than trusting in God's provision and protection, the believer's actions deem God incapable to accomplish the matter without the individual contributing his *"carefulness."*

DEVOTIONAL THOUGHTS

- **(For children):** God made all things *(John 1:3)*, owns all things *(Psalm 50:12)*, knows what we need *(Matthew 6:32b)*, and is more

☐ Completion Date Carefulness • 19

than able to give it to us *(Ephesians 3:20)*. For instance, consider His care for His children when they were in the wilderness *(Deuteronomy 8:15-16; Deuteronomy 29:5)*.
- **(For everyone):** Why is it a sin to worry? What message does our worry send to the Lord? What is an alternate plan for worry *(Philippians 4:6)*?
- The absence of worry does not suggest the absence of effort on the part of man. It merely suggests a different foundation of hope. In whom does worry place its hope? In whom does faith place its hope?

PRAYER THOUGHTS
- Ask God to give you victory over the sin of being full of cares.
- Ask the Lord to show you when you are consumed by worry.

SONG: *'TIS SO SWEET TO TRUST IN JESUS*

Day 17: (Tuesday)
Cast Your Care upon Him

1 Peter 5:7 Casting all your care upon him; for he careth for you.

INTRODUCTORY THOUGHTS

Prayer serves as the greatest remedy for worry and fears. In *Philippians 4:6*, God's word tells us to *"Be careful for nothing; but in every thing by prayer and supplication with thanksgiving let your requests be made known unto God."* This truth is reaffirmed in *1 Peter 5:7* where the Bible says, *"Casting all your **care** upon him; for **he careth for you.**"* A man can expend time and strength caring for the things of this world including the necessities of life, or he can make a conscious decision to obediently cast those same cares upon the Lord. This allows the Lord to show Himself strong toward the individual by caring for His child. According to *Philippians 4:7*, by choosing to pray, the cares and worries of man are replaced with *"the peace of God."* The Bible describes this peace as one that keeps the believer's heart and mind through Christ Jesus and even passes one's ability to comprehend its depths and riches.

DEVOTIONAL THOUGHTS
- **(For children):** God does not want us troubled or afraid *(John 14:27)*. When you are afraid, God wants you to turn to Him and talk to Him.

David called on the Lord many times to help him during fearful times *(Psalm 3:1, 4-6; Psalm 34:4)*.
- **(For everyone):** How does prayer hinder worry? How does worry hinder prayer? What are the benefits of choosing prayer versus the consequences of choosing to worry?
- What does *1 Peter 5:7* mean when it says, *"for he* [the Lord] *careth for you"*? Is it possible that prayer makes your cares God's responsibility rather than your own?

PRAYER THOUGHTS
- Ask God to help you choose prayer over worry.
- Ask the Lord to replace your cares with the peace of God.

SONG: *TELL IT TO JESUS*

Day 18: Church Night

2 Corinthians 7:11 For behold this selfsame thing, that ye sorrowed after a godly sort, **what carefulness it wrought in you,** *yea, what clearing of yourselves, yea, what indignation, yea, what fear, yea, what vehement desire, yea, what zeal, yea, what revenge! In all things ye have approved yourselves to be clear in this matter.*

Day 19: (Thursday)
Worry Is Vain

Psalm 127:1 Except the LORD build the house, they labour in vain that build it: except the LORD keep the city, **the watchman waketh but in vain.**

2 **It is vain** *for you* **to rise up early, to sit up late, to eat the bread of sorrows***: for so he giveth his beloved sleep.*

INTRODUCTORY THOUGHTS

God tasks the watchman with some tremendous responsibilities. He has to remain alert for troubles at all hours of his watch and cannot slacken his resolve to stay attentive. Yet, we are told that if the Lord chooses not to intervene, all of the watchman's worries and efforts are simply in vain. Interestingly, the watchman's job is to worry! The fear of trouble keeps him up at night and causes him to rise up early in the morning to do his duty. Eventually, however, this worry produces physical ailments within the individual. With these negative outcomes, the worry and anxiety also provide no solution for the problems of this life. Worrying has deprived many good people of restfulness and sleep without offering the desperately sought after solutions. It is important to note that help has never come simply as a result of one's worry, and no problems ever resolved themselves simply due to the magnitude of one's worry. Bottom line: except the Lord intervenes in the problems at hand, no help will be forthcoming. Worry is vain!

Devotional Thoughts
- **(For children):** Read *Matthew 8:23-26*. The disciples were afraid because of a storm. Yet, Jesus was with them. He said that they should not have been afraid. Since He is always with us, we too should not worry or be afraid *(Deuteronomy 31:6)*.
- **(For everyone):** Can you list any benefits you personally received from the time you spent in worry? How have your problems been solved with worry? How has your family been helped by your worry?
- How does worry disregard the greatest help available? How does prayer consult the greatest help available? Which one will you choose?

Prayer Thoughts
- Thank the Lord for the option of prayer.
- Ask God to help you realize the vanity of worry.

SONG: *SUFFICIENT UNTO THE DAY*

Day 20: (Friday)
The Goal of the Adversary

1 Samuel 1:6 **And her adversary also provoked her sore, for to make her fret, because the LORD had shut up her womb.**

Introductory Thoughts

Elkanah had two wives, one named Hannah and the other Peninnah. Peninnah had children, but Hannah remained barren. Peninnah used this opportunity of Hannah's barren state to provoke her, hoping that she could trouble her rival. The Christian's primary adversary is much different from Peninnah, but Satan's goal and resolve is identical to this example. The adversary, the Devil *(1 Peter 5:8)*, wants believers to live troubled, fretful, and defeated lives. If he can cause a believer to fret and to worry and to complain, he has a much greater chance of turning that believer's heart against the Lord *(Proverbs 19:3)*. The Devil knows that if he turns the heart, he might be able to cause that believer to curse the Lord *(Isaiah 8:21)*. Satan uses worry as one of the foundational elements in his multipronged attack to bring about his greater objective. He wants to turn hearts against God! Those believers who struggle most with worry offer Satan the greatest chance of success.

DEVOTIONAL THOUGHTS

- **(For children):** The king of Assyria sent a letter to Hezekiah trying to make him doubt that God could help when he attacked. He wanted Hezekiah to fear and give up without a fight. Read what Hezekiah did with those threats *(2 Kings 19:14-19)* and how God heard the prayer and delivered His people *(2 Kings 19:35)*.
- **(For everyone):** How can worry lead to greater sins for the believer? How could a person who began by worrying eventually curse the Lord? How will Satan's ultimate plan for your life be accomplished through worry?
- Does worry come from God or from Satan? Does faith originate with God or Satan? Whose will do you choose to implement when you choose to worry? How is this a dangerous start down a dangerous path?

PRAYER THOUGHTS

- Ask the Lord to help you recognize the attacks of Satan.
- Ask the Lord to put a hedge of protection about you.

SONG: *WITH CHRIST, I SMILE AT THE STORM*

Day 21: (Saturday)
Fretting Because of Others

Psalm 37:1 *Fret not thyself because of evildoers*, neither be thou envious against the workers of iniquity.

☐ Completion Date

INTRODUCTORY THOUGHTS

Although the Bible repeatedly warns against fretting, believers fret because of others. Sadly, one's worry can make the sin of others seem more desirable. We should not fret because of *"evildoers" (Psalm 37:1)*, or *"him who prospereth in his way (Psalm 37:7)*, or *"the man who bringeth wicked devices to pass" (Psalm 37:7)*, or even *"evil men" (Proverbs 24:19)*. Some believers may fret about these people because of their fears, but the scripture offers another reason why believers fret over the wicked. According to *Psalm 37:1* and *Proverbs 24:19*, fretting over the wicked is directly associated to one's envy toward them. Perhaps believers worry about these people so much because there is a deep-rooted desire to become like them. This desire can be rooted in the fact that those whom we fear are viewed as more powerful, more in control, and even more confident. Eliminate the envy and you will eliminate the fear.

DEVOTIONAL THOUGHTS

- **(For children):** Do you know children who have more to play with than you do? God does not want us to be upset when we do not have what others have *(Galatians 5:26)*. What we have we get from Him *(John 3:27; James 1:17)*. He wants us to be content with what we have *(Hebrews 13:5)*.
- **(For everyone):** What are reasons believers might fret over the wicked? Why do you personally fret over the wicked? Is it possible that you harbour some envy toward them?
- Fretting is the opposite of resting in the Lord and waiting patiently for Him *(Psalm 37:7)*. Which will you choose? Will you choose to fret or choose to trust?

PRAYER THOUGHTS

- Ask the Lord to show you the desires of your heart.
- Ask God to help you trust Him in all matters of life.

SONG: *SIMPLY RESTING*

Notes: _____

_____

_____

_____

• Carefulness   ☐ Completion Date

Notes:

Quotes from the next volume

(VOLUME 4, WEEK 3)

Subject: Anger

The source of God's anger and the means by which He acts upon His anger sets the standard for what is truly a righteous anger.

Anger is not sinful, yet the source of one's anger sometimes does manifest the sinfulness of the heart.

4
Appetite

Appetite—The word itself is only found four times in scripture, but the subject matter is covered using a wide variety of terminology.

Variations: appetite

First usage: *Job 38:39* (appetite)

Last usage: *Isaiah 29:8* (appetite)

Defined: The longing for or desire of something; in this particular case, the study relates to the appetite for food.

Interesting fact: Historically, the lamb has been the prey of other animals *(Amos 3:12)*. In the coming kingdom, animal diets will miraculously be altered *(Isaiah 11:7)*. During this period, the Bible says that the wolf will dwell with the lamb; the young of the cow and the bear shall also lie down together *(Isaiah 11:6-7)*.

Bible study tip: Differences found within the scripture do not mean that the Bible contains any contradictions. Many times the differences exist to provide additional details or to provide a distinction in emphasis. At other times, differences exist because of changes in God's dealing with man over time. Though it is true God never changes, His plan for man and the means by which He brings about that plan do change over time. A prime example concerns the dieting restrictions in the old covenant which do not apply to this age!

Sunday, Day 22—Church Day (no devotional)
Monday, Day 23—*Receive It with Thanksgiving*
Tuesday, Day 24—*How Many Meals Should Be Eaten?*
Wednesday, Day 25—Church Night (no devotional)
Thursday, Day 26—*Dietary Restrictions upon Believers*
Friday, Day 27—*Vegetarianism, a Doctrine of Devils*
Saturday, Day 28—*The Sin of Gluttony*

Day 22: Church Day

Proverbs 23:1 *When thou sittest to eat with a ruler, consider diligently what is before thee:*
2 And put a knife to thy throat, ***if thou*** *be* ***a man given to appetite****.*
3 Be not desirous of his dainties: for they are deceitful meat.

Day 23: (Monday)
Receive It with Thanksgiving

1 Timothy 4:4 For ***every creature of God*** *is* ***good****, and nothing to be refused,* ***if it be received with thanksgiving****:*

INTRODUCTORY THOUGHTS

The Bible says that God provides food for His people ***(Matthew 6:26)***. This God-given provision has been that way since the beginning of man's existence on earth ***(Genesis 1:29)***. Interestingly, the Bible also says that God provides food for the animal kingdom ***(Psalm 147:9)***. One might declare that "the animals must go out and search for food to eat" and "men must go to work and earn wages in order to purchase their food." However, a good response to this mind-set would be to focus on how men and animals are able to get their food: "Who gives the animals the strength and the prowess to find the food?" or "Who gives man the health and ability to work his job, earn his wages, and purchase his food?" With a more objective mind-set, you can see why man owes God thanks for the food that he eats. Every Christian should bow his head and give thanks to God for His provision before partaking of any meal.

Devotional Thoughts

- **(For children):** *Ephesians 5:20* says, *"Giving thanks always for all things unto God."* This thankfulness includes giving God thanks for the food we eat. Jesus gave thanks before He fed the 4,000 *(Matthew 15:36)* and also gave thanks before feeding the 5,000 *(John 6:11)*.
- **(For everyone):** What does it mean to receive food with thanksgiving? What kinds of food are to be refused? How often do you pause and thank God for your food before eating?
- Although some people choose to use scare tactics to get others to pray before eating, what are some things that might actually happen when one forgets to thank God for his food?

Prayer Thoughts

- Thank God for His provision for your food.
- Ask God to help you be mindful that your food comes from Him.

SONG: *COUNT YOUR BLESSINGS*

Day 24: (Tuesday)
How Many Meals Should Be Eaten?

Judges 19:5 And it came to pass on the fourth day, when they arose early in the morning, that he rose up to depart: and the damsel's father said unto his son in law, Comfort thine heart with a morsel of bread, and afterward go your way.

Introductory Thoughts

The various dieting trends push for several additional times that man should eat. The Bible clears up any question concerning the number of meals an individual should eat in a single day. Believers should be very careful not to accept the latest trends as though they are the best or even from the Lord. Within scripture, one finds someone partaking of the meal commonly called breakfast *(Judges 19:5)*, at other times, one finds someone partaking of a meal at noon *(Genesis 43:16)*, and at other times, partaking of an evening meal *(Luke 24:29-30)*. In the case of Elijah, the Lord only fed him twice a day *(1 Kings 17:6)*. The most important truth to realize and consider: know that food purposes to give man the necessary strength to fulfil the will of the Lord.

Devotional Thoughts

- **(For children):** Job called food *"necessary" (Job 23:12b)*. We need it for strength and health. Consider the following Bible stories: *1 Kings 19:5-8; Luke 8:52-55; Acts 27:33-38*.
- **(For everyone):** What is the purpose of food? When should people eat? What happens when people eat too much? Do they gain more strength or feel more sluggish?
- Why is it important to allow the Bible to be your authority in all matters including your diet? Is it possible that God knows more about the body than the modern doctors and scientists?

Prayer Thoughts

- Thank the Lord for the strength He gives you through meals.
- Ask God to help you find the proper balance in your diet.

SONG: *WHILE HERE I LIVE, I LIVE TO THEE*

Day 25: Church Night

Ecclesiastes 6:7 **All the labour of man is for his mouth, and yet the appetite is not filled.**

Day 26: (Thursday)
Dietary Restrictions upon Believers

1 Timothy 4:4 **For every creature of God is good, and nothing to be refused,** *if it be received with thanksgiving:*

Introductory Thoughts

Throughout mankind's history, God has placed various dietary restrictions upon people. In the beginning, God gave man herbs and fruit for meat *(Genesis 1:29)*. Under the law, the diet expanded, yet still excluded certain animals that the Lord deemed unclean *(Leviticus 11:1-23)*. The issue was so important that questions concerning dietary restrictions were raised in the early church. In the end, the only restrictions specifically given for the New Testament church were that they should not partake of food knowingly offered to idols, and they should refrain from eating the blood *(Acts 15:20, 29; Acts 21:25)*. *1 Timothy 4:4* confirms these truths by stating that no creature is to be refused based upon some man-made mandate.

Devotional Thoughts

- **(For children):** The Lord ate meat with Abraham *(Genesis 18:2, 8, 22)* and with His disciples *(Luke 24:36-43)*. The apostle Paul told the Romans that it was permissible to eat all things *(Romans 14:14a)*. He said those who thought you could only eat herbs were weak in what they believed *(Romans 14:1-2)*.
- **(For everyone):** What are some situations where it might be a concern if you were eating food offered to idols? What does it mean that believers should refrain from blood?
- According to *1 Timothy 4:4*, what foods should be refused? What does this imply concerning those who preach and teach that believers should exclude meat from their diets?

Prayer Thoughts

- Thank the Lord for the food He gives you.
- Ask God to help you avoid the fads of refusing meats.

SONG: *MY HEART, O GOD, BE WHOLLY THINE*

Day 27: (Friday)
Vegetarianism, a Doctrine of Devils

1 Timothy 4:1 Now the Spirit speaketh expressly, that in the latter times some shall depart from the faith, giving heed to seducing spirits, and **doctrines of devils**;

2 Speaking lies in hypocrisy; having their conscience seared with a hot iron;

3 Forbidding to marry, and **commanding to abstain from meats**, *which God hath created to be received with thanksgiving of them which believe and know the truth.*

30 • Appetite ☐ Completion Date

Introductory Thoughts

Every generation has their own set of ritualistic practices: vegetarianism, the refusal to eat meat, and veganism, the refusal to eat any animal product, are increasingly popular today. The problems arise when proponents of these practices seek to promote the idea that meat eating is evil and should be eliminated. Today's passage proves that the scriptures teach just the opposite. In fact, any individual preaching or teaching a necessary abstinence from eating meat is preaching a doctrine of devils. Regardless of what the modern doctors, scientists, or latest fad diets prescribe, the Bible clearly states that God does not intend for His people to abstain from eating meat. Much of the modern movement stems from an idolatrous view of the animal kingdom. Yet, God clearly provided animals for man's survival and continuation.

Devotional Thoughts

- **(For children):** Read *Psalm 139:14*. When you eat, your body gets rid of anything it cannot use *(Matthew 15:17)*. What you eat has nothing to do with God accepting you or not accepting you *(Romans 14:17)*. God is more concerned with the sin in your heart *(Matthew 15:18-19)* and only He can cleanse that *(1 John 1:8-10)*.
- **(For everyone):** Have you ever had someone try to convince you that it was ungodly to eat meat? Where did they get their authority for their position? Was it from scripture taken in context?
- God gave beasts to man for food. How would it then be offensive for someone to suggest it is evil to eat the flesh of animals? Why would God call it a doctrine of devils?

Prayer Thoughts

- Ask the Lord to protect you from those who would choose to deceive you.
- Ask the Lord to put a hedge of protection about you.

SONG: *BEHOLD, THE HERETICK APPEARS*

Day 28: (Saturday)
The Sin of Gluttony

Proverbs 23:19 Hear thou, my son, and be wise, and guide thine heart in the way.

20 **Be not** *among winebibbers;* **among riotous eaters of flesh***:*

21 For the drunkard and **the glutton** *shall come to poverty: and drowsiness shall clothe a man with rags.*

Introductory Thoughts

Scripture misconceptions are frequently based upon superficial understanding of Bible texts and truths. For example, very few Bible teachers seem to grasp the biblical definition of *gluttony*. Most people consider gluttony as referring to the sin of overeating. However, the Bible's built-in dictionary suggests a completely different scenario. Consider the two parallels within our text. ***Proverbs 23:21*** defines the drunkard as someone *among winebibbers* in verse 20. Additionally, ***Proverbs 23:21*** defines the *glutton* as someone among *riotous eaters of flesh* in verse 20. This context shows us that gluttony is not determined so much by the amount of food eaten, but the manner of food consumption. The fact that gluttony and drunkenness are mentioned every time together further confirms this truth ***(Deuteronomy 21:20; Proverbs 23:21; Matthew 11:19; Luke 7:34).*** Notice that the last two references in Matthew and Luke refer to the false accusations hurled toward the Saviour. When Christ's accusers referred to Him as a gluttonous man and a winebibber, they were referring to His associations with the publicans and sinners, not His personal eating and drinking habits!

Devotional Thoughts

- **(For children):** God meant for you to enjoy eating and drinking *(Ecclesiastes 5:18)*. It needs to be done with the right purposes in mind *(Ecclesiastes 10:17)*. God brings judgment when we do not eat and drink for the right reason *(Exodus 32:6-8, 19-20, 26-28)*.
- **(For everyone):** Read *1 Corinthians 10:31*. What does this suggest about the importance of diet? How can a person eat to the glory of God?

- Individuals should be careful about the amount of food eaten, but not because of fear of being gluttonous. From the scripture, what is the scene in which someone would be gluttonous?

Prayer Thoughts
- Ask the Lord to help you be scriptural in every facet of life.
- Thank the Lord for the built-in dictionary of His word.

SONG: *SINCE YE ARE NOT YOUR OWN*

Notes: _____

Quotes from the next volume

(VOLUME 4, WEEK 4)

Subject: Anger (con't)

The believer should not only abstain from ungodly anger within his own heart but also guard himself against making friends with those who are angry.

An angry man thrives in an environment where strife is prevalent.

Godly anger can put a stop to sin.

5

Appetite (con't)

Appetite—The word itself is only found four times in scripture, but the subject matter is covered using a wide variety of terminology.

Variations: appetite

Interesting fact: In *1 Corinthians 5:11*, the apostle Paul warned the Corinthian believers *"not to eat"* with *"any man that is called a brother"* if he be *"a fornicator, or covetous, or an idolater, or a railer, or a drunkard, or an extortioner."* On the surface, this may seem like the strictest of commands. Yet, the context directly refers to breaking fellowship with disobedient or rebellious brethren. It may also allude to not partaking of the Lord's Supper with them.

Bible study tip: Generally speaking, a people group that came forth from a particular place is designated by taking that place or person's name and adding *ite(s)* to the end. For instance, the *Canaanites* were from the land of *Canaan*, etc. *(Genesis 15:19-21)*. At other times, beings are designated with words ending in *im(s)* *(Genesis 14:5)*. The diligent Bible student will take note of these usages and search the context for hints as to why these differences are incorporated into the text.

Sunday, Day 29—Church Day (no devotional)
Monday, Day 30—*The Power of Food*
Tuesday, Day 31—*Whose God Is Their Belly*
Wednesday, Day 32—Church Night (no devotional)
Thursday, Day 33—*Keep Under Your Body*
Friday, Day 34—*Loss of Appetite*
Saturday, Day 35—*Round About Thy Table*

Day 29: Church Day

*Proverbs 16:26 He that laboureth laboureth for himself; for **his mouth craveth it of him**.*

Day 30: (Monday)
The Power of Food

*Genesis 25:29 And **Jacob sod pottage**: and Esau came from the field, and he was faint:*

*30 And **Esau said to Jacob, Feed me**, I pray thee, with that same red pottage; for I am faint: therefore was his name called Edom.*

*31 And **Jacob said, Sell me this day thy birthright**.*

*32 And **Esau said, Behold, I am at the point to die**: and what profit shall this birthright do to me?*

*33 And Jacob said, Swear to me this day; and he sware unto him: **and he sold his birthright unto Jacob**.*

34 Then Jacob gave Esau bread and pottage of lentiles; and he did eat and drink, and rose up, and went his way: thus Esau despised his birthright.

INTRODUCTORY THOUGHTS

Food is a necessity for sustaining life. Interestingly, the Bible records several instances where a man's need for food became a source of great temptation. For instance, Esau was willing to sell his birthright because he considered one meal more valuable than his future inheritance. The Bible also records several instances where the children of Israel allowed their desire for food to incite rebellion against the Lord *(**Numbers 11:4-6**)*. Another very important example of appetite involves the earliest narratives recorded in Genesis involving an overwhelming appetite. In the garden, Eve partook of the forbidden fruit when she *"saw that the tree was good for food" **(Genesis 3:6)**.* Due to the many examples of inordinate appetite leading to sin, it comes as no surprise that the Devil first sought to tempt the Lord by commanding stones to be made bread **(Luke 4:3)** after He had fasted for forty days.

DEVOTIONAL THOUGHTS

- **(For children):** The children of Israel allowed their lust for food and lack of faith to cause them to disobey God. The Lord gave His people explicit instructions. He provided manna every morning and told them to take only what was necessary for each day and not save any for the next day. Some of the people allowed their appetite to rule them **(Exodus 16:14-20)**. Read Solomon's prayer about food **(Proverbs 30:8c-9)**.
- **(For everyone):** How can man's need for food cause him to sin? How can it be used against believers in their time of weakness (i.e., persecution)?
- How often do you complain against the Lord because of the food that He has provided for you? Does allowing your appetite for food to be more important than pleasing the Lord upset you?

PRAYER THOUGHTS

- Thank God for the food that He supplies.
- Ask God to keep your appetite from being a source of sin.

SONG: *WHY SHOULD I THE TEMPTER FEAR?*

Day 31: (Tuesday)
Whose God Is Their Belly

Philippians 3:18 *(For **many walk**, of whom I have told you often, and now tell you even weeping, that they are the enemies of the cross of Christ:*

*19 Whose end is destruction, **whose God is their belly**, and whose glory is in their shame, who mind earthly things.)*

Appetite (con't)

Introductory Thoughts

Paul's description of the enemies of the cross suggests that they were controlled by their bellies. Paul may have meant something other than appetite when he used the word *belly*, but there can be no doubt that the idea is included. In **Romans 16:18**, Paul said that *"they that are such serve not our Lord Jesus Christ, but their own belly."* In other words, those who are divisive and doctrinally unsound are led by their own lusts. The outcomes of their desires focus upon fulfilling their own lusts which Proverbs and Ecclesiastes reinforce. In **Proverbs 16:26**, the Bible says that man *"laboureth for himself; for his mouth craveth it of him."* This is repeated in **Ecclesiastes 6:7** where the Bible says, *"All the labour of man is for his mouth, and yet the appetite is not filled."* These are just a few biblical examples of those ruled by appetite.

Devotional Thoughts

- **(For children):** Jesus performed many miracles while on earth that definitely proved He was the Son of God. After feeding the 5,000, some continued to follow Him, not to become His true disciples, but because they wanted their bellies full without working *(John 6:26)*.
- **(For everyone):** How much are you controlled by your belly? If you don't know, try fasting. Food is necessary for sustenance, but the Lord still wants control of every aspect of your body.
- What drastic things have men done historically in order to satisfy their hunger *(2 Kings 6:25, 28-29)*? What would you be willing to do if you had no food?

Prayer Thoughts

- Ask God to show you when you are under your belly's control.
- Ask God to lead you in all things by His Spirit.

SONG: *WHEREVER HE LEADS I'LL GO*

Day 32: Church Night

Proverbs 25:16 Hast thou found honey? ***eat so much as is sufficient for thee****, lest thou be filled therewith, and vomit it.*

☐ Completion Date   Appetite (con't) • 37

Day 33: (Thursday)
Keep Under Your Body

***1 Corinthians 9:27** But **I keep under my body, and bring it into subjection**: lest that by any means, when I have preached to others, I myself should be a castaway.*

INTRODUCTORY THOUGHTS

A believer should be controlled only by the Lord. At no point should a man be controlled by the cravings of his body, even that of his appetite. No doubt, Paul's words above covered a much broader scope than simply a man's appetite, but he too understood the need to control one's cravings. The Bible records several instances where Paul was hungry and had nothing to eat *(**2 Corinthians 11:27**)*. Solomon warned his son about the need for controlling one's appetite when seated before rulers at a meal. He admonished, *"When thou sittest to eat with a ruler, consider diligently what is before thee: And put a knife to thy throat, if thou be a man given to appetite" **(Proverbs 23:1-2)**.*

DEVOTIONAL THOUGHTS

- **(For children):** The king of Babylon took the best of the male captives from the children of Israel and wanted them trained for his service. He offered them a variety of food and drink which God did not allow. All of the captives chose to eat the king's meat except Daniel and his three friends. God blessed them greatly for their obedience ***(Daniel 1:8-20)***.
- **(For everyone):** What are some instances when it might be extremely important to guard your appetite? What does an inability to control one's appetite suggest about the person in general?
- How can an excessive appetite hinder serving the Lord? How could these excesses become a hindrance to a pastor, missionary, or evangelist?

PRAYER THOUGHTS

- Ask God to help you control your appetite.
- Ask God to help you *"keep under"* your body.

SONG: *MY HEART'S THE SEAT OF WAR*

Day 34: (Friday)
Loss of Appetite

Psalm 102:1 *Hear my prayer, O LORD, and let my cry come unto thee.*

2 Hide not thy face from me in the day when I am in trouble; incline thine ear unto me: in the day when I call answer me speedily.

3 For my days are consumed like smoke, and my bones are burned as an hearth.

4 ***My heart is smitten****, and withered like grass;* ***so that I forget to eat my bread.***

INTRODUCTORY THOUGHTS

Man's appetite can serve as a powerful motivator. Yet, there are times when the body is so troubled because of difficulties that it will either forget its desire to eat or lose its desire to eat altogether. The psalmist said that his heart was smitten to the point that he forgot to eat his bread **(Psalm 102:4)**. In **Psalm 107:18**, the Bible speaks of men who abhor *"all manner of meat"* and that *"draw near unto the gates of death."* Other Bible characters serve as appropriate examples. Hannah was so distraught by Peninnah's mocking over her barrenness that she refused to eat **(1 Samuel 1:7)**. David refused to eat while pleading with the Lord for the life of his child **(2 Samuel 12:16-17)**. At other times, illness may cause a severe reduction in appetite.

DEVOTIONAL THOUGHTS

- **(For children):** Saul refused food for a day and a night to seek an answer from God about an impending battle. Because Saul had sinned against the Lord, God would not give him the answer he sought. Samuel told Saul of God's judgment and the terrible news took away Saul's appetite. Others had to compel or forcefully urge Saul to eat **(1 Samuel 28:18-23)**.
- **(For everyone):** Do you ever remember a time when you lost your appetite? What caused you to lose your appetite? What became the sole focus of your attention?
- When are you most susceptible to your appetite taking control? How can getting busy for the Lord help to withstand your desire to overindulge on food?

☐ Completion Date   Appetite (con't) • 39

PRAYER THOUGHTS
- Ask God to give you strength even when your appetite is gone.
- Thank the Lord for His faithfulness.

SONG: *GOD WILL TAKE CARE OF YOU*

Day 35: (Saturday)
Round About Thy Table

Psalm 128:1 *Blessed is every one that feareth the LORD; that walketh in his ways.*

2 For thou shalt eat the labour of thine hands: happy shalt thou be, and it shall be well with thee.

3 Thy wife shall be as a fruitful vine by the sides of thine house: thy children like olive plants **round about thy table***.*

4 Behold, that thus shall the man be blessed that feareth the LORD.

INTRODUCTORY THOUGHTS

Two of the greatest opportunities within godly homes revolve around time spent at the family altar and time spent together at the supper table. Both interactions help to develop a cohesive family unit and an unbreakable bond. The family altar helps the family to get to know the Lord while the family table enables the family to get to know each other. The psalmist speaks of the blessing of having children around the table **(Psalm 128:3)**. Some may wonder if this is some other table, but the context of **Psalm 128:2** is that of a meal. Families historically placed great importance upon gathering together around the table as much as possible. Today's disintegrating familial unit usually has each person grabbing his or her own food only to rush off into some other room for work or pleasure. These times of gathering need to be given precedence in order to offer any hope of restoring the family unit.

DEVOTIONAL THOUGHTS
- **(For children):** Eating and drinking serves as one of the purposes of the home **(1 Corinthians 11:22a, 34a)**. This is why mealtime is an excellent opportunity to bring together a distracted family. Job understood this and thought back to a time that made him happy **(Job 29:2a, 5b)**. While at the table with family, try to keep the conversa-

tion pleasant. Do not spend time speaking of problems and troubles. When we eat with the Lord, it will be a happy time *(Revelation 19:9)*.
- **(For everyone):** How often does your entire family gather together around the table for a meal? Would you describe your family as close knit? Is it possible that the two are connected?
- Do you hasten to finish eating to get away from the supper table? Or do you use this time as an opportunity to eat and enjoy the time spent with your loved ones? Are you willing to slow down and let God work in your home?

PRAYER THOUGHTS
- Thank God for giving you a family with which to eat.
- Ask God to help you see the importance of family meals.

SONG: *GOD, GIVE US CHRISTIAN HOMES*

Notes: _____

Quotes from the next volume
(VOLUME 4, WEEK 5)
Subject: Appearance

All true fellowship, consecration, and sanctification originates within the heart; however, it will eventually work its way to the outside.

Believers are not to speak, look, think, or act like the world. In every way possible, believers are to remain separate.

All of the believer's endeavours should be done for the Lord and not unto men.

6
Appetite (con't)

Appetite—The word itself is only found four times in scripture, but the subject matter is covered using a wide variety of terminology; this particular study focuses upon partaking of or abstaining from alcoholic beverages.

Variations: appetite

Interesting fact: Multitudes of people have been deceived into thinking that Jesus turned water into fermented wine *(John 2:1-11)*. However, for the Lord to have done so would have been to place Himself under the *"Woe"* of **Habakkuk 2:15** which states, *"Woe unto him that giveth his neighbour drink, that puttest thy bottle to him, and makest him drunken also."* Furthermore, this would mean that the Lord Jesus, contrary to scripture, willingly tempted men with evil *(James 1:13)*. Additionally, the context and record of the event proves that the wine was an unfermented product. Those at the wedding had drunk all the wine until there was no wine left and yet their taste buds remained intact to note the superiority of that which the Saviour had made *(John 2:10)*.

Bible study tip: Some have wrongfully suggested that Jesus could not drink wine because He was a Nazarite. Though it is certain that Jesus did not drink fermented wine, He could have partaken of unfermented wine. Additionally, every

Bible student should note the distinct difference between a *Nazarene*—one born in Nazareth **(Matthew 2:23)** and a *Nazarite*—one who takes the God-ordained vow recorded in **Numbers 6:2-3**. Jesus was a Nazarene by birth, but there exists no record of Him ever taking the vow of the Nazarite.

Sunday, Day 36—Church Day (no devotional)
Monday, Day 37—*Deceived by Wine*
Tuesday, Day 38—*Be Not Drunk, but Be Filled*
Wednesday, Day 39—Church Night (no devotional)
Thursday, Day 40—*Tarrying Long at the Wine*
Friday, Day 41—*Stumbling in Judgment*
Saturday, Day 42—*A Little Wine for Thy Stomach's Sake*

Day 36: Church Day

Habakkuk 2:15 Woe unto him that giveth his neighbour drink, that puttest thy bottle to him, and makest him drunken also, that thou mayest look on their nakedness!

Day 37: (Monday)
Deceived by Wine

Proverbs 20:1 Wine is a mocker, strong drink is raging: and whosoever is deceived thereby is not wise.

INTRODUCTORY THOUGHTS

Throughout history, millions of people have been deceived by the influence of wine and strong drink, including many Christians. These multitudes have been duped into thinking that they have the power to start and stop their consumption at will. All of them underestimated the power and the control of alcohol. Alcoholic consumption at the first seems to pose no threat to the individual, but as man continues to give himself to it, he discovers its deadly side. This is confirmed in **Proverbs 23:32** where the Bible says, "At the last it biteth like a serpent, and stingeth like an adder." A man who submits himself to wine or strong drink eventually discovers that partaking in these substances turns to his own demise. He will lose his God-given self-control and find himself at the mercy of the unmerciful strong drink.

Devotional Thoughts

- **(For children):** The Bible compares using strong drink to a painful adder's bite. ***Genesis 49:17*** tells us that the bite of an adder will cause a horse to rear (rise up on his hind legs) causing the rider to be thrown off backward. If an adder's bite causes great pain for such a large animal like a horse, strong drink will definitely not be good for people.
- **(For everyone):** Would you willingly choose to play with a serpent that has been known to bite? Or would you stay away just in case it might harm you? Making the choice to drink yields some very dangerous outcomes.
- What does it mean to mock someone? Why does the Bible say that wine is a mocker? What does it mean to rage? Why does the Bible say that strong drink is raging?

Prayer Thoughts

- Ask God to protect you from the dangers of strong drink.
- Ask God to give you the wisdom to trust His word.

SONG: *WHATEVER I NEED IN JESUS DWELLS*

Day 38: (Tuesday)
Be Not Drunk, but Be Filled

Ephesians 5:18 *And **be not drunk with wine**, wherein is excess; but be filled with the Spirit;*

Introductory Thoughts

Man cannot be drunk with wine and simultaneously filled with the Spirit. The two elements are completely inconsistent and stand in direct conflict. Man will be either yielded to the control of the Spirit or yielded to the control of alcohol but cannot be yielded simultaneously to both. *"[B]e not drunk with wine"* is a commandment to avoid sin. *"[B]e filled with the Spirit"* is a commandment to yield to righteousness. This dichotomy should be an easy choice for each and every believer to identify and formulate. On one hand, the individual can choose to indulge in alcoholic beverages, resulting in a choice to displease the Saviour. On the other hand, he can yield to the Holy Ghost, resulting in a decision pleasing to His Lord. No believer should ever be deceived into believing that he can fill himself with both the world's drink and God's Spirit. It does not work, it will not work, and it cannot not work!

DEVOTIONAL THOUGHTS

- **(For children):** In *1 Corinthians 3:16-17*, God says your body is His temple and that you are not to defile it—make it unclean. Daniel said he would not defile himself with the king's wine which the king offered as a daily provision with the meals *(Daniel 1:5, 8)*.
- **(For everyone):** What might happen if a person was drunk with wine? What might happen if a person was filled with the Spirit of God? Make a list and see how the list differs.
- Why is alcohol contrary to God's will for a person's life? How will it hinder a believer from serving the Lord to the best of his ability?

PRAYER THOUGHTS

- Ask God to help you choose to be filled with the Spirit.
- Thank God for preserving you from the evils of alcohol.

SONG: *FAREWELL VAIN WORLD*

Day 39: Church Night

Hosea 4:11 Whoredom and **wine and new wine take away the heart.**

Day 40: (Thursday)
Tarrying Long at the Wine

Proverbs 23:29 **Who hath woe?** *who hath sorrow? who hath contentions? who hath babbling? who hath wounds without cause? who hath redness of eyes?*

30 **They that tarry long at the wine;** *they that go to seek mixed wine.*

INTRODUCTORY THOUGHTS

The world has falsely presented alcoholic consumption as a thing pleasurable, similar to the now politically incorrect cigarette advertise-

☐ Completion Date   Appetite (con't) • 45

ments of a few decades ago. Contrary to the one marketed to the world, the Bible presents a completely opposing portrait. Though changes subtly occur, alcohol eventually takes control of those who choose to continue their early participation. The Bible says, *"Woe unto them that rise up early in the morning, that they may follow strong drink; that continue until night, till wine inflame them!" (Isaiah 5:11)*. Drinking may begin as a source of pleasure and stress reduction but it rarely, if ever, ends there. The ultimate outcome of the intake of alcohol is its consumption by a person from daytime until he drinks himself silly at night. The Bible describes some of the physical effects of this practice as contentions, babbling, and redness of eyes. It also describes some of the by-products as woe, sorrow, and wounds without cause. A sane world obedient to God would reject such outcomes if only they knew, understood, and obeyed the truth.

DEVOTIONAL THOUGHTS

- **(For children):** A person addicted to alcohol cannot live without it. ***Proverbs 23:35*** presents a sad story as does ***Isaiah 56:12***. God does not want sin to control you ***(Romans 6:12)***. He wants you to allow Him to be in control of your life ***(Romans 6:22)***.
- **(For everyone):** Would you ever start drinking if you knew the possibility existed that you would get to the point where you had to drink more and more and longer and longer in order to fulfil your dependence?
- Have you ever spent time around those who partake of alcohol in excess? Have you noticed the woe, sorrow, and contentions that have afflicted them resulting from the alcohol use?

PRAYER THOUGHTS

- Thank God for joy and peace.
- Pray for those you know who have submitted to alcohol and its controlling effects.

SONG: *HAPPY THE MEN WHOSE BLISS SUPREME*

Day 41: (Friday)
Stumbling in Judgment

*Isaiah 28:7 But **they also have erred through wine, and through strong drink are out of the way; the priest and the prophet have erred through strong drink**, they are swallowed up of wine, they are out of the way through strong drink; they err in vision, **they stumble in judgment**.*

INTRODUCTORY THOUGHTS

There are many stories of those overcome with a sense of embarrassment resulting from their actions while under the influence. As they increasingly yielded to the power of strong drink, they did things they later regretted once sober. This is what the Bible means about alcohol when it says it causes men to *"stumble in judgment."* No doubt many of God's people like Noah *(Genesis 9:21-25)* and Lot *(Genesis 19:31-36)* had regrets as they became sober. The Bible tells of Nabal who *"was very drunken"* and foolishly refused to help king David *(1 Samuel 25:1-17, 36)*. When he came to himself, Abigail told her husband all that had transpired during his drunken stupor. After he heard of his foolish actions, the Bible says that *"his heart died within him" (1 Samuel 25:37)*.

DEVOTIONAL THOUGHTS

- **(For children):** Strong drink causes people to forget what is right and do what is wrong *(Proverbs 31:4-5; Isaiah 5:22-23)*. When Ahasuerus had wine, he asked his wife to do something he normally would not have asked her to do *(Esther 1:10-12)*. When she refused, he was angry and had her dethroned. Later, he could not change his mind *(Esther 2:1)*.
- **(For everyone):** What are some foolish decisions that people might make while under the influence of alcohol? Is it possible that some of those decisions are irreversible?
- Have you ever been around others who were controlled by alcohol? Did they make decisions later regretted once they came to their senses?

☐ Completion Date   Appetite (con't) • 47

PRAYER THOUGHTS
- Ask God to show you the wickedness of alcohol.
- Ask God to give you the wisdom to do right.

SONG: *CLEANSE ME*

Day 42: (Saturday)
A Little Wine for Thy Stomach's Sake

*1 Timothy 5:23 Drink no longer water, but **use a little wine for thy stomach's sake and thine often infirmities**.*

INTRODUCTORY THOUGHTS

Many carnal believers quoting **1 Timothy 5:23** have attempted to justify their unscriptural use of alcohol. Yet, a careful look at the scriptures proves that they wrest (or twist) the scripture to their own destruction **(2 Peter 3:16)**. From the passage, we understand that Timothy was plagued by some chronic health problems. Paul specifically mentioned stomach problems, but there were other infirmities that beset him as well. Drinking water was not curing Timothy's ailments, so Paul, perhaps with doctor Luke's guidance and recommendation, suggested *"a little wine"* for Timothy's *often* infirmities. What purpose did the wine serve? It was strictly medicinal and not social or pleasurable. In other words, Paul said that Timothy needed some medicine to facilitate his recovery. Paul was not offering Timothy or us an excuse to drink but a prescription of medicine for recovery from debilitating ailments.

DEVOTIONAL THOUGHTS

- **(For children):** God gave doctors and medicine to help us **(Matthew 9:12; Proverbs 17:22a)**. He also said not to do anything that even looks evil because you might cause others to justify their sin **(1 Thessalonians 5:22; Romans 14:21)**. Timothy was to take a *"little"* wine. Thus God was not approving strong drink.
- **(For everyone):** Why do carnal people seek to twist the scripture to make it say what they want it to say? How does God feel when people mess with His word attempting to justify their sin and failings?

- If a believer is sick, he should take medicine. How could the purchase of any kind of alcoholic beverage hurt your testimony? How could the Devil use alcohol to hurt your witness to the lost?

PRAYER THOUGHTS
- Ask God to help you trust His word as it is written.
- Ask God to give you the wisdom to guard your testimony.

SONG: *ALL THE WAY MY SAVIOUR LEADS ME*

Notes: _____

_____

_____

_____

_____

_____

_____

_____

_____

Quotes from the next volume

(VOLUME 4, WEEK 6)

Subject: Authority

Authority resides with those who have the right to rule but not always with those who have the ability to rule.

When the Lord Jesus spoke, men marvelled. Why? Because the Lord did not speak like the other religious leaders, instead He spoke with authority!

The godly believer is certain of his beliefs because he is certain of the authority behind those beliefs.

7
Bereavement

Bereavement—found thirteen times in twelves verses; Note: In order to gain a more complete study of bereavement, Bible students should also consider studying sorrow, consolation, and mourning.

Variations: bereave, bereaved, bereaveth

First usage: *Genesis 42:36* (bereaved)

Last usage: *Hosea 13:8* (bereaved)

Defined: to be deprived of something or to have it taken away; Note: This study is particularly focused upon the loss of loved ones.

Interesting fact: A lamentation is a specific statement concerning someone mourning for another *(Jeremiah 22:18)*, often made for the dead *(Genesis 50:10)*. Interestingly, an entire book of the Bible was written to serve as a lamentation and is so named. It opens with a lamentation for Judah: *"How doth the city sit solitary, that was full of people! how is she become as a widow! She that was great among the nations, and princess among the provinces, how is she become tributary!"* **(Lamentations 1:1)**.

Bible study tip: Pay particular attention to any statistical peculiarities within scripture. For example, the book of Lamentations contains five chapters. The first two chapters and the last two chapters each contain twenty-two verses. The middle chapter is made up of sixty-six verses (twenty-two x three). What is the significance of the numbers five, twenty-two, and sixty-six in scripture? How do these statistical features relate to the message of Lamentations?

Sunday, Day 43—Church Day (no devotional)
Monday, Day 44—*Praying for Sick Loved Ones*
Tuesday, Day 45—*What Happens at Death*
Wednesday, Day 46—Church Night (no devotional)
Thursday, Day 47—*Mourning for Those Departed*
Friday, Day 48—*Lamenting over the Deceased*
Saturday, Day 49—*Sorrowing Not as the World*

Day 43: Church Day

Job 1:20 Then Job arose, and rent his mantle, and shaved his head, and fell down upon he ground, and worshipped,

21 And said, Naked came I out of my mother's womb, and naked shall I return thither: **the LORD gave, and the LORD hath taken away; blessed be the name of the LORD.**

Day 44: (Monday)
Praying for Sick Loved Ones

2 Samuel 12:15 And Nathan departed unto his house. And the LORD struck the child that Uriah's wife bare unto David, and it was very sick.

16 **David** *therefore* **besought God for the child***; and David fasted, and went in, and lay all night upon the earth.*

17 And the elders of his house arose, and went to him, to raise him up from the earth: but he would not, neither did he eat bread with them.

☐ Completion Date   Bereavement • 51

18 And it came to pass on the seventh day, that the child died. And the servants of David feared to tell him that the child was dead: for they said, Behold, while the child was yet alive, we spake unto him, and he would not hearken unto our voice: how will he then vex himself, if we tell him that the child is dead?

19 But when David saw that his servants whispered, David perceived that the child was dead: therefore David said unto his servants, Is the child dead? And they said, He is dead.

20 Then David arose from the earth, and washed, and anointed himself, and changed his apparel, and came into the house of the LORD, and worshipped: then he came to his own house; and when he required, they set bread before him, and he did eat.

21 Then said his servants unto him, What thing is this that thou hast done? thou didst fast and weep for the child, while it was alive; but when the child was dead, thou didst rise and eat bread.

22 And he said, While the child was yet alive, I fasted and wept: for I said, Who can tell whether GOD will be gracious to me, that the child may live?

23 But now he is dead, wherefore should I fast? can I bring him back again? I shall go to him, but he shall not return to me.

INTRODUCTORY THOUGHTS

One of the more difficult things any individual faces in this life involves watching loved ones suffer. Yet, this life is filled with suffering and death. David witnessed just such a tragedy when his child became ill and eventually died. While the child was alive, David implored the Lord for the child's recovery. No doubt, he was asking God to heal the child and restore health. In addition to praying for the child, David fasted and wept for the life of his newborn. In the end, the Lord decided to take the child. David understood that he could not bring the child back but would one day go to where the child already was. As soon as the child passed, David refocused upon living. He ceased praying for the child and began to comfort his grieving wife.

DEVOTIONAL THOUGHTS

- **(For children):** The word *beseech* means to request earnestly. When Jesus was on earth, many besought Him to heal their sick loved ones

(Matthew 8:5-7; Luke 4:38-39; John 4:46-47). The Lord wants us to come to Him with such requests *(Philippians 4:6-7)*.
- **(For everyone):** Have you ever had a loved one suffer from a serious illness or injury? Did you merely sit around and worry about his or her condition, or did you earnestly pray?
- Why did David cease to pray for the child as soon his baby died? What did he do next? Why is it important that we follow the same type of pattern that David set forth?

PRAYER THOUGHTS
- Pray for any loved ones who are ill or seriously injured.
- Thank God for the privilege of prayer.

SONG: WHAT A FRIEND WE HAVE IN JESUS

Day 45: (Tuesday)
What Happens at Death

*1 Thessalonians 5:23 And the very God of peace sanctify you wholly; and I pray God **your whole spirit and soul and body** be preserved blameless unto the coming of our Lord Jesus Christ.*

INTRODUCTORY THOUGHTS

Man is made up of three parts: spirit, soul, and body. Death takes place when the soul *(Genesis 35:18)* and the spirit *(Genesis 25:8)* leave the body. This event happens to everyone regardless of the individual's spiritual state at death. Saved or lost, a person's spirit returns to God who gave it *(Ecclesiastes 3:21; Ecclesiastes 12:7)*. However, the soul's destination is based upon whether or not a person has trusted Jesus Christ as Saviour during this life. There exists no midpoint between earth and heaven (or hell) to purge one's sins, including places invented by religions to do so. For a saved person, the Bible declares that to be absent from the body is to be present with the Lord *(2 Corinthians 5:8)*. Unfortunately for the lost, this same outcome is not true. Following death, the Bible reveals that the lost man's soul immediately goes to hell *(Luke 16:23)*.

Devotional Thoughts

- **(For children):** If you are sad over a saved person's death, read *Ecclesiastes 7:1*. Why does the Bible say that the day of death is better than the day of one's birth? The person's troubles are over. If saved, the individual is with God *(Philippians 1:21, 23)*. The sadness experienced at someone's death is really for ourselves because we miss our loved one. Our saved loved one is happy and would not choose to return to earth.
- **(For everyone):** Why is it important to pray for the salvation of loved ones before they die? How can we also use times of illness and serious injury to remind our loved ones of their need to be saved?
- Why should scriptural knowledge of death help us in the departure of saved loved ones? How should it sober us in the departure of lost loved ones?

Prayer Thoughts

- Pray for your loved ones who may be lost.
- Thank God that death only temporarily separates the saved.

SONG: *ABSENT FROM FLESH! O BLISSFUL THOUGHT!*

Day 46: Church Night

*2 Samuel 18:33 And **the king was much moved**, and went up to the chamber over the gate, **and wept**: and as he went, thus he said, O my son Absalom, my son, my son Absalom! **would God I had died for thee**, O Absalom, my son, my son!*

Day 47: (Thursday)
Mourning for Those Departed

Genesis 23:1 And Sarah was an hundred and seven and twenty years old: these were the years of the life of Sarah.

*2 And **Sarah died** in Kirjatharba; the same is Hebron in the land of Canaan: and **Abraham came to mourn for Sarah, and to weep for her**.*

Introductory Thoughts

When a loved one passes away, mourning serves as an important part of the healing process. However, believers should never sorrow in the same fashion as the world *(1 Thessalonians 4:13)*, yet mourning is acceptable and proper when grieving the death of someone. In Bible times, people seemed to take mourning very seriously. In fact, the initial mourning period at times was quite lengthy *(Genesis 50:3; Numbers 20:29; Deuteronomy 34:8)*. There were even people whose purpose it was to assist in the mourning of those departed *(Jeremiah 9:17)*. Grieving is a natural part of man's process in dealing with the loss of loved ones. Failure to give time to properly mourn often prolongs the process and hinders the individual from dealing with the loss.

Devotional Thoughts

- **(For children)**: Mary and Martha were very sad. Their brother Lazarus had died. Friends came to comfort them. Jesus also came. Even though He knew He would raise Lazarus from the dead, He wept with them. He felt their sorrow. It is okay to cry when someone dies *(John 11:19, 31-36)*.
- **(For everyone)**: Have you ever lost a loved one to death? How did you handle the loss? Did you take time to mourn? If not, did you find that the pain of the loss lingered over a longer period?
- Why is it crucial that we take the appropriate amount of time to mourn the loss of our loved ones? How can God help us during the time of mourning?

Prayer Thoughts

- Ask God to help you see the importance of dealing with death.
- Thank God for the help He gives us in times of mourning.

SONG: *DOES JESUS CARE?*

Day 48: (Friday)
Lamenting over the Deceased

*2 Samuel 1:17 And **David lamented with this lamentation over Saul and over Jonathan** his son:*

18 (Also he bade them teach the children of Judah the use of the bow: behold, it is written in the book of Jasher.)

19 The beauty of Israel is slain upon thy high places: how are the mighty fallen!

20 Tell it not in Gath, publish it not in the streets of Askelon; lest the daughters of the Philistines rejoice, lest the daughters of the uncircumcised triumph.

21 Ye mountains of Gilboa, let there be no dew, neither let there be rain, upon you, nor fields of offerings: for there the shield of the mighty is vilely cast away, the shield of Saul, as though he had not been anointed with oil.

22 From the blood of the slain, from the fat of the mighty, the bow of Jonathan turned not back, and the sword of Saul returned not empty.

23 Saul and Jonathan were lovely and pleasant in their lives, and in their death they were not divided: they were swifter than eagles, they were stronger than lions.

24 Ye daughters of Israel, weep over Saul, who clothed you in scarlet, with other delights, who put on ornaments of gold upon your apparel.

25 How are the mighty fallen in the midst of the battle! O Jonathan, thou wast slain in thine high places.

26 I am distressed for thee, my brother Jonathan: very pleasant hast thou been unto me: thy love to me was wonderful, passing the love of women.

27 How are the mighty fallen, and the weapons of war perished!

INTRODUCTORY THOUGHTS

In Bible times, the mourning process often included a time of lamentation. Although lamentations were diverse, scripture points to a time set aside for speaking about the deceased. Today's passage shows that David lamented the passing of Saul and Jonathan. He spoke positively about their efforts in battle *(2 Samuel 1:25)*, their usefulness to Israel *(2 Samuel 1:24)*, and their beauty *(2 Samuel 1:23)*. Apparently, part of the healing process includes speaking of those who have departed. Perhaps it would lead to rejoicing in the good memories and crying at the mention of sad times. Regardless, it is clear that talking about the deceased helps those still alive in a time of mourning.

DEVOTIONAL THOUGHTS

- **(For children):** The Bible records that Josiah was the last king of Judah who truly wanted to follow God. He rid the land of idolatry, cleansed and repaired God's house, read the book of the law to the people, and

wept over sins. When Josiah died in battle, Jeremiah the prophet and the people lamented over him *(2 Chronicles 35:24-25)*.
- **(For everyone):** How could it be helpful to talk about loved ones who have departed? How could it be harmful to refuse to speak of those who have gone on before us?
- How do you handle the passing of loved ones? Do you try to get through the hurt without speaking of those who have died? Have you found this to be helpful?

Prayer Thoughts
- Ask God to help you properly deal with the loss of loved ones.
- Ask God to help you minister to others as they deal with death.

SONG: *BE STILL, MY SOUL*

Day 49: (Saturday)
Sorrowing Not as the World

1 Thessalonians 4:13 But **I would not have you to be ignorant, brethren, concerning them which are asleep, that ye sorrow not, even as others which have no hope.**

14 For if we believe that Jesus died and rose again, even so **them also which sleep in Jesus will God bring with him.**

15 For this we say unto you by the word of the Lord, that we which are alive and remain unto the coming of the Lord shall not prevent them which are asleep.

16 For the Lord himself shall descend from heaven with a shout, with the voice of the archangel, and with the trump of God: and the dead in Christ shall rise first:

17 Then we which are alive and remain shall be caught up together with them in the clouds, to meet the Lord in the air: and so shall we ever be with the Lord.

18 **Wherefore comfort one another with these words.**

Introductory Thoughts

The death of someone is a sorrowful event, but much more so for those who do not know God (the lost). Believers, on the other hand, understand that the separation of death is only temporary. For this reason,

☐ Completion Date   Bereavement • 57

believers should find much hope after losing a loved one who knew the Lord. This loss serves as another reminder to look forward to the joys of heaven awaiting God's people. The scenario is much different for the lost. When a lost person loses a loved one, there is no reason for hope. Yet, God offers hope! If the departed loved one was saved, the hope for a reunion is both real and anticipated; however, if the loved one was never saved, hell will not be a place for any joyous reunions. It is terrible to witness others lose loved ones to death without the wonderful hope offered by God to His children.

Devotional Thoughts

- **(For children)**: Read *Proverbs 14:32b*. Martha knew of that hope when her brother Lazarus died *(John 11:23-27)*. The Pauline epistles also describe the hope that every Christian has *(1 Corinthians 15:51-52, 57)*.
- **(For everyone)**: Why do believers have hope in the loss of a saved friend or family member? Where do the deceased go when they die? How do their circumstances compare with those that are left behind?
- Have you ever been to a funeral for someone who did not know the Lord? Have you ever witnessed lost people as they mourn the passing of a loved one? Did it make you thankful for the hope that God has promised to His children?

Prayer Thoughts

- Thank God for the hope He has given to us in death.
- Ask God to help you witness to the lost concerning death.

SONG: *MY TIMES OF SORROW AND OF JOY*

Notes: _____

_____
_____
_____
_____
_____

Notes:

Quotes from the next volume
(VOLUME 4, WEEK 7)
Subject: Authority (con't)

One of the most dangerous things a believer can do is seek to implement authority that does not belong to him.

Those who know the Lord ought to be the first to obey, submit to *(Hebrews 13:17)*, and pray for *(1 Timothy 2:1-2)* those in authority.

8
Comfort

Comfort—found 131 times in 119 verses

Variations: comfort, comfortable, comfortably, comforted, comfortedst, comforter, comforters, comforteth, comfortless, comforts

First usage: *Genesis 5:29* (comfort)

Last usage: *2 Thessalonians 2:17* (comfort)

Defined: commonly defined as a feeling of relief, but more accurately comfort involves inner strength that an individual can carry with him along the way

Interesting fact: Comfort is a wonderful gift from God. However, there are times when individuals are so distraught that they refuse the comfort offered to them. Out of the 131 times *comfort* (or its variations) is found in scripture, three times you will find that someone *"refused to be comforted" (Genesis 37:35; Psalm 77:2; Jeremiah 31:15)*.

Bible study tip: The Lord is not opposed to the asking of questions. One of the greatest inquiries mankind can make revolves around "why?" In God's word, the Lord graciously makes statements only to follow those statements with the reason or cause for the previous statement. For example, the

Lord *"comforteth us in all our tribulation"* THAT *"we may be able to comfort them which are in any trouble" (2 Corinthians 1:4).*

Sunday, Day 50—Church Day (no devotional)
Monday, Day 51—*What Is Comfort?*
Tuesday, Day 52—*The God of All Comfort*
Wednesday, Day 53—Church Night (no devotional)
Thursday, Day 54—*The Comforter, Which Is the Holy Ghost*
Friday, Day 55—*Comfort of the Scriptures*
Saturday, Day 56—*Comfort One Another*

Day 50: Church Day

*Psalm 119:76 Let, I pray thee, **thy merciful kindness be for my comfort**, according to thy word unto thy servant.*

Day 51: (Monday)
What Is Comfort?

*Genesis 24:67 And Isaac brought her into his mother Sarah's tent, and took Rebekah, and she became his wife; and he loved her: and **Isaac was comforted** after his mother's death.*

INTRODUCTORY THOUGHTS

The world places a premium on the concept of living comfortably. For instance, people desire comfortable clothes, comfortable beds, comfortable cars, comfortable furniture, etc. The list is unending. There are even foods designated as "comfort foods." Yet, with this great emphasis upon comfort, the world seems to experience so little of true comfort. So, what exactly is comfort? Why is speaking of comfort so trendy and yet so hard to achieve? The word *comfort* is easily defined by breaking it down into two parts: *com* and *fort*. The prefix *com* means "with" and the word *fort* means "strength." Simply put, comfort involves a strength that a person can carry with him. Immediately, every Christian should recognize that very little true comfort exists in this world. True comfort stems from the Lord and not that offered outside of Him.

☐ Completion Date Comfort • 61

Devotional Thoughts

- **(For children):** Ruth was a poor stranger in a strange and distant land. God led Ruth to glean in Boaz' field to get food. Boaz comforted her: spoke kindly, offered her to gather barley every day in his field, offered her protection, and even offered food and drink when the workers ate *(Ruth 2:8-14)*.
- **(For everyone):** Have you ever experienced a time when you needed some comfort? Why did Isaac need to be comforted in *Genesis 24:67*? How did his comfort come from the Lord?
- What are some times, other than the loss of a loved one, when an individual might need to be comforted? What are some ways in which you could offer comfort?

Prayer Thoughts

- Ask God to help you be a comfort to others in their time of need.
- Thank God for the times He has comforted you.

SONG: *TURN YOUR EYES UPON JESUS*

Day 52: (Tuesday)
The God of All Comfort

*2 Corinthians 1:3 Blessed be God, even the Father of our Lord Jesus Christ, the Father of mercies, and **the God of all comfort;***

***4** Who comforteth us in all our tribulation, that we may be able to comfort them which are in any trouble, by the comfort wherewith we ourselves are comforted of God.*

Introductory Thoughts

The Bible clearly states that all comfort comes either directly or indirectly from the Lord. The Bible says that He is *"the Father of mercies, and the God of all comfort" (2 Corinthians 1:3)*. Any true and lasting comfort man receives originates with and through the Lord *(James 1:17)*, and the comfort given by God can comfort each of us in any and all tribulation *(2 Corinthians 1:4)*. Unfortunately, man seems to think that every problem he faces requires a different area of study with various solutions. Yet, the Bible contradicts this line of thinking by stating that every tribulation has only one source of comfort. It is important to note that the comfort received by one person can be passed on to help others regardless of the trouble faced. That is the power of God's comfort!

DEVOTIONAL THOUGHTS
- **(For children):** God gave each of us a mother for many reasons, but one reason involves the comfort each of us so desperately needs. Mom may not always be near, but God is always with us and wants to comfort us *(Isaiah 66:13a)*.
- **(For everyone):** What troubles are you presently facing? At first thought, what sources would you think you need in order to receive comfort? Why is it crucial that you realize your comfort comes from God?
- How have you taken God's comfort to others? What did you learn about God's comfort during a time of loss? How did you use that comfort to help someone else who had lost a loved one?

PRAYER THOUGHTS
- Thank God for the comfort He offers in every trouble.
- Ask God to help you pass His comfort to others.

SONG: *COME, YE DISCONSOLATE*

Day 53: Church Night

Psalm 23:4 *Yea, though I walk through the valley of the shadow of death,* **I will fear no evil:** *for thou art with me;* **thy rod and thy staff they comfort me.**

Day 54: (Thursday)
The Comforter, Which Is the Holy Ghost

John 14:26 *But* **the Comforter, which is the Holy Ghost,** *whom the Father will send in my name, he shall teach you all things, and bring all things to your remembrance, whatsoever I have said unto you.*

INTRODUCTORY THOUGHTS
The Bible never directly addresses the Lord Jesus as *"the Comforter,"* yet the Lord alluded to this title. The Lord told His followers that the coming of the Holy Ghost would be God's means of sending them

"another Comforter" (John 14:16). Evidently, the Lord Jesus served as the Comforter and the Holy Ghost would function as *another* Comforter. During His earthly ministry, the Lord Jesus worked in the lives of those who followed Him. He was their Comforter. When He went to the Father, the Father sent *"another Comforter"* and He is the Holy Ghost. Each person who is born again by the grace of God has the Holy Ghost dwelling within *(Romans 8:9)*. When troubles come, and they will, the believer has within himself a person of the Godhead that specializes in comforting those afflicted.

Devotional Thoughts

- **(For children):** The Holy Ghost is God *(1 John 5:7; Acts 5:3-4)*. He lives inside every single believer *(John 14:17)*. Since God has the power to make everything *(Job 33:4; Psalm 33:6-9)*, He has the power to comfort you in anything *(Isaiah 51:12-13)*.
- **(For everyone):** If comfort is strength that you can carry with you, how does the Holy Ghost perfectly fit the description of *"the Comforter"*? How is He strength that can be carried with you?
- How can the comfort of the Holy Ghost be a wonderful evidence of salvation? Where does a lost person get his comfort? How is comfort different in the life of a saved person?

Prayer Thoughts

- Thank God for sending the Holy Ghost to be your *"Comforter."*
- Ask God to help you submit to the comfort of the Spirit.

SONG: *ABIDE WITH ME*

Day 55: (Friday)
Comfort of the Scriptures

*Romans 15:4 For whatsoever things were written aforetime were written for our learning, **that we through patience and comfort of the scriptures might have hope.***

Introductory Thoughts

Far too many people wrongly assume that the Bible lacks relevance in addressing modern problems. However, the Bible declares that things written *aforetime* were written for comfort in present troubles. Though the Bible does not deal specifically with every modern trouble, the work of God in past believers' lives offers the comfort necessary to face any trouble. This is one of many reasons why it is imperative that believers read the entire Bible and not limit it to the New Testament or certain epistles within it. God's workings in the lives of Job, Abraham, and Jeremiah can offer just as much comfort as God's workings in the lives of Paul or John. No matter the trouble faced, an open Bible with a receptive heart serves as man's greatest opportunity for experiencing the ever allusive comfort.

DEVOTIONAL THOUGHTS

- **(For children):** The story of Joseph is comforting because it lets us know that God is in charge no matter what we may experience. Joseph was rejected by his brothers, sold into slavery, imprisoned, and forgotten in that prison for two more years by someone who promised to help him. None of his troubles were his fault or deserved and yet he remained true to God.
- **(For everyone):** How has the word of God been a comfort to you in times of weakness? What Bible verses has God used to bring you through some difficult times?
- If God's word is a comfort to you, don't you think it would be a comfort to others? How could you prepare to help others in their times of trouble?

PRAYER THOUGHTS

- Thank God for giving you a perfect Bible that offers comfort.
- Ask God to teach you how to comfort others with the Bible.

SONG: *OUR GOD, OUR HELP*

Day 56: (Saturday)
Comfort One Another

1 Thessalonians 5:11 Wherefore **comfort yourselves together**, and edify one another, even as also ye do.

12 And we beseech you, brethren, to know them which labour among you, and are over you in the Lord, and admonish you;

☐ Completion Date

13 And to esteem them very highly in love for their work's sake. And be at peace among yourselves.

*14 Now we exhort you, brethren, warn them that are unruly, **comfort the feebleminded**, support the weak, be patient toward all men.*

15 See that none render evil for evil unto any man; but ever follow that which is good, both among yourselves, and to all men.

INTRODUCTORY THOUGHTS

God comforts believers expecting that they, in turn, will extend that heaven-sent comfort toward others during their times of need. Believers are admonished to *"comfort the feebleminded, support the weak, and be patient toward all men"* **(1 Thessalonians 5:14)**. Stronger believers are encouraged to bear the infirmities of those who are weak **(Romans 15:1)**. When one believer weeps as a result of the trials and troubles of this life, the body of Christ should weep with that brother or sister **(Romans 12:15)**. Every member of the body of Christ should be available to the strengthening and support of other members of the body, for in doing so, believers fulfil the law of Christ **(Galatians 6:2)**.

DEVOTIONAL THOUGHTS

- **(For children):** When we know people are hurting (physically or in their hearts), we should consider how they feel and help them if we can **(1 Corinthians 12:26)**. Job did **(Job 30:25; Job 29:15-16)**. Abraham knew what to do to comfort weary travelers **(Genesis 18:1-5)**.
- **(For everyone):** How can you comfort other believers? What trials has God helped you through? How can you take His help for you and offer it to others in need?
- Who do you know that might be going through a difficult time? What could you do to comfort them? Have you been through that difficulty before, and if not, how could you still be a comforter?

PRAYER THOUGHTS

- Thank God for believers who have helped you.
- Ask God to use *"the Comforter"* to make you a comforter.

SONG: *BLEST BE THE TIE THAT BINDS*

Notes: _____

Quotes from the next volume

(VOLUME 4, WEEK 8)
Subject: Blame

In Christ, believers bear no guilty responsibility for sins they have committed. Instead, believers are viewed and accepted in the righteousness of Christ *(Ephesians 1:6)*.

The saints of God are positionally blameless in Christ, but practically, each believer must strive daily to *"be blameless and harmless, . . . in the midst of a crooked and perverse nation."*

9

Confusion

Confusion—found twenty-eight times in twenty-seven verses

Variations: confused, confusion

First usage: *Leviticus 18:23* (confusion)

Last usage: *James 3:16* (confusion)

Defined: the state of bewilderment or uncertainty

Interesting fact: The Bible associates confusion with the face five times *(Ezra 9:7; Psalm 44:15; Jeremiah 7:19; Daniel 9:7, 8)*. Perhaps this association reveals that a man's face serves as the window to his mind. Confusion, though housed in the mind, clearly manifests itself upon one's face to others.

Bible study tip: Paul's epistles commonly incorporated lists in order to drive home a particular point of emphasis. *2 Timothy 3:1-5* contains one such list. When studying these lists, consider the number of items listed, the inclusion or exclusion of the coordinating conjunctions like "and," and the overall theme expressed. While considering each part, try not to lose sight of the greater message being conveyed.

Sunday, Day 57—Church Day (no devotional)
Monday, Day 58—*What Is Confusion?*

Tuesday, Day 59—*Confusion and Sin*
Wednesday, Day 60—Church Night (no devotional)
Thursday, Day 61—*The Author of Confusion*
Friday, Day 62—*Where There Is Envying and Strife*
Saturday, Day 63—*A Prayer for Confusion*

Day 57: Church Day

Jeremiah 3:25 *We lie down in our shame, and **our confusion covereth us**: **for we have sinned against the LORD our God**, we and our fathers, from our youth even unto this day, and have not obeyed the voice of the LORD our God.*

Day 58: (Monday)
What Is Confusion?

Acts 19:29 *And **the whole city was filled with confusion**: and having caught Gaius and Aristarchus, men of Macedonia, Paul's companions in travel, they rushed with one accord into the theatre.*

30 And when Paul would have entered in unto the people, the disciples suffered him not.

31 And certain of the chief of Asia, which were his friends, sent unto him, desiring him that he would not adventure himself into the theatre.

*32 **Some therefore cried one thing, and some another: for the assembly was confused**; and the more part knew not wherefore they were come together.*

INTRODUCTORY THOUGHTS

Paul's stedfastness in the gospel message caused a stir throughout Asia. He boldly declared that the people's idols were no gods at all. Such preaching so angered the local craftsmen that they met together to discuss how to stop Paul and end his message's impact of their livelihood. The mass confusion intensified the fear as it spread throughout the city. As some of Paul's companions were ushered into the theatre, the crowd cried out conflicting things to the point that many had no idea why they had even gathered together. The people's confusion escalated. Because of conflicting reports, they were unable to discern the reality of the situation. Confusion thrives when conflicting statements or feelings are present and people fail to discern the truth.

DEVOTIONAL THOUGHTS
- **(For children):** The book of Kings tells of a man of God who was given specific instructions about a message he was to deliver at the altar in Bethel. He repeated the instructions to Jeroboam and to a prophet whom he later met. He was confused when the prophet lied and told him something different than what God had instructed him. He should have listened to God and ignored the lies *(1 Kings 13:7-10, 15-26; Galatians 1:8)*.
- **(For everyone):** Have you ever had mixed feelings about a particular issue to the point that you were confused? Where did the mixed feelings originate?
- Eve must have been confused in the garden. She had heard that she would die if she partook of the forbidden fruit, but the Devil told her she would not. Whose voice did she obey?

PRAYER THOUGHTS
- Ask God for a clear mind in the presence of conflicting thoughts.
- Ask God to guard you from confusion.

SONG: *AMAZING GRACE!*

Day 59: (Tuesday)
Confusion and Sin

Daniel 9:7 O Lord, righteousness belongeth unto thee, but unto us confusion of faces, as at this day; to the men of Judah, and to the inhabitants of Jerusalem, and unto all Israel, that are near, and that are far off, through all the countries whither thou hast driven them, **because of their trespass that they have trespassed against thee.**

8 O Lord, to us belongeth confusion of face, to our kings, to our princes, and to our fathers, **because we have sinned against thee.**

INTRODUCTORY THOUGHTS

Confusion does not always result directly from personal sin, but sin surely causes a great deal of confusion. In today's passage, we find Daniel making this point as he contrasted God and man. Daniel pointed out that righteousness belonged to the Lord and confusion belonged to the people. Why? Simply because God's people chose to sin against the Lord. Sin blurs and transforms an otherwise clear and indisputable reality into corruption and vagaries. Committing sin blurs the broad chasm between sin and righteousness. This blurring makes it more difficult for a child of God to discern the perfect will of God. Therefore, only those believers who eschew evil can and will experience clarity of mind. Those who embrace evil reap uncertainty.

DEVOTIONAL THOUGHTS
- (**For children**): Peter would not believe what was going to happen to Jesus *(Matthew 16:21-23)* nor what Jesus told him he would do when that time came *(Matthew 26:31-35)*. Once Peter denied the Lord in the first instance, it became easier to do it a second and third time.
- (**For everyone**): Do you find it difficult to discern the difference between right and wrong? Was there a time in your life when it seemed much easier than it does now? What changed?
- What are some ways in which sin can bring confusion? Why does sin bring confusion? What does it do to your fellowship with God? How does this yield confusion?

PRAYER THOUGHTS
- Thank God for the clarity He offers and provides.
- Ask God to guard you from sin that would bring confusion.

SONG: *HEAVENLY SUNLIGHT*

Day 60: Church Night

Psalm 71:1** In thee, O LORD, do I put my trust:* **let me never be put to confusion.*

Day 61: (Thursday)
The Author of Confusion

***1 Corinthians 14:33** For **God is not the author of confusion**, but of peace, as **in all churches of the saints**.*

☐ Completion Date   Confusion • 71

INTRODUCTORY THOUGHTS

The Bible plainly points out that God is not the author (or originator) of the confusion in the life of any believer. In fact, God desires for every individual to have clarity of mind when it comes to the truths found in His word. He wants man to know for a certainty concerning his eternal destination, whether heaven or hell. God furthermore wants man to have perfect clarity in distinguishing sin from righteousness. Simply put, God has no desire for believers to live in a confused state of mind. Had sin never entered into the world, there would be no conflicting feelings or voices introducing the confusion so prevalent today. Yet, God's truth becomes even more essential in order to clear up the confusion caused by sin and Satan.

DEVOTIONAL THOUGHTS

- **(For children):** God is not willing that any should perish *(2 Peter 3:9)*. He said if we really want to find Him, we will *(Jeremiah 29:13-14a)*. He wants us to know for sure we are saved. He does not want us to live with doubts or confusion *(1 John 5:11-13)*.
- **(For everyone):** Have you ever blamed confusion on the Lord? Have you ever suggested that the Lord was leading you to do something contrary to the revealed words of God?
- Why is it important to realize that God is not the author of confusion? What does this mean you can assume when confusion enters into your mind and heart?

PRAYER THOUGHTS

- Thank God for the clarity of truth.
- Ask God to help you know that confusion is not sent by Him.

SONG: *ALL THE WAY MY SAVIOUR LEADS ME*

Day 62: (Friday)
Where There Is Envying and Strife

***James 3:16** For where envying and strife is, there is confusion and every evil work.*

Introductory Thoughts

Where envy finds its breeding grounds, there grows confusion. Rather than churches, homes, and individuals choosing the blessings of peace, many have chosen the struggles resulting from envy and strife. In doing so, they reap the resultant confusion. Where strife oozes from the people, so will a mass state of confusion. This fact definitely accounts for the magnitude of Christians living outside the will of God with no opportunity to even discern what it is. *The church* should be a haven of truth, a place that clears up the confusion outside of its fellowship. *The Christian home* should be a place of clarity that serves to protect from the confusion perpetrated by the world, the flesh, and the Devil. Yet, far too many Christians have chosen rather to accept the curse of confusion.

Devotional Thoughts

- **(For children):** Saul's envy of David *(1 Samuel 18:5-9)* brought confusion. He tried to kill David and even tried to smite his own son who knew David was not to blame *(1 Samuel 19:4-5; 1 Samuel 20:32-34)*. Saul's home could have been happy if not for envy.
- **(For everyone):** Why are churches splitting over foolish things? Why are families fighting, often over things that really do not even matter? Why are individuals more confused now than perhaps ever before?
- Do you enjoy envy and strife? Do you find confusion to be an enjoyable thing? If not, what can you do to know the clarity of mind that God desires for you?

Prayer Thoughts

- Ask God to protect your home or church from envy and strife.
- Ask God to give you clarity of mind.

SONG: *I NEED THEE EVERY HOUR*

Day 63: (Saturday)
A Prayer for Confusion

***Psalm 35:1** Plead my cause, O LORD, with them that strive with me: fight against them that fight against me.*

2 Take hold of shield and buckler, and stand up for mine help.

☐ Completion Date Confusion • 73

3 Draw out also the spear, and stop the way against them that persecute me: say unto my soul, I am thy salvation.

4 Let them be confounded and put to shame that seek after my soul: let them be turned back and brought to confusion that devise my hurt.

Introductory Thoughts

It is not a common practice for people to desire or pray for confusion. Yet, there are times in the word of God when believers pleaded with the Lord in hopes that He might send confusion to their enemies. For instance, David entreated the Lord to send confusion to those who devised *(Psalm 35:4)*, desired *(Psalm 70:2)*, and rejoiced at his hurt *(Psalm 35:26)*. Perhaps those chasing David would be led by the Lord in the wrong direction. Perhaps the Lord would allow David's enemies to turn against each other rather than being united together in killing David. Regardless, David knew there would be times when his enemies would have the ability to overtake him. In those times, he asked the Lord to intervene on his behalf by confusing them.

Devotional Thoughts

- **(For children):** Elisha told Israel's king where the Syrians were going to attack. Syria's king sent a great host to surround Elisha at Dothan. Elisha prayed for the Lord to smite the army with blindness and he led the army to the king of Israel *(2 Kings 6:8-14, 18-19)*.
- **(For everyone):** Has there ever been a time when you needed the Lord to confuse someone who was trying to harm you? Did you know that you could ask the Lord to work on your behalf?
- How would this be a good prayer for missionaries who are working in closed countries like China, Israel, or the Arab nations? How would it be a good prayer for those who seek to give the gospel in troublesome times?

Prayer Thoughts

- Thank God for the times He has confused the enemy.
- Ask God to put a hedge about you as you serve Him.

SONG: *ETERNAL FATHER, STRONG TO SAVE*

Notes: _____

Quotes from the next volume

(VOLUME 4, WEEK 9)

Subject: Blame (con't)

The apostle Paul spent much of his life persecuting the church of God, but when the Lord saved him, he spent the remainder of his life attentive to protecting the testimony of the ministry.

Paul thought his testimony was so important that he would rather suffer personally than bring any reproach or blame upon himself or the work of God.

10

Contention or Strife

Contention—found twenty times in twenty verses

Strife—found eighty-nine times in eighty-two verses

Variations: contention, contentions, contentious, strife, strifes, strive, strived, striven, striveth, striving, strivings, strove

First usage of contention: *Proverbs 13:10* (contention)

Last usage of contention: *Titus 3:9* (contentions)

First usage of strife: *Genesis 6:3* (strive)

Last usage of strife: *James 3:16* (strife)

Defined: conflict, strife, or the act of contending

Interesting fact: In the late 1600s, poet and playwright William Congreve wrote *"Heaven has no rage, like love to hatred turned, Nor hell a fury, like a woman scorned."* The latter part of the phrase is commonly paraphrased to say, *"Hell hath no fury like a woman scorned."* In similar fashion, the scripture identifies the difficulties of living with a contentious woman stating that her contentions are like a continual dropping **(Proverbs 19:13; Proverbs 27:15)** and that it would be better to dwell in the wilderness *(Proverbs 21:19)* or in the corner of the housetop than with her *(Proverbs 21:9; Proverbs 25:24)*.

Bible study tip: In modern English, sentences begin with a capital letter, however, in scripture this is not always the case. In some cases, an exclamation point *(1 Samuel 4:8)* or question mark *(Genesis 4:10)* might be followed by a lower case letter. A period, however, will never be followed by a lower case letter. This pattern also holds true in many of the old hymns of the faith. Take time to consider why these differences might be used within any particular passage.

Sunday, Day 64—Church Day (no devotional)
Monday, Day 65—*What Is Strife?*
Tuesday, Day 66—*By Pride Cometh Contention*
Wednesday, Day 67—Church Night (no devotional)
Thursday, Day 68—*Strive Not Without Cause*
Friday, Day 69—*The Castle Bars*
Saturday, Day 70—*Strife Harms the Innocent*

Day 64: Church Day

*Proverbs 17:14 The beginning of strife is as when one letteth out water: therefore **leave off contention**, before it be meddled with.*

Day 65: (Monday)
What Is Strife?

Genesis 13:5 And Lot also, which went with Abram, had flocks, and herds, and tents.

*6 And **the land was not able to bear them, that they might dwell together**: for their substance was great, so that they could not dwell together.*

*7 And **there was a strife** between the herdmen of Abram's cattle and the herdmen of Lot's cattle: and the Canaanite and the Perizzite dwelled then in the land.*

☐ Completion Date   Contention or Strife • 77

*8 And Abram said unto Lot, **Let there be no strife**, I pray thee, between me and thee, and between my herdmen and thy herdmen; for we be brethren.*

9 Is not the whole land before thee? separate thyself, I pray thee, from me: if thou wilt take the left hand, then I will go to the right; or if thou depart to the right hand, then I will go to the left.

Introductory Thoughts

As Abram and Lot travelled together, it became increasingly obvious that the multitude of their possessions would make it difficult for them to dwell together. Eventually, the herdmen of the two men began to strive with each other over the pastures for their cattle. No doubt, both groups of herdmen were primarily concerned with the well-being of their own master's cattle. Neither was willing to compromise their own needs or wishes in order to accommodate the needs of the other group. As Abram witnessed the relationship decay, he knew that he must concede to the inevitability of separating the two groups. He asked Lot to choose another piece of land in which to dwell.

Devotional Thoughts

- **(For children):** Paul and Barnabas had a sharp disagreement on whether or not to take John Mark with them on their second missionary journey. The matter did not get settled at that time. They split up and went different directions, Barnabas going with Mark and Paul going with Silas *(Acts 15:36-41)*.
- **(For everyone):** Why was there strife between the herdmen of Abram and Lot? Why were the herdmen unable to settle the dispute? Does it appear that either group would give any ground to the other?
- What might have happened if Abram had not stepped in to solve the dispute between herdmen? How did Abram demonstrate wisdom in solving the problem?

Prayer Thoughts

- Ask God to help you understand how strife begins.
- Ask God for wisdom to settle disputes for His glory.

SONG: *MIGHTY GOD! THOU GREAT AND GOOD*

Day 66: (Tuesday)
By Pride Cometh Contention

Proverbs 13:10 Only by pride cometh contention*: but with the well advised is wisdom.*

INTRODUCTORY THOUGHTS

Contention comes when two parties have conflicting desires or points of view and are unwilling to amicably resolve them. Oftentimes, pride hinders either party from admitting their errors or even the possibility of their being partially to blame. Contention ceases in the absence of pride. When Rehoboam, Solomon's son, became king, the people of God came to him requesting relief from the heavy burden of taxes that had been placed upon them by Solomon. The older men counselled Rehoboam to do as the people requested, but the younger men instructed Rehoboam to reject the wishes of the people. Rehoboam contentiously responded to the people's request with pride; strife understandably followed *(1 Kings 12:1-16)*.

DEVOTIONAL THOUGHTS

- **(For children):** Haman was full of pride and became angry because Mordecai (a Jew who worshipped God only) would not bow down to him. Haman caused much strife in the land by wanting to destroy all the Jews *(Esther 3:1-6)*.
- **(For everyone):** Have you ever witnessed contention where both sides were wrong? Why would neither side admit that they were wrong? Why would neither side suffer the wrong to bring peace?
- If contention comes by pride, what does this suggest about most relationship problems? Why is their strife between a husband and wife, or a parent and a child?

PRAYER THOUGHTS

- Ask the Lord to help you avoid the sin of pride.
- Ask God to show you when to suffer the wrong to bring peace.

SONG: *BEWARE, YE SONS OF GOD, BEWARE*

Day 67: Church Night

***Proverbs 22:10** Cast out the scorner, and contention shall go out; yea, strife and reproach shall cease.*

Day 68: (Thursday)
Strive Not Without Cause

***Proverbs 3:27** Withhold not good from them to whom it is due, when it is in the power of thine hand to do it.*

28 Say not unto thy neighbour, Go, and come again, and to morrow I will give; when thou hast it by thee.

29 Devise not evil against thy neighbour, seeing he dwelleth securely by thee.

*30 **Strive not with a man without cause, if he have done thee no harm**.*

Introductory Thoughts

There are times when strife remains an unavoidable option; however, no believer should ever strive with others without a just cause and purpose. Today's passage gives instructions for dealing with a neighbour as this relationship is more likely than any other to encounter strife. The Lord instructs a man to never devise evil against his neighbour. In like manner, a man should never instigate strife when his neighbour has done him no harm. There are many examples in the Bible of those who chose not to heed this admonition. Nabal, the husband of Abigail, was a wicked man who refused to provide provisions for David's men ***(1 Samuel 25:1-38)***. David and his men had done no harm to Nabal or his belongings. In fact, David's men had been a blessing and help to Nabal's shepherds. Fortunately, the wisdom of Nabal's wife subdued David's desire for strife.

Devotional Thoughts

- **(For children):** The Lord Jesus Christ is the greatest example of someone hated for no cause ***(John 15:24-25; Psalm 69:4; Psalm 109:3)***. He always did good and right among the people ***(Acts 10:38; Acts 2:22-23)***.

- **(For everyone):** Most strife occurs between those who really have no reason to fight. Why do you have strife with your loved ones? Is there generally a just cause for your actions?
- Why did Nabal refuse to help David's men? What was David planning to do because of Nabal's foolishness? What stopped David from harming Nabal?

PRAYER THOUGHTS

- Ask the Lord to keep you from strife that is without cause.
- Ask God to give you wisdom in times when strife is possible.

SONG: *JESUS, CEMENT OUR HEARTS AS ONE*

Day 69: (Friday)
The Castle Bars

Proverbs 18:19 *A brother offended is harder to be won than a strong city: and their* **contentions are like the bars of a castle**.

INTRODUCTORY THOUGHTS

In Bible times, the greatest form of defence for a city was to remain strong and surrounded by high walls. If a people group or nation had high walls and a strong city, they were extremely difficult to conquer. During these times, the barriers were imperative for a strong national defense. The Lord considered this scenario as an appropriate picture to demonstrate the state of an offended brother, resulting from contention. The Lord likens this contention to the bars on a castle. Even if the enemy were capable of getting into the strong city, other obstacles existed making it impossible to break through to its core. These included the bars erected to avoid someone from entering the castle. In like manner, contention makes it almost impossible to break through to the heart of an offended brother.

DEVOTIONAL THOUGHTS

- **(For children):** Jacob tricked his father into giving him the blessing meant for his elder brother Esau. For this deception, Esau hated Jacob and planned on killing him. Jacob had to flee for his life and safety ***(Genesis 27:41-45)***. Twenty years later, Jacob returned home still fear-

ing Esau *(Genesis 32:11)*. Fortunately for Jacob, the Lord took care of Esau's bitterness *(Genesis 33:4)*.
- **(For everyone)**: Bars of a castle would keep the enemy out, but they could also work as a prison for those whom they supposedly protect. How is this a perfect picture of contention?
- Have you offended somebody with contentions? Have you tried to make things right? How is the relationship now? Have you been able to remove the bars of the castle?

PRAYER THOUGHTS
- Ask God to protect you from strife.
- Ask God to give you wisdom to see the dangers of contention.

SONG: *THROW OUT THE LIFE-LINE*

Day 70: (Saturday)
Strife Harms the Innocent

Exodus 21:22 If men strive, and hurt a woman with child, so that her fruit depart from her, and yet no mischief follow: he shall be surely punished, according as the woman's husband will lay upon him; and he shall pay as the judges determine.
23 And if any mischief follow, then thou shalt give life for life,
24 Eye for eye, tooth for tooth, hand for hand, foot for foot,
25 Burning for burning, wound for wound, stripe for stripe.

INTRODUCTORY THOUGHTS

The Lord gave laws to protect innocent life and punish those guilty of harming others. In the midst of these laws, the Bible has a section devoted to a scenario of what might occur when two men strive with each other. During their conflict, they might hurt a woman who was with child causing her to lose her unborn child. The conflict is literal or physical and the problems resulting are literal or physical, but one cannot miss the spiritual truth disclosed. When two people strive, those not even involved in the initial conflict suffer consequences. Before two people decide to take part in strife, they would be wise to consider how their contentious behaviour affects the innocent people around them.

82 • Contention or Strife ☐ Completion Date

Devotional Thoughts

- **(For children):** Adam and Eve loved their sons very much. They suffered when Cain killed his brother Abel. Abel was dead and Cain had to leave home and wander from place to place *(Genesis 4:1-12)*.
- **(For everyone):** Have you ever been hurt by strife although you were not directly involved? Was your hurt any less than that of those who took part in the strife?
- What are some good examples where strife harms the innocent (i.e., church, home, workplace)? Why is it important to think about the consequences of strife before partaking in it?

Prayer Thoughts

- Ask God to protect the innocent in times of strife.
- Thank God for the times He has shielded you from harm.

SONG: *BREAK THESE HEARTS OF STONE*

Notes: _____

_____
_____
_____
_____
_____
_____
_____

Quotes from the next volume

(VOLUME 4, WEEK 10)

Subject: Conscience

Sin makes a terrible mess of man's conscience.

Only the blood of Jesus Christ can purge a man's conscience from dead works to serve the living God.

11

Contention or Strife (con't)

Contention—found thirteen times in the Old Testament and seven times in the New Testament

Strife—found sixty times in the Old Testament and twenty-nine times in the New Testament

Variations: contention, contentions, contentious, strife, strifes, strive, strived, striven, striveth, striving, strivings, strove

Last usage of *contention* in the Old Testament: *Habakkuk 1:3* (contention)

First usage of *contention* in the New Testament: *Acts 15:39* (contention)

Last usage of *strife* in the Old Testament: *Habakkuk 1:3* (strife)

First usage of *strife* in the New Testament: *Matthew 12:19* (strive)

Interesting fact: Strife is likened to the letting out of water *(Proverbs 17:14)*, taking a dog by the ears *(Proverbs 26:17)*, and fire *(Proverbs 26:20-21)*. It should be of no surprise that the Bible says, *"every fool will be meddling" (Proverbs 20:3).*

84 • Contention or Strife (con't) ☐ Completion Date

Bible study tip: At times, the Lord chose to use all capital letters in a word or phrase. For example, God said of Himself, *"I AM THAT I AM" (Exodus 3:14)*. One day the Lord shall be called *"THE LORD OUR RIGHTEOUSNESS" (Jeremiah 23:6)*. And one day the woman of Revelation chapter 17 will have *"MYSTERY, BABYLON THE GREAT, THE MOTHER OF HARLOTS AND ABOMINATIONS OF THE EARTH"* written upon her forehead *(Revelation 17:5)*. Consider why these and other such unique instances might exist and why God would use ALL CAPS in some places and choose not to do so in others.

Sunday, Day 71—Church Day (no devotional)
Monday, Day 72—*Strife, a Sign of Carnality*
Tuesday, Day 73—*Love of Strife*
Wednesday, Day 74—Church Night (no devotional)
Thursday, Day 75—*Let Us Not Walk in Strife*
Friday, Day 76—*A Froward Man Soweth Strife*
Saturday, Day 77—*Stirring Up Strife*

Day 71: Church Day

Proverbs 17:1 Better is a dry morsel, and quietness therewith, than an house full of sacrifices with strife.

Day 72: (Monday)
Strife, a Sign of Carnality

1 Corinthians 3:1 And I, brethren, could not speak unto you as unto spiritual, but as unto carnal, even as unto babes in Christ.

2 I have fed you with milk, and not with meat: for hitherto ye were not able to bear it, neither yet now are ye able.

3 For ye are yet carnal: for whereas there is among you envying, and strife, and divisions, are ye not carnal, and walk as men?

4 For while one saith, I am of Paul; and another, I am of Apollos; are ye not carnal?

☐ Completion Date   Contention or Strife (con't) • 85

INTRODUCTORY THOUGHTS

The apostle Paul wanted to educate the Corinthians concerning the deeper things of God; however, he was unable to do so because of their inability to grasp such spiritual truths *(1 Corinthians 3:1-2)*. These believers displayed a carnality like none other found within the scriptures. As a result of their carnality, they also exhibited envy, strife, and divisions *(1 Corinthians 3:3)*. As their boasting concerning the individuals they chose to follow escalated, the divisiveness also increased. Some of them boasted of following Paul, while others boasted of following Apollos *(1 Corinthians 3:4)*. They were full of pride and Paul had to enlighten them concerning the foolishness of this strife. The strife birthed from pride yielded a foolish behaviour. Strife was all the evidence Paul needed to rebuke these believers concerning their carnality.

DEVOTIONAL THOUGHTS

- **(For children):** Jesus taught His disciples what it meant to be great *(Mark 10:43-45; John 13:13-17)*. Nonetheless, the disciples because of their pride chose to strive amongst themselves *(Luke 22:24)*. The disciples were carnal in their thinking.
- **(For everyone):** Since strife is an obvious indicator of spiritual immaturity, our partaking in strife should cause us to turn to a self-evaluation.
- Paul wanted to teach the Corinthians deeper spiritual truths. Why did he say he was unable to do so? Do you partake in strife? If so, you are likely missing the deeper spiritual truths that God intends for you to learn.

PRAYER THOUGHTS

- Ask God to show you if you are carnal.
- Ask God to help you mature beyond carnality.

SONG: *THE UNITY OF THE SPIRIT*

Day 73: (Tuesday)
Love of Strife

***Proverbs 17:19** He loveth transgression that loveth strife: and he that exalteth his gate seeketh destruction.*

86 • Contention or Strife (con't)   ☐ Completion Date

INTRODUCTORY THOUGHTS

   Understanding man's true nature makes today's verse understandable and comprehensible. Ignoring the true reality of man's constitution will lead the reader to refuse this Bible truth. Surely no man, woman, boy, or girl would love strife! Strife seems to be contrary to something we would deem lovable. After all, the Bible likens strife to the bars of a castle *(Proverbs 18:19)*, creating a prison for some and an impossible barrier for others. It is birthed through pride *(Proverbs 13:10)* and harms those most innocent *(Exodus 21:22-25)*. With these thoughts in mind, how could anyone *love* strife? The answer is quite simple. Man's flesh desires to rebel against the laws of God. It finds pleasure in transgression and satisfaction in displeasing the Lord. So man, although aware of strife's downfalls and pitfalls, craves strife and the resultant conflict.

DEVOTIONAL THOUGHTS

- **(For children):** Even though King Herod was a Jew, he cared nothing for God's laws. The wise men asked him, *"Where is he that is born King of the Jews?"* Herod's curiosity and pride caused him to *"seek the young child to destroy him."* He chose to harm the innocent by slaying all male children two years old and under in Bethlehem *(Matthew 2:16)*.
- **(For everyone):** Do you enjoy seeing people argue? Do you enjoy participating in arguments? Do you seek to stop arguments even if it means you must swallow your pride in order to achieve a resolution?
- Would you ever admit that you love strife? Would you seek to stir it up once it seems to be dying out? Do you recognize this as sin and understand that you need to repent?

PRAYER THOUGHTS

- Ask God to forgive you for loving strife.
- Ask God to convict you when you participate in strife.

SONG: *OFT HAVE I TURNED MY EYES WITHIN*

Day 74: Church Night

Proverbs 26:17 He that passeth by, and **meddleth with strife belonging not to him, is like one that taketh a dog by the ears.**

20 *Where no wood is, there the fire goeth out: so* **where there is no talebearer, the strife ceaseth.**

21 As coals are to burning coals, and wood to fire; so is a contentious man to kindle strife.

Day 75: (Thursday)
Let Us Not Walk in Strife

***Romans 13:11** And that, knowing the time, that now it is high time to awake out of sleep: for now is our salvation nearer than when we believed.*

12 The night is far spent, the day is at hand: let us therefore cast off the works of darkness, and let us put on the armour of light.

*13 **Let us walk** honestly, as in the day; not in rioting and drunkenness, not in chambering and wantonness, **not in strife and envying**.*

14 But put ye on the Lord Jesus Christ, and make not provision for the flesh, to fulfil the lusts thereof.

INTRODUCTORY THOUGHTS

Time is short! The time of Christ's return is approaching quickly *(Romans 13:11-12)*. There is no time for petty strife amongst believers. This is not the time to stir up the troops one against another, but rather the time to rally them under the same banner admonishing them to adorn the same armour *(Romans 13:12)*. This is the time for believers to walk honestly *(Romans 13:13)*. The battle has been raging for some time, and this battle leaves no time for participation in the rioting and drunkenness found in society *(Romans 13:13)*. There is far too much at stake. The believers who choose to participate in strife and envy may feel as though they are winning the battle, but they fail to realize how they are losing the war. It is time for believers to crucify the flesh and serve Christ *(Romans 13:14)*.

DEVOTIONAL THOUGHTS

- **(For children):** The church at Philippi was a good church. Paul wanted it to stay that way. In his letter to them, Paul mentioned two women by name who could not get along and told them to be of the same mind *(Philippians 4:2)*. Their strife hurt the church and needed to be addressed.
- **(For everyone):** What are you supposed to be doing for the Lord (i.e., witnessing, praying, studying the Bible, ministering to others)? Why

would anyone choose to spend their time and strength stirring up strife?
- As Christ's return draws nearer, God's people should get more serious about the things of God. Are you growing increasingly serious about serving God?

PRAYER THOUGHTS
- Ask the Lord to awake you from carnality.
- Ask God to renew your zeal to serve Him.

SONG: *MY CHRISTIAN FRIENDS IN BONDS OF LOVE*

Day 76: (Friday)
A Froward Man Soweth Strife

Proverbs 16:28 A froward man soweth strife: and a whisperer separateth chief friends.

INTRODUCTORY THOUGHTS

During Bible times, even the average individual understood a great deal concerning agriculture. This meant that the laws of sowing and reaping were quite familiar to them. They understood that sowing seed was done in hopes of reaping a harvest of that which was sown. Today's passage explains that the froward man chooses to sow strife. In other words, there are some in society who look for strife and where it does not exist, they will sow the seeds of strife so that it sprouts even where it did not originally exist. Why would they do this? Some people revel in seeing the fruits of arguments, wars, strife, envy, debate, and other such things. The froward man simply finds a way to instigate problems and exploit situations by creating lies or exaggerations to accomplish his sordid purposes.

DEVOTIONAL THOUGHTS
- **(For children):** Jezebel was a wicked queen. She stirred up strife against Naboth because he refused to sell a vineyard to her husband. She wrote letters to the rulers of the city telling them to hire men to lie about Naboth hoping that he would be eliminated. Jezebel's actions caused Naboth to be stoned *(1 Kings 21:8-13)*.

- **(For everyone):** Do you know people who choose to sow strife? What has he or she done in order to sow strife? Has this person lied? Has this person twisted others' words in order to create conflict?
- How can you help to solve the problems caused by those who revel in sowing strife? Are others buying the lies of the froward? Can you help to stop the strife? How might you be able to do so?

Prayer Thoughts
- Ask God to convict you if you sow seeds of strife.
- Ask God to help you repair the damage of the froward.

SONG: *COME, DEAREST JESUS, COME*

Day 77: (Saturday)
Stirring Up Strife

Proverbs 15:18 A wrathful man stirreth up strife: but he that is slow to anger appeaseth strife.

Introductory Thoughts

No doubt about it: the world is full of problems. Every day, people choose to say and do things that they should not say or do. Their actions contain all of the necessary ingredients for strife. The Bible says a wrathful man looks for the possibility of strife and does whatever necessary to stir it up *(Proverbs 15:18)*. Why does he do this? The Bible points out that he is proud of heart *(Proverbs 28:25)* and full of hatred *(Proverbs 10:12)*. The Bible further describes this work in ***Proverbs 26:20-21*** where it says, "Where no wood is, there the fire goeth out: so where there is no talebearer, the strife ceaseth. As coals are to burning coals, and wood to fire; so is a contentious man to kindle strife." A contentious man seeks to rekindle the flames as he notices the fires of strife beginning to be extinguished.

Devotional Thoughts
- **(For children):** The Jews who hated Paul's gospel stirred up the people in their own cities: Antioch *(Acts 13:50)* and Iconium *(Acts 14:1, 2, 5-7)*. They even followed Paul to another city (Lystra) to stir up trouble *(Acts 14:19)*.

- **(For everyone):** Have you ever had a conflict with someone? Has it been resolved? Do you find that it seems to be fixed but then spirals out of control again? If so, someone is likely stirring up strife.
- Do you look for ways to turn people against one another? Do you seek to draw things out of people only to tell others and stir up trouble? If so, you need to repent and get right with the Lord!

PRAYER THOUGHTS

- Ask God to forgive you for times you have stirred up strife.
- Ask God to help you see when someone is trying to cause strife.

SONG: *JESUS, I COME*

Notes: _____

_____

_____

_____

_____

_____

_____

_____

Quotes from the next volume

(VOLUME 4, WEEK 11)

Subject: Conscience (con't)

A man's conscience is within himself, but its testimony can be seen by others.

A man's conscience is much like a muscle. When a man exercises his conscience, it becomes strong and increasingly useful.

As men depart from the faith and give heed to seducing spirits and doctrines of devils, their consciences become so weak that they show little to no sign of life.

12

Contention or Strife (con't)

Contention—found eleven times in eleven verses in Proverbs

Strife—found seventeen times in sixteen verses in Proverbs

Variations: contention, contentions, contentious, strife, strifes, strive, strived, striven, striveth, striving, strivings, strove

First usage of *contention* in Proverbs: *Proverbs 13:10* (contention)

Last usage of *contention* in Proverbs: *Proverbs 27:15* (contentious)

First usage of *strife* in Proverbs: *Proverbs 3:30* (strive)

Last usage of *strife* in Proverbs: *Proverbs 30:33* (strife)

Interesting fact: Because of a lack of drinking water, the children of Israel murmured in Exodus chapter 17. After the Lord supernaturally provided water out of a rock, the place became known as *Meribah (Exodus 17:7)*. The Bible's built-in dictionary reveals that Meribah is closely associated with strife. This is why the Bible describes this place and the waters as *the place of* or *the waters of strife (Numbers 20:13, 24; Numbers 27:14; Deuteronomy 33:8; Psalm 106:32; Ezekiel 47:19; Ezekiel 48:28)*. This place was located in the desert or wilderness of Zin *(Numbers 27:14)* which "coincidentally" is identified as the wilderness of Sin *(Exodus 17:1)*.

Bible study tip: *"A good name is rather to be chosen than great riches, and loving favour rather than silver and gold" (Proverbs 22:1).* The phrase a "good name" refers to more than a mere title by which a man is addressed because names and reputations (or circumstances) were more closely associated historically. Sometimes a man's birth name depicts his reputation. At other times, a man's name is changed to match his character or reputation. When studying the life of a Bible character, always consider the meaning and purpose of his or her name.

Sunday, Day 78—Church Day (no devotional)
Monday, Day 79—*Contention Separates*
Tuesday, Day 80—*Let Nothing Be Done Through Strife*
Wednesday, Day 81—Church Night (no devotional)
Thursday, Day 82—*The Honour of Ceasing from Strife*
Friday, Day 83—*When It Is Right to Strive*
Saturday, Day 84—*Striving for No Profit*

Day 78: Church Day

Proverbs 22:10 Cast out the scorner, and contention shall go out; yea, strife and reproach shall cease.

Day 79: (Monday)
Contention Separates

Acts 15:36 And some days after Paul said unto Barnabas, Let us go again and visit our brethren in every city where we have preached the word of the Lord, and see how they do.

*37 And **Barnabas determined to take with them John**, whose surname was Mark.*

*38 But **Paul thought not good to take him with them**, who departed from them from Pamphylia, and went not with them to the work.*

☐ Completion Date   Contention or Strife (con't) • 93

*39 And **the contention was so sharp between them, that they departed asunder one from the other**: and so Barnabas took Mark, and sailed unto Cyprus;*

40 And Paul chose Silas, and departed, being recommended by the brethren unto the grace of God.

INTRODUCTORY THOUGHTS

The church at Antioch sent out Paul and Barnabas *(Acts 13:1-4)*. These men were missionaries seeking to win the lost and edify the children of God. They travelled far and wide on their first missionary journey and then returned to Antioch to offer the believers a report of the work *(Acts 15:30)*. Soon thereafter, Paul determined that he and Barnabas should make a second trip to check on the growth of those to whom they previously ministered *(Acts 15:36)*. Barnabas sincerely desired to accompany Paul but also thought it wise to take John Mark (who had previously quit on Paul and Barnabas). Paul disagreed with taking John Mark and the Bible describes that the *"contention was so sharp between them, that they departed asunder one from the other" (Acts 15:39)*.

DEVOTIONAL THOUGHTS

- **(For children):** King Saul and his son Jonathan loved David *(1 Samuel 16:21-22; 1 Samuel 18:1-2)*; however, Saul's love quickly turned to hatred *(1 Samuel 18:8-9)*. David had to flee for his life. He only saw Saul twice more after that (not under good conditions) and only saw Jonathan one more time.
- **(For everyone):** Have you ever spent time serving the Lord with someone only to have the fellowship broken as a result of some kind of strife? What kind of an effect did it have on you and the work of the Lord?
- Who was wrong in the conflict between Paul and Barnabas? What was the outcome of their conflict? In the end, does it really matter who was right and who was wrong?

PRAYER THOUGHTS

- Ask God to protect you from such splits.
- Ask the Lord to give you grace with other believers.

SONG: *MAY THIS CHURCH OF THINE*

Day 80: (Tuesday)
Let Nothing Be Done Through Strife

***Philippians 2:1** If there be therefore any consolation in Christ, if any comfort of love, if any fellowship of the Spirit, if any bowels and mercies,*

2 Fulfil ye my joy, that ye be likeminded, having the same love, being of one accord, of one mind.

*3 **Let nothing be done through strife or vainglory**; but in lowliness of mind let each esteem other better than themselves.*

4 Look not every man on his own things, but every man also on the things of others.

5 Let this mind be in you, which was also in Christ Jesus:

6 Who, being in the form of God, thought it not robbery to be equal with God:

7 But made himself of no reputation, and took upon him the form of a servant, and was made in the likeness of men:

8 And being found in fashion as a man, he humbled himself, and became obedient unto death, even the death of the cross.

INTRODUCTORY THOUGHTS

For a variety of reasons, people do the things they choose to do. Sometimes their motives are right and godly, and at other times, their motives are simply wrong. The motive should never result from strife or vainglory in the Lord's service. The Lord Jesus Christ, of course, offers the perfect example of someone whose motives were always pure and holy. People often assumed the worst and said untrue things about Him. He certainly had the right and the wherewithal each and every time to correct their errors. He could have won any and every argument without mercy or grace. Yet, His service was not motivated by selfishness or pride. In fact, the Bible points out that He was equal with God, but made Himself of no reputation ***(Philippians 2:6-7)***. He knew He was always right but allowed Himself to be defamed for the greater cause.

DEVOTIONAL THOUGHTS

- **(For children):** God gave Moses the position of leading the children of Israel ***(Acts 7:25; Exodus 3:10)***. Miriam and Aaron attempted to usurp this position ***(Numbers 12:2)***. They would have been serving

out of pride, but God quickly stopped their words of strife *(Numbers 12:4-15)*.
- **(For everyone):** Do you ever do things "for the Lord" seeking to prove yourself to others? Do you claim to be serving Christ while really trying to show others that you are better than they are?
- Why do you serve the Lord? Do you serve the Lord when no one else notices or only when others are watching? What is your motive for serving?

PRAYER THOUGHTS
- Ask God to help you serve Him with a pure motive.
- Ask the Lord to keep you from competition in His service.

SONG: *I GAVE MY LIFE FOR THEE*

Day 81: Church Night

James 3:13 Who is a wise man and endued with knowledge among you? let him shew out of a good conversation his works with meekness of wisdom.

*14 But **if ye have bitter envying and strife in your hearts, glory not**, and lie not against the truth.*

15 This wisdom descendeth not from above, but is earthly, sensual, devilish.

*16 For **where envying and strife is, there is confusion and every evil work**.*

Day 82: (Thursday)
The Honour of Ceasing from Strife

Proverbs 20:3 It is an honour for a man to cease from strife: but every fool will be meddling.

INTRODUCTORY THOUGHTS

In a world filled with competition and pride, the peacemaker is often wrongly accused of being unable to handle the conflict or the fight. This is why many people consider backing down from strife a sign of weakness. Once again, God and man are at complete opposite ends of the spectrum. While many men consider it commendable to continue strife, God thinks it honourable to cease from strife. In other words, the greater man or woman brings conflict to a close rather than further instigating it. According to the Bible, it is a fool who continues to meddle in hopes of prolonging the conflict. It is up to each believer to determine whether to accept God's way or man's way of thinking.

DEVOTIONAL THOUGHTS

- **(For children):** Read *1 Peter 2:21-23*. People mistreated Jesus throughout His trial and crucifixion. He could have stopped it *(Matthew 26:53)*, yet He came to earth to be our Saviour. Stemming from His great love for us, He chose not to strive *(Matthew 26:62-63a; Matthew 27:12-14, 39-44; Luke 23:34)*.
- **(For everyone):** How is it possible to be more honourable in ceasing from strife? What kind of strength does it take to swallow your pride and take the wrong even if you are not the only one at fault or completely at fault?
- Do you find joy in reconciling others or in stirring up their conflicts? How could this general attitude lead to problems in your desire to see others reconciled to God?

PRAYER THOUGHTS

- Ask God to give you a desire to cease from strife.
- Ask the Lord to help you adopt His way of thinking.

SONG: *HOME, SWEET HOME*

Day 83: (Friday)
When It Is Right to Strive

1 Corinthians 9:25 **And every man that striveth for the mastery** *is temperate in all things. Now they do it to obtain a corruptible crown; but we an incorruptible.*

INTRODUCTORY THOUGHTS

Our studies reveal that the Bible places great emphasis upon the evils of strife. Any sincere believer should recognize that this negative strife is often based upon pride, hatred, and a love for transgression. Yet, there are times when the opposite holds true. Striving can be done out of a holy desire to please the Lord. Perhaps the most significant aspect concerns the enemy with whom believers strive. The apostle Paul said that he *"strived to preach the gospel" **(Romans 15:20)*** and desired for believers to *"strive together with"* him in prayers to God ***(Romans 15:30)***. He further illustrated his point concerning striving by pointing out some opposing parallels: the world strives for mastery in order to gain a corruptible crown, but believers should strive to gain an incorruptible crown.

Devotional Thoughts

- **(For children):** The rulers commanded Peter and John not to preach about Jesus *(Acts 4:18-20)*. Yet, they kept on striving to preach because it was the right thing to do *(Acts 4:29; Acts 5:27-29, 40-42)*.
- **(For everyone):** Do you find that you strive more for ungodly causes or for godly causes? Why is it wrong to strive in evil ways? Why is it right and necessary to strive in godly warfare?
- How can the Christian life be described as striving? What areas of your spiritual life require diligent striving on your part? Are you faithfully striving in those areas?

Prayer Thoughts

- Ask the Lord for courage in the spiritual battle.
- Ask God to help you strive in witnessing, prayer, etc.

SONG: *SOUND THE BATTLE CRY!*

Day 84: (Saturday)
Striving for No Profit

Titus 3:8 *This is a faithful saying, and these things I will that thou affirm constantly, that they which have believed in God might be careful to maintain good works. These things are good and profitable unto men.*

*9 But **avoid** foolish questions, and genealogies, and contentions, and **strivings about the law; for they are unprofitable and vain**.*

Introductory Thoughts

In the Christian warfare, there are times where strife is both necessary and right. There are things for which preachers, teachers, moms and dads, and young people need to take a stand even if taking a stand brings about conflict. These particular positions are only to take place in times where the stand is good and profitable unto men *(Titus 3:8)*. Unfortunately, most conflict, especially amongst the religious, falls under a completely different category. It often stems from *"foolish questions, and genealogies, and contentions, and strivings about the law"* and these strivings *"are unprofitable and vain"* **(Titus 3:9)**. Before entering into conflict, the believer should question the possible profit gained in such a battle.

DEVOTIONAL THOUGHTS

- **(For children):** Arguing over what kind of fruit Adam and Eve ate from the tree of the knowledge of good and evil is foolish because the Bible does not say what it was. It is more important to know that they were warned by God; they were disobedient; and their disobedience was punished **(Genesis 2:17; Genesis 3:16-19)**.
- **(For everyone):** What kind of strife do you find yourself in with other believers? Does it profit either party to be correct? Will it harm either party to be wrong?
- What issues are most important to you? For which ones are you willing to contend? How crucial are these issues in the word of God? Are they worth splitting with other believers?

PRAYER THOUGHTS

- Ask God to help you strive when there is true profit.
- Ask the Lord for wisdom in knowing when to strive.

SONG: *TO ARMS! TO ARMS!*

Quotes from the next volume

(VOLUME 4, WEEK 12)

Subject: Conviction

One of the greatest misperceptions concerning conviction is that one man can cause conviction upon another man.

By definition, conviction is the work of God to convince an individual of the validity of and accountability for truth.

Much attention has been given to the outward appearance of conviction, but the initial work of conviction remains invisible to the eyes of men.

13

Envy

Envy—found forty times in thirty-nine verses

Variations: envied, envies, enviest, envieth, envious, envy, envying, envyings

First usage: *Genesis 26:14* (envied)

Last usage: *1 Peter 2:1* (envies)

Defined: hatred or resentment over the possessions or achievements of others

Interesting fact: Envy is a matter of the heart. Although many of the warnings concerning envy warn the righteous about envying the wicked, the first mention of envy attributes this act to the Philistines concerning the possessions of Isaac *(Genesis 26:12-14)*. Therefore, it stands to reason that not only is envy something the righteous often feel toward the wicked, but it is also a behaviour the righteous learned from the wicked.

Bible study tip: Pay close attention to the order of events contained within a verse. This order often teaches a greater doctrinal truth. Consider this truth as it pertains to *Genesis 30:1*. First, *"Rachel saw that she bare Jacob no children."* Then, she *"envied her sister."* Lastly, she *"said unto Jacob, Give* *me children, or else I die."* By understanding the context, we see that Rachel said what she said because of the envy within her heart. She felt the envy in her heart because she became obsessed about having no children. The root problem causes the other issues.

Sunday, Day 85—Church Day (no devotional)
Monday, Day 86—*Be Not Thou Envious*
Tuesday, Day 87—*Envy or Godly Fear*
Wednesday, Day 88—Church Night (no devotional)
Thursday, Day 89—*I Was Envious When I Saw*
Friday, Day 90—*Envy Yields Action*
Saturday, Day 91—*Spiritual Osteoporosis*

Day 85: Church Day

Proverbs 27:4 *Wrath is cruel, and anger is outrageous; but who is able to stand before envy?*

Day 86: (Monday)
Be Not Thou Envious

Proverbs 24:1 Be not thou envious against evil men, *neither desire to be with them.*

Introductory Thoughts

Although jealously is one of God's attributes, envy is not. Rather, envy is a product of a sinful nature found only in mankind. It is important to note that long before envy manifests itself outwardly, it first devises its plan within the heart *(Mark 7:21-23)*. Unfortunately, this characteristic is not limited exclusively to the wicked but also frustrates the righteous. This reveals why Solomon warned his son to guard his heart against the dangers of envy. According to Job, envy slays *(Job 5:2)*, and it often slays the instigator with the victim. Every believer must battle daily to avoid allowing envy to overtake his heart and defile him.

☐ Completion Date   Envy • 101

Devotional Thoughts

- **(For children)**: Because Joseph's brothers envied him, they wanted to kill him. Instead, they decided to sell him as a slave *(Genesis 37:11, 18, 20, 26-27)*. He spent thirteen years as a slave or prisoner. Rather than envying his brothers still living in the comforts and security of home, he chose to serve God in present circumstances. When he was later reunited with his brothers, he helped them rather than envying them *(Genesis 50:21)*.
- **(For everyone)**: Do you envy others? What do you think causes you to envy them? Does this envy please the Lord? Will the things for which you envy others help or hurt you at the final judgment?
- How does envy suggest a state of dissatisfaction on the part of the believer? How does God feel about it when believers fail to be satisfied with how God has blessed them?

Prayer Thoughts

- Ask God to help you guard your heart from envy.
- Ask the Lord to help you be satisfied with His will for your life.

SONG: *DRAW ME NEARER*

Day 87: (Tuesday)
Envy or Godly Fear

*Proverbs 23:17 **Let not thine heart envy** sinners: but be thou in the fear of the LORD all the day long.*

Introductory Thoughts

Life is full of polar opposites that cannot simultaneously reside within the believer's heart and life (i.e., truth and lies, love and hate, holiness and sin). Some of these conflicts are familiar and easily identifiable. Yet, the Bible indicates that a similar conflict exists in an individual's life concerning envy and the fear of the Lord. When a man reflects upon the life of the wicked with envy, he ceases to walk in the fear of the Lord. Why? A man who fears the Lord considers the coming judgment directed toward those who know not God. Every person will stand before the Lord and those who fear the Lord and know the end of the story do not desire to have the lot of the wicked pertaining to this judgment. Every man must choose. Does he choose to walk in the fear of the Lord or does he envy the wicked because his eyes veered away from the Lord?

DEVOTIONAL THOUGHTS

- **(For children):** A neighbourhood boy gets a lot of toys by stealing them. You may be envious of the toys, but you remember *Exodus 20:15* and know that it is wrong to steal. Fearing God means that you hate evil *(Proverbs 8:13)* and realize that no one gets away with his sin *(Ecclesiastes 12:13-14)*.
- **(For everyone):** What does it mean to envy? Why is it impossible to walk in the fear of the Lord while envying others? What does it mean to walk in the fear of the Lord?
- Do you look at others and wish that you could live like they live or have what they have? Do the lives of those people you envy please God? Will the judgment be a pleasant time for them?

PRAYER THOUGHTS

- Ask God to help you choose the fear of the Lord.
- Ask the Lord to help you see the dangers of choosing envy.

SONG: *LORD OF OUR LIFE, GOD WHOM WE FEAR*

Day 88: Church Night

1 Peter 2:1 *Wherefore laying aside all malice, and all guile, and hypocrisies, and envies, and all evil speakings,*

2 As newborn babes, desire the sincere milk of the word, that ye may grow thereby:

Day 89: (Thursday)
I Was Envious When I Saw

Psalm 73:3 *For I was envious at the foolish, when I saw the prosperity of the wicked.*

4 For there are no bands in their death: but their strength is firm.

5 They are not in trouble as other men; neither are they plagued like other men.

☐ Completion Date   Envy • 103

Introductory Thoughts

The Bible points out that judgment or punishment against an evil work during one's lifetime is not always executed speedily *(Ecclesiastes 8:11)*. This has made some people think that the wicked can live with seeming impunity from the consequences of their actions. At times it might seem as though the wicked are in fact rewarded for their wickedness while the righteous are punished for diligent, holy living. Believers must live cautiously in order to avoid getting their focus off the Lord and becoming envious of the supposed conquests of the wicked. Although troubles may come to the righteous in spite of their goodness, and help to the wicked in spite of their wickedness, Christians must not and cannot envy the wicked. This dichotomy has caused many once strong Christians to choose the devil's deceitfulness over God's goodness.

Devotional Thoughts

- **(For children):** Hannah, who was childless, could have become envious at Peninnah who had children. In fact, things became even more difficult when Peninnah mocked Hannah because of her barrenness. Even though this wounded Hannah, she did not cause trouble but prayed to the Lord *(1 Samuel 1:2-20)*.
- **(For everyone):** Asaph said he was envious because of something he "*saw.*" Are things always as they seem through your eyes? Why is it important to guard against trusting in what you perceive to be true?
- How can you be sure to temper the perceptions you hold? What is our authority for truth? How can that authority keep you from being tempted to envy the wicked?

Prayer Thoughts

- Ask God for wisdom to see the end of the wicked.
- Thank the Lord for helping you overcome envy.

SONG: *AMIDST THY WRATH REMEMBER LOVE*

Day 90: (Friday)
Envy Yields Action

***Proverbs 3:31** **Envy** thou not the oppressor, and choose none of his ways.*

Introductory Thoughts

Envy is a heart problem that if caught early should never outwardly manifest itself to others. However, failure to recognize the existence of envy in one's life and repent swiftly will yield to much greater future problems. Solomon's first admonition to his son was that he not envy the oppressor. This warning was followed by a second admonition against choosing the oppressor's ways. If a man envies the wicked, he will eventually be convinced to travel the direction that he once only envied. Long before an individual outwardly turns from righteousness to worldliness, he does so within his unrestrained thoughts. Failure to repent of these thoughts eventually yields to the unholy actions once deemed unacceptable.

Devotional Thoughts

- **(For children):** An unchristian neighbour brags to you and others that he is having more fun camping on the weekends than you have going to church. If you envy his words and actions, you might find yourself soon quitting church in order to seek worldly pleasures. You must remember that God will reward your faithfulness *(Psalm 31:19, 23)*. If your neighbour does not know God, his future is bleak with nothing to look forward to *(Romans 6:23)*.
- **(For everyone):** Have you allowed known sin within your life to overtake you? Did you first find yourself envying others who were partaking in the very sin of which you are now guilty?
- Are you currently envious of anyone in your heart? Are you willing to repent of this sin before it goes beyond repair? What will happen if you refuse to repent?

Prayer Thoughts

- Ask God to help you see the end result of envy.
- Ask the Lord to show you when envy creeps into your heart.

SONG: *BEWARE, YE SONS OF GOD, BEWARE*

Day 91: (Saturday)
Spiritual Osteoporosis

Proverbs 14:30 *A sound heart is the life of the flesh: but envy the rottenness of the bones.*

Introductory Thoughts

Physically speaking, the life of the flesh involves a sound heart ***(Proverbs 14:30)*** and blood ***(Leviticus 17:11)***. Without these, a man will not long survive. In like manner, much emphasis is also placed upon the importance of sound bone structure. A man who has problems with his bone density and strength finds his quality of life greatly hindered. According to the Bible, we can draw a parallel between bone strength and spirituality. The Bible says that envy is the rottenness of the bones. As bone strength declines, the individual becomes prone to falls and injury. In like manner, as a person allows envy to take root within his heart, he becomes unstable and prone to falling and personal injury. Those who refuse to repent of envy will ultimately lead themselves into an untimely spiritual death.

Devotional Thoughts

- **(For children):** Absalom's pride caused him to envy his father's position as king. He spoke against his father, stole the hearts of the people, and prepared an army with the intent of killing king David. Even though he appeared outwardly strong, his heart within was not right with God ***(Proverbs 6:12-19)*** and he died in battle.
- **(For everyone):** How has envy weakened your walk with the Lord? How long have you allowed it to go unrestrained? Will you allow it to continue to harm you?
- If you had a bone disease would you seek treatment in order to increase your quality of life? What would you do if you had a spiritual bone disease?

Prayer Thoughts

- Ask the Lord to help you avoid the sin of envy.
- Ask God to protect your walk with Him.

SONG: *HIS WAY WITH THEE*

Notes: _____

Quotes from the next volume
(VOLUME 4, WEEK 13)
Subject: Conviction (con't)

Man's personal viewpoint always becomes increasingly realistic once confronted by the presence of the Holy One.

Conviction testifies of guilt and transgression. It testifies that God is just and man is vile.

14

Envy (con't)

Envy—found twenty-one times in twenty Old Testament verses and nineteen times in as many verses in the New Testament

Variations: envied, envies, enviest, envieth, envious, envy, envying, envyings

Last usage in the Old Testament: *Ezekiel 35:11* (envy)

First usage in the New Testament: *Matthew 27:18* (envy)

Interesting fact: The apostle Paul uniquely implements lists of items to convey important emphases. Some of these lists can be found in ***Romans 1:29-31; Romans 13:13; 2 Corinthians 12:20;*** and ***Galatians 5:19-21***. Interestingly, each of these passages contains some form of the word *envy* within their lists.

Bible study tip: Not everything in the Bible is true; however, everything in the Bible is correctly, accurately, and precisely recorded. This statement concerning any untruths found in scripture may at first cause some concern, but those who choose to wholeheartedly trust in the wisdom of God know what this means. For example, consider ***Genesis 3:4***. What the serpent said to Eve was not true; however, the Bible accurately and faithfully records the serpent's lies. Understanding this concept becomes imperative when considering the Book of Job.

Sunday, Day 92—Church Day (no devotional)
Monday, Day 93—*Who Is Able to Stand Before Envy?*
Tuesday, Day 94—*For Envy They Delivered Him*
Wednesday, Day 95—Church Night (no devotional)
Thursday, Day 96—*Envy Persecutes Believers*
Friday, Day 97—*Charity Envieth Not*
Saturday, Day 98—*When We Were Envious*

Day 92: Church Day

*Romans 13:13 Let us walk honestly, as in the day; not in rioting and drunkenness, not in chambering and wantonness, **not in strife and envying**.*

Day 93: (Monday)
Who Is Able to Stand Before Envy?

*Proverbs 27:3 A stone is heavy, and the sand weighty; but **a fool's wrath** is heavier than them both.*
*4 Wrath is cruel, and anger is outrageous; but **who is able to stand before envy?***

INTRODUCTORY THOUGHTS

The book of Proverbs offers many profound truths and sometimes conveys these truths through the implementation of comparisons and contrasts. Today's proverb is a case in point. The Lord uses this structure to assist man's venturing from the familiar to that which is unfamiliar. Those concepts recognizable to mankind can be used to help convey and explain deeper truths known only to the Lord. For instance, man easily understands what is meant by saying that a stone is heavy and sand is weighty, but the Lord wants man to comprehend the heaviness of a fool's wrath. Man knows that wrath is cruel and anger is outrageous, but God wants man to realize that envy is crueler and more outrageous than both wrath and anger. During times of anger and wrath, merciful moments

☐ Completion Date

might be displayed; however, envy relentlessly pursues its victim without mercy.

DEVOTIONAL THOUGHTS

- **(For children):** When Isaac was in the land of the Philistines, they envied his wealth and drove him from their territory *(Genesis 26:12-17)*. Cain was envious of Abel because God accepted Abel's offering. Envy led Cain to kill his brother *(1 John 3:11-12; Genesis 4:3-8)*.
- **(For everyone):** In what ways could envy be more dangerous than wrath or anger? What does it mean to be cruel or outrageous? How is the inability to stand before envy more severe?
- How can envy be so severe that man would be unable to stand before it? What are some things that a man might be willing to do to another man as envy controls his emotions?

PRAYER THOUGHTS

- Ask God to protect you from the envy of others.
- Ask the Lord to show you the dangers of envy.

SONG: *JESUS! WHAT A FRIEND FOR SINNERS*

Day 94: (Tuesday)
For Envy They Delivered Him

*Matthew 27:18 For he knew that **for envy they had delivered him***.

INTRODUCTORY THOUGHTS

During the Lord's earthly ministry, His most malicious enemies were not common men or even the Roman government. His greatest enemies were the religious leaders charged with maintaining the spiritual purity of the people of God. How could those most religious create discord with the very One who gave them the dictates for the Jewish religion they claimed to defend? The answer is simple. It was envy! According to **John 11:48**, the religious leadership of Israel determined that they could not allow Jesus to continue teaching, preaching, and ministering to others. These leaders realized that all men would believe on Him causing the Romans to demote them. They would not allow this to happen. How far would they go to keep their place and nation? The Bible reveals that they would even cause the crucifixion of the innocent Son of God.

Devotional Thoughts

- **(For children)**: Satan was full of pride and envy. He desperately wanted to become God himself but was unsuccessful in his attempts *(Ezekiel 28:14-15; Isaiah 14:12-15)*. He even tried to destroy God manifest in the flesh *(Matthew 2:16; Luke 4:28-30; Luke 22:3-4; John 19:15-16)*. Again, he was unsuccessful *(Acts 10:39-42)*.
- **(For everyone)**: To what extent did the religious leaders go to protect their seat of authority in Israel? How did Pilate know that they delivered Jesus to him because of envy?
- To what extremes will men go because of envy? What are some of these things you might remember from the Bible? What about Joseph, for example? What are some of the things you might remember from recent news?

Prayer Thoughts

- Ask the Lord to help you see the wickedness of envy.
- Ask God to help you repent of any envy present within your heart.

SONG: *GRACE GREATER THAN OUR SIN*

Day 95: Church Night

*Galatians 5:26 Let us not be desirous of vain glory, provoking one another, **envying one another**.*

Day 96: (Thursday)
Envy Persecutes Believers

Acts 13:42 And when the Jews were gone out of the synagogue, the Gentiles besought that these words might be preached to them the next sabbath.

43 Now when the congregation was broken up, many of the Jews and religious proselytes followed Paul and Barnabas: who, speaking to them, persuaded them to continue in the grace of God.

44 And the next sabbath day came almost the whole city together to hear the word of God.

45 *But **when the Jews saw the multitudes, they were filled with envy**, and spake against those things which were spoken by Paul, contradicting and blaspheming.*

INTRODUCTORY THOUGHTS

As the apostle Paul boldly preached the word of God, his most receptive audience consisted of the common people. Both Jews and Gentiles were intrigued by his message and desired to hear more. From week to week, the numbers continued to grow. The multitudes simply wanted to hear what this former blasphemer had to say about the faith he had once sought to exterminate. As the fame of Paul's message increased, so did the opposition from the religious leaders of his day. The success of the gospel message caused many of the Jews to be filled with envy. They began contradicting and blaspheming Paul's message. When their efforts failed to hinder the message, they stirred up the people in the cities against the truth. These groups began to assault the believers *(Acts 17:1-9)*.

DEVOTIONAL THOUGHTS

- **(For children):** Daniel still prayed to God although he knew that men, envious of his position, had tricked the king into passing a law which would require that Daniel be cast into a den of lions. (See Daniel chapter 6.)
- **(For everyone):** History is replete with testimonies of believers persecuted because of the envy of political and religious leaders. What are some examples that you can remember?
- How could your stand for the truth lead to persecution in the area in which you live? Are you bold enough in your faith to cause others to envy?

PRAYER THOUGHTS

- Ask God for the boldness like that found in the lives of early believers.
- Thank God for giving us a holy faith and a holy cause.

SONG: *ABLE TO DELIVER*

Day 97: (Friday)
Charity Envieth Not

1 Corinthians 13:4 Charity suffereth long, and is kind; ***charity envieth not****; charity vaunteth not itself, is not puffed up,*

5 Doth not behave itself unseemly, seeketh not her own, is not easily provoked, thinketh no evil;

6 Rejoiceth not in iniquity, but rejoiceth in the truth;

7 Beareth all things, believeth all things, hopeth all things, endureth all things.

Introductory Thoughts

Charity is the peak of Christianity *(2 Peter 1:5-7)*. The Bible says that after salvation, charity is to be desired above all other things *(1 Peter 4:8)* and is the bond of perfectness *(Colossians 3:14)*. Yet far too many people, Christians included, know so little about charity. God has not left man without answers, both simple and profound. First Corinthians chapter 13 offers the most vivid description of charity: charity suffereth long and is kind *(1 Corinthians 13:4)*. It rejoiceth not in iniquity but in the truth *(1 Corinthians 13:6)*. It beareth, believeth, hopeth, and endureth all things *(1 Corinthians 13:7)*. Out of all the wonderful things associated to charity, the Bible makes it clear that charity will have no part with envy.

Devotional Thoughts

- **(For children):** When someone receives a blessing, it is because God allows it *(John 3:27; James 1:17)*. We should be happy for others, knowing God wanted them to experience this blessing *(Romans 12:15a)*. We should not envy but be satisfied with what God has given us *(Hebrews 13:5)*.
- **(For everyone):** If charity is the peak of Christianity, every believer ought to desire it. Since envy hinders charity, it ought to be avoided by every believer. Which of the two do you desire?
- Do you find charity or envy most prevalent in your life? What happens when charity prevails? What happens when envy prevails? As a believer, which of the two is most enjoyable?

☐ Completion Date

PRAYER THOUGHTS
- Ask the Lord to strengthen you in charity.
- Ask God to protect your heart from envy.

SONG: *O! TO BE LIKE THEE*

Day 98: (Saturday)
When We Were Envious

Titus 3:3 *For **we ourselves also were sometimes** foolish, disobedient, deceived, serving divers lusts and pleasures, **living in malice and envy**, hateful, and hating one another.*

INTRODUCTORY THOUGHTS

The Bible often speaks of sin as a thing of the past pertaining to the believer's life prior to salvation. This is not because believers are without sin, but the goal of every believer should be to depart from and avoid the sins which once controlled his life prior to salvation. These past actions which helped us to see our lost condition should be viewed as the friend of our past and the enemy of our present and future. This is exactly how Paul spoke of envy in his epistle to Titus. According to Paul, *"we . . . were sometimes foolish, disobedient, deceived, serving divers lusts and pleasures, living in malice and envy, hateful, and hating one another."* Concerning the sins of the past, Paul further admonishes: *"let it not be once named among you, as becometh saints"* (***Ephesians 5:3***).

DEVOTIONAL THOUGHTS
- **(For children):** God wants us to learn and obey His word. By learning and obeying God's word, we grow up on the inside (***1 Peter 2:2***). We all have a desire to envy (***James 4:5***), and letting God help us put away envy is an important aspect of our spiritual growth (***1 Corinthians 13:4, 11; 1 Corinthians 3:1-3***).
- **(For everyone):** Have you trusted Christ as your Saviour? What is different about you now? Do you still view and partake in the sins that first caused you to recognize your wretchedness?
- Are you envious of other believers? Are you envious of the world? Are you willing to repent of this sin and ask God to help you get victory over it?

• Envy (con't) ☐ Completion Date

PRAYER THOUGHTS
- Thank God for the change He wrought in you at salvation.
- Ask God to continue to help you grow in His grace.

SONG: *ONLY A SINNER*

Notes: _____

_____
_____
_____
_____
_____
_____
_____
_____
_____
_____
_____
_____

Quotes from the next volume

(VOLUME 4, WEEK 14)

Subject: Finances

The Bible mentions true riches thus implying that false riches exist also. Much of what the world considers riches simply serves as a veil for true poverty.

Only the Lord has the infallible wisdom to determine the riches each man can rightfully possess in order to bring God the greatest glory.

15

Heresy

Heresy—found five times in five verses; Note: two other subjects assist this study of heresy: false doctrine and false teachers.

Variations: heresies, heresy, heretick

First usage: *Acts 24:14* (heresy)

Last usage: *2 Peter 2:1* (heresies)

Defined: doctrines contrary to the established teachings found within God's word

Interesting fact: Throughout scripture, a departure from the truths of God and the loss of fellowship with God have been likened to that of an adulterous relationship. For instance, the Bible says that Israel had *"gone a whoring" (Leviticus 17:7; Ezekiel 23:30)* and *"played the harlot" (Jeremiah 3:1)*. Additionally, the New Testament warns against those that would *"seduce"* believers concerning the truth *(1 Timothy 4:1; 2 Timothy 3:13; 1 John 2:26)*. One's acceptance of God's truths corresponds to entering into a covenant with the giver of those truths.

Bible study tip: As you study a chapter or a psalm, break down the combined verses into their individual sentences. Failing to recognize when a thought continues from the previous verse or expands into the next verse has caused Bible students to miss the direct and entire context. It is always dangerous to ignore or miss the true context of any passage.

Sunday, Day 99—Church Day (no devotional)
Monday, Day 100—*Thy Word Is Truth*
Tuesday, Day 101—*The Commandments of Men*
Wednesday, Day 102—Church Night (no devotional)
Thursday, Day 103—*Carried About with Doctrine*
Friday, Day 104—*Hold Fast*
Saturday, Day 105—*Spoiled by False Doctrine*

Day 99: Church Day

Titus 3:10 A man that is an heretick after the first and second admonition reject;

*11 Knowing that **he that is such** is subverted, and sinneth, being condemned of himself.*

Day 100: (Monday)
Thy Word Is Truth

*John 17:17 Sanctify them through thy truth: **thy word is truth**.*

INTRODUCTORY THOUGHTS

The world is full of ideas, theories, and teachings, yet each individual must conscientiously separate the truth from all the confusion. In order to do so, man must first recognize the only proper authority for truth's existence. As Pilate stood before the Lord doubting truth's very existence, he asked the all-important question, *"What is truth?"* Of course, the Lord answered this question before the question was ever asked when He said, *"**I am** the way, **the truth**, and the life" (John 14:6)*. In like manner, as today's verse indicates, the word of God is truth. The authority for truth must be God and His perfect word. Every teaching must be compared with it to validate or deny its accuracy. Simply put, apart from God and His holy word, there exists no other true and infallible authority.

☐ Completion Date   Heresy • 117

Devotional Thoughts

- **(For children):** No one likes to be lied to, and fortunately God cannot lie *(Titus 1:2)*. He wrote the Bible *(2 Peter 1:21; 2 Timothy 3:16a)* and it, too, is completely true *(Psalm 119:160a)* and without error. You can trust what He says. The psalmist tells us that is why he loved God's word *(Psalm 119:163)*.
- **(For everyone):** What is your authority? Do you accept things based upon your feelings or based upon your opinions or that of others? Do you check the things you hear or believe against the scripture?
- What happens when your opinion or way of life contradicts the scripture? Which one do you accept as truth? If it is not the Bible, then the Bible is not your authority.

Prayer Thoughts

- Ask the Lord to help you have the proper authority.
- Ask God to give you a stronger faith in His word.

SONG: *THE BIBLE STANDS*

Day 101: (Tuesday)
The Commandments of Men

Matthew 15:7 Ye hypocrites, well did Esaias prophesy of you, saying,

8 This people draweth nigh unto me with their mouth, and honoureth me with their lips; but their heart is far from me.

9 But in vain they do worship me, teaching for doctrines the commandments of men.

Introductory Thoughts

The world is not short on teachings. Men have commandments. Some of these are decent and harmless, while others are dangerous. The problem comes when men elevate their doctrines or teachings to the level of God's word. This is exactly what the religious leaders did during the Lord's earthly ministry. They elevated their own writings, thoughts, and opinions to the level of the word of God until they would eventually give more reverence to their commandments than to the scripture. This is the propagation of false doctrine. Even now, there are multitudes of people propagating the commandments of men as though they are the words of God.

DEVOTIONAL THOUGHTS
- **(For children):** Read *Mark 7:1-9*. The Pharisees found fault with Jesus' disciples because they did not wash their hands. This washing was not meant to eliminate germs, but an action performed with no real importance other than following the precepts of man. God always prefers that we first be clean within our hearts.
- **(For everyone):** Why is it so important for us to check the words of men against the words of God? When should we reject the words of men? When should we reject the words of God?
- What is the worst thing that could happen to someone who accepts the commandments of men rather than the words of God? How should this thought encourage us to stand for truth?

PRAYER THOUGHTS
- Ask the Lord to help you keep the Bible as your authority.
- Ask God to help you discern right from wrong.

SONG: *THY TESTIMONY'S MY DELIGHT*

Day 102: Church Night

1 Timothy 4:1 Now the Spirit speaketh expressly, that in the latter times some shall depart from the faith, giving heed to seducing spirits, and doctrines of devils;

2 Speaking lies in hypocrisy; having their conscience seared with a hot iron;

*3 **Forbidding to marry, and commanding to abstain from meats,** which God hath created to be received with thanksgiving of them which believe and know the truth.*

Day 103: (Thursday)
Carried About with Doctrine

***Ephesians 4:14** That **we henceforth be no more children, tossed to and fro, and carried about with every wind of doctrine**, by the sleight of men, and cunning craftiness, whereby they lie in wait to deceive;*

Introductory Thoughts

God wants everyone to be firmly established in sound doctrine. The more time an individual spends in his Bible, the better grounded in truth he becomes. With the importance placed upon establishing believers, God warned about being *"carried about with divers and strange doctrines" (**Hebrews 13:9**)* and about being *"tossed to and fro, and carried about with every wind of doctrine" (**Ephesians 4:14**)*. The Devil hates Christians who become rooted and grounded in the truth. This is why he weakens and destroys believers by propagating doctrines contrary to scripture. Men may be the facilitators of false doctrines but the ultimate plan of deception is crafted by the Devil himself.

Devotional Thoughts

- **(For children):** God wants us to study His word so we know when someone is telling us the truth. Some people say we have to worship primarily on Saturdays rather than Sundays, that we cannot eat meats, and that good works or getting baptized allows us access to heaven. These false teachings are only overcome by those who learn the Bible. *(Acts 20:27-31; 2 Timothy 2:15)*.
- **(For everyone):** What does it mean to be established? How does reading the Bible establish you in the truth? Are you taking advantage of your opportunities to be rooted in the truth?
- Why would the Devil desire to craft false doctrines? Why would he hope to persuade believers to accept these false doctrines? How do false doctrines hinder propagation of the truth?

Prayer Thoughts
- Ask God to protect you from false doctrines.
- Ask the Lord to establish you in the truth.

SONG: *STANDING ON THE PROMISES*

Day 104: (Friday)
Hold Fast

2 Timothy 1:13 Hold fast the form of sound words, which thou hast heard of me, in faith and love which is in Christ Jesus.

INTRODUCTORY THOUGHTS

As the world, the flesh, and the Devil war against the truth and those who propagate the truth, believers must determine to hold fast to the very words under attack. The apostle Paul expressed this truth to two young preachers. The verse above shows that Paul admonished Timothy to *"hold fast the form of sound words"* which he had heard from Paul. He also admonished Titus and all those desiring the office of a bishop to hold *"fast the faithful word" (Titus 1:9)*. As the battle for men's minds and souls rages, the ultimate objective is to get believers to turn loose of the words of life. Those desiring to deceive use various means with the propagation of false doctrine being one of their primary tools. Each believer must diligently hold fast the faithful, sound words given by God.

DEVOTIONAL THOUGHTS

- **(For children):** To *"hold fast"* means to continue in the truth that you have learned from others and from the Bible *(2 Timothy 1:5; 2 Timothy 3:14-16)*. Like Ezra, each of us should have a heart for the word of God *(Ezra 7:10)*.
- **(For everyone):** What is the best way to stand against false doctrine? How likely are you to accept false doctrine while holding fast the form of sound words?
- What does it mean to hold something fast? How can you hold fast the word of God? How could this also help others to avoid the snare of false doctrine?

PRAYER THOUGHTS

- Ask the Lord to help you hold fast His word.
- Ask God to protect you and your family from false doctrine.

SONG: *I'LL NOT GIVE UP THE BIBLE*

☐ Completion Date   Heresy • 121

Day 105: (Saturday)
Spoiled by False Doctrine

Colossians 2:8 Beware lest any man spoil you *through philosophy and vain deceit,* ***after the tradition of men,*** *after the rudiments of the world, and not after Christ.*

INTRODUCTORY THOUGHTS

When one side defeats another in battle, to the victor goes the spoils. This means that the victor enters the camp of the defeated and takes its valuable possessions (including women, children, material goods, etc.). With this truth in mind, the apostle Paul warned the believers at Colosse to be on guard, knowing that men would seek to spoil them through philosophy and vain deceit. In other words, accepting the philosophies of men, or false doctrines, is likened to losing a battle and allowing the enemy to rob the believer of his most valuable possessions. It is important to understand that although a believer can never lose his salvation, he can be robbed of his stability, growth, peace, and joy.

DEVOTIONAL THOUGHTS

- **(For children):** The churches of Galatia accepted sound doctrine on how to be saved. Then, false teachers told them they had to work to maintain their salvation, and they believed the lie. No one can work for salvation nor can they work to keep it ***(Galatians 3:1-3; Ephesians 2:8-9)***.
- **(For everyone):** Do you know anyone who has been spoiled through philosophy or vain deceit? What did he or she lose when spoiled? What specific issue brought the damage?
- What have you gained from learning sound doctrine? What are some things you might lose if spoiled by philosophy or vain deceit? What should you do to stand for the truth?

PRAYER THOUGHTS

- Thank God for the sound doctrine He has given you.
- Ask God to help you to be aware of the ongoing battle.

SONG: *THE BIBLE, WHAT A PRECIOUS BOOK*

Notes:

Quotes from the next volume
(VOLUME 4, WEEK 15)
Subject: Finances (con't)

Some televangelists teach that God wants everyone wealthy which is simply not true. However, if wealth is gained through scriptural means, it can be used of the Lord to do much good (by supporting missionaries, helping those in need, furthering the gospel, etc.).

When possible, believers should be willing to help the poor, but they must keep in mind that they will never eliminate the problem of poverty.

16
Heresy (con't)

Heresy—found five times in five verses; Note: two other subjects assist this study of heresy: false doctrine and false teachers.

Variations: heresies, heresy, heretick

Interesting fact: Fifty-nine times in fifty-four verses the Bible uses a form of the word *blasphemy*. People blaspheme both the name of God and word of God. Many of the expressed acts that cause this blasphemy come as no surprise, but two lesser known acts of blasphemy involve disobedient servants **(1 Timothy 6:1)** and wives **(Titus 2:5)**.

Bible study tip: The Bible records many prayers; however, there are times when the Bible does not specifically mention prayer taking place but the actions within the passage are a prayer. These instances offer the reader opportunity to learn the doctrine of prayer along with a practical education on the benefits of prayer during times of difficulty (see the ***Psalm 102*** subtitle and then read ***Psalm 102:1-28***).

Sunday, Day 106—Church Day (no devotional)
Monday, Day 107—*Transformed into an Apostle*
Tuesday, Day 108—*Deceiving the Hearts of the Simple*
Wednesday, Day 109—Church Night (no devotional)

124 • Heresy (con't)

Thursday, Day 110—*The Effects of False Teachers*
Friday, Day 111—*They Will Not Endure Sound Doctrine*
Saturday, Day 112—*Some Shall Depart from the Faith*

Day 106: Church Day

2 Timothy 3:13 **But evil men and seducers shall wax worse and worse, deceiving, and being deceived.**

14 **But continue thou in the things which thou hast learned and hast been assured of,** knowing of whom thou hast learned them;

Day 107: (Monday)
Transformed into an Apostle

2 Corinthians 11:13 **For such are false apostles,** deceitful workers, **transforming themselves into the apostles of Christ.**

INTRODUCTORY THOUGHTS

The sorry state of biblical spirituality in the world today clearly reflects the fact that too many people think far too highly of their levels of discernment. In fact, many of the most beloved teachers when compared to the Bible would be considered false teachers. Yet, scriptural ignorance insures that the masses will never realize the extent of the deception. For this reason, multitudes are led away from faith in the words of God. The apostle Paul insured that believers are warned of the impending dangers by pointing out that Satan himself is transformed into an angel of light *(2 Corinthians 11:14)*. For this reason, believers should not marvel when his followers are also *"transformed as the ministers of righteousness" (2 Corinthians 11:15)*. This should serve as a sober warning to the saints of God that the Devil has his minions doing his bidding. In fact, they tend to be the most expressly and outwardly religious. These people serve Satan within churches all over the world with the sole purpose of leading people astray.

DEVOTIONAL THOUGHTS

- **(For children):** The book of Acts says the Bereans searched the scriptures daily to see if what Paul and Silas were preaching was true *(Acts 17:10-11)*. Read what Jesus said about false teachers *(Matthew 7:15)*.

God wants us to be like the Bereans who measured all truth according to what saith the scriptures.
- **(For everyone):** If Satan's ministers can be transformed into ministers of righteousness, how can the saints of God identify those propagating false doctrine?
- Why is it important that believers have the scripture as their authority in all matters? What happens when we become followers of men (even if those men are currently following the scripture)?

PRAYER THOUGHTS
- Ask the Lord to protect your church from false teachers.
- Ask God to give you discernment concerning error.

SONG: *THE BIBLE IS DIVINE*

Day 108: (Tuesday)
Deceiving the Hearts of the Simple

***Romans 16:18** For **they** that are such **serve** not our Lord Jesus Christ, but **their own belly; and by good words and fair speeches deceive the hearts of the simple**.*

INTRODUCTORY THOUGHTS

The enemies of God and of His people have always sought to conquer those weak in the faith by destroying their faith. Even now, false teachers seek to deceive the hearts of the simple—those who lack knowledge, understanding, and wisdom *(**Proverbs 8:5; Proverbs 9:4, 13**)*. According to the scripture, these teachers do so *"by good words and fair speeches."* It is not some raving, ranting lunatic that is most dangerous; it is the sweet talking, kind, loving, liar. In order to gain a following, a teacher must only appeal to others by sounding intelligent and offering *"fair speeches"* sprinkled with truth. If he can present things new to his audience, whether factual or not, the simple will become enamoured with his abilities and follow his teachings. This is why the Bible warns believers to have no fellowship with those who teach things contrary to the scripture. Any world religious leader who speaks softly and kindly yet fails to proclaim the true gospel probably lives more like a devil in private. The Bible calls these people wolves in sheep's clothing.

126 • Heresy (con't) ☐ Completion Date

Devotional Thoughts
- **(For children):** Read *Proverbs 14:15*. God wants us to know if what we hear is right by comparing it to His words. If a friend says it is acceptable to pretend you are sick so you will not have to do chores, you are simple if you believe that. You are wise if you remember and obey *Colossians 3:9a*.
- **(For everyone):** Are you simple? Are you following the precepts of man or following the scripture? What does a man have to do in order to earn your respect as a teacher of the word of God?
- What measures can you take to ensure that you are not deceived by those propagating false doctrines? How can you also insure that your family or church is not one of those who circulates falsehoods?

Prayer Thoughts
- Ask God to give you knowledge, understanding, and wisdom.
- Ask God to show you the importance of following scripture only.

SONG: *LAY NOT THIS BOOK ASIDE!*

Day 109: Church Night

*Proverbs 14:25 A true witness delivereth souls: but **a deceitful witness speaketh lies.***

Day 110: (Thursday)
The Effects of False Teachers

Titus 1:11 Whose mouths must be stopped, who subvert whole houses, teaching things which they ought not, for filthy lucre's sake.

Introductory Thoughts

False teachers are extremely dangerous because they undermine truth! Their rotten fruit may not surface for some time, but when allowed to continue unchecked, they will deceive individuals, whole families, and good churches. Paul warned Titus that such teachers had already seen some success and that their mouths must be stopped. Regretfully, whole houses had already been subverted with the false teachers still at work. A similar situation is recorded in *Acts 15:24* where the saints of God were *"troubled"* by the words of false teachers. There is no telling

☐ Completion Date   Heresy (con't) • 127

how many of God's people have walked away from sound doctrine because of false teachers. Worse yet, how many souls are burning right now in hell because they trusted in a false gospel?

Devotional Thoughts

- **(For children):** False teachers taught that the dead rise not. Paul said if that were true, our faith is vain and we would be miserable *(1 Corinthians 15:12, 16-19)*. Some taught the resurrection was past causing others to give up what they believed *(2 Timothy 2:17-18)*.
- **(For everyone):** Why would the Devil seek to deceive you into believing false doctrines? Why does the Devil desire to get you to become a follower of man?
- Do you know anyone who has been deceived into believing false doctrine? How has it affected that individual? Has it affected that person's family, or church?

Prayer Thoughts

- Thank God for giving you light concerning the danger of false teaching.
- Ask the Lord to guard you from deception.

SONG: *HOLD THE FORT*

Day 111: (Friday)
They Will Not Endure Sound Doctrine

*2 Timothy 4:3 For **the time will come when they will not endure sound doctrine**; but after their own lusts shall they heap to themselves teachers, having itching ears;*

Introductory Thoughts

The apostle Paul warned of a time when people would no longer endure sound doctrine. Because of their lusts, they would actively seek after teachers who turned them unto fables. In fact, much of this is accomplished by people using the truth as a source for teaching things contrary to the very truth they supposedly uphold. Far too frequently people have been turned away from the truth in the name of truth. These Bible teachers elevate themselves as the authority while creating fables generally based upon certain verses of scripture. The tragedy may begin subtly, but eventually, many people seek after these teachers rather than scripture. This is why Paul admonished Timothy to *"Preach the word" (2 Timothy 4:2)* to delay the onset of this spiritually desolate period.

Devotional Thoughts

- **(For children):** People do not like God's word because it tells them they need to be saved and do what God wants. Consider some of the different reactions from those who did not want to hear God's word: **Psalm 50:17; Jeremiah 5:31; Jeremiah 36:21-25; Acts 7:54-57.**
- **(For everyone):** If both sound doctrine and fables originate from the same source, how can we know the difference between the two? What can you do to ensure that you are not led away from the truth?
- Paul warned that people would seek teachers rather than scripture. Is this happening today? Has it happened to you? Where is your allegiance? Who is your authority?

Prayer Thoughts

- Ask the Lord to help you to endure sound doctrine.
- Ask the Lord to help you to seek scripture over teachers.

SONG: *THE SACRED PAGE*

Day 112: (Saturday)
Some Shall Depart from the Faith

1 Timothy 4:1 Now the Spirit speaketh expressly, that **in the latter times some shall depart from the faith,** *giving heed to seducing spirits, and doctrines of devils;*

Introductory Thoughts

It is always a painful experience to see those who once walked with the Lord now walking contrary to Him. Families and friends are hurt because of those now living contrary to God's dictates. Paul warned Timothy that this departure from the faith would take place *in the last days*. A firm and consistent stand for the faith would give way to an increase in the influence of seducing spirits and doctrines of devils. No doubt, this has occurred since the inception of the New Testament church, but Paul warned that it would increase to its apex in the latter times. In response to the coming danger, Paul admonished the young preacher to be *"nourished up in the words of faith and of good doctrine"* **(1 Timothy 4:6)**. This shows that the best defense against departing from the truth is a consistent feasting upon the truth.

Devotional Thoughts

- **(For children)**: False teachers teach heresy (a denial of the truth of God's word). Peter tells us they will even deny the Lord. Their end is destruction and many will follow them to this destruction **(2 Peter 2:1-2)**. Growing in grace and knowledge helps us recognize false teachers **(2 Peter 3:15-18)**.
- **(For everyone)**: How do you feel when others walk away from the truth? Why do people walk away? Are they generally spiritually seduced gradually or quickly?
- How can we ensure that we are *"nourished up in the words of faith and of good doctrine"* **(1 Timothy 4:6)**? How can this help us be steadfast in the faith?

Prayer Thoughts

- Ask the Lord to nourish you in His word.
- Ask the Lord to strengthen the saints of God at your church.

SONG: *THE DEAR VOLUME OF THY BOOK*

Notes:

Notes:

Quotes from the next volume

(VOLUME 4, WEEK 16)

Subject: Hope

All men live their lives based upon hope; however, not all hope is the same. One man's hope might be that there is no life after death. Another might place his hope solely in the payment for sin provided by the Lord Jesus Christ.

The Devil blinds the lost to keep them from being born again; he distracts the saved to keep them from successfully serving the Lord. Interestingly, he accomplishes both elements using the same means – giving men misplaced hopes.

Once a man dies, all hope ceases. His destination and his reward are settled, but until that point in time, there is hope for salvation, hope for growth, and hope for spiritual change.

17

Hypocrisy

Hypocrisy—found forty times in forty verses

Variations: hypocrisies, hypocrisy, hypocrite, hypocrites, hypocrite's, hypocritical

First usage: *Job 8:13* (hypocrite's)

Last usage: *1 Peter 2:1* (hypocrisies)

Defined: the act of pretending to be something one is not; an imitation

Interesting fact: Matthew contains sixteen of the forty instances of the various forms of the words *hypocrite* or *hypocrisy* found in scripture. The first fifteen of these references in Matthew describe the character and work of the hypocrite. The sixteenth and final usage reveals the hypocrite's end where *"there shall be weeping and gnashing of teeth"* **(Matthew 24:51)**.

Bible study tip: Take note of virtues demonstrated or benefits enjoyed as these things pertain to an individual or type of individual. It is also very important to take note of the duration of those benefits. For example, the hypocrite has *"hope,"* but this hope *"shall perish"* **(Job 8:13)**. He has *"joy,"* but his joy is only *"for a moment"* **(Job 20:5)**.

Sunday, Day 113—Church Day (no devotional)
Monday, Day 114—*The Hypocrite Forgets God*
Tuesday, Day 115—*The Joy of the Hypocrite*
Wednesday, Day 116—Church Night (no devotional)
Thursday, Day 117—*An Hypocrite Destroyeth His Neighbour*
Friday, Day 118—*Practising Hypocrisy*
Saturday, Day 119—*Wisdom Without Hypocrisy*

Day 113: Church Day

1 Peter 2:1 *Wherefore **laying aside all** malice, and all guile, and **hypocrisies**, and envies, and all evil speakings,*

Day 114: (Monday)
The Hypocrite Forgets God

Job 8:13 *So are **the paths of all that forget God**; and the hypocrite's hope shall perish:*

INTRODUCTORY THOUGHTS

The Bible-believing student rejects any notion of coincidences within scripture. He chooses rather to believe that every word of God was specifically chosen by the Lord to convey His intended message. In today's passage, the Lord revealed the root of the hypocrite's problems—he is likened to *"all that forget God."* The hypocrite is a person who presents himself one way, when in reality, he is altogether something far different than the perception he imitates. For instance, he may fast to convey the message that he loves the Lord, but his spirituality is only a façade for men to see. He may pray, but does so to be heard by men. In the end, his greatest problem is that he has forgotten that the all-seeing, all-knowing God knows the difference between heartfelt actions and hypocrisy.

DEVOTIONAL THOUGHTS

- **(For children):** Whatever we do should be done for the Lord **(Colossians 3:22-23)**. The Pharisees seemed religious but their hearts were not right because they simply desired the praise of men **(Matthew 6:2; Matthew 23:5a)**. Jesus compared them to dirty cups **(Luke 11:39)** and whited sepulchres **(Matthew 23:27-28)**.

- **(For everyone):** In what way does a hypocrite forget God? Who becomes the focus of the hypocrite's attention rather than God? How does it ultimately cause him to fall?
- Whom should we seek to please? How would a desire to please God change how we live? How would it affect the parts of our lives not seen by men?

Prayer Thoughts

- Ask the Lord to help you seek to please Him.
- Ask God to guard you against forgetting Him.

SONG: *TURN YOUR EYES UPON JESUS*

Day 115: (Tuesday)
The Joy of the Hypocrite

*Job 20:5 That the triumphing of the wicked is short, and **the joy of the hypocrite but for a moment**?*

Introductory Thoughts

The hypocrite lives for the present by seeking his reward from the praise of man *(Matthew 6:2)*. He finds his greatest joy only when men shower him with the praise he so desperately seeks. According to scripture, this joy is only temporary. As soon as the hypocrite does something to gain the praise of man, he becomes jealous as he sees others accomplish greater feats. When the hypocrite loses man's attention and praise, he becomes distraught and seeks more aggressive ways to win men's lost admiration. Only those ignorant of God's ways would want to live such a horrible existence! This life yields no lasting peace or joy which is the very outcome offered by God for those who live for Him and love Him. For the hypocrite, nothing remains constant. His standard is always changing and bar ever raising while the faithful Christian joyfully seeks to please the never-changing God *(Malachi 3:6)*.

Devotional Thoughts

- **(For children):** Haman was promoted by king Ahasuerus but lived miserably inside because Mordecai refused to praise him *(Esther 3:1-2; Esther 5:11-13)*. He reaped what he sowed when his wicked plan to kill Mordecai turned against him *(Esther 7:10)*.

- **(For everyone):** Do you have lasting joy? Are you constantly trying to gain the admiration of others? Whom are you ultimately supposed to live to please?
- What are some other reasons why the joy of a hypocrite might only last for a moment of time? How is this different from the joy of the believer as noted in **Psalm 16:11**?

PRAYER THOUGHTS
- Ask the Lord to give you lasting joy.
- Ask God to show you when you are acting the hypocrite's part.

SONG: *JOY UNSPEAKABLE*

Day 116: Church Night

Matthew 15:7 Ye **hypocrites,** *well did Esaias prophesy of you, saying,*
8 This people **draweth nigh unto me with their mouth, and honoureth me with** *their* **lips; but their heart is far from me.**

Day 117: (Thursday)
An Hypocrite Destroyeth His Neighbour

Proverbs 11:9 An **hypocrite with his mouth destroyeth his neighbour***: but through knowledge shall the just be delivered.*

INTRODUCTORY THOUGHTS

Hypocrites desperately desire the praise of men, yet they are unwilling to put forth the right efforts to obtain any legitimate praise. Instead, they choose to elevate themselves by demeaning others. The actions of the Pharisee found in **Luke 18:11-13** best illustrate this truth. While the Pharisee was hypocritically thanking the Lord that he was not wicked like the publican, the publican was busy confessing to God how wicked he was. In order to exalt himself, the Pharisee determined to belittle his neighbour thinking that this comparison made him look better. This practice of exalting oneself while demeaning others is as old as man himself. People today choose to inflate their own pride or position by undermining others.

Devotional Thoughts

- **(For children):** Mary poured some expensive ointment upon the Lord to anoint His body for burial. Judas complained that the ointment should have been sold and the money given to the poor. In reality, Judas revealed his hypocrisy because he cared nothing for the poor; he was simply a thief *(John 12:1-8).*
- **(For everyone):** Have you ever sought to destroy others so that you could be exalted in the mind of God or man? Did your unsavoury behaviour prick your conscience? Why or why not?
- Did the Pharisee gain any favour with God by attempting to destroying the publican? How did the publican gain favour with God and go away justified?

Prayer Thoughts

- Ask God to help you edify others with your mouth.
- Ask God to show you your own hypocrisy.

SONG: *I WANT A PRINCIPLE WITHIN*

Day 118: (Friday)
Practising Hypocrisy

Isaiah 32:6 ***For the vile person will speak villany, and his heart will work iniquity, to practise hypocrisy,*** *and to utter error against the LORD, to make empty the soul of the hungry, and he will cause the drink of the thirsty to fail.*

Introductory Thoughts

Hypocrisy requires more effort than most people realize. In fact, the level of effort expended by the hypocrite frequently exceeds what would be necessary to simply do right. Unfortunately, man's sinful heart will frequently choose hypocrisy over genuine righteousness. As an individual chooses to live hypocritically, his practice of hypocrisy becomes more proficient. Young children do not often understand hypocrisy. They innocently speak and do things regardless of how it may negatively impact others. Eventually, these same children, taught by adults, learn how to hide things and pretend to be something that they are not. Eventually, the honest, transparent child grows into a deceptive, hypocritical adult unless the parents consistently direct the child away from this behaviour. How do people avoid this transformation from taking place? The individual must actively and consistently attempt to live a life without deception by allowing God to control his life.

Devotional Thoughts

- **(For children):** Absalom aggressively attempted to take the kingdom from his father David. He appeared as though he was good but was actually false and faithless *(2 Samuel 15:1-12)*.
- **(For everyone):** Is there a balance between always speaking one's mind and completely covering up what one truly thinks? How can anyone consistently find this balance?
- How can adults cease from practising hypocrisy? When is the practise of hypocrisy usually started? What can parents do to help their children avoid this pitfall that comes from living a lie?

Prayer Thoughts

- Ask God to help you stop practising hypocrisy.
- Ask the Lord to show you the dangers of hypocrisy.

SONG: *TEMPLES OF THE HOLY GHOST*

Day 119: (Saturday)
Wisdom Without Hypocrisy

*James 3:17 But **the wisdom that is from above is** first pure, then peaceable, gentle, and easy to be intreated, full of mercy and good fruits, without partiality, and **without hypocrisy**.*

Introductory Thoughts

The Bible mentions two types of wisdom: worldly wisdom *(1 Corinthians 3:19)* and godly wisdom *(James 1:5)*. These distinct wisdoms oppose each other in several aspects including their relationship to hypocrisy. Man claims to live wisely and yet encourages something that counteracts true wisdom—hypocrisy. This is because God's wisdom operates only when hypocrisy is absent. At first, this might seem quite difficult to achieve, yet righteousness is never accomplished through sinful means. The only way to demonstrate true wisdom is to do so with purity and mercy void of partiality and hypocrisy.

☐ Completion Date   Hypocrisy • 137

Devotional Thoughts

- **(For children):** A friend tells you he plans to get even with a child who broke his toy. Because you also do not like this child, you choose to say and do nothing. However, godly wisdom always chooses God's word over how we feel. Consider these scriptures *(Ephesians 4:32; Romans 12:17a)*. What should be said or done to this child?
- **(For everyone):** What should a person say when asked for his opinion concerning something sinful? Should he remain silent? Should he avoid offending the person asking the question? Should he rather choose to utter all his mind?
- What kind of wisdom are you manifesting? Does hypocrisy exist in your wisdom?

Prayer Thoughts

- Ask God for godly wisdom.
- Ask God to teach you more about wisdom and hypocrisy.

SONG: *THE MORE I KNOW OF THEE*

Notes: _____

_____
_____
_____
_____
_____
_____
_____
_____
_____
_____
_____
_____

☐ Completion Date

Notes:

Quotes from the next volume

(VOLUME 4, WEEK 17)

Subject: Hope (con't)

The world looks at those who read the Bible and wonders why anyone would desire to read about the lives of those who lived thousands of years ago. Yet, the testimonies found in scripture concerning God's provisions continue to provide hope for man today.

Man continues to experience a sense of emptiness more prevalent today than at any other time in history. Every day, people expend an enormous amount of time, strength, and money hoping to obtain the ever illusive happiness.

Regardless of man's circumstances, hope can put a song in man's heart and praise upon his lips.

18
Hypocrisy (con't)

Hypocrisy—found fourteen times in fourteen verses in the Old Testament and twenty-six times in twenty-six verses the New Testament

Variations: hypocrisies, hypocrisy, hypocrite, hypocrites, hypocrite's, hypocritical

Last usage in the Old Testament: *Isaiah 33:14* (hypocrites)

First usage in the New Testament: *Matthew 6:2* (hypocrites)

Interesting fact: The Book of Job incorporates a form of the word *hypocrite* more times than any other book with the exception of Matthew's gospel. In Matthew's gospel, the mention of hypocrisy was generally directed toward the religious leaders. Additionally, we find it eight times within the Book of Job. The majority of the Book of Job expresses the conversation and interaction between Job and his three *"friends."* Bible students recognize that hypocrisy revolved around the counsel of these *"friends."* Not surprisingly, each of the main speakers found in the Book of Job used a form of the word *hypocrite* on at least one occasion.

Bible study tip: Animals are frequently used in scripture as representations of various types of men and devils. For instance, a sly ruler was depicted by a fox *(Luke 13:32)*. Birds were implemented to convey truths concerning the devil or devils *(Matthew 13:4, 19)*. Wolves often depicted false prophets *(Matthew 7:15; Acts 20:29)*. Be sure to recognize when and why the context plainly uses the animal kingdom to describe or depict a certain characteristic in man.

Sunday, Day 120—Church Day (no devotional)
Monday, Day 121—*The Desire of the Hypocrite*
Tuesday, Day 122—*The Discernment of the Hypocrite*
Wednesday, Day 123—Church Night (no devotional)
Thursday, Day 124—*Compassing Sea and Land for One*
Friday, Day 125—*Leaving the Weightier Matters Undone*
Saturday, Day 126—*Laying Aside All Hypocrisies*

Day 120: Church Day

*Job 27:8 For **what is the hope of the hypocrite**, though he hath gained, when God taketh away his soul?*

Day 121: (Monday)
The Desire of the Hypocrite

*Matthew 6:2 Therefore when thou doest thine alms, do not sound a trumpet before thee, as **the hypocrites** do in the synagogues and in the streets, that they may **have glory of men**. Verily I say unto you, **They have their reward**.*

INTRODUCTORY THOUGHTS

The Bible points out that the hypocrite has forgotten God *(Job 8:13)*. Therefore, the hypocrite shows little to no concern for receiving the praise of God. His natural desire to please God has instead been replaced with a desire to receive praise and glory from other men. This desire affects everything the hypocrite does. He gives, in hopes that others will admire his generosity *(Matthew 6:2-4)*. He prays, hoping someone will notice the eloquence with which he calls upon God *(Matthew 6:5-8)*. He fasts, but not in hopes of moving the Lord; rather, he wants others to marvel at the dedication with which he has devoted himself to God *(Matthew 6:16-18)*.

Devotional Thoughts

- **(For children):** Some of the chief rulers believed that Jesus was the Son of God but would not say so because they loved the praise of men more than the praise of God and did not want to be put out of the synagogue *(John 12:42-43)*.
- **(For everyone):** In Matthew chapter 6, the phrase *"they have their reward"* occurs three times *(Matthew 6:2, 5, 16)*, each time speaking of hypocrites. What does it mean that the hypocrite already has his reward?
- Whom are you seeking to please? What does it suggest if you are seeking to please men (see *Galatians 1:10*)? What happens when you make it your goal to please men?

Prayer Thoughts

- Ask the Lord to make it your goal to please Him.
- Ask the Lord to show you the areas of hypocrisy in your life.

SONG: *BE THOU MY VISION*

Day 122: (Tuesday)
The Discernment of the Hypocrite

Matthew 16:1 The Pharisees also with the Sadducees came, and tempting desired him that he would shew them a sign from heaven.

2 He answered and said unto them, When it is evening, ye say, It will be fair weather: for the sky is red.

3 And in the morning, It will be foul weather to day: for the sky is red and lowring. O **ye hypocrites, ye can discern the face of the sky; but can ye not discern the signs of the times?**

Introductory Thoughts

The Lord commended the hypocrite for his discernment in certain areas of life but rebuked him for his lack of discernment in the most needful areas. As such, the hypocrite readily recognizes problems in others but remains blind to those same inadequacies within his own life. Though some might accuse the hypocrite of merely ignoring his own deficiencies, it is likely that he cannot discern the presence of these problems as they appear within his own life. This is most likely caused by the blindness produced by Satan. After all, Satan has no problem when a man finds fault in others so long as that man remains oblivious to his own failures. Without God's help, the hypocrite will never discern that his hypocrisy is his problem.

DEVOTIONAL THOUGHTS
- **(For children):** God sent the prophet Nathan to tell king David a story about a rich man who had wronged a poor man. David became angry and expressed his disgust for what the rich man had done. God was using the story to help David realize that he must confess his own sin *(2 Samuel 12:1-7a).*
- **(For everyone):** How easy is it for you to find fault in others? What are some areas in which you have problems? Is it easier for you to see the problems in others than those that exist within your own life?
- What are some areas in which you see problems in others but fail to recognize your guilt in the same area? Do you judge others more severely than yourself?

PRAYER THOUGHTS
- Ask the Lord to help you repent of your own problems.
- Ask God to give you grace in dealing with others.

SONG: *GOD IS A RIGHTEOUS JUDGE BE SURE*

Day 123: Church Night

*Matthew 22:18 But **Jesus** perceived their wickedness, and **said**, Why tempt ye me, ye **hypocrites**?*

Day 124: (Thursday)
Compassing Sea and Land for One

*Matthew 23:15 Woe unto you, scribes and Pharisees, **hypocrites!** for **ye compass sea and land to make one proselyte**, and when he is made, ye make him twofold more the child of hell than yourselves.*

INTRODUCTORY THOUGHTS

The Bible depicts the hypocrite as someone who may work hard. Yet, the efforts of hypocrites are directed toward the wrong things. The Lord

Jesus pointed out that the hypocrites would *"compass sea and land to make one proselyte."* This conveys hard work. Think about the difference that Christians could make by labouring that hard to win *"one"* soul to the Lord! The hypocrite promotes unholy things contrary to the will of God. Believers need to take the right lesson away from studying the hypocrite. Each of us should be working hard to lead others to Christ and then to teach sound Bible doctrine. Yet, we should spend a lot less time finding fault in others. If we did, churches would be full of converts growing in the grace and knowledge of Jesus Christ.

Devotional Thoughts

- **(For children):** When missionaries survey the land to which they are called to serve, they often find a number of false religions with no true church in existence. We need to pray for workers *(Matthew 9:36-38)*, better yet, have a heart like Isaiah *(Isaiah 6:8)*.
- **(For everyone):** In what areas of service for the Lord are you putting forth your greatest efforts? Are you witnessing to the lost? Are you seeking the Lord in prayer? Are you reading your Bible?
- Do you find yourself working hard to get the praise of men? Are you working tirelessly to find the faults in others while ignoring them in your own life?

Prayer Thoughts

- Ask God to help you labour for right things.
- Ask God to show you when you are acting like a hypocrite.

SONG: *WHO IS ON THE LORD'S SIDE?*

Day 125: (Friday)
Leaving the Weightier Matters Undone

Matthew 23:23 Woe unto you, scribes and Pharisees, **hypocrites!** *for ye pay tithe of mint and anise and cummin, and* **have omitted the weightier matters of the law, judgment, mercy, and faith:** *these ought ye to have done, and not to leave the other undone.*

Introductory Thoughts

Hypocrites often reveal themselves as detail oriented people. However, though they might notice something small and insignificant, they often fail to recognize the extremely obvious necessities of faithful service. When dealing with the hypocrites of His day, the Lord Jesus declared this very truth. The hypocrites paid tithes of mint, anise, and cummin but omitted judgment, mercy, and faith *(Matthew 23:23)*. They would *"strain at a gnat,"* but *"swallow a camel" (Matthew 23:24)*. They were obedient in the strictest sense of their religion in certain aspects, but oblivious to their disobedience in the more obvious areas of life. Even today, a hypocrite often becomes overzealous in his obedience in one area of life while failing to recognize his rebellion in other important areas.

Devotional Thoughts

- **(For children):** The Jews would not work on the sabbath. They found fault with Jesus because He healed people on the sabbath. Jesus pointed out that they helped animals on the sabbath and rightly so. People in need should be helped also *(Luke 13:10-17; Luke 14:1-6)*.
- **(For everyone):** Do you work hard to be obedient in smaller matters while ignoring your rebellion to weightier commands? What was the Lord's counsel to the hypocrites? What should you do?
- Do you work hard to perform the letter of the law (tithe of mint, anise, and cummin) while completely ignoring the spirit of the law (judgment, mercy, faith)?

Prayer Thoughts

- Ask the Lord to help you avoid the errors of the hypocrite.
- Ask God to help you obey the smaller and weightier matters.

SONG: *ABOVE THE TREASURES OF THIS WORLD*

Day 126: (Saturday)
Laying Aside All Hypocrisies

*1 Peter 2:1 Wherefore **laying aside all** malice, and all guile, and **hypocrisies**, and envies, and all evil speakings,*

*2 As newborn babes, **desire the sincere milk of the word**, that ye may grow thereby:*

3 If so be ye have tasted that the Lord is gracious.

☐ Completion Date   Hypocrisy (con't) • 145

Introductory Thoughts

Peter admonished *"newborn babes"* in Christ to lay aside all hypocrisies. It is a natural battle that every babe in Christ must face. A new believer might have an inappropriate longing to please the one who led him to the Lord rather than giving the Lord preeminence. He might perform actions in hopes that his spiritual mentor will take notice. Eventually, this fault blossoms to the point where he begins to see problems in others while failing to realize the same problems exist in his own life. He might work hard to obey the strictest of commands while missing the overall desire of the Lord in his own life. Even as a babe in Christ, he must work to lay aside hypocrisy. Until he does, he will never grow into the mature believer the Lord wants him to be.

Devotional Thoughts

- **(For children):** God wants us to examine our hearts *(1 Corinthians 11:28a; 2 Corinthians 13:5a; Psalm 139:23-24)*. When we have sin in our hearts and do not confess that sin, but rather see everyone else's faults, that is hypocrisy *(Luke 6:41-42)*.
- **(For everyone):** If hypocrisy is a battle faced by *"newborn babes,"* does one constantly battling with hypocrisy suggest some need for spiritual growth? Should you be facing the battles of a newborn babe or should those battles become a thing of the past?
- Has the Lord used the scripture to show you that hypocrisy exists in your life? Does this offend you? Are you willing to lay aside your hypocrisy and grow in the Lord?

Prayer Thoughts

- Ask God to help you repent of your hypocrisy.
- Ask the Lord to help you grow into a mature believer.

SONG: *MORE ABOUT JESUS*

Notes: _____

_____

_____

_____

_____

Notes: _____

Quotes from the next volume

(VOLUME 4, WEEK 18)
Subject: Jealousy

The Bible student understands that jealousy cannot always be sinful because God says that He is a jealous God *(Nahum 1:2)*.

Biblically speaking, a man's name is equal to his character *(Proverbs 22:1)*. God's character is often defined by His name.

As man provokes the Lord to jealousy, the Lord responds with judgment.

19

Liberality

Liberality—found ten times in eight verses

Variations: liberal, liberality, liberally

First usage: *Deuteronomy 15:14* (liberally)

Last usage: *James 1:5* (liberally)

Defined: something done in an unrestricted manner

Interesting fact: The biblical mentions of liberality involve taking of one's possessions or monies and distributing them to others who are in a specific time of need *(Deuteronomy 15:14; 1 Corinthians 16:3; 2 Corinthians 8:2; 2 Corinthians 9:13)*. Societies have become increasingly enamored by those who claim to take from the rich and give to the poor. However, liberality is never defined as one man taking another's possessions and monies in order to assist others who might have unmet needs. Furthermore, it is completely unscriptural to give (including even the basic necessities of life) to those who refuse to work *(2 Thessalonians 3:10)*.

Bible study tip: The more we depart from daily Bible reading, the more we veer away from understanding and implementing sound biblical terminology. The consequences of this departure from biblical terminology are twofold: (1)

we improperly identify people (i.e., liberals, scholars, sodomites) and acts, and (2) we then tend to interpret scripture based upon our flawed understanding of Bible vocabulary. With this in mind, we should never underestimate the influence of daily Bible reading upon in-depth Bible study.

Sunday, Day 127—Church Day (no devotional)
Monday, Day 128—*Mislabeled Liberals*
Tuesday, Day 129—*The Liberal Soul Shall Be Made Fat*
Wednesday, Day 130—Church Night (no devotional)
Thursday, Day 131—*Liberality in Giving*
Friday, Day 132—*Liberality Yields Thanksgiving*
Saturday, Day 133—*A Liberal God*

Day 127: Church Day

Proverbs 28:27 He that giveth unto the poor shall not lack: *but he that hideth his eyes shall have many a curse.*

Day 128: (Monday)
Mislabeled Liberals

*Isaiah 32:5 The **vile person shall be no more called liberal**, nor the churl said to be bountiful.*

6 For the vile person will speak villany, and his heart will work iniquity, to practise hypocrisy, and to utter error against the LORD, to make empty the soul of the hungry, and he will cause the drink of the thirsty to fail.

7 The instruments also of the churl are evil: he deviseth wicked devices to destroy the poor with lying words, even when the needy speaketh right.

*8 But **the liberal deviseth liberal things; and by liberal things shall he stand**.*

INTRODUCTORY THOUGHTS

The first part of Isaiah chapter 32 speaks of a future time when the Lord will right wrongs that exist in societies. Isaiah points out that the

Lord will reign in righteousness *(Isaiah 32:1)* and mankind will no longer be blinded by sin *(Isaiah 32:3-4)*. Though many wrongs will be made right, the Lord specifically mentions that the *vile* will no longer be called *liberal (Isaiah 32:5)*. How did the Lord know in Isaiah's day that the label *liberal* would be inappropriately used to address the vile? Perhaps this was already taking place or the Lord was merely demonstrating His infinite knowledge and prophetic aptitude. Liberals are not Bible corrupters, nor are they politicians holding nonconservative points of view. Quite simply, a liberal is a person who gives generously.

Devotional Thoughts

- **(For children)**: Read what the Lord Jesus said about giving *(Acts 20:35)*. In Romans, Paul was taking a contribution for needy saints at Jerusalem *(Romans 15:25-26)*. Giving freely is called *liberality (1 Corinthians 16:1-4)*.
- **(For everyone)**: Would you want to be labeled as liberal? How has the misuse of the word affected you by infecting your thinking? With the Bible definition, do you see the label *liberal* as one meant for praise or meant for reproach?
- Would you be considered a liberal in the scriptural sense? Why should God's people be the most liberal people in the world? In what ways should we be liberal?

Prayer Thoughts

- Ask the Lord to help you learn to be liberal.
- Thank God for the promise of righting the wrongs of this world.

SONG: *IS THY CRUSE OF COMFORT WASTING?*

Day 129: (Tuesday)
The Liberal Soul Shall Be Made Fat

***Proverbs 11:25** The liberal soul shall be made fat: and he that watereth shall be watered also himself.*

Introductory Thoughts

The book of Proverbs frequently incorporates the tools of comparison and contrast for the purpose of teaching specific truths. In today's passage, a *liberal* soul is likened to one who waters. The passage also mentions that being made fat is likened to being watered. In other words, a liberal reaps the benefits of his own liberality. Proverbs chapter 3 also sets forth the principle of sowing and reaping as man is told to *"Honour the LORD with thy substance, and with the firstfruits of all thine increase: So shall thy barns be filled with plenty, and thy presses shall burst out with new wine" (Proverbs 3:9-10).* When a man with a sincere heart liberally cares for the Lord and His people, the Lord will return his liberality back to him.

Devotional Thoughts

- **(For children):** Over and over again, God promises to bless His people that give to Him and also give to those in need *(Proverbs 19:17; Proverbs 22:9; Proverbs 28:27; Hebrews 6:10)*. God even invites us to test the truth of what He says *(Malachi 3:10)*. He cannot lie *(Titus 1:2)*.
- **(For everyone):** The rewards of liberality do not make sense to the world. How could giving to the Lord actually yield an increase to the giver? Have you ever experienced this truth?
- Liberality often requires personal sacrifice. In what ways have you personally sacrificed to be liberal in your giving to the Lord and His work?

Prayer Thoughts

- Ask the Lord to show you the benefits of liberality.
- Ask God to give you a desire to be liberal in your giving.

SONG: *LORD, THOU LOVEST THE CHEERFUL GIVER*

Day 130: Church Night

Romans 12:6 Having then gifts differing according to the grace that is given to us, whether prophecy, let us prophesy according to the proportion of faith;

7 Or ministry, let us wait on our ministering: or he that teacheth, on teaching;

8 Or he that exhorteth, on exhortation: **he that giveth, let him do it with simplicity;** *he that ruleth, with diligence;* **he that sheweth mercy, with cheerfulness.**

☐ Completion Date

Day 131: (Thursday)
Liberality in Giving

Exodus 36:5 And they spake unto Moses, saying, ***The people bring much more than enough*** *for the service of the work, which the LORD commanded to make.*

INTRODUCTORY THOUGHTS

In Moses' day, when the people of God were called upon to give to the work of God, they gave abundantly. Ultimately, the men doing God's work came to Moses suggesting that the people refrain from giving anything more. Any person with the right heart who believes in the work of God will not have to be begged to give. He will give liberally. This type of liberality manifested itself again in the early church. The Bible describes the people of God at that time as being *"of one heart and of one soul" (Acts 4:32).* Amazingly, many of them sold their houses and lands and brought the money to the apostles *(Acts 4:34).* This liberality greatly assisted the work of God and helped the people of God.

DEVOTIONAL THOUGHTS

- **(For children):** The Bible gives examples of those who loved God so much that they gave even when it might have been difficult to give more. Some examples would be the Macedonians *(2 Corinthians 8:1-4)* and the widow woman *(Mark 12:41-44).*
- **(For everyone):** Would your giving be classified as liberal? Are you more concerned about possessing the things of this world or contributing to the work of God?
- What would you be willing to sacrifice in order to help other believers? What would you give up in order to help missionaries fulfill their calling?

PRAYER THOUGHTS

- Ask the Lord to teach you how to give sacrificially.
- Ask God to give you joy in giving.

SONG: *AND MUST I PART WITH ALL I HAVE?*

Day 132: (Friday)
Liberality Yields Thanksgiving

2 Corinthians 9:6 But this I say, He which soweth sparingly shall reap also sparingly; and he which soweth bountifully shall reap also bountifully.

*7 **Every man according as he purposeth in his heart, so let him give; not grudgingly, or of necessity: for God loveth a cheerful giver.***

8 And God is able to make all grace abound toward you; that ye, always having all sufficiency in all things, may abound to every good work:

9 (As it is written, He hath dispersed abroad; he hath given to the poor: his righteousness remaineth for ever.

10 Now he that ministereth seed to the sower both minister bread for your food, and multiply your seed sown, and increase the fruits of your righteousness;)

11 Being enriched in every thing to all bountifulness, which causeth through us thanksgiving to God.

*12 For **the administration of this service not only supplieth the want of the saints, but is abundant also by many thanksgivings unto God;***

*13 Whiles by the experiment of this ministration **they glorify God** for your professed subjection unto the gospel of Christ, and **for your liberal distribution unto them, and unto all men;***

14 And by their prayer for you, which long after you for the exceeding grace of God in you.

15 Thanks be unto God for his unspeakable gift.

INTRODUCTORY THOUGHTS

Modern Christianity has terribly corrupted both the meaning and beauty of liberality. Giving has turned into a show designed to bring honour and praise to those doing the giving. God never intended giving to be so perverted. For this reason, the apostle Paul declared that the bountiful giving of the saints caused thanks to be given to God ***(2 Corinthians 9:11)***. The more they gave, the more thanks God would receive ***(2 Corinthians 9:12)***. The Corinthians recognized that man should not receive personal glory for giving especially when considering the fact that one's ability to give does not exist apart from God's enabling. This is not to say that an individual who obeys God should not be appreciated for his obedience to God. Yet, all praise and thanks belong to God. Men should give abundantly in hopes that the Lord would receive the glory and receive many thanks.

DEVOTIONAL THOUGHTS
- **(For children):** Paul was thankful to God for the church at Philippi *(Philippians 1:3)*. One reason was their liberality *(Philippians 4:15-16)*. Paul used the money to help in his ministry of telling people how to be saved *(Philippians 4:17)*.
- **(For everyone):** Does your giving bring glory to you or glory to God? Do you give liberally to a point where it is obvious that God is the one who gets the glory rather than man?
- Does your service to God bring glory and attention to you or glory and attention to the Lord? What could you do differently in order to redirect attention and focus upon the Lord?

PRAYER THOUGHTS
- Ask God to teach you to do things in a way that gives Him glory.
- Thank the Lord for using you to get believers to give Him thanks.

SONG: *TO GOD BE THE GLORY*

Day 133: (Saturday)
A Liberal God

*James 1:5 If any of you lack wisdom, let him ask of **God**, that **giveth to all men liberally**, and upbraideth not; and it shall be given him.*

INTRODUCTORY THOUGHTS

God exhibits the perfect standard of righteousness through His character and work. Any person desiring to know the right way to do something should look to the Lord for his example. The Bible says that God gives liberally to man. If one needs wisdom, all he need do is to ask the Lord for wisdom and God promises to give man the wisdom and to give it in a liberal fashion. Fortunately, this promise is not in any way restricted exclusively to wisdom but also includes the manner in which God gives to man in other areas of life. Look no further than Calvary for proof of this truth. At Calvary, God gave liberally in the sacrifice of

154 • Liberality ☐ Completion Date

His Son. As a result of that sacrifice, God promises that whosoever will can come to God for salvation. Since God gives so liberally to man, how should man give to God?

Devotional Thoughts

- **(For children):** *Psalm 68:19* tells us God *"daily loadeth us with benefits."* Can you name some of those benefits? No matter what you give to the Lord, He gives back more abundantly to you. That is the meaning of *Luke 6:38*.
- **(For everyone):** In what areas has God given to you in a liberal manner? Have you ever found God to be stingy when you asked Him for anything? Was it something that you needed?
- Do you follow God's example in giving? Do you give liberally to the Lord like He gives liberally to you? How does your liberality reflect your thankfulness to God or lack thereof?

Prayer Thoughts

- Thank God for giving liberally to you.
- Ask God to increase your love for Him.

SONG: *I GAVE MY LIFE FOR THEE*

Notes: _____
_____
_____
_____

Quotes from the next volume

(VOLUME 4, WEEK 19)

Subject: Jealousy (con't)

Jealousy can be likened to a weapon. When this weapon rests in the bosom of someone with righteous motives, lives are spared. When it rests in the bosom of a fool, it leads to unjust destruction.

When men worship false gods, the Lord is stirred to jealousy.

20

Loyalty

Loyalty—The word *loyalty* is not found in scripture, but the concept is related to faithfulness which is found 111 times in 107 verses.

Variations: faithful, faithfully, faithfulness, unfaithful, unfaithfully

First usage: *Numbers 12:7* (faithful)

Last usage: *Revelation 22:6* (faithful)

Defined: faithful, honourable, or law-abiding

Interesting fact: The phrases *"true and faithful"* or *"faithful and true"* occur five times in scripture. Twice the Bible uses the phrase *"true and faithful"* **(Jeremiah 42:5; Revelation 21:5)**. Three times the order is reversed as it refers to something or someone as *"faithful and true"* **(Revelation 3:14; Revelation 19:11; Revelation 22:6)**. Biblical loyalty must be both true and faithful.

Bible study tip: John chapters 14 through 17 have been identified as some of the most beautiful passages in all of scripture. Do not fail to recognize that Judas Iscariot departed in order to betray Christ in **John 13:30** and did not return with guards until **John 18:3**. Always consider the audience because this may help understand the doctrine and import of the truths conveyed. In this instance, the Lord expressed some of His most personal teachings when the twelve were present minus one—Judas, the betrayer.

Sunday, Day 134—Church Day (no devotional)
Monday, Day 135—*I Will Never Leave Thee*
Tuesday, Day 136—*Thou Shalt Have No Other Gods*
Wednesday, Day 137—Church Night (no devotional)
Thursday, Day 138—*Faithful unto Death*
Friday, Day 139—*The Sheep Shall Be Scattered*
Saturday, Day 140—*The Cost of Loyalty*

Day 134: Church Day

Psalm 12:1 Help, LORD; for the godly man ceaseth; for **the faithful fail from among the children of men**.

Day 135: (Monday)
I Will Never Leave Thee

Hebrews 13:5 Let your conversation be without covetousness; and be content with such things as ye have: for **he hath said, I will never leave thee, nor forsake thee**.

INTRODUCTORY THOUGHTS

God offered man the greatest statement of loyalty when Christ promised never to leave the believer. The Lord did not promise some type of reciprocating loyalty conditioned upon man's loyalty toward Him. Rather, the Lord promised He will *"never leave . . . nor forsake."* Man's frailty offers God numerous reasons and opportunities to justify leaving and forsaking, but God's character overrides man's frailty. If the Lord promises loyalty, He fulfils that promise without requiring reciprocity. According to **2 Peter 3:9**, *"The Lord is not slack concerning his promise."* Once a man is born again, he becomes a child of God and immediately becomes the beneficiary of promised loyalty given to him by the Son of God.

Devotional Thoughts

- **(For children):** The Lord will always be there for you *(Psalm 37:28)*. He was there for David when his men turned against him *(1 Samuel 30:6)*. When others forsook Paul, the Lord was there for him *(2 Timothy 4:16-17)*.
- **(For everyone):** What have you done to earn this promise of loyalty from the Lord Jesus Christ? How has He earned your loyalty? Does He actually have your loyalty?
- What does it mean to you that the Lord will NEVER leave you? When is the last time you meditated upon the Lord's faithfulness to you?

Prayer Thoughts

- Ask the Lord to teach you the true meaning of loyalty.
- Thank the Lord for promising never to leave you.

SONG: *CONSTANTLY ABIDING*

Day 136: (Tuesday)
Thou Shalt Have No Other Gods

Exodus 20:1 *And God spake all these words, saying,*

*₂ **I am the LORD thy God**, which have brought thee out of the land of Egypt, out of the house of bondage.*

*₃ **Thou shalt have no other gods before me**.*

₄ Thou shalt not make unto thee any graven image, or any likeness of any thing that is in heaven above, or that is in the earth beneath, or that is in the water under the earth:

*₅ Thou shalt not bow down thyself to them, nor serve them: **for I the LORD thy God am a jealous God**, visiting the iniquity of the fathers upon the children unto the third and fourth generation of them that hate me;*

Introductory Thoughts

God expects loyalty from man. He is not interested in "worship" that involves Him being one of man's many gods. In fact, He adamantly opposed this position within the Ten Commandments. There the Lord admonished His people to *"have no other gods before"* Him *(Exodus 20:3)*. He then warned them not to make nor bow in worship to idols *(Exo-*

dus 20:4-5). The Lord earned Israel's loyalty in many ways, but the Bible specifically points to His delivering them from Egypt. It is important to note that God does not expect blind loyalty from man, but He certainly deserves this type of loyalty. He earned man's loyalty by being his Creator. Yet His ultimate claim to loyalty stems from His offering to redeem fallen man though man is completely unworthy.

DEVOTIONAL THOUGHTS

- **(For children)**: God is the only true God *(Isaiah 44:6)*. He knows idols cannot help anyone *(Psalm 115:3-9)*. Remember Elijah's contest *(1 Kings 18:25-39)*. God told His people to break the idols *(Exodus 34:13-14)* and not even to speak of them *(Exodus 23:13)*.
- **(For everyone)**: What are some reasons why you should be loyal to the Lord? What has He done to earn your loyalty? How loyal have you been to Him?
- How is it disloyal to have other gods before the Lord? How is it disloyal to bow down to or worship things other than the Lord? Have you been disloyal to the Lord? Has He been disloyal to you?

PRAYER THOUGHTS

- Thank God for being loyal to you!
- Ask the Lord to teach you what it means to be loyal.

SONG: *O WORSHIP THE KING!*

Day 137: Church Night

Proverbs 20:6 *Most men will proclaim every one his own goodness: but **a faithful man who can find?***

Day 138: (Thursday)
Faithful unto Death

Revelation 2:10 *Fear none of those things which thou shalt suffer: behold, the devil shall cast some of you into prison, that ye may be tried; and ye shall have tribulation ten days: **be thou faithful unto death**, and I will give thee a crown of life.*

Introductory Thoughts

True loyalty never wavers without sound justification. The book of Revelation reveals that believers in Smyrna were going to face various difficulties such as imprisonment, trials, and perhaps even martyrdom. In the midst of these calamities, the Lord admonished them to be *"faithful unto death."* God's people have always had their loyalty to the Lord tested. If loyalty occurred naturally, everyone would exhibit loyalty. True loyalty is not something a believer possesses in the absence of adversity. Rather, adversity provides the means for loyalty to excel. In fact, it was in the face of the adversity of crucifixion that the Lord Jesus Christ exemplified His loyalty to both mankind and the Father. In doing so, He set forth an example that every believer ought to willingly follow and exemplify.

Devotional Thoughts

- **(For children):** Shadrach, Meshach, and Abednego were told to bow to an idol or burn in the furnace. We know that the Lord did deliver them out of the furnace. However, they did not know for sure in advance that He would. They simply made up their minds to be faithful unto death whether or not God chose to deliver them **(Daniel 3:14-29)**.
- **(For everyone):** The Lord saw your need for salvation and did something about it. How might that be considered loyalty? How far was He willing to go to secure your salvation?
- In what ways has the world tested your loyalty to the Lord? Did you remain loyal in spite of these tests? If not, would you say that you were probably never loyal in the first place?

Prayer Thoughts

- Thank the Lord for being loyal to the point of death.
- Ask the Lord to help you follow His example.

SONG: *LOYALTY TO CHRIST*

Day 139: (Friday)
The Sheep Shall Be Scattered

*Mark 14:27 And Jesus saith unto them, All ye shall be offended because of me this night: for it is written, **I will smite the shepherd, and the sheep shall be scattered**.*

Introductory Thoughts

Sometimes the Bible conveys some disheartening truths including man's inability to love the Lord during difficult times. Regrettably, believers are easily offended and sometimes even scattered from the Lord because of a lack of resolve. The Lord prophesied in **Zechariah 13:7** concerning His followers' reaction to His rejection. Though the Lord knows the future, consider how this rejection must have grieved Him when it actually transpired. At a time when any faithful disciple should have been loyal to his Master, those closest to the Lord were instead scattered. The One that fed them when they were hungry *(Mark 6:35-44)*, healed family members when ill *(Mark 1:29-31)*, calmed the troubled waters during the storms *(Mark 4:37-41)*, and taught them many wonderful truths was now the cause of their offence.

Devotional Thoughts

- **(For children):** We know what the Lord has done for us. Yet sometimes, like the disciples, we fear men and do not appropriately react to adversity *(Proverbs 29:25)*. The Bible tells us whom to fear *(Luke 12:4-5; Hebrews 13:6)*. Who feared God in the story of the man born blind: the parents *(John 9:18-23)* or their son *(John 9:24-34)*?
- **(For everyone):** How has the Lord blessed you? Has He been faithful to you through the good times and the bad? How can you be anything other than loyal to Him?
- What would it take to cause you to stop walking with the Lord? What troubles would keep you from serving the Lord? Would you have been scattered from the Lord (see *Mark 14:29-31*)?

Prayer Thoughts

- Ask the Lord to help you to be loyal through good times and bad.
- Ask the Lord to show you if your loyalty is faulty.

SONG: *TO THE WORK!*

Day 140: (Saturday)
The Cost of Loyalty

Hebrews 11:32 *And what shall I more say? for the time would fail me to tell of Gedeon, and of Barak, and of Samson, and of Jephthae; of David also, and Samuel, and of the prophets:*

33 Who through faith subdued kingdoms, wrought righteousness, obtained promises, stopped the mouths of lions,

34 Quenched the violence of fire, escaped the edge of the sword, out of weakness were made strong, waxed valiant in fight, turned to flight the armies of the aliens.

35 Women received their dead raised to life again: and others were tortured, not accepting deliverance; that they might obtain a better resurrection:

36 And others had trial of cruel mockings and scourgings, yea, moreover of bonds and imprisonment:

37 They were stoned, they were sawn asunder, were tempted, were slain with the sword: they wandered about in sheepskins and goatskins; being destitute, afflicted, tormented;

38 (Of whom the world was not worthy:) they wandered in deserts, and in mountains, and in dens and caves of the earth.

Introductory Thoughts

Loyalty sometimes comes at the steepest of prices! For some, the cost may seem minimal, but for others it has cost them deeply, dearly, and sometimes completely. Throughout history, the people of God have endured mocking, persecution, and even martyrdom. God offers us the record of many who chose to suffer rather than recant their proclaimed faith in the Creator. Many things have changed since ancient times, but those choosing to walk with the Lord today will likewise see an escalation in all forms of persecution. This tribulation from the world will become increasingly worse as man continues to be influenced by ungodliness. Believers should willingly endure whatever cost loyalty may require by keeping in mind the ultimate price paid when Christ gave Himself for mankind. Though the list in Hebrews chapter 11 has been closed, the Lord continues to track the actions of those loyal to Him.

Devotional Thoughts

- **(For children):** The apostle Paul suffered many things because of his faith in the Lord *(2 Corinthians 11:23-28)*. His faithfulness even cost him his life *(2 Timothy 4:6-7)*. Let's ask the Lord to help us willingly live for Him *(2 Timothy 3:12)*.
- **(For everyone):** What price can you honestly say you have paid because of your loyalty to the Lord? What price would you be willing to pay in order to maintain your loyalty to Him?
- Who is your favorite Bible character? Was he or she loyal to the Lord? What did he or she endure resulting from his or her loyalty? What could you learn from that person's loyalty?

Prayer Thoughts

- Ask the Lord to give you a willingness to pay the price of loyalty.
- Ask God to give you strength in times of persecution.

SONG: *AM I A SOLDIER OF THE CROSS?*

Notes: _____

_____

_____

_____

Quotes from the next volume

(VOLUME 4, WEEK 20)

Subject: Life

Science frequently uses natural reasoning and ordinary terminology to explain away the hand of God as He interacts with mankind.

The world sometimes views children as a burden. The parents of many larger families have been questioned for their strange or foolish behaviour in birthing so many children into the world. God, however, views children in a completely opposite fashion than that of the world.

21
Loyalty (con't)

Loyalty—The word *loyalty* is not found in scripture, but the concept is related to faithfulness which occurs fifty-six times in fifty-six Old Testament verses and fifty-five times in fifty-one New Testament verses.

Variations: faithful, faithfully, faithfulness, unfaithful, unfaithfully

Last usage in the Old Testament: *Hosea 11:12* (faithful)

First usage in the New Testament: *Matthew 24:45* (faithful)

Interesting fact: Mordecai was loyal to king Ahasuerus before he was a recipient of Ahasuerus' favour *(Esther 2:21-23)*. At first, the loyalty seemed to go unnoticed, but at the most needful time, the Lord insured that Ahasuerus learned of Mordecai's loyalty *(Esther 6:1-3)*. Mordecai's loyalty while in obscurity led to his life being spared *(Esther 6:4-11; Esther 7:1-10)* and ultimately to his promotion in the kingdom *(Esther 8:1-2)*. It is important to note that all this took place while in a pagan land under a pagan king.

Bible study tip: *"Where art thou?"* serves as the first question asked of Adam by God following Adam's sinful act *(Genesis 3:9)*. This particular question serves to point out to the reader that Adam was noticeably missing, yet this is not the first occasion. Many sermons have been preached and commentaries written presenting Eve's failure to properly communicate God's word when confronted by the serpent *(Genesis 3:1-5)*. However, though seemingly present with his wife during the sinful act *(Genesis 3:6)*, Adam was missing or just silent from any of the recorded conversation. Concerning Bible study, we should not only take notice of that which is clearly present but also consider any unexpected missing element.

Sunday, Day 141—Church Day (no devotional)
Monday, Day 142—*Honour Calls for Loyalty*
Tuesday, Day 143—*Inherited Loyalty*
Wednesday, Day 144—Church Night (no devotional)
Thursday, Day 145—*David, a Man of Loyalty*
Friday, Day 146—*Loyalty Killed Uriah*
Saturday, Day 147—*Loyalty Is Contagious*

Day 141: Church Day

Proverbs 17:11 An evil man seeketh only rebellion: *therefore a cruel messenger shall be sent against him.*

Day 142: (Monday)
Honour Calls for Loyalty

*Numbers 27:20 And **thou shalt put some of thine honour upon him, that all the congregation of the children of Israel may be obedient**.*

INTRODUCTORY THOUGHTS

Man's loyalty must be first and foremost directed toward the Lord; however, an aspect of one's loyalty to the Lord also involves a certain loyalty toward man. At times, these loyalties might conflict. During those instances, each person should heed the words of Simon Peter when he admonished, *"We ought to obey God rather than men" **(Acts 5:29)**.* When one's loyalty to God does not conflict with any loyalty toward man, the Lord admonishes men to be loyal toward one another. When Moses placed his honour upon Joshua, he did so in order to encourage obedience, respect, and loyalty on the part of the people of God. In similar fashion, the Lord has crowned man with glory and honour *(Psalm 8:5)*. As such, the Lord has naturally put within man a desire to be loyal toward the Lord and others.

DEVOTIONAL THOUGHTS

- **(For children):** God expects children to love, respect, and obey their parents. This was so important, God had Moses write it as the fifth commandment *(Exodus 20:12)*. Jesus taught it *(Matthew 15:4)*. Paul taught it *(Ephesians 6:1-2)*. In addition, Jesus offered a great example when He was growing up *(Luke 2:51)*.
- **(For everyone):** Why should children be loyal to their parents? Why should parents be loyal to their children? Why should husbands be loyal to their wives, and wives to their husbands?
- Are you loyal to others? If you are a child, are you loyal to your parents? If you are an adult, are you loyal to your boss, spouse, government, and pastor when such loyalty does not conflict with loyalty to God?

PRAYER THOUGHTS

- Thank the Lord for the honour He has placed on man.
- Ask God to strengthen your loyalty to others.

SONG: *BLEST BE THE TIE THAT BINDS*

Day 143: (Tuesday)
Inherited Loyalty

Numbers 27:20 And thou shalt put some of thine honour upon him, that all the congregation of the children of Israel may be obedient.

INTRODUCTORY THOUGHTS

As the people had honoured the Lord, they had honoured Moses. When Moses placed his honour upon Joshua, he did so in order to encourage the people's obedience and loyalty toward Joshua. Moses wanted the same loyalty that had been directed toward him now directed toward Joshua. God's people could have risen up against Joshua thinking that he had not accomplished enough to merit their loyalty. Yet, the people respected the fact that Moses had directly placed his own honour upon his minister Joshua. The people emphatically accepted Moses' message as reflected by their answer to Joshua: *"According as we hearkened unto Moses in all things, so will we hearken unto thee: only the LORD thy God be with thee, as he was with Moses"* **(Joshua 1:17).**

DEVOTIONAL THOUGHTS

- **(For children):** We know we should honour and obey God, but we must also honour and obey those whom God has chosen to be over us. This includes pastors **(Acts 20:28; Hebrews 13:7)** and people in office **(Romans 13:1-2; 1 Peter 2:17).**
- **(For everyone):** To some degree, all loyalty owed to man is inherited by God placing His honour upon His creation. Do you honour those whom you should honour? Are you loyal to them?
- Why were the people loyal to Joshua? To what extent were they loyal (see **Joshua 1:16-18**)? If loyalty to man does not conflict with loyalty to God, to what extent should we be loyal?

PRAYER THOUGHTS

- Ask the Lord to give you wisdom concerning your level of loyalty.
- Thank the Lord for giving us people worthy of loyalty.

SONG: *TRUST AND OBEY*

Day 144: Church Night

Esther 2:21 In those days, **while Mordecai sat in the king's gate, two of the king's chamberlains,** *Bigthan and Teresh, of those which kept the door,* **were wroth, and sought to lay hand on the king Ahasuerus.**

22 And **the thing was known to Mordecai, who told it unto Esther the queen; and Esther certified the king thereof in Mordecai's name.**

23 And **when inquisition was made of the matter, it was found out; therefore they were both hanged on a tree***: and it was written in the book of the chronicles before the king.*

☐ Completion Date   Loyalty (con't) • 167

Day 145: (Thursday)
David, a Man of Loyalty

1 Samuel 24:1 *And it came to pass, when Saul was returned from following the Philistines, that it was told him, saying, Behold, David is in the wilderness of Engedi.*

2 Then Saul took three thousand chosen men out of all Israel, and went to seek David and his men upon the rocks of the wild goats.

3 And he came to the sheepcotes by the way, where was a cave; and Saul went in to cover his feet: and David and his men remained in the sides of the cave.

4 And **the men of David said unto him, Behold the day of which the LORD said unto thee, Behold, I will deliver thine enemy into thine hand, that thou mayest do to him as it shall seem good unto thee. Then David arose, and cut off the skirt of Saul's robe privily.**

5 And **it came to pass afterward, that David's heart smote him, because he had cut off Saul's skirt.**

6 And **he said unto his men, The LORD forbid that I should do this thing unto my master,** *the LORD'S anointed, to stretch forth mine hand against him, seeing he is the anointed of the LORD.*

7 **So David stayed his servants** *with these words,* **and suffered them not to rise against Saul.** *But Saul rose up out of the cave, and went on his way.*

8 David also arose afterward, and went out of the cave, and cried after Saul, saying, My lord the king. And when Saul looked behind him, David stooped with his face to the earth, and bowed himself.

9 And **David said to Saul,** *Wherefore hearest thou men's words, saying, Behold, David seeketh thy hurt?*

10 **Behold, this day thine eyes have seen how that the LORD had delivered thee to day into mine hand in the cave: and some bade me kill thee: but mine eye spared thee; and I said, I will not put forth mine hand against my lord; for he is the LORD'S anointed.**

11 Moreover, my father, see, yea, see the skirt of thy robe in my hand: for in that I cut off the skirt of thy robe, and killed thee not, know thou and see that there is neither evil nor transgression in mine hand, and I have not sinned against thee; yet thou huntest my soul to take it.

12 The LORD judge between me and thee, *and the LORD avenge me of thee:* **but mine hand shall not be upon thee.**

13 As saith the proverb of the ancients, Wickedness proceedeth from the wicked: but mine hand shall not be upon thee.

Introductory Thoughts

Men frequently focus upon David's extreme failures but fail to realize that he also exemplified a tremendous example of someone who understood loyalty. King Saul's antics would have allowed most people to justify not affording Saul the loyalty his position warranted. Even many of David's men held to this position. Yet, we read that David felt and acted otherwise. Although Saul repeatedly attempted to kill David, David did not take advantage of any of his opportunities to kill Saul. The Bible says that he refused to stretch forth his hand against the LORD'S anointed. Instead, David decided to send a message to Saul by cutting off the skirt of Saul's robe. Because of David's loyalty, even this act immediately smote his heart. His godly character trumped his personal frustrations toward the very man who sought to bring him grave, personal harm. Although David's men were prepared and able to take the most aggressive actions, David advised against it.

Devotional Thoughts

- **(For children):** We may not like those who have the authority over us. They may not even love God or personally care for us, but God still expects us to honour them when possible *(Titus 3:1; 1 Peter 2:13-14, 18)*. Joseph, Nehemiah, and Daniel worked for pagan kings, yet they practiced *Titus 3:2a*.
- **(For everyone):** Did Saul deserve David's loyalty? If not, why was David loyal toward him? What did David do that brought conviction to his heart? What would it take to bring conviction to your heart when you fail to obey?
- David's men were loyal to David to the point that they were ready to kill Saul. How would David's loyalty to Saul be a wonderful example and edification to his own men?

Prayer Thoughts

- Ask the Lord to teach you what it means to be loyal.
- Ask God for strength of character.

SONG: *FOOTPRINTS OF JESUS*

☐ Completion Date

Day 146: (Friday)
Loyalty Killed Uriah

2 Samuel 11:6 *And David sent to Joab, saying, Send me Uriah the Hittite. And Joab sent Uriah to David.*

7 And when Uriah was come unto him, David demanded of him how Joab did, and how the people did, and how the war prospered.

8 And David said to Uriah, Go down to thy house, and wash thy feet. And Uriah departed out of the king's house, and there followed him a mess of meat from the king.

*9 But **Uriah slept at the door of the king's house with all the servants of his lord, and went not down to his house**.*

*10 And **when they had told David, saying, Uriah went not down unto his house, David said unto Uriah, Camest thou not from thy journey? why then didst thou not go down unto thine house?***

*11 And **Uriah said** unto David, **The ark, and Israel, and Judah, abide in tents; and my lord Joab, and the servants of my lord, are encamped in the open fields; shall I then go into mine house, to eat and to drink, and to lie with my wife? as thou livest, and as thy soul liveth, I will not do this thing**.*

12 And David said to Uriah, Tarry here to day also, and to morrow I will let thee depart. So Uriah abode in Jerusalem that day, and the morrow.

13 And when David had called him, he did eat and drink before him; and he made him drunk: and at even he went out to lie on his bed with the servants of his lord, but went not down to his house.

INTRODUCTORY THOUGHTS

Loyalty is a godly trait, and like most godly traits, difficulties can accompany it. The story of David and Uriah serves as a prime example. David sinned against the Lord when he committed adultery with Bathsheba, Uriah's wife. His actions caused her to become expectant with child. In an attempt to cover his wickedness, he sent for Uriah, his faithful soldier. David knew that his only opportunity to hide his sin from man was for Uriah to go home to Bathsheba. However, Uriah was a faithful soldier. He simply refused to enjoy the comforts of being with his wife while his fellow soldiers were enduring the hardness of battle. Uriah instead chose to sleep at the door of the king's house. This loyalty caused David to reevaluate his devious plan and escalate the consequences. He decided to order Uriah to the hottest part of the battle insuring certain death. It was not just the enemy that killed Uriah, but also his loyalty to an unfaithful man!

DEVOTIONAL THOUGHTS

- **(For children):** Many men in the Bible lost their lives because they were loyal to God. A few examples are John the Baptist *(Luke 9:9)*, Stephen *(Acts 7:57-59)*, James *(Acts 12:1-2)*, and Paul *(2 Timothy 4:6)*. Can you think of any others?
- **(For everyone):** What would have happened had Uriah been unfaithful to his fellow soldiers and David? How would we think differently of Uriah if he had proven disloyal?
- Urias (Uriah) is mentioned in the genealogy of Christ *(Matthew 1:6)*. Read the account to see what is so unique about his inclusion. Why do you think the Lord put him in the genealogy of Christ?

PRAYER THOUGHTS

- Thank the Lord for the faithful example of Uriah.
- Ask the Lord to teach you that loyalty is worth the cost.

SONG: *IF, ON A QUIET SEA*

Day 147: (Saturday)
Loyalty Is Contagious

2 Samuel 15:19 Then said the king to Ittai the Gittite, Wherefore goest thou also with us? return to thy place, and abide with the king: for thou art a stranger, and also an exile.

20 Whereas thou camest but yesterday, should I this day make thee go up and down with us? seeing I go whither I may, return thou, and take back thy brethren: mercy and truth be with thee.

*21 And **Ittai answered the king, and said, As the LORD liveth, and as my lord the king liveth, surely in what place my lord the king shall be, whether in death or life, even there also will thy servant be.***

☐ Completion Date   Loyalty (con't) • 171

INTRODUCTORY THOUGHTS

David was loyal and his loyalty was certainly infectious. Throughout his life, he had those who attempted great feats in order to assist or protect him. Others wanted to simply be a blessing to him. First Chronicles chapter 11 provides insight into such events. One of these examples involved David's three mighty men performing a life threatening effort simply because David thirsted for a drink of water from the well of Bethlehem *(1 Chronicles 11:15-19)*. Consider that level of loyalty that would inspire men to risk their lives simply because their king expressed a thirst for some particular water. In addition to the men who were willing to risk their lives for David's safety, there were many others who merely wanted to be by David's side. Such was the testimony of Ittai.

DEVOTIONAL THOUGHTS

- **(For children)**: Timothy was loyal to God and to Paul. Paul had led him to a saving knowledge of Jesus Christ and subsequently trained him. They were like father and son. Paul could trust him *(Philippians 2:19-22)*. Another loyal friend to Paul was Onesiphorus *(2 Timothy 1:16-18)*.
- **(For everyone)**: What have you done to demonstrate your loyalty to the Lord Jesus Christ? What have you done to demonstrate your loyalty to others the Lord has given you?
- Are you loyal? Has your loyalty encouraged others to likewise be loyal? Have you allowed others to see the benefits of loyalty in your own life?

PRAYER THOUGHTS

- Thank God for those who were loyal before you.
- Ask God to make you an example of loyalty.

SONG: *WHATEVER MY LOT MAY BE*

Notes: _____
_____
_____
_____
_____

Notes: _____

Quotes from the next volume

(VOLUME 4, WEEK 21)
Subject: Life (con't)

Though some things have changed, the Old Testament Law declares and expresses the mind of God. It demonstrates God's hatred for sin and His desire for just judgment.

The world is consumed with "saving the earth." They have multiple plans to purify the water, the air, the ground, the food, etc. Unfortunately, they are ignorant of the green plan laid out in the Bible. According to scripture, the land is polluted from the shedding of blood. The Bible says in **Numbers 35:33** that "*blood . . . defileth the land.*"

Capital punishment is not done to the exclusion of God's grace, but rather as an act of God's just judgment.

22
Loyalty (con't)

Loyalty—Although the Bible does not contain the word *loyalty*, the concept is related to faithfulness which occurs twice in two separate verses in the Law (Genesis-Deuteronomy), twelve times in twelve verses in the Prophets (Isaiah-Malachi), twenty-one times in twenty-one verses in the Psalms, and thirty-one times in thirty verses in Paul's writings (Romans-Hebrews).

Variations: faithful, faithfully, faithfulness, unfaithful, unfaithfully

Interesting fact: Before David, Moses, or Elisha had ministries or kingdoms of their own, they exercised loyalty with the possessions of others. A man disloyal toward others will never be worthy of his own authority, nor will he be worthy of loyalty from others.

Bible study tip: When looking into the New Testament for an Old Testament person or place, consider that the spelling could vary from one testament to the next. For example, Isaiah in the Old Testament *(Isaiah 53:1)* is Esaias in the New *(Romans 10:16)*; Elijah *(1 Kings 19:10-18)* is Elias *(Romans 11:2)*; Messiah *(Daniel 9:25)* is Messias *(John 4:25)*; and Joshua is Jesus *(Hebrews 4:8)*. This difference in spelling happens when the original languages differ in translation from each language into English. The variation remains intact because of the honesty and integrity of the King James translators.

Sunday, Day 148—Church Day (no devotional)
Monday, Day 149—*Loyalty Conquers Rebellion*
Tuesday, Day 150—*Loyalty Gives Honour*
Wednesday, Day 151—Church Night (no devotional)
Thursday, Day 152—*Great Men Are Loyal*
Friday, Day 153—*Loyalty Overcomes Obstacles*
Saturday, Day 154—*Loyalty Yields Reward*

Day 148: Church Day

Hebrews 13:5 Let your conversation be without covetousness; and be content with such things as ye have: for **he hath said, I will never leave thee, nor forsake thee.**

Day 149: (Monday)
Loyalty Conquers Rebellion

2 Samuel 17:15 Then said **Hushai unto Zadok and to Abiathar the priests, Thus and thus did Ahithophel counsel Absalom and the elders of Israel; and thus and thus have I counselled.**
16 Now therefore send quickly, and tell David, saying, Lodge not this night in the plains of the wilderness, but speedily pass over; lest the king be swallowed up, *and all the people that are with him.*

INTRODUCTORY THOUGHTS

Absalom rebelled against king David (his father) by seeking to take over David's kingdom and end his life. Ahithophel, who had previously served as an advisor to David, gave counsel to Absalom that could have eliminated David and his followers *(2 Samuel 17:1-4)*. The counsel pleased Absalom, but he chose to request a second opinion from Hushai. Yet, Hushai was still a loyal friend of David, unbeknownst to Absalom, who was actually working undercover in Absalom's kingdom *(2 Samuel 15:31-37)*. Thankfully, Absalom asked for his counsel. Hushai proceeded to tell Absalom the shortcomings of Ahithophel's counsel and offered his own counsel that would protect king David. After hearing the counsel of both Ahithophel and Hushai, Absalom unwisely determined that Hushai's counsel was better. Hushai's loyalty to the king and God conquered Absalom's rebellion and eventually ended it.

DEVOTIONAL THOUGHTS

- **(For children):** Abigail's loyalty and wisdom kept David from seeking vengeance against her wicked husband Nabal. David thanked Abigail because he would have regretted such a shameful deed. Abigail's loyalty saved Nabal's household *(1 Samuel 25:2-38)*.
- **(For everyone):** In a home, how could one child's loyalty to his parents conquer the rebellion of siblings? In a workplace, how could one person's loyalty overcome the rebellion of others?
- How can one believer's loyalty to the Lord overcome the rebellion of others? How are you working for the Lord in order to fight against the rebellion of this world?

PRAYER THOUGHTS

- Ask the Lord to help you to be loyal when others rebel.
- Ask the Lord to give you the loyalty of Hushai.

SONG: *COME, WE THAT LOVE THE LORD*

Day 150: (Tuesday)
Loyalty Gives Honour

2 Samuel 18:1 And David numbered the people that were with him, and set captains of thousands and captains of hundreds over them.

2 And David sent forth a third part of the people under the hand of Joab, and a third part under the hand of Abishai the son of Zeruiah, Joab's brother, and a third part under the hand of Ittai the Gittite. **And the king said unto the people, I will surely go forth with you myself also.**

3 But **the people answered, Thou shalt not go forth: for if we flee away, they will not care for us; neither if half of us die, will they care for us: but now thou art worth ten thousand of us:** *therefore now it is better that thou succour us out of the city.*

4 And the king said unto them, What seemeth you best I will do. And the king stood by the gate side, and all the people came out by hundreds and by thousands.

INTRODUCTORY THOUGHTS

In spite of the rebellion of others, David's men remained loyal to their king. David's followers honoured him with their loyalty despite Absalom's rebellion which caused David and his men to flee from Jerusalem *(2 Samuel 15:13-15)*. David's men wanted to protect the true king so much that they wanted him to avoid endangering himself by going into battle. David's men were ready and willing to sacrifice their lives for him but wanted his life preserved at all costs. Their loyalty to David caused them to elevate his desires and needs far above their own needs, wants, and even safety. Unlike many kingdoms of the world, the soldiers were more concerned about the life of the king and the preservation of his kingdom.

DEVOTIONAL THOUGHTS

- **(For children):** One time when the Philistines warred with Israel, David went to battle but felt faint. When one of the sons of the giant attacked him, Abishai came to his rescue. His men reminded him that he was too important to perish in battle *(2 Samuel 21:15-17)*.
- **(For everyone):** How did the loyalty of David's followers cause them to honour him? How would your loyalty to the Lord cause you to honour Him?
- In what ways would it be proper for your loyalty to cause you to honour others? How could this be taken too far and become a problem? To whom is your priority in loyalty?

PRAYER THOUGHTS

- Thank the Lord for the example given by David's men.
- Ask the Lord to help you see the importance of loyalty.

SONG: *CROWN HIM WITH MANY CROWNS*

Day 151: Church Night

***Proverbs 24:21** My son, fear thou the LORD and the king: and meddle not with them that are given to change:*

Day 152: (Thursday)
Great Men Are Loyal

2 Samuel 19:31 And Barzillai the Gileadite came down from Rogelim, and went over Jordan with the king, to conduct him over Jordan.

*32 Now **Barzillai** was a very aged man, even fourscore years old: and **he had provided the king of sustenance while he lay at Mahanaim; for he was a very great man.***

INTRODUCTORY THOUGHTS

Loyalty to David likely placed a bounty on a man's head. As David fled from Absalom and the city of Jerusalem, it became increasingly dangerous to offer any type of assistance to David. Barzillai, regardless of the personal danger, chose to risk everything for David *(2 Samuel 17:27-29)*. When it came time for David to travel back to reclaim his throne, Barzillai journeyed part of the way with David. Scripture identifies Barzillai as *"a very great man."* Perhaps this description identifies him as materially wealthy, but it no doubt also speaks of his character. His character is further manifested in his final conversation with David *(2 Samuel 19:33-38)*. When David regained his authority, he sought any opportunity to return favour for Barzillai's loyalty. No matter the accolades or advantage, Barzillai did not help David for personal gain.

DEVOTIONAL THOUGHTS

- **(For children):** Jonathan was not afraid to speak well of David to his father Saul when Saul wanted to kill David *(1 Samuel 19:4; 1 Samuel 20:31-33)*. Jonathan was willing to give up his hopes of being king when he knew David was God's choice *(1 Samuel 23:15-18)*.
- **(For everyone):** What do you think would have been your opinion of Barzillai had you known him? Would you have considered him to be a great man? What is the common opinion others have of you?
- To whom did Barzillai demonstrate loyalty in his last dealings with David? Can you see any loyalty toward Barzillai's city or family? Can you see loyalty to Chimham?

PRAYER THOUGHTS

- Ask God to show you the greatness of loyalty.

- Ask the Lord to help you to be loyal, even when it is not a popular position.

SONG: *COME, THOU FOUNT OF EVERY BLESSING*

Day 153: (Friday)
Loyalty Overcomes Obstacles

2 Samuel 23:13 And three of the thirty chief went down, and came to David in the harvest time unto the cave of Adullam: and the troop of the Philistines pitched in the valley of Rephaim.

14 And **David was then in an hold, and the garrison of the Philistines was then in Bethlehem.**

15 And **David longed, and said, Oh that one would give me drink of the water of the well of Bethlehem, which is by the gate!**

16 And **the three mighty men brake through the host of the Philistines, and drew water out of the well of Bethlehem, that was by the gate, and took it, and brought it to David:** *nevertheless he would not drink thereof, but poured it out unto the LORD.*

17 And he said, Be it far from me, O LORD, that I should do this: is not this the blood of the men that went in jeopardy of their lives? therefore he would not drink it. These things did these three mighty men.

INTRODUCTORY THOUGHTS

Loyalty is a beautiful trait. Loyalty leads men to do significant things for others although the reasons for doing so could be considered insignificant. The actions of David's men offer a prime example when David was in exile from his throne. Perhaps David was simply reminiscing when he mentioned his longing for a drink of water from the well of Bethlehem. Why not get a drink from any well? What was so special about the water from Bethlehem's well? Regardless of these minor details, three of David's mighty men heard the desire of their king. Their loyalty compelled them to go. These men had to break through the host of the Philistines in order to get the water from the well of David's desire. They risked their lives and for what? Was it merely a drink of water? To them it was much more than that—it was a special loyalty they each had for their king!

Devotional Thoughts

- **(For children):** Jonathan's armourbearer was loyal to him and willing to go with Jonathan to attack a garrison of the Philistines *(1 Samuel 14:6-14)*. Ruth was loyal to Naomi and returned with her to Bethlehem although Ruth was a complete stranger. She would also have to work hard in order to support Naomi *(Ruth 1:14-17)*.
- **(For everyone):** Loyalty for David caused the mighty men to risk their lives. What has your loyalty for the Lord Jesus Christ caused you to do? Would loyalty send you to some field of service for the Lord?
- Why did David's men break through the hosts of the Philistines? What had David done for them that caused them to be loyal? What has the Lord done for you? Are you loyal toward Him?

Prayer Thoughts

- Thank the Lord for dying on the cross for your sins.
- Ask God to make you a mighty man for him.

SONG: *MY JESUS, I LOVE THEE*

Day 154: (Saturday)
Loyalty Yields Reward

***Esther 2:21** In those days, **while Mordecai sat in the king's gate, two of the king's chamberlains**, Bigthan and Teresh, of those which kept the door, **were wroth, and sought to lay hand on the king Ahasuerus**.*

*22 And **the thing was known to Mordecai, who told it unto Esther the queen; and Esther certified the king thereof in Mordecai's name**.*

*23 And **when inquisition was made of the matter, it was found out; therefore they were both hanged on a tree**: and it was written in the book of the chronicles before the king.*

Introductory Thoughts

Loyalty may seem to go unobserved but eventually yields unexpected and momentous dividends. The story of Esther's uncle uniquely exemplifies this point. Mordecai sat in the king's gate in Shushan. One day, while he sat in the gate, he overheard two men plotting to kill the king. When Mordecai heard the news, he immediately repeated these words to Queen Esther, thus foiling the plot. The two men were tried, found guilty, and ultimately executed. At first, Mordecai's loyalty seemed to remain unnoticed, but one night the king was troubled and could not sleep. His servants, by divine providence, read the record of Mordecai's loyalty to him *(Esther 6:1-3)*. Soon thereafter, Mordecai's loyalty was rewarded *(Esther 6:4-11)*. His loyalty most likely saved his life and spared the lives of countless Jews (see Esther chapter 7).

Devotional Thoughts

- **(For children):** Jonathan's loyalty did not go unnoticed by David. Following Jonathan's death in battle, David rewarded Jonathan by taking care of his son Mephibosheth (read 2 Samuel chapter 9). God also noticed Jonathan's loyalty as He does ours *(2 Chronicles 15:7; Ephesians 6:8; Hebrews 6:10)*.
- **(For everyone):** Have you been loyal to the Lord Jesus Christ? Does it seem as though sometimes your loyalty goes unnoticed? When will your loyalty yield rewards?
- In what ways did Mordecai's loyalty eventually help others? How could your loyalty to the Lord be a blessing to others? Who could be hurt if you ceased to be loyal?

Prayer Thoughts

- Ask the Lord to help you to be loyal when it seems nobody notices.
- Ask God to remind you that your labour for Him is not in vain.

SONG: *FROM THE CROSS TO THE CROWN*

Quotes from the next volume
(VOLUME 4, WEEK 22)
Subject: Life (con't)

Many people seek to keep the law in the strength of their own flesh, but the Bible says the law is *"comprehended in this saying, namely, Thou shalt love thy neighbour as thyself."*

The Lord places such a high value upon the lives of others that He gave His own Son. The Devil puts so much value in himself that he seeks to take the lives of others.

23

Meddling

Meddling—found twelve times in twelve Old Testament verses

Variations: intermeddle, intermeddleth, meddle, meddled, meddleth, meddling

First usage: *Deuteronomy 2:5* (Meddle)

Last usage: *Proverbs 26:17* (meddleth)

Defined: to interfere with or involve oneself in the affairs or business of others

Interesting fact: The Bible specifically identifies two types of people with which a man should never meddle: (1) one who flatters with his lips *(Proverbs 20:19)*, and (2) one who is given to change *(Proverbs 24:21)*. In both instances, the more emphatic warning is directed toward those who meddle with such people. This is why the Bible refers to the individual who *"will be meddling"* as a fool *(Proverbs 20:3)*.

Bible study tip: The Bible often uses the same word to indicate several distinct meanings. For example, the word *world* can refer to the entire universe *(2 Samuel 22:16)* or the people inhabiting the universe *(John 3:16)*. The word *house* can refer to the individuals who comprise a family *(Genesis 7:1)*, or it can indicate the place in which the family dwells *(Genesis 19:3)*. The Bible student should always consider the context in order to determine the intended usage.

Sunday, Day 155—Church Day (no devotional)
Monday, Day 156—*Meddling with God*
Tuesday, Day 157—*Meddling to Thy Hurt*
Wednesday, Day 158—Church Night (no devotional)
Thursday, Day 159—*The Dangers of Meddling*
Friday, Day 160—*Every Fool Will Be Meddling*
Saturday, Day 161—*Intermeddling with All Wisdom*

Day 155: Church Day

Proverbs 26:17 He that passeth by, and **meddleth with strife belonging not to him, is like one that taketh a dog by the ears**.

Day 156: (Monday)
Meddling with God

2 Chronicles 35:21 But he sent ambassadors to him, saying, What have I to do with thee, thou king of Judah? I come not against thee this day, but against the house wherewith I have war: for **God commanded me to make haste: forbear thee from meddling with God, who is with me, that he destroy thee not**.

INTRODUCTORY THOUGHTS

As Necho, king of Egypt, was on his way to fight against Carchemish, king Josiah of Judah came out against him for battle. Necho assured Josiah that the battle did not involve Judah and that the Lord had commanded him to make haste against the house of Carchemish. In order to turn Josiah's intervention, Necho reminded Josiah that his intervention would be meddling with the will of God. Josiah refused to listen to the warning and meddled in these matters costing him his life *(2 Chronicles 35:22-24)*. Gamaliel, a doctor of the law, expressed a similar statement

☐ Completion Date　　　　　　　　　　　　　　　　　　　Meddling • 183

when he told his peers that they should let the apostles alone lest they fight against God *(Acts 5:34-39)*.

Devotional Thoughts

- **(For children):** It is a useless endeavour to fight against God *(2 Chronicles 13:12b; Isaiah 46:9-10)*. The enemies of Jesus tried to interfere with the resurrection of Jesus Christ *(Matthew 27:62-66)*, but it was in God's plan and they could not stop it *(Matthew 28:1-6)*.
- **(For everyone):** In what ways might we involve ourselves in the Lord's work and end up fighting against the Lord? How should we involve ourselves in the Lord's work to insure that we do not meddle with Him?
- God's plan is not open to discussion. How did Josiah's intervention turn to meddling with God? What kind of man had Josiah been in his life? How should this serve as a warning to all?

Prayer Thoughts

- Ask God to help you further His work rather than hindering it.
- Ask God for wisdom to know when you are meddling with Him.

SONG: *I SET MYSELF AGAINST THE LORD*

Day 157: (Tuesday)
Meddling to Thy Hurt

*2 Kings 14:10 Thou hast indeed smitten Edom, and thine heart hath lifted thee up: glory of this, and tarry at home: for **why shouldest thou meddle to thy hurt**, that thou shouldest fall, even thou, and Judah with thee?*

Introductory Thoughts

The scripture offers a negative connotation of meddling. After all, meddling is the unnecessary involvement of oneself in the affairs of others. Unfortunately, it has been a common practice in the history of nations to provoke others to battle when war was unnecessary and often contrary to God's will. For instance, Amaziah, king of Judah, sent messengers to Jehoash, king of Israel, asking for a face-to-face meeting. Jehoash responded with wisdom saying, *"tarry at home: for why shoul-*

dest thou meddle to thy hurt." Amaziah refused to heed the counsel and meddled to his own hurt. History is full of such testimonies both on a national and individual level.

DEVOTIONAL THOUGHTS

- **(For children)**: Do you like to suffer? Some sufferings glorify God *(1 Peter 4:12-14, 16)*. Some do not. Read what kind of suffering God forbids which includes being a busybody in the matters of others *(1 Peter 4:15)*. If you suffer in this way, it is your own fault.
- **(For everyone)**: Have you ever meddled (unnecessarily involved yourself) in someone else's business? How did that turn out for you? Has this meddling often come back to hurt you in the end?
- Josiah refused to heed Necho's warning *(2 Chronicles 35:21-24)*. How did it turn out for him? Amaziah refused to heed Jehoash's warning. How did it turn out for him?

PRAYER THOUGHTS

- Ask the Lord to give you wisdom to cease from meddling.
- Ask God to help you deal with your own problems.

SONG: *YIELD NOT TO TEMPTATION*

Day 158: Church Night

***Proverbs 24:21** My son, fear thou the LORD and the king: and meddle not with them that are given to change:*

Day 159: (Thursday)
The Dangers of Meddling

***Proverbs 17:14** The beginning of strife is as when one letteth out water: therefore **leave off contention, before it be meddled with**.*

INTRODUCTORY THOUGHTS

Meddling in the problems of others is a dangerous practice resulting in unforeseen outcomes. The Bible uses two comparisons to help convey the danger involved with meddling. ***Proverbs 17:14*** compares meddling to the letting out of previously restrained water. The idea is that med-

☐ Completion Date   Meddling • 185

dling with the problems belonging to others is like personally opening the gates once restraining a large body of water. The second comparison is found in **Proverbs 26:17**. The Bible says, *"He that passeth by, and meddleth with strife belonging not to him, is like one that taketh a dog by the ears."* When someone does this, the dog turns upon the individual. Both of these warnings demonstrate the grievous dangers involved in unnecessarily meddling in the affairs of others.

Devotional Thoughts

- **(For children)**: Even before Rebekah bore her twins, she knew that the family leader would be Jacob, the younger of the two *(Genesis 25:22-26)*. When it appeared that Isaac would bless Esau, she meddled in the outcome by tricking Isaac into blessing Jacob. Jacob had to run for his life and never saw his mother again (see Genesis chapter 27).
- **(For everyone)**: What would happen if you personally opened a gate (like a great dam) to let water out that had been previously restrained? What could happen if you went up and grabbed a dog by the ears? How does this give a vivid representation of the dangers of meddling?
- In whose problems are you currently meddling? Are you willing to ask the Lord to help you repent of this dangerous practice?

Prayer Thoughts

- Thank God for the warnings about meddling.
- Ask God for wisdom to cease from meddling.

SONG: *NOTHING BETWEEN*

Day 160: (Friday)
Every Fool Will Be Meddling

Proverbs 20:3 *It is an honour for a man to cease from strife: but every fool will be meddling.*

Introductory Thoughts

The world constantly and consistently contradicts the truths of God. For instance, it has convinced mankind that it is manly to start a fight and cowardly to cease from strife. As is almost always the case, the world's natural way of thinking stands in stark contrast to true scriptural teachings. According to scripture, *"It is an honour for a man to cease from strife."* This reveals that the most honourable of men are those who through God-given wisdom are able to bring strife to a peaceable resolution without the need for war. A fool, however, continues to meddle until a fight breaks out. The Bible clearly states the dangers of meddling, yet a fool chooses to ignore the scriptural warning to his own hurt.

Devotional Thoughts

- **(For children):** A fool does not cease with his words until he has provoked a fight *(Proverbs 18:6)*. The Bible tells us that the best way to prevent a fight is with kind words *(Proverbs 15:1; Proverbs 25:15b)*.
- **(For everyone):** How would you describe the Lord's viewpoint on meddling? What verses would you use to support your perspective? What should you do if you are presently meddling in the affairs of others?
- Why does the Bible say that a *"fool"* will continue to meddle? What makes a person a fool? Does a fool choose to do what he wants regardless of the wise warnings from scripture?

Prayer Thoughts

- Ask the Lord to keep you from being a fool.
- Ask God for the wisdom necessary to cease from strife.

SONG: *I AM RESOLVED*

Day 161: (Saturday)
Intermeddling with All Wisdom

*Proverbs 18:1 Through desire a man, having separated himself, seeketh and **intermeddleth with all wisdom**.*

Introductory Thoughts

The scripture never offers a positive viewpoint of meddling. One might consider intermeddling with wisdom as a good thing, yet the scripture teaches otherwise. Today's passage states that a man through desire seeks and intermeddles with *"all"* wisdom. According to James, there are two major types of wisdom, earthly *(James 3:15)* and heavenly

(James 3:17). According to *Proverbs 18:1*, the man intermeddles with all wisdom, including the earthly. He separates himself from the pure truth and opens his mind to all the various types of wisdom that the world offers. Just as the scriptural teaching on meddling in other places, the man has no business involving himself with the world's wisdom.

Devotional Thoughts

- **(For children):** God made Solomon the wisest man that ever lived *(1 Kings 3:12)*. Toward the end of his life, he forsook God's wisdom and turned toward worldly wisdom thinking it was acceptable to worship other gods. The Lord was angry with him *(1 Kings 11:4-9)*.
- **(For everyone):** Man should involve himself only in God's wisdom. Read *Romans 16:19*. How does this verse confirm that man should not intermeddle with *"all"* wisdom?
- Do you know someone who has separated himself for the purpose of studying and meddling in the world's wisdom? How has this person benefited? Is that person you?

Prayer Thoughts

- Ask the Lord to help you seek only His wisdom.
- Thank the Lord for His warnings against meddling.

SONG: *MORE ABOUT JESUS*

Notes: _____

Notes:

Quotes from the next volume
(VOLUME 4, WEEK 23)
Subject: Martyrdom

It takes a special person with strong conviction to be willing to die for a just cause.

It is not only possible to glorify God in one's life but equally possible to glorify God in death.

An individual is not truly ready to live for the Lord until he is ready to die for Him.

24

The Home

The Home—This study focuses on the hierarchy and relationships of the husband, his wife, and their children.

Interesting fact: There is a difference between a man that is married and an husband. Twice in Genesis chapter two *(Genesis 2:24, 25)*, Adam and Eve were identified as *"a man"* and *"his wife"* or *"the man and his wife."* The word *husband* speaks of a man's work—his vineyard as depicted in **Psalm 128:3**. Adam is first addressed as an husband in **Genesis 3:6** where it becomes obvious that he has failed to properly tend to his vineyard.

Bible study tip: Pay particular attention to the manner in which the apostles introduced themselves within the opening lines of their epistles. The various adopted titles are purposeful conveying a particular message for God's intended audience. For instance, Paul's self-ascribed title in his epistle to Philemon is *"a prisoner of Jesus Christ"* **(Philemon 1)**. Compare this to Paul's opening address to the Galatians **(Galatians 1:1)**. Why would Paul choose *prisoner* in one place and *apostle* in another?

Sunday, Day 162—Church Day (no devotional)
Monday, Day 163—*Order in the Home*
Tuesday, Day 164—*The Spiritual Leader*

Wednesday, Day 165—Church Night (no devotional)
Thursday, Day 166—*A Praying Man*
Friday, Day 167—*If Any Provide Not for His Own*
Saturday, Day 168—*The Protector*

Day 162: Church Day

*Colossians 3:18 **Wives, submit yourselves unto your own husbands**, as it is fit in the Lord.*

*19 **Husbands, love your wives**, and be not bitter against them.*

*20 **Children, obey your parents** in all things: for this is well pleasing unto the Lord.*

*21 **Fathers, provoke not your children to anger**, lest they be discouraged.*

Day 163: (Monday)
Order in the Home

*1 Corinthians 11:3 But I would have you know, that **the head of every man is Christ**; and **the head of the woman is the man**; and **the head of Christ is God**.*

INTRODUCTORY THOUGHTS

As the world seeks to further weaken any distinctions between men and women, it becomes even more important to stand firm upon God's principles. God has a defined order in the home and the worldly attitudes do not alter God's precepts. Someone has to be the leader of each home and bear the responsibility. According to *1 Corinthians 11:3*, the proper order is a woman submitted to a man, who is submitted to Christ, who is submitted to the heavenly Father. Christ's submission to the Father in no way suggested inferiority to the Father, nor does a submissive wife indicate any type of inferiority to her husband. In fact, it takes a stronger woman to follow God's plan of submission. A godly home follows the scripture even when it contradicts the generally accepted teachings of the day.

☐ Completion Date

Devotional Thoughts

- **(For children):** God is not the author of confusion *(1 Corinthians 14:33)*. How could anyone play "Follow the Leader" if everyone decided that they wanted to be the leader? God set up the order of leadership in the home *(Ephesians 5:22-23; Ephesians 6:1)*.
- **(For everyone):** The order of the home was established in *Genesis 3:16*, if not earlier. Why is it important that the husband/father be the head of the home?
- The fact that the man is to be the head of the home in no way suggests that he is better than the wife/mother. How can this be proven from *1 Corinthians 11:3*?

Prayer Thoughts

- Ask the Lord to restore the proper order to your home.
- Ask God to help each member of the family to fulfil his/her role.

SONG: *GOD, GIVE US CHRISTIAN HOMES*

Day 164: (Tuesday)
The Spiritual Leader

Genesis 18:18 Seeing that **Abraham** *shall surely become a great and mighty nation, and all the nations of the earth shall be blessed in him?*

19 For I know him, that he **will command his children and his household after him, and they shall keep the way of the LORD, to do justice and judgment**; *that the LORD may bring upon Abraham that which he hath spoken of him.*

Introductory Thoughts

As the head of the home, the man bares the responsibility for the biblical training of every individual within his home. Yet, many homes today have no man in them. Regardless of society's disintegration, there is never a time when the man ever relinquishes his accountability to God as the spiritual leader of his home. In today's passage, we read of Abraham bearing his personal responsibility. According to God's testimony, Abraham bore that responsibility well. The Lord testified that Abraham would command his children and household after him. Abraham's family would keep the way of the LORD and would do justice and judgment. Unfortunately, the same cannot be expressed for far too many modern Christian homes. In fact, church pews are overflowing with faithful women while their men are absentee husbands expressing little to no interest in the things of God.

DEVOTIONAL THOUGHTS

- **(For children):** To nurture means to train. Read *Ephesians 6:4*. To whom did God give the responsibility of training up children concerning the things of the Lord? Timothy's father was not a believer *(Acts 16:1)*; therefore, his mother took the responsibility of training young Timothy *(2 Timothy 1:5; 2 Timothy 3:15)*.
- **(For everyone):** Who is the spiritual leader of your home? Do you have a home where there is no husband/father or one where he shows little interest in the things of God? If so, how can you help the situation?
- With leadership comes responsibility. How is the spiritual leader accountable to God? Who will answer to the Lord for the biblical principles taught within the home?

PRAYER THOUGHTS

- Ask the Lord to strengthen the spiritual leader in your home.
- Ask God for strength to follow His order for your home.

SONG: *HAPPY THE HOME, WHEN GOD IS THERE*

Day 165: Church Night

Psalm 128:1 *Blessed is every one that feareth the LORD; that walketh in his ways.*

2 For thou shalt eat the labour of thine hands: happy shalt thou be, and it shall be well with thee.

*3 **Thy wife shall be as a fruitful vine by the sides of thine house: thy children like olive plants round about thy table.***

☐ Completion Date

Day 166: (Thursday)
A Praying Man

Job 1:5 *And it was so, when the days of their feasting were gone about, that **Job** sent and sanctified them, and **rose up early in the morning, and offered burnt offerings according to the number of them all: for Job said, It may be that my sons have sinned, and cursed God in their hearts. Thus did Job continually.***

INTRODUCTORY THOUGHTS

Job's home was certainly not a perfect home, but God testified to this man's faithfulness. The Bible points to prayer as one of Job's most faithful qualities. Job continually sought the Lord on his children's behalf with offerings and prayer. One might consider this a simple task if the family loves and serves God together. Yet, Job's wife is the only indicator we have of Job's family and she mocked Job's faithfulness ***(Job 2:9)***. Some husbands and fathers are quick to point out the errors of those within their home, but could only be moved to prayerful intercession before the Lord by a tragic event. A man who fails to pray for his God-given family is really no man at all.

DEVOTIONAL THOUGHTS

- **(For children):** The Bible offers many examples of fathers praying for their children, both born and unborn. King David fasted and prayed for a sick child ***(2 Samuel 12:15-16)***. He also prayed for his son Solomon to follow God's ways ***(1 Chronicles 29:19)***. Manoah prayed that God would direct him how to raise his unborn child ***(Judges 13:8)***.
- **(For everyone):** Are you the head of your home? If so, do you regularly pray for your wife and/or children? How could Job's wife have better handled the tragedies in their family?
- Read the account of the father in ***Matthew 17:14-18***. What did the father do to help his son? How could this be a picture of a father praying for his child?

PRAYER THOUGHTS

- Ask the Lord to help you be faithful in prayer.
- Ask God to strengthen each member of the family.

SONG: *FROM EVERY STORMY WIND*

Day 167: (Friday)
If Any Provide Not for His Own

*1 Timothy 5:8 But **if any provide not for his own**, and specially for those of his own house, **he hath denied the faith, and is worse than an infidel**.*

INTRODUCTORY THOUGHTS

The Bible explicitly emphasizes the spiritual responsibility of providing for one's family. Sometimes believers wrongfully distinguish between the ministry work and any so-called secular work, but both are accomplished scripturally and prayerfully to please the Lord. *1 Timothy 5:8*, in the direct context, deals with the responsibilities of providing for a household member who is a widow; yet, the emphasis upon *"those of his own house"* broadens the scope. A man who fails or refuses to provide for the needs of his family has *"denied the faith"* and said to be *"worse than an infidel."* That is certainly a stiff and stern rebuke. It remains the man's responsibility to provide for his family regardless of how far societal norms move away from God's precepts. This does not mean that the woman cannot assist in the provision *(Proverbs 31:13-16)* but that the responsibility still belongs to the man.

DEVOTIONAL THOUGHTS

- **(For children):** God told Adam to work in the garden *(Genesis 2:15)*. After Adam and Eve sinned, the responsibility to work still fell upon the man *(Genesis 3:16-19)* but the work would be much harder. *Genesis 3:19* was spoken to Adam although Eve would also be affected.
- **(For everyone):** Do you provide for your family? Do you see it as a spiritual responsibility given to you by the Lord? Do you labour so that your family can have what they need to serve the Lord?
- Do both the husband and wife in your home work? Is it because it is necessary, or is it so you can satisfy your desires beyond what is necessary? Are you willing to do what's right, even if it costs you financially?

PRAYER THOUGHTS

- Ask the Lord to give good health and strength to your provider.
- Ask God to make your home an example of godliness.

SONG: *HOW CLOSELY JOINED ARE MAN AND WIFE*

☐ Completion Date   The Home • 195

Day 168: (Saturday)
The Protector

*Genesis 33:1 And **Jacob lifted up his eyes, and looked, and, behold, Esau came, and with him four hundred men**. And he divided the children unto Leah, and unto Rachel, and unto the two handmaids.*

*2 And **he put** the handmaids and their children foremost, and Leah and her children after, and **Rachel and Joseph hindermost**.*

3 And he passed over before them, and bowed himself to the ground seven times, until he came near to his brother.

4 And Esau ran to meet him, and embraced him, and fell on his neck, and kissed him: and they wept.

5 And he lifted up his eyes, and saw the women and the children; and said, Who are those with thee? And he said, The children which God hath graciously given thy servant.

6 Then the handmaidens came near, they and their children, and they bowed themselves.

7 And Leah also with her children came near, and bowed themselves: and after came Joseph near and Rachel, and they bowed themselves.

INTRODUCTORY THOUGHTS

A normal man naturally desires to protect what God has given to him. Jacob was not always the best example of godliness, but he had the right desire to protect his family from harm. The Bible reveals to us how he reacted when he could see his brother Esau approaching. Unsure of how this reunion might disintegrate into harm, Jacob divided his family with the most precious at the rear. As his family's protector, Jacob led the caravan. If there was going to be trouble, he would have an opportunity to intervene offering his family an opportunity to flee for safety. According to ***Ephesians 5:25***, a man's protection should include a willingness to lay down his life for his wife. A godly man will always intercede between his home and the impending danger.

DEVOTIONAL THOUGHTS

- **(For children):** Noah protected his family by believing God and obediently building the ark ***(Genesis 7:5, 7)***. God made men stronger than women ***(1 Peter 3:7)***. Women need help and protection both physi-

cally *(Genesis 29:7-10; Exodus 2:16-19; Mark 16:1-3)* and spiritually *(1 Timothy 2:12-14)*.
- **(For everyone):** Do those in your home feel safe? Why or why not? Do you have someone who would willingly provide protection in the unfortunate case that trouble comes?
- What are some ways in which a husband and father can protect those within his home? Is this protection always physical, or should he protect them spiritually and emotionally too?

Prayer Thoughts

- Thank the Lord for giving you a protector.
- Ask the Lord to help you be a good protector.

SONG: *FOLLOW ON*

Notes: _____

Quotes from the next volume

(VOLUME 4, WEEK 24)

Subject: Martyrdom (con't)

There comes a time in each person's life when two loves conflict and one must be chosen as the superior love.

The Lord honours those who strongly sealed what they believed with the loss of their own lives.

25

The Home (con't)

The Home—This study focuses on the hierarchy and relationships of the husband, his wife, and their children.

Interesting fact: On the surface, it might appear that the marriage relationship was created for man. After all, the Lord said, *"It is not good that the man should be alone; I will make him an help meet for him" **(Genesis 2:18)**.* Paul further testified, *"For the man is not of the woman; but the woman of the man. Neither was the man created for the woman; but the woman for the man" **(1 Corinthians 11:8-9)**.* This seems further confirmed when we consider the initial creation of the woman out of man and her subsequent presentation to the man **(Genesis 2:18-22; Mark 10:6-9)**. It seems obvious that the primary impetus behind the institution and formation of the marriage relationship was for man and for his benefit. However, it is important to consider that everything created has a higher purpose. **Revelation 4:11** states, *"Thou art worthy, O Lord, to receive glory and honour and power: for thou hast created all things, and for thy pleasure they are and were created."* Marriage, like every other thing created, was instituted to bring pleasure to the Lord Jesus Christ.

Bible study tip: Repetition used in scripture serves to teach and emphasize important truths. The repetition can be obvious and impossible to miss but not always. For instance, the Bible will, at times, use repetition as bookends to a chapter or a verse. By opening and closing a passage with repetition, the student's attention is directed upon a singular subject. Psalm 113 offers a fine example. It opens and closes with the phrase *"Praise ye the LORD"* **(Psalm 113:1, 9)**.

Sunday, Day 169—Church Day (no devotional)
Monday, Day 170—*The Selfless Woman*
Tuesday, Day 171—*Known for Love*
Wednesday, Day 172—Church Night (no devotional)
Thursday, Day 173—*The Wife Shall Honour Her Husband*
Friday, Day 174—*Wives, Submit Yourselves*
Saturday, Day 175—*Prone to Contention*

Day 169: Church Day

Proverbs 14:1 Every wise woman buildeth her house: but the foolish plucketh it down with her hands.

Day 170: (Monday)
The Selfless Woman

Proverbs 31:25 Strength and honour are her clothing; **and she shall rejoice in time to come.**
26 She openeth her mouth with wisdom; and in her tongue is the law of kindness.
27 **She looketh well to the ways of her household***, and eateth not the bread of idleness.*

INTRODUCTORY THOUGHTS

A good wife and mother will exemplify a type of selflessness like no one else upon the earth. Proverbs offers a wonderful examination into her life and ways. Her life is one of sacrifice, often putting the needs and wants of her household ahead of her own. She labours to take care of her family **(Proverbs 31:16-19)**. She looks well to the ways of her household while enjoying little to no idle time **(Proverbs 31:27)**. Yet at day's end, she rises up to give meat to her household *(Proverbs 31:15)*. All the while, she can open her mouth with wisdom with the law of kindness in her tongue *(Proverbs 31:26)*. The Bible points to her only reward as the praise of her husband and children *(Proverbs 31:28)*. This reward may seem insignificant to the world, but to her the love of her family is both sufficient and worth the effort.

DEVOTIONAL THOUGHTS

- **(For children):** Name some of the things that your mother does for you from the time you get up in the morning until the time you go back to bed. A godly mother always has something to do: she takes care of the home *(Titus 2:5)*; she teaches and brings up children *(Proverbs 31:1; 1 Timothy 5:10)*; she guides the home *(1 Timothy 5:14)*; she comforts her children *(Isaiah 66:13)*.
- **(For everyone):** Consider the actions of the two women in *1 Kings 3:26*. Which one exemplified a godly love for the child? Do you as a wife and mother in your home exemplify this kind of selflessness?
- What was Moses' mother willing to sacrifice to insure the well-being of Moses *(Exodus 2:3)*? What are you willing to sacrifice for the sake of those within your household?

PRAYER THOUGHTS

- Thank the Lord for the godly wife/mother in your home.
- Ask God to give you a selfless heart.

SONG: *IS YOUR ALL ON THE ALTAR?*

Day 171: (Tuesday)
Known for Love

Isaiah 49:15 Can a woman forget her sucking child, that she should not have compassion on the son of her womb? yea, they may forget, yet will I not forget thee.

INTRODUCTORY THOUGHTS

Godly ladies are known for the love they express toward others. *Isaiah 49:15* might be used to argue otherwise, but the Lord references a mother's love to depict the peak of earthly love. This passage simply points out that the mother's love only fails to reach the pinnacle when compared to God's own love toward His creation. God made a woman's heart tender, but sin can harden this tender heart. For this reason, the older women within the New Testament church are instructed to nurture this particular trait within the younger women by teaching them how to love their husbands and their children *(Titus 2:4)*. When things are spiritually right, the godly woman makes it her priority to care for those whom God has given her, and she does so in love. Examples of this love permeate the pages of scripture.

DEVOTIONAL THOUGHTS
- **(For children):** Timothy's grandmother showed love by teaching his mother about God and His word. Timothy's mother, in turn, taught him *(2 Timothy 1:5; 2 Timothy 3:15)*. When children are sick, mothers show love by praying, caring, and seeking help for them *(2 Kings 4:18-22; Mark 7:25-30)*.
- **(For everyone):** What did Hannah do each year to demonstrate her love for Samuel *(1 Samuel 2:19)*? How did Hagar demonstrate love for Ishmael in *Genesis 21:16*? What are some ways in which the wife or mother of your home demonstrates love?
- What is so special about a mother's love? How does it differ from that of a father? Who made the woman to love like that?

PRAYER THOUGHTS
- Ask the Lord to increase the love in your home.
- Thank God for putting it in the heart of women to love.

SONG: *A CHRISTIAN HOME*

Day 172: Church Night

Proverbs 15:17 Better is a dinner of herbs where love is, than a stalled ox and hatred therewith.

Day 173: (Thursday)
The Wife Shall Honour Her Husband

Esther 1:20 And when the king's decree which he shall make shall be published throughout all his empire, (for it is great,) **all the wives shall give to their husbands honour,** *both to great and small.*

☐ Completion Date

Introductory Thoughts

The Bible shows us that even heathen kings know it is proper for a woman to honour her husband. Some might suggest that because these words were spoken by a heathen, the reader should discount them, but these truths are supported elsewhere in scripture. For instance, ***Ephesians 5:33*** says that the wife is to reverence her husband. Sara honoured Abraham, even to the point of calling him lord ***(1 Peter 3:6)***. Even Abigail, who had a husband that was a man of Belial, honoured her husband when she kept David from ending Nabal's life ***(1 Samuel 25:23-33)***. A woman who honours her husband honours the Lord. She does so because the Lord commands it, not because her husband necessarily deserves her honour.

Devotional Thoughts

- **(For children):** Honour means to treat with respect. God made the woman to be a help to her husband ***(Genesis 2:18)***. As such, she will do him good all the days of her life ***(Proverbs 31:12)***. This includes both her actions and her speech.
- **(For everyone):** What kind of a man was Nabal? How could Abigail honour him when he was so wicked? What would have caused her to be a good wife to a bad man?
- If you are a wife, do you honour your husband? What kind of message does this send to your children? How does this please or displease the Lord?

Prayer Thoughts

- Ask the Lord to make your home more scriptural.
- Ask God to help each member of your family to please Him.

SONG: *HOW CLOSELY JOINED ARE MAN AND WIFE*

Day 174: (Friday)
Wives, Submit Yourselves

Ephesians 5:22 Wives, submit yourselves unto your own husbands, as unto the Lord.

23 For the husband is the head of the wife, even as Christ is the head of the church: and he is the saviour of the body.

24 Therefore **as the church is subject unto Christ, so let the wives be to their own husbands in every thing**.

INTRODUCTORY THOUGHTS

The Lord gave specific commandments to both the husband and the wife. The Lord, knowing that man's foremost love was, by nature, himself, commanded the man to *"love"* his wife as Christ loved the church **(Ephesians 5:25)**. Additionally, the Lord, knowing that a woman would not naturally desire to submit, commanded the wife to submit to her own husband, as unto the Lord. This does not suggest that she only goes along with her husband so long as she agrees with his decisions, neither does it mean that she can never offer input into the decision-making process. But, in the end, she follows her husband's leading, trusting the Lord to bless her faithfulness.

DEVOTIONAL THOUGHTS

- **(For children):** To submit means to willingly put yourself under the authority of another. According to **Titus 2:5**, to whom should wives be obedient and why? When God lays down the order in the home **(Genesis 3:16)** and wives do not follow this precept, they are despising His word and may cause others to do the same through their bad example.
- **(For everyone):** What happens when a godly lady submits to her godly husband? Read what the Bible says could happen when a godly lady submits to an ungodly husband **(1 Peter 3:1-4)**.
- What should happen if a husband's leadership is in direct rebellion to the plain teachings of scripture? How could **Acts 5:29** be applied to this scenario? How could it be dangerous if misapplied?

PRAYER THOUGHTS

- Ask the Lord to help you be obedient to His commandments.
- Thank God for the opportunity to have a biblical home.

SONG: *TRUST AND OBEY*

Day 175: (Saturday)
Prone to Contention

Proverbs 19:13 *A foolish son is the calamity of his father: and **the contentions of a wife are a continual dropping.***

Introductory Thoughts

With all the difficult challenges that a woman faces within the home, it should not be surprising that the Lord repeatedly gave warnings against a woman with a contentious spirit. How does the downward spiral begin? She may spend her life serving others with little to no thanks. She may honour and submit to a husband who deserves little honour or authority. If she does not continually walk with the Lord, she can become disillusioned with the Lord and with her duties as a mother and wife. She might begin to be contentious ***(Proverbs 21:9; Proverbs 25:24; Proverbs 27:15)*** causing greater problems in the home, perhaps to the point of causing those she loves to become bitter against her ***(Colossians 3:19)***.

Devotional Thoughts

- **(For children):** A woman with a meek and quiet spirit *"is in the sight of God of great price"* **(1 Peter 3:4)**. A hateful, argumentative woman disquiets (takes peace away from) the earth ***(Proverbs 30:21, 23a)***. It is impossible to hide her ***(Proverbs 27:15-16)***.
- **(For everyone):** Is there peace or contention in your home? Have you done things as a husband or child to cause the wife/mother in your home to grow weary in well doing? Why not unilaterally change and trust God to fix the situation?
- Are you a wife and mother? Are you contentious with those within your home? What happened to cause you to become disobedient to God's commands?

Prayer Thoughts

- Ask God to help you walk with Him in the good times and in the bad.
- Thank God for giving you a Christian home.

SONG: *LIKE A RIVER GLORIOUS*

Notes:

Quotes from the next volume

(VOLUME 4, WEEK 25)

Subject: Motives

The Lord is just as concerned with *why* a man does what he does as He is concerned with *what* the man does.

Many times asking and answering the simple question, "Why?" is the best way to expose one's motives.

It is always right to do right, but it is more perfectly right to do right for the right reasons.

26

The Home (con't)

The Home—This study focuses on the hierarchy and relationships of the husband, his wife, and their children.

Interesting fact: God's admonition concerning child rearing is twofold: (1) nurturing and (2) admonishing *(Ephesians 6:4)*. It is similar to the relationship of law to grace. God's designed emphasis—law followed by grace—teaches us the correct relationship of the two primary aspects of child rearing. Children properly raised must first learn via the application of law before they will ever appreciate the grace afforded them. Parents often fail to find a proper balance between the admonishing and nurturing of their children. This results in an unstable and insecure child. Erring one way or the other will produce a child who is either too rigid or too soft but definitely unbalanced.

Bible study tip: Combining the words *from* and *to* together in scripture demonstrates boundaries as it pertains to places, people, or time. The words used in that order separated by names, times, places, or things are meant to identify the boundaries being emphasized. For example, **Psalm 41:13** says, "Blessed be the LORD God of Israel **from** everlasting, and **to** everlasting. Amen, and Amen." In other words, the Lord can be traced as far back as eternity past and as far forward as eternity future. This particular example emphasizes one truth, but other examples serve to emphasize differing truths. The key is to note what is being emphasized and its intended purpose.

Sunday, Day 176—Church Day (no devotional)
Monday, Day 177—*Suffer Children to Come unto Me*
Tuesday, Day 178—*In the Days of Thy Youth*
Wednesday, Day 179—Church Night (no devotional)
Thursday, Day 180—*Honour Thy Father and Mother*
Friday, Day 181—*What Can I Do for the Lord?*
Saturday, Day 182—*Misbehaving Children*

Day 176: Church Day

Proverbs 20:11 Even a child is known by his doings, whether his work be pure, and whether it be right.

Day 177: (Monday)
Suffer Children to Come unto Me

Matthew 19:14 But Jesus said, **Suffer little children,** *and forbid them not,* **to come unto me***: for of such is the kingdom of heaven.*

INTRODUCTORY THOUGHTS

The Lord Jesus is the King of kings, the Lord of lords, and the Creator of the universe. Yet, during His earthly ministry, the Lord made it known that He cared for the *"little ones"* **(Matthew 18:6, 10, 14).** Perhaps the disciples thought the Master would be too busy or have more important things to do than to take time for the children. The Lord rebuked His disciples for such erroneous thinking. After all, the Lord loved children and wanted them to come to Him. It grieved Him to think that His disciples would forbid any child from coming to Him. Even now, the Lord wants little children to come to Him. No disciple should ever forbid children to come to the Lord. Even with all of life's distractions, the Bible admonishes young people to remember their Creator in the days of their youth *(Ecclesiastes 12:1).*

☐ Completion Date   The Home (con't) • 207

Devotional Thoughts

- **(For children):** The Lord says, *"he careth for you"* **(1 Peter 5:7)**. The Lord died for everyone and wants them to be saved **(1 Timothy 2:4)**. In **Romans 10:13**, *"whosoever"* means you! You may, can, and should be saved when you are young **(Proverbs 8:17; Jeremiah 29:13)**.
- **(For everyone):** Have you trusted the Lord as Saviour? Have you talked to someone about trusting the Lord for salvation only to have that person turn you away? Why were you turned away?
- Why is it important that children not be turned away when they are seeking the Lord? What should we do to help them better understand salvation without turning them away?

Prayer Thoughts

- Thank the Lord for caring for the little children.
- Ask God to work in the hearts of the young ones in your family.

SONG: *JESUS LOVES EVEN ME*

Day 178: (Tuesday)
In the Days of Thy Youth

Ecclesiastes 12:1 Remember now thy Creator in the days of thy youth, while the evil days come not, nor the years draw nigh, when thou shalt say, I have no pleasure in them;

Introductory Thoughts

NOW is the ideal time to love and serve the Lord. Some unwise counsel has suggested that young people should go out and experience the world in their youth before they later settle down and serve God once mature. An equally erroneous teaching proclaims that godly parents should raise their children to love and serve the Master at some future time. Both have misled far too many homes! The Lord wants young people to love and serve Him now. One should begin early in life to learn the most important lessons of life. As a child, one should learn *"the fear of the LORD"* **(Psalm 34:11)**, to *"praise the name of the LORD"* **(Psalm 148:12-13; Matthew 21:15)**, and to *"remember"* his Creator **(Ecclesiastes 12:1)**. Like Samuel, children should grow and be *"in favour both with the LORD, and also with men"* **(1 Samuel 2:26)**.

Devotional Thoughts

- **(For children):** *Proverbs 3:1-4* tells how to find favour with God and man. Jesus is a good example for us *(Luke 2:51-52)*. Finding favour with God and man can also be summed up in *James 1:22*.
- **(For everyone):** What could a young person do for the Lord? How could a young person walk with the Lord, fear the Lord, praise the Lord, and remember his or her Creator?
- What are some things that Samuel did, even as a youth, to find favour with the Lord and with men? What could you do in youth to find the same type of favour?

Prayer Thoughts

- Ask the Lord to help young people give God their youth.
- Ask God to encourage young people to grow in Him.

SONG: *LOYALTY TO CHRIST*

Day 179: Church Night

Proverbs 29:17 Correct thy son, and he shall give thee rest; yea, he shall give delight unto thy soul.

Day 180: (Thursday)
Honour Thy Father and Mother

Ephesians 6:1 Children, obey your parents in the Lord: for this is right.

*2 **Honour thy father and mother**; (which is the first commandment with promise;)*

Introductory Thoughts

The Bible has much to say concerning the dangers of improper family relationships. "There is a generation that curseth their father, and doth not bless their mother" **(Proverbs 30:11)**. "The son dishonoureth the father, the daughter riseth up against her mother" **(Micah 7:6)**, "the eye . . . mocketh at his father, and despiseth to obey his mother" **(Proverbs 30:17)**. Yet, the first commandment with promise was to "honour thy father and mother" **(Ephesians 6:1-2)**. This honour can be demonstrated by hearkening to **(Proverbs 23:22)** and obeying one's parents **(Colossians 3:20)**. As parents seek the Lord's direction, God will lead them as to how to lead their individual homes **(Ezra 8:21)**. The child's responsibility is directed toward submitting to and learning of the Lord by obeying the parents.

Devotional Thoughts

- **(For children):** Esther was raised by her cousin Mordecai. She was obedient to him *(Esther 2:5-7, 20)*. Even later, she listened to his wisdom and saved her people from a wicked plan *(Esther 4:7-8, 16)*. For many generations, the Rechabites obeyed what their father commanded and the Lord rewarded them *(Jeremiah 35:5-10; 18-19)*.
- **(For everyone):** How is a young person's relationship with the Lord directly related to his or her relationship to parents (or guardians)? What is the first concept a young person will often have of God?
- Why does God begin life with youth? Why did God establish life so that it would begin with a child's reliance upon parents? What are some of the responsibilities of youth?

Prayer Thoughts

- Ask the Lord to help the children in your home to be obedient.
- Thank God for the family structure He established.

SONG: *GOD, GIVE US CHRISTIAN HOMES*

Day 181: (Friday)
What Can I Do for the Lord?

John 6:9 There is a lad here, which hath five barley loaves, and two small fishes: but what are they among so many?

Introductory Thoughts

Young people often underestimate how the Lord might use them for His glory even at an early age. Yet, the Lord frequently used children and young people to accomplish great feats. One such case is the testimony of the unnamed lad who supplied five barley loaves and two small fishes. Though his name and age are unknown, his selflessness and availability are not. The Lord took his insignificant meal and multiplied it until it was able to feed five thousand men, plus women and children. The Lord did not refuse the lad for service due to his inexperience or inabilities. He merely needed the lad's availability. In like manner, God desires to use young people today. All He needs is for a young person to make himself available and leave the results to God.

DEVOTIONAL THOUGHTS
- **(For children)**: A little maid who was being held captive in a foreign land saw her master suffering and told her master's wife that God could help him. This brought about Naaman's healing and introduced him to the Lord of the little maid *(2 Kings 5:1-19)*. You too can help people by simply telling them to read God's word and go to the house of God.
- **(For everyone)**: Has the Lord ever used you to accomplish His work? How did it feel to be used by God? Do you want Him to continue to use you in His service?
- Name some other children or young people from the Bible who served the Lord. Why did the Lord use them? Why would He use you?

PRAYER THOUGHTS
- Ask God to use you in His service.
- Thank God for His ability to use you regardless of your age.

SONG: *WHO IS ON THE LORD'S SIDE?*

Day 182: (Saturday)
Misbehaving Children

Isaiah 3:5 And the people shall be oppressed, every one by another, and every one by his neighbour: **the child shall behave himself proudly against the ancient**, *and the base against the honourable.*

INTRODUCTORY THOUGHTS

Much of a young person's character or lack thereof is demonstrated in his behaviour toward adults and especially the elderly. In Isaiah chapter 3, the Bible speaks of a time when the judgment of God will be upon His people, and one of the characteristics of the day will be that *"the child shall behave himself proudly against the ancient."* The prophet Elisha

☐ Completion Date   The Home (con't) • 211

dealt with such children when they came out of the city mocking him saying, *"Go up, thou bald head; go up, thou bald head"* **(2 Kings 2:23)**. Apparently, Job endured a similar problem as he said, *"young children despised me; I arose, and they spake against me"* **(Job 19:18)**. Children can be cruel, and in doing so they reveal an evil heart displeasing to the Lord. It is never a good idea to encourage children to be insolent and impolite toward adults.

Devotional Thoughts

- **(For children):** People can tell what kind of child you are by the way you act **(Proverbs 20:11)**. Before the Lord returns, people will turn away from God more and more. Paul referred to this as perilous times. One way the youth will turn away involves being *"disobedient to parents"* **(2 Timothy 3:1-2)**. Will you choose to obey or disobey **(Luke 11:28)**?
- **(For everyone):** For what did the children mock Elisha? Why did the children likely despise Job? Did these men have any control over these areas of their lives? How does this demonstrate cruelty?
- How should children treat adults? What kind of relationship should they seek with the elderly? Should there ever be a time when a young person mocks or disrespects an adult?

Prayer Thoughts

- Ask God to raise up a respectful generation of young people.
- Ask the Lord to convict you for foolish mockery.

SONG: *DEAR CHILDREN HEARKEN TO MY WORDS*

Notes: _____
_____
_____
_____
_____
_____
_____

Notes:

Quotes from the next volume

(VOLUME 4, WEEK 26)

Subject: Motives (con't)

The Bible clearly points out that the natural man is guided by self-serving motives.

It is imperative that each believer not only do what is right, but also examine himself to make sure that he is doing what is right for the right reasons.

27

Resolution

Resolution—The word *resolution* does not appear within scripture; however, the concept of problem or conflict resolution frequently appears.

Defined: the act of problem solving

Interesting fact: Proper problem resolution requires godly wisdom. Man's greatest obstacle in resolving problems takes place when he attempts to solve any problem in a self-serving manner or in ways providing only short-term solutions and ignoring the long-term consequences. For a case in point, consider the desire of the disciples to call down fire upon those who did not initially receive the Lord *(Luke 9:52-54)*. The Lord rebuked their suggested solution because it created long-term consequences *(Luke 9:55-56)*.

Bible study tip: Believers have become increasingly careless with their Bible study, especially with the introduction of Bible study software. Word studies, both in the original languages and in English, have preempted contextual study. Word studies should not be viewed negatively unless they neglect contextual study as an integral aspect of study. A word study only works when the student takes the time to study the context of each occurrence within scripture. True

Bible study requires work *(2 Timothy 2:15)* during this computer age and before.

Sunday, Day 183—Church Day (no devotional)
Monday, Day 184—*Problems Are a Reality of Life*
Tuesday, Day 185—*Problems Will Not Just Go Away*
Wednesday, Day 186—Church Night (no devotional)
Thursday, Day 187—*Hiding Does Not Resolve the Problem*
Friday, Day 188—*Take Your Problems to the Lord*
Saturday, Day 189—*All Problems, No Solutions*

Day 183: Church Day

Proverbs 15:1 A soft answer turneth away wrath*: but grievous words stir up anger.*

Day 184: (Monday)
Problems Are a Reality of Life

1 Peter 4:12 Beloved, ***think it not strange concerning the fiery trial which is to try you****, as though some strange thing happened unto you:*

INTRODUCTORY THOUGHTS

Problems are a reality of life. The Lord cautioned concerning this truth when He said, *"In the world ye shall have tribulation" **(John 16:33)***. Simon Peter echoed this sentiment when he said, *"Beloved, think it not strange concerning the fiery trial which is to try you, as though some strange thing happened unto you" **(1 Peter 4:12)***. Problems, trials, and tribulations occur because of sin's presence, and so long as sin remains within this world, men will face difficulties. Though the nature of these problems varies, the foundational solutions are the same: problems must be faced, and spiritual, scriptural solutions must be sought. Failure to do so only increases the presence and impact of the problems.

DEVOTIONAL THOUGHTS

- **(For children):** No one escapes having problems *(Job 14:1)*. The apostle Paul had been stoned at Lystra. After preaching in another town,

☐ Completion Date

he returned to Lystra and warned his disciples that problems would come, but they should continue serving God *(Acts 14:19-22)*.
- **(For everyone):** What are some problems you are presently facing? Are you able to identify the source of any of these problems? What are you doing to resolve the problems?
- What is your first reaction when a serious problem arises? Do you try to hide or ignore the problem in hopes it will disappear? Does that appear to be working?

PRAYER THOUGHTS
- Ask the Lord to help you solve the problems that you face.
- Ask God for wisdom in settling troubling conflicts.

SONG: *OUR GOD, OUR HELP*

Day 185: (Tuesday)
Problems Will Not Just Go Away

Mark 6:34 And Jesus, when he came out, saw much people, and was moved with compassion toward them, because they were as sheep not having a shepherd: and he began to teach them many things.

35 And **when the day was now far spent, his disciples came unto him, and said, This is a desert place, and now the time is far passed***:*

36 **Send them away,** *that they may go into the country round about, and into the villages, and buy themselves bread:* **for they have nothing to eat.**

37 **He answered and said unto them, Give ye them to eat.** *And they say unto him, Shall we go and buy two hundred pennyworth of bread, and give them to eat?*

INTRODUCTORY THOUGHTS

Man can, at times, readily recognize problems that arise, but often initially reacts with solutions to remove the problem out of sight. As the disciples looked out over the multitude in today's passage, they saw thousands in a desert place with a lack of provisions. They quickly viewed what seemed to them as an insurmountable problem. As evening approached, they came to the Lord and suggested that He send the people away. The disciples were more comfortable with the problem if it was out of sight, out of mind, and not theirs to face. Their suggestion was an unacceptable solution. For this reason, the Lord put the problem back upon the disciples when He said to them, *"Give ye them to eat"* **(Mark 6:37)**. In other words, the problem would not go away or solve itself. The Lord directed the disciples to find a solution and their turning a blind eye was completely unacceptable.

DEVOTIONAL THOUGHTS

- **(For children):** Man does not want to face his sin problem. He tries to put it out of sight by getting rid of God's word or anyone who points out the problem *(Jeremiah 36:21-26; John 19:15a; Acts 7:52; Acts 22:22)*. Ignoring the sin problem is dangerous *(Romans 6:23)*.
- **(For everyone):** What is a problem that you are currently facing? Up to this point, what has been your solution in dealing with the problem? Have you tried to send the problem away?
- What additional problems could have occurred if the Lord sent the people away? Is it possible that some of the people would have experienced significant problems by leaving without food?

PRAYER THOUGHTS

- Ask the Lord to show you that problems cannot be sent away.
- Ask God to help you see the complications of ignoring problems.

SONG: *DARE TO BE A DANIEL*

Day 186: Church Night

*Proverbs 22:10 Cast out the scorner, and contention shall go out; yea, **strife and reproach shall cease**.*

Day 187: (Thursday)
Hiding Does Not Resolve the Problem

*Genesis 3:6 And when **the woman** saw that the tree was good for food, and that it was pleasant to the eyes, and a tree to be desired to make one wise, she took of the fruit thereof, and did eat, **and** gave also unto **her husband** with her; and he did eat.*

☐ Completion Date   Resolution • 217

*7 And **the eyes of them both were opened, and they knew that they were naked**; and they sewed fig leaves together, and made themselves aprons.*

*8 And **they heard the voice of the LORD God walking in the garden in the cool of the day: and Adam and his wife hid themselves** from the presence of the LORD God amongst the trees of the garden.*

Introductory Thoughts

The Devil would have man believe that hiding from problems provides an adequate solution. This is a lie! Adam and Eve created problems for themselves by partaking of the fruit. Their initial efforts to resolve the problem further confirmed that they had created an unresolved situation of their own doing. As they heard the voice of the Lord walking in the garden, they hid themselves amongst the trees in hopes that these efforts would protect them in some way. They hoped the problem would pass unnoticed without them having to face the fact that they had sinned against the Lord. The Lord would not allow them to hide; instead, He called for Adam to show himself resulting in both Adam and Eve directly facing the problem.

Devotional Thoughts

- **(For children):** When God's people conquered Jericho, Joshua had warned them earlier not to take anything for themselves *(Joshua 6:18)*. Achan took a garment and some money. He thought by hiding it in his tent, he would not get caught. God knew all about his sin *(Joshua 7:11, 19-22; Jeremiah 16:17; Proverbs 28:13)*.
- **(For everyone):** Have you ever had a problem and thought that hiding from the problem would make it go away? How did that work for you? Did the problem get better or grow worse?
- Why is it so important that we face our problems? What can happen to them if we face them? What can happen if we attempt to hide from them?

Prayer Thoughts

- Ask the Lord to give you boldness to face your problems.
- Ask God to help you see that hiding does not solve problems.

SONG: *GOD WILL TAKE CARE OF YOU*

Day 188: (Friday)
Take Your Problems to the Lord

1 Peter 5:7 Casting all your care upon him; for he careth for you.

INTRODUCTORY THOUGHTS

God expects man to face his problems, but He does not expect man to resolve those problems independently. Ultimately, God desires to hear the burdens of the heart even if the burdens or cares have been brought upon man by his own wrongdoing. God, knowing the condition of Adam and Eve, made a point to visit them. He obviously knew Adam's location but knew it was best for Adam to acknowledge the problem. He wanted Adam to tell Him about the problems brought on by sin. In like manner, God knows what man has need of before it is ever brought to Him in prayer *(Matthew 6:8)*, but He still desires for man to come to Him for help.

DEVOTIONAL THOUGHTS

- **(For children):** Saul's jealousy caused David to flee. He made the cave Adullam his headquarters and hid there from Saul. David took his problems to the Lord *(Psalm 142:1-7)*. Read what Hezekiah did when threatened by the king of Assyria *(2 Kings 19:9b-19)*.
- **(For everyone):** Where is the first place you go to find a solution to your problems? Do you first seek counsel from friends and family, or do you take your problem to the Lord?
- How could prayer possibly be an important step in resolving problems or potential problems? How can God's intervention help us keep from creating additional problems?

PRAYER THOUGHTS

- Ask God to teach you the necessity of prayer in problem solving.
- Thank God for His willingness to help you solve problems.

SONG: *DOES JESUS CARE?*

☐ Completion Date

Day 189: (Saturday)
All Problems, No Solutions

*Numbers 11:4 And **the mixt multitude** that was among them **fell a lusting**: and **the children of Israel also wept** again, and said, Who shall give us flesh to eat?*

*5 **We remember** the fish, which **we did eat in Egypt freely;** the cucumbers, and the melons, and the leeks, and the onions, and the garlick:*

INTRODUCTORY THOUGHTS

Most men have no trouble creating and recognizing the trouble they have created but often experience great difficulty in finding any necessary solutions. In the wilderness, the children of Israel readily identified problems, but rarely, if ever, offered suitable solutions for these problems. Their expectation was that someone else could provide the solutions so long as they found satisfaction in complaining. Even today, this scenario repeats itself in businesses, churches, and family lives. People can complain about problems and often lack the ambition or the wherewithal for finding any lasting solutions. The average person finds enjoyment in expressing his complaints but leaves the solutions to others. This has greatly troubled the workplace, the home, the church, and every nation.

DEVOTIONAL THOUGHTS

- **(For children):** In *Acts 6:1*, we read about a problem in the early church. The ones who complained only offered a problem but no solution. Eventually, the apostles had to solve the problem *(Acts 6:2-5)*.
- **(For everyone):** How does it demonstrate a lack of character when we are willing to offer up complaints but unwilling to be a part of the solution to the problems we identify?
- Why is it that man naturally causes or is involved in problems but has little to no concept of how to resolve those problems? How could one improve in this area?

PRAYER THOUGHTS

- Ask God to teach you how to solve problems.
- Ask God to build this character in you and your loved ones.

SONG: *I AM RESOLVED*

Notes:

Quotes from the next volume
(VOLUME 4, WEEK 27)
Subject: Suffering and Death

On this side of eternity, few men ever grasp the purposes or the benefits of suffering affliction.

Trials are certain to come; heartaches are unavoidable, but the believer must praise the Lord despite the difficulties.

Trials, afflictions, and heartaches presently abound, but those who know the Lord can rejoice in knowing those things are only *"for a season" (1 Peter 1:6)*.

28

Resolution (con't)

Resolution— The word *resolution* does not appear within scripture; however, the concept of problem or conflict resolution frequently appears.

Interesting fact: Have you ever wondered how the Israelites convinced the Egyptians to let them **borrow** *"jewels of silver, and jewels of gold, and raiment" **(Exodus 3:22)***? The answer is found in ***Exodus 3:21*** where the Lord promised, *"I will give this people favour in the sight of the Egyptians: and it shall come to pass, that,* **when ye go, ye shall not go empty."** A lack of faithfulness to God usually serves as the greatest hindrance to finding favour with men. First, follow the Lord and, then, He will assist with men. The Bible promises, *"When a man's ways please the LORD, he maketh even his enemies to be at peace with him"* ***(Proverbs 16:7)***.

Bible study tip: Typology is the study of how a person, place, thing, or event pictures some future person, place, thing, or event. This is one of the many scripturally sound and enjoyable ways to study scripture. In fact, the Lord Jesus encouraged typology when He said, *"as Moses lifted up the serpent in the wilderness, even so must the Son of man be lifted up"* ***(John 3:14; see also Numbers 21:4-9)***. The serpent being lifted up was a type of Christ being lifted up on the cross to become a curse for man. Though typology is useful, it does not exist without its own set of dangers. The most common danger is attributing a type in scripture to which the Bible never alludes. Another temptation, perhaps not as common, is to elevate the actual type to the status of the antitype (that which is being pictured). For instance, the Israelites had no idea that the serpent was a future type of Christ's sacrifice and burned incense to it. At this, Hezekiah was greatly distraught and broke the serpent in pieces calling it *"Nehushtan"* which basically means brasen thing **(2 Kings 18:4)**. Every type will fall short in some way or another of its antitype. Otherwise, it would become equal to the antitype and eventually superior to it.

Sunday, Day 190—Church Day (no devotional)
Monday, Day 191—*The Root of the Problem*
Tuesday, Day 192—*Wrong Solutions Yield New Problems*
Wednesday, Day 193—Church Night (no devotional)
Thursday, Day 194—*Solutions Are Not Always Easy*
Friday, Day 195—*The Necessity of Patience*
Saturday, Day 196—*God Uses Problems*

Day 190: Church Day

Proverbs 17:1 *Better is a dry morsel, and quietness therewith, than an house full of sacrifices with strife.*

Day 191: (Monday)
The Root of the Problem

Genesis 3:9 *And the LORD God called unto* **Adam***, and said unto him,* **Where art thou?**

10 And he said, **I heard thy voice in the garden, and I was afraid, because I was naked; and I hid myself.**

11 And he said, **Who told thee that thou wast naked? Hast thou eaten of the tree, whereof I commanded thee that thou shouldest not eat?**

12 And the man said, **The woman whom thou gavest to be with me, she gave me of the tree, and I did eat.**

☐ Completion Date

13 And the LORD God said unto the woman, **What is this that thou hast done?** *And* **the woman said, The serpent beguiled me, and I did eat.**

14 And the LORD God said unto the serpent, Because thou hast done this, thou art cursed above all cattle, and above every beast of the field; upon thy belly shalt thou go, and dust shalt thou eat all the days of thy life:

INTRODUCTORY THOUGHTS

When a problem presents itself, it is very important for man to consider the root of the problem. In scripture, the Lord would often accomplish this through inquiry. Before entering the garden, the Lord of course knew what had taken place. Yet, the first thing the Lord did was to ask Adam where he was. The Lord did this not to locate Adam, but He knew that Adam needed to get to the root of the problem. Adam did acknowledge what transpired to bring about the current problem but failed to take personal responsibility for the problem. When a problem presents itself, man should take the time to seek the cause of the problem. He should do so by willingly taking personal responsibility.

DEVOTIONAL THOUGHTS

- **(For children):** While Moses was receiving the Law from God, the Israelites were at the foot of the mountain behaving foolishly *(Exodus 32:1-8)*. Moses went down to see what was happening. When questioned, Aaron blamed the people instead of facing his fear of man and his compromise. His answer was also dishonest *(Exodus 32:21-24)*.
- **(For everyone):** Why is it so important for people to strongly consider the root of a problem? How could this consideration possibly prevent a second occurrence of the same problem in the future?
- A problem cannot be solved long term without considering what initially brought about the problem. What does this suggest about solutions that do not consider the root of the problem?

PRAYER THOUGHTS

- Ask the Lord to help you identify the root of your problems.
- Ask God to help you take responsibility for your problems.

SONG: *I SURRENDER ALL*

Day 192: (Tuesday)
Wrong Solutions Yield New Problems

*Genesis 16:1 Now **Sarai Abram's wife bare him no children: and she had an handmaid**, an Egyptian, whose name was Hagar.*

*2 And **Sarai said unto Abram, Behold now, the LORD hath restrained me from bearing: I pray thee, go in unto my maid; it may be that I may obtain children by her**. And Abram hearkened to the voice of Sarai.*

*3 And **Sarai Abram's wife took Hagar her maid the Egyptian, after Abram had dwelt ten years in the land of Canaan, and gave her to her husband Abram to be his wife.***

*4 And **he went in unto Hagar, and she conceived: and when she saw that she had conceived, her mistress was despised in her eyes.***

*5 And **Sarai said unto Abram, My wrong be upon thee:** I have given my maid into thy bosom; and when she saw that she had conceived, I was despised in her eyes: the LORD judge between me and thee.*

*6 But **Abram said unto Sarai, Behold, thy maid is in thy hand; do to her as it pleaseth thee. And when Sarai dealt hardly with her, she fled from her face.***

INTRODUCTORY THOUGHTS

Most problems have multiple solutions, yet some of the solutions yield newer and greater problems. Abram and Sarai knew the Lord wanted to give them a son. All they needed to do was to trust God to accomplish what He had promised. The problem—Sarai bare Abram no children. Instead of seeking the Lord for the proper solution to the problem, Sarai conceived what she believed to be a good plan. She wanted her maid Hagar to bare a son for them. This solution was indeed a solution to the problem, but it was not God's solution. Hagar had a son, but this son turned out to be a thorn in the flesh of Abram and Sarai's son Isaac. The problems resulting from their solution have lingered for millennia and continue to this day.

DEVOTIONAL THOUGHTS

- **(For children):** When Saul failed to wait for Samuel to make a sacrifice before going to battle, he brought problems on his own household *(1 Samuel 13:8-14; 1 Samuel 31:1-2, 6).*

- **(For everyone):** What problems did Abram and Sarai have before introducing Hagar into their solution? What new problems arose because of their decision to have a son through Hagar?
- What should Abram and Sarai have done in order to find a proper solution? What would likely have been the solution given by the Lord? Would God's solution have created these new problems?

Prayer Thoughts

- Ask God to show you new problems caused by your self-conceived solutions.
- Ask the Lord to show you His solutions to your problems.

SONG: *WHERE HE LEADS I'LL FOLLOW*

Day 193: Church Night

Proverbs 15:18 A wrathful man stirreth up strife: but he that is slow to anger appeaseth strife.

Day 194: (Thursday)
Solutions Are Not Always Easy

*Numbers 16:23 And **the LORD spake unto Moses**, saying,*

*24 **Speak unto the congregation, saying, Get you up from about the tabernacle of Korah, Dathan, and Abiram.***

*25 And **Moses** rose up and went unto Dathan and Abiram; and the elders of Israel followed him.*

*26 And he **spake unto the congregation, saying, Depart, I pray you, from the tents of these wicked men, and touch nothing of theirs, lest ye be consumed in all their sins.***

*27 **So they gat up from the tabernacle of Korah, Dathan, and Abiram, on every side**: and Dathan and Abiram came out, and stood in the door of their tents, and their wives, and their sons, and their little children.*

Introductory Thoughts

Sometimes the right decisions are the easiest to see and the most difficult to make. In the case of Korah's rebellion, many of the people at that time recognized the ease of making the right decision. The person who understood and saw God's impending judgment knew that the only proper solution was the one offered by the Lord—separate from the tents of the rebels. The proper solution was also quite easy to perform. However, there were many family members of these men involved in the rebellion who had to make a difficult choice. The solution was made known unto them, the details were clear, but their choices were not easy. Why? The right decision involved walking away from a father and family whom they may have loved dearly. According to the psalms, at least some of the sons of Korah chose to do the right thing and separate from their family.

DEVOTIONAL THOUGHTS

- **(For children):** King Asa wanted to serve the Lord. To do so, he had to make a choice that was not easy *(1 Kings 15:11, 13)*. The widow woman made a difficult decision when asked to give away her last meal. God blessed her for it *(1 Kings 17:8-16)*.
- **(For everyone):** What determines whether or not something is a right solution? Does ease of choice determine the scriptural nature of a solution? Is the proper solution always easy?
- Put yourself in the place of Korah's sons. What would have crossed your mind in deciding whether or not to walk away from your father? How did God bless their choice to do right?

PRAYER THOUGHTS

- Ask the Lord to give you courage to choose right.
- Thank God for giving you understanding as to right solutions.

SONG: *AM I A SOLDIER OF THE CROSS?*

Day 195: (Friday)
The Necessity of Patience

Genesis 8:1 And God remembered Noah, and every living thing, and all the cattle that was with him in the ark: and **God made a wind to pass over the earth, and the waters asswaged;**

2 The fountains also of the deep and the windows of heaven were stopped, and the rain from heaven was restrained;

☐ Completion Date   Resolution (con't) • 227

3 And the waters returned from off the earth continually: **and after the end of the hundred and fifty days the waters were abated.**

4 And the ark rested in the seventh month, on the seventeenth day of the month, upon the mountains of Ararat.

5 And the waters decreased continually until the tenth month: in the tenth month, on the first day of the month, were the tops of the mountains seen.

6 And **it came to pass at the end of forty days, that Noah opened the window of the ark which he had made***:*

7 And **he sent forth a raven, which went forth to and fro, until the waters were dried up from off the earth.**

8 **Also he sent forth a dove from him, to see if the waters were abated from off the face of the ground;**

9 But the dove found no rest for the sole of her foot, and she returned unto him into the ark, for the waters were on the face of the whole earth: then he put forth his hand, and took her, and pulled her in unto him into the ark.

10 And **he stayed yet other seven days; and again he sent forth the dove out of the ark***;*

11 And **the dove came in to him in the evening; and, lo, in her mouth was an olive leaf pluckt off: so Noah knew that the waters were abated from off the earth.**

12 And **he stayed yet other seven days***; and sent forth the dove; which returned not again unto him any more.*

13 And it came to pass in the six hundredth and first year, in the first month, the first day of the month, the waters were dried up from off the earth: and Noah removed the covering of the ark, and looked, and, behold, the face of the ground was dry.

14 And in the second month, on the seven and twentieth day of the month, was the earth dried.

Introductory Thoughts

Oftentimes the right solutions do not resolve the problems overnight—consider Noah, the ark, and the flood. Patience is a necessity! They all knew God's plan involved drying the earth and sending them forth from the ark. No doubt, each passing day made it increasingly difficult to wait upon the Lord to resolve the problem that kept them locked in the ark. A man who demands a hasty solution to his problems often fails to find God's ultimate solution. God's solutions almost always require time and patience. The problems arose over a period of time and finding their solutions takes time also. The areas of life where troubles most often appear (i.e., sin, family, job, finances) are rarely solved apart from time and patience.

DEVOTIONAL THOUGHTS

- **(For children):** The book of James tells us that Job went through his trouble with patience *(James 5:11)*. Even though he did not understand why his problems came upon him, he waited for God to answer and he is an example for us. Read *Job 1:20-22; Job 2:9-10*.
- **(For everyone):** What problems are you currently facing? Is there a solution that would solve the problem but require patience? Are you willing to exercise the necessary patience to solve your problems?
- How could hasty solutions create new problems? Why do we often desire quick, easy solutions rather than godly solutions that may not offer immediate gratification?

PRAYER THOUGHTS

- Ask the Lord to increase your patience.
- Ask God for wisdom in problem solving.

SONG: *BE STILL, MY SOUL*

Day 196: (Saturday)
God Uses Problems

*Genesis 13:5 And **Lot** also, which **went with Abram**, had flocks, and herds, and tents.*

*6 **And the land was not able to bear them, that they might dwell together: for their substance was great, so that they could not dwell together.***

*7 And **there was a strife between the herdmen of Abram's cattle and the herdmen of Lot's cattle**: and the Canaanite and the Perizzite dwelled then in the land.*

☐ Completion Date   Resolution (con't) • 229

*8 And **Abram said unto Lot, Let there be no strife**, I pray thee, between me and thee, and between my herdmen and thy herdmen; for we be brethren.*

*9 Is not the whole land before thee? **separate thyself, I pray thee, from me: if thou wilt take the left hand, then I will go to the right; or if thou depart to the right hand, then I will go to the left.***

10 And Lot lifted up his eyes, and beheld all the plain of Jordan, that it was well watered every where, before the LORD destroyed Sodom and Gomorrah, even as the garden of the LORD, like the land of Egypt, as thou comest unto Zoar.

*11 Then **Lot chose him all the plain of Jordan**; and Lot journeyed east: and they separated themselves the one from the other.*

*12 **Abram dwelled in the land of Canaan**, and Lot dwelled in the cities of the plain, and pitched his tent toward Sodom.*

13 But the men of Sodom were wicked and sinners before the LORD exceedingly.

*14 **And the LORD said unto Abram, after that Lot was separated from him, Lift up now thine eyes, and look from the place where thou art northward, and southward, and eastward, and westward:***

*15 **For all the land which thou seest, to thee will I give it, and to thy seed for ever.***

16 And I will make thy seed as the dust of the earth: so that if a man can number the dust of the earth, then shall thy seed also be numbered.

17 Arise, walk through the land in the length of it and in the breadth of it; for I will give it unto thee.

18 Then Abram removed his tent, and came and dwelt in the plain of Mamre, which is in Hebron, and built there an altar unto the LORD.

Introductory Thoughts

God often allows problems to enter people's lives in order to facilitate His initial plans. For example, God had already expressed His desire to Abram for him to separate from his kindred. For various reasons, Abram had not obeyed God up until this point. In order to bring about God's desired will, He allowed conflict to enter between the herdmen of Abram and those of Lot. The solution to this unnecessary conflict was quite simple. Abram suggested that they part ways (God's initial plan) and Abram turned toward the land of Canaan (God's initial plan). The Lord used the same tactic in the early church to get them to spread out and to preach His word outside of Jerusalem (see *Acts 1:8* and *Acts 8:1*).

DEVOTIONAL THOUGHTS

- **(For children)**: The apostle Paul wrote several epistles from prison, one of which was Philippians. Read what he had to say about his problems *(Philippians 1:12-14)*. John was in prison and wrote the book of Revelation *(Revelation 1:9, 19)*. Joseph's problems eventually enabled him to save his own brethren *(Genesis 50:20-21)*.
- **(For everyone)**: What was God's will for Abram? What could have happened had the problem not come along between the herdmen of Abram and those of Lot?
- Has God ever allowed problems to enter your life only to bring about His desired will as part of the solution? How does this demonstrate God's love and wisdom?

PRAYER THOUGHTS

- Ask the Lord to help you see His plan in your problems.
- Thank God for sending problems that bring about His will.

SONG: *TRUSTING JESUS*

Quotes from the next volume
(VOLUME 4, WEEK 28)

Subject: Suffering and Death (con't)

As man's decision maker, the soul is the part of man that will live for all eternity in heaven *(2 Corinthians 5:8)* or exist forever in hell *(Luke 16:23)*.

A man's body is the house or dwelling place for his soul and his spirit.

The Bible is the mind of God. As such, it frequently presents things from a perspective contrary to the common line of thinking and teaching.

29

Communication

Communication—found forty-six times in forty-five verses; Communication can involve financial giving, but these studies focus upon communication as it pertains to one's words.

Variations: commune, communed, communicate, communicated, communication, communications, communing, communion

First usage: *Genesis 18:33* (communing)

Last usage: *Hebrews 13:16* (communicate)

Defined: to make something common

Interesting fact: Some Bible teachers have suggested that the early church practiced a form of communism in that *"they had all things common" (Acts 4:32)*. This is just simply not the case! In fact, financial communication (amongst believers) was never forced upon any of the believers by a government entity or by the apostles. Rather, financial communication was a personal choice on the part of each individual believer so it cannot be classified as a form of communism *(Galatians 6:6; Philippians 4:14-15; 1 Timothy 6:18)*.

Bible study tip: Every English student understands that phrases like *"God's righteousness"* can also be understood as the *"righteousness of God"* **(Romans 10:3)**. However, in the scriptures, that rule does not always apply. For instance, *"the Lord's day"* **(Revelation 1:10)** spoken of by the apostle John in Revelation does not refer to *"the day of the LORD"* as prophesied by many of God's messengers **(Zechariah 14:1)**.

Sunday, Day 197—Church Day (no devotional)
Monday, Day 198—*Communication Makes Common*
Tuesday, Day 199—*Straight from the Heart*
Wednesday, Day 200—Church Night (no devotional)
Thursday, Day 201—*Communication Yields Words*
Friday, Day 202—*God Desires Our Communication*
Saturday, Day 203—*The World Needs Our Communication*

Day 197: Church Day

Colossians 3:8 *But now ye also **put off** all these; anger, wrath, malice, blasphemy, **filthy communication out of your mouth**.*

Day 198: (Monday)
Communication Makes Common

Psalm 77:6 *I call to remembrance my song in the night: **I commune with mine own heart**: and **my spirit made diligent search**.*

Introductory Thoughts

To communicate is to make something common. Communication can be accomplished in a variety of fashions. Communication can be between (1) an individual and his or her heart, (2) a person and the Lord, or (3) two or more people. According to **Psalm 77:6**, to commune with someone or something is to make *"diligent search."* This thought may seem a bit foreign or odd today, but consider what takes place when people communicate. When someone communicates, words or thoughts are exchanged. Since words or thoughts originate in the heart **(Matthew 12:34)**, communication is the searching and revealing of the heart. Communication discovers and makes known things of the heart to both participants.

Devotional Thoughts

- **(For children):** Naomi's daughters-in-law were both going back to Bethlehem with her. She did not really know how they felt about continuing with her until she communicated with them. Orpah, then, did not go, but Ruth communicated what was in her heart *(Ruth 1:8-18)*.
- **(For everyone):** Why is it crucial that people know how to communicate with others? What problems can arise when families, friends, coworkers, or brothers and sisters in Christ fail to communicate with one another?
- What is in the heart of your loved ones? What troubles them? What causes them to rejoice? How could you discover these things? Why is it important for you to know about these things?

Prayer Thoughts

- Ask God to teach you to communicate with others.
- Ask the Lord to teach you how to communicate with Him.

SONG: *MY HEART'S THE SEAT OF WAR*

Day 199: (Tuesday)
Straight from the Heart

Psalm 4:4 *Stand in awe, and sin not:* **commune with your own heart** *upon your bed, and be still. Selah.*

Introductory Thoughts

It is very important that a man learns his spiritual heart condition. The Bible characterizes man's heart as being naturally full of lies and deception *(Jeremiah 17:9)*. A man cannot afford to leave off communication with his heart because he needs to find the truth of what lies within. Many fail to commune with their own hearts for fear of what they might discover. The psalmist was so concerned about this communication that he sought God's help in searching his heart to determine its contents *(Psalm 139:23-24)*. The idea of communing with one's own heart might seem absurd to some people, but it is scriptural and imperative (see ***Psalm 77:6; Psalm 4:4***). In fact, this communication aids in every other form of communication.

Devotional Thoughts

- **(For children):** God forgave David for many evil things including that of murder. When David's son Absalom murdered his brother Amnon, Absalom fled from David's presence for three years *(2 Samuel 13:37-39)*. When David allowed Absalom to return home, David waited an additional two years before seeing him *(2 Samuel 14:1, 21-24, 28)*. The end result of David and Absalom's failure to communicate was disastrous. Had David communicated with Absalom, he might have seen what was in Absalom's heart, enabling David to help Absalom.
- **(For everyone):** What is in your heart? Are you bitter? Are you envious of the wicked? Why is it important that you be able to commune with your own heart?
- What happens when we cease to communicate with our own hearts? How does that allow the heart to convince us that everything is alright when in reality it is not?

Prayer Thoughts

- Ask God to teach you to commune with your own heart.
- Ask the Lord to reveal the wickedness that resides within your heart.

SONG: *CLEANSE ME*

Day 200: Church Night

*Matthew 5:37 But **let your communication be, Yea, yea; Nay, nay**: for **whatsoever is more than these cometh of evil**.*

Day 201: (Thursday)
Communication Yields Words

*Job 4:2 If **we assay to commune** with thee, wilt thou be grieved? but who can withhold himself from speaking?*

Introductory Thoughts

All of today's gadgets have caused the world to lack the basic communication skills necessary to properly function. Communication takes place through various means but is most frequently accomplished by the articulation of words between two or more people. Often in scripture, the words *commune* and *communication* are followed by the word *say-*

ing which suggests that communication generally involves one person speaking to another person. The more a society or an individual experiences a breakdown in their understanding of words, the more they will experience a breakdown in communication. When the individuals within society grow up without face-to-face interaction with other people, that society will lack the ability to communicate. Ultimately, this hinders every facet of life.

Devotional Thoughts

- **(For children):** For three years, Daniel and his friends competed with others to determine who might be the best to serve in the king's palace. In order to win, they had to be able to effectively communicate *(Daniel 1:18-20)*. Jonathan *communed* with Saul when trying to change Saul's mind about killing David *(1 Samuel 19:2-7)*.
- **(For everyone):** Do you have trouble communicating with others, especially face-to-face using words? Why? Are you able to convey the thoughts of your heart with others using spoken words or do you depend upon society's gadgets?
- What has greatly hindered our ability to communicate with others? How does this weaken our ability to stand when confronted with wickedness?

Prayer Thoughts

- Ask the Lord to give you boldness to communicate.
- Ask God to teach you what communication is.

SONG: *PRECIOUS PROMISE*

Day 202: (Friday)
God Desires Our Communication

*Exodus 25:22 And there I will meet with thee, and **I will commune with thee** from above the mercy seat, from between the two cherubims which are upon the ark of the testimony, of all things which I will give thee in commandment unto the children of Israel.*

Introductory Thoughts

Since the garden in Eden, God has longed for fellowship with the very people He created *(Genesis 3:8)*. In fact, one of the great reasons

God desires for people to learn to communicate with others is so they can, in turn, understand how to better communicate with Him. Communication with God takes place in two major forms. Man communicates with God through prayer. Prayer can take place simply within one's heart or verbally but can only be accomplished when a man conveys his thoughts or concerns to the Lord. God, on the other hand, communicates with man through the scriptures. Before Eve, communication existed between a man (Adam) and his God. Even in eternity, it appears that the greatest form of communication will exist between God and the redeemed.

Devotional Thoughts

- **(For children):** God invites you to talk with Him *(Jeremiah 33:3)*. His ears are open to you *(Psalm 34:15)*. The apostle Paul encouraged people to pray anytime *(1 Thessalonians 5:17)*. Always be truthful with the Lord *(Psalm 51:6; Psalm 145:18)*.
- **(For everyone):** Do you struggle to communicate with the Lord in prayer? Do you find it difficult to convey the burdens of your heart? What hinders you from being able to communicate with God?
- What kind of communication takes place in your home? How can this affect the ability of your family to communicate with God?

Prayer Thoughts

- Thank God for His desire to communicate with you.
- Ask God to give you a longing to talk to Him on a daily basis.

SONG: *COME UNTO ME (JONES)*

Day 203: (Saturday)
The World Needs Our Communication

***Philemon 6** That **the communication of thy faith** may become effectual by the acknowledging of every good thing which is in you in Christ Jesus.*

Introductory Thoughts

God has called the saved to be His ambassadors *(2 Corinthians 5:20)*, and as such, Christians are to take God's truth to a lost and dying world. This message must be communicated. Due mostly to man's ever

☐ Completion Date | Communication • 237

increasing dependence upon technology, Christians have lost their effectiveness in communicating with others. This may seem insignificant, until one considers how it has weakened our ability to communicate our faith. Fewer people today will knock on a door and tell a stranger that he must be born again. Even fewer will stand upon a street corner and communicate the words of God to those who pass by. The saved must once again become willing to go forth and tell family and stranger alike that Jesus saves.

Devotional Thoughts

- **(For children):** In *Psalm 89:1*, the psalmist said he would use his mouth to tell what God had done for him. We should not fear for God is with us *(Isaiah 41:13)*. Read some of the examples from the book of Acts of people who used their mouths for the Lord *(Acts 5:18-21; Acts 8:35; Acts 16:32; Acts 18:26)*.
- **(For everyone):** Are you saved? If so, do you ever communicate the gospel to those who do not know Jesus as their Saviour? Are you ashamed of the gospel of Christ *(Romans 1:16)*?
- What hinders you from telling others about what the Lord has done in your life? Why are you so fearful of telling them that Jesus Christ came to die for their sins?

Prayer Thoughts

- Ask the Lord to conquer your fears so you can witness to others.
- Ask God to teach you how to communicate your faith.

SONG: *NEVER BE AFRAID*

Notes: _____

Notes:

Quotes from the next volume

(VOLUME 4, WEEK 29)

Subject: Profanity

The words that enter a man's ears eventually fill his heart and mind with thoughts of good or bad. It is, therefore, crucial that a man guards not only the words that exit his mouth but also the words that enter his ears.

As ambassadors for Christ, it is imperative that believers speak only those things which are righteous and becoming of the gospel of Christ.

The world consistently blasphemes the name of the Lord. To them, God's name is nothing more than a word to be included in their cursing.

30

Chastening or Punishment

Chastening or Punishment—found 137 times in 122 verses

Variations: chasten, chastened, chastenest, chasteneth, chastening, chastise, chastised, chastisement, chastiseth, punish, punished, punishment, punishments, unpunished

First usage: *Genesis 4:13* (punishment)

Last usage: *Revelation 3:19* (chasten)

Defined: Though punishment and chastening are considered by some to be identical, there appears to be a great diversity between the two. *Punishment* seems to be the infliction of a penalty upon another individual. *Chastening*, on the other hand, emphasizes the correction of inappropriate behaviour.

Interesting fact: A form of the word *punish* appears nine times in nine New Testament verses. Of these nine occurrences, only four of them reference punishment from the Lord to men *(Matthew 25:46; 2 Thessalonians 1:9; Hebrews 10:29; 2 Peter 2:9)*. These four instances speak of God's judgment toward those who refuse to trust Christ for salvation. At least in the New Testament, the judgment of God's people is never identified as punishment but always as chastening.

This is vitally important when studying the context of Hebrews chapter 10.

Bible study tip: The study of scripture can be divided into three primary applications: (1) practical or devotional, (2) historical, and (3) doctrinal (including prophetic). It is likely *2 Timothy 3:16* links the historical and doctrinal applications together as *doctrine*. The practical application is identified as *reproof, correction, and instruction in righteousness*. Though practical or devotional applications of Bible study are godly and important, they should never neglect the historical or doctrinal applications of study.

Sunday, Day 204—Church Day (no devotional)
Monday, Day 205—*Chastening or Punishment*
Tuesday, Day 206—*The Recipients of Punishment*
Wednesday, Day 207—Church Night (no devotional)
Thursday, Day 208—*The Recipients of Chastening*
Friday, Day 209—*The Proofs of Chastening*
Saturday, Day 210—*The Purpose of Chastening*

Day 204: Church Day

Proverbs 3:11 My son, **despise not the chastening of the LORD; neither be weary of his correction:**

Day 205: (Monday)
Chastening or Punishment

Leviticus 26:24 Then will I also walk contrary unto you, and **will punish you yet seven times for your sins.**
28 Then I will walk contrary unto you also in fury; and I, even I, **will chastise you seven times for your sins.**

INTRODUCTORY THOUGHTS

The words *chastening* and *punishment* are like many Bible words that share an overlapping meaning but also exhibit certain variants. A

Bible-believer always trusts that God carefully chose His words to accomplish His expressed purpose in any given passage. On the surface, it would seem like the words *punish (Leviticus 26:24)* and *chastise (Leviticus 26:28)* seem completely interchangeable, but a thorough study of the whole counsel of God reveals distinctions. One area in which there appears to be a distinction involves the intended purpose of execution. Punishment is the infliction of judgment for the sake of *justice*, while chastening is the application of judgment for the sake of *correction*.

Devotional Thoughts

- **(For children):** The thieves crucified on either side of Jesus were being justly punished *(Luke 23:39-41)*. Jonah wanted the Ninevites destroyed. Read what God used to chastise Jonah and what He said to correct Jonah's wrong attitude (see Jonah chapter 4).
- **(For everyone):** Why is it important for Bible students to study any differences that may exist between the words *punish* and *chastise*? Do you currently know of any differences that exist?
- Why does God punish? Why does He chasten? Why should believers want to know the purpose of each? How can that information make us better Christians?

Prayer Thoughts

- Ask God to teach you the meaning and purpose of chastening.
- Ask the Lord to help you do right at all times.

SONG: *AFFLICTIONS DO NOT COME ALONE*

Day 206: (Tuesday)
The Recipients of Punishment

*Genesis 4:13 And **Cain said** unto the LORD, **My punishment** is greater than I can bear.*

Introductory Thoughts

In the most basic sense, punishment is directed toward those who have done wrong. Though any particular punishment may seem harsh by those receiving the punishment, God intended it to be a calculated response toward wrongdoing. Though there are some passages in the Old Testament that indicate punishment was directed toward the people of God *(Ezra 9:13; Hosea 12:2)*, the vast majority of references demonstrate that it was intended for the enemies of God *(Psalm 149:7; Proverbs 11:21; Isaiah 10:12; Isaiah 13:11; Isaiah 24:21; Isaiah 26:21; Isaiah 27:1; Jeremiah 25:12; Jeremiah 46:25)*. A careful study of the New Testament will strengthen the distinction as there are no references to God punishing His people.

DEVOTIONAL THOUGHTS

- **(For children)**: The Bible points out that those who are not saved are ungodly and are God's enemies *(Romans 5:6, 8, 10)*. If they die without accepting God's plan of salvation, they will be forever punished *(2 Thessalonians 1:7-9; Revelation 21:7-8)*.
- **(For everyone)**: Why would there be no references to God punishing His people in the New Testament? Why would the shed blood of Christ eliminate and negate the implementation of punishment for the saints of God?
- Look up the word *punish* and its various forms in the New Testament. When will God punish the wicked? How long will their punishment last?

PRAYER THOUGHTS

- If saved, thank God that you will not know His punishment.
- If lost, ask God to open your eyes to your need for salvation.

SONG: *RESCUE THE PERISHING*

Day 207: Church Night

Proverbs 11:21 Though hand join in hand, **the wicked shall not be unpunished**: but the seed of the righteous shall be delivered.

Day 208: (Thursday)
The Recipients of Chastening

Deuteronomy 8:5 Thou shalt also consider in thine heart, that, **as a man chasteneth his son, so the LORD thy God chasteneth thee**.

Introductory Thoughts

Chastening is best associated to a parent-child relationship *(Deuteronomy 8:5; 2 Samuel 7:14; Proverbs 13:24; Proverbs 19:18; Hebrews 12:6-8)*. As such, God's chastening, at least within the New Testament, is only intended for those He calls His sons *(1 John 3:2)*. God chastens His children, not to administer justice, but to strengthen and correct them. The believer does not receive some type of punishment from the Lord resulting from the believer's sins because these sins have been completely atoned through the shed blood of Christ. However, the saint's continued practice of sin requires the chastening hand of the Lord in order to conform him into the image of Christ. While chastening is reserved exclusively for sons, a lost man receives only punishment or salvation.

Devotional Thoughts

- **(For children):** Children need to be taught the truth so they can make wise choices between good and evil *(1 Peter 2:2; Hebrews 5:14)*. When you choose the wrong, you need to be corrected. Your correction is that of a child being corrected and you certainly remain a member of your family and very much loved. Consider these verses and be grateful that dad and mom care for you: ***Proverbs 22:15; Proverbs 23:13-14***.
- **(For everyone):** Why is it a blessing to know that chastening rather than punishment is the product of being a believer? What does this suggest about God's purpose in dealing with you?
- If chastening is meted out by the Lord as a Father to a son, how should you react to His chastening? How can you be grateful in the midst of His chastening?

Prayer Thoughts

- Thank God for His chastening.
- Ask the Lord to help you see the blessings of chastening.

SONG: *AMIDST THY WRATH REMEMBER LOVE*

Day 209: (Friday)
The Proofs of Chastening

*Hebrews 12:6 For **whom the Lord loveth he chasteneth, and scourgeth every son whom he receiveth.***

*7 **If ye endure chastening, God dealeth with you as with sons;** for what son is he whom the father chasteneth not?*

*8 But **if ye be without chastisement,** whereof all are partakers, **then are ye bastards, and not sons.***

INTRODUCTORY THOUGHTS

Chastening is not merely a means of judgment implemented by the Lord for wrongdoing, but also serves as a proof of sonship. According to **Hebrews 12:6**, at some point in every child of God's life, he will experience the chastening hand of the Lord. Any individual able to freely do wrong without God's chastening should examine whether or not he is in the faith. The absence of chastening suggests that a person is not a son of God **(Hebrews 12:8)**. Just as any good father will not allow his son to get away with wrongdoing, God the Father does not allow His children to do wrong without suffering the consequences of such actions. Chastisement may be delayed, but it is inevitable.

DEVOTIONAL THOUGHTS

- **(For children):** When we get saved, we become sons of God **(John 1:12)**. God chastens us out of love because we are sons **(Proverbs 3:11-12)**.
- **(For everyone):** How can someone become a son of God? What is the eternal destination of someone who is born again? Why is it a blessing that the Lord offers proofs of sonship for the believer?
- Upon what is God's chastening based **(Revelation 3:19)**? What should we gather from the fact that God chastens us when we sin against His law?

PRAYER THOUGHTS

- Ask the Lord to show you His love through chastening.
- Thank God for caring enough to correct you when wrong.

SONG: *BREAK FORTH, O JOYFUL HEART*

Day 210: (Saturday)
The Purpose of Chastening

*Hebrews 12:10 For **they verily for a few days chastened us after their own pleasure; but he for our profit, that we might be partakers of his holiness**.*

Introductory Thoughts

Earthly parents sometimes chasten their children according to their own pleasure, but the Lord chastens His children ONLY for their profiting. In addition, earthly parents will sometimes err by disciplining their children for convenience to end the child's inconvenience brought upon the parent. The end goal turns out to be the satisfaction of the parent rather than the sole good of the child. However, in God's dealings with His children, He chastens for the benefit of the one receiving the chastening. He uses His chastening to help make His children partakers of His holiness. When they have done wrong, He wants them to repent *(Revelation 3:19)*. When they have gone astray, He wants them to find correction *(Job 5:17)*. God, as a Father, always chooses to do what is best for His children. It is always exclusively for their profit!

Devotional Thoughts

- **(For children):** God had to chasten Jonah for his disobedience. Jonah then repented and obeyed *(Jonah 1:1-3, 17; Jonah 2:1-2; Jonah 3:1-3)*. Zacharias was chastised for not believing God's promise *(Luke 1:13, 18-20, 57-64)*. God chastens us so we will learn to keep His word *(Psalm 94:12; Psalm 119:67)*.
- **(For everyone):** What are some reasons your earthly father had for chastening you in the past? What was his motive? How is this different from God's chastening?
- How does God's chastening make you better? How can His chastening be profitable for you? What happens if He refuses to chasten you?

Prayer Thoughts

- Ask God to teach you the benefits of chastening.
- Ask God to help you see how chastening is an act of love.

SONG: *COME, THOU FOUNT OF EVERY BLESSING*

Notes:

Quotes from the next volume

(VOLUME 4, WEEK 30)

Subject: Government and Nations

There are many nations led by many leaders, but there is only one *"whose name alone is JEHOVAH,"* and He it is that is *"the most high over all the earth"* **(Psalm 83:18)**.

Military might, a sound economy, a good job market, and great leadership will offer no resistance once the Lord has set His mind against any nation.

Only one nation (Israel) holds a promise from God that it will never be utterly destroyed; every other nation must fervently guard its affairs to ensure its continued and future existence.

31
Chastening or Punishment (con't)

Chastening or Punishment—found 116 times in 102 Old Testament verses and twenty-one times in twenty New Testament verses

Variations: chasten, chastened, chastenest, chasteneth, chastening, chastise, chastised, chastisement, chastiseth, punish, punished, punishment, punishments, unpunished

Last usage in the Old Testament: *Zechariah 14:19* (punishment)

First usage in the New Testament: *Matthew 25:46* (punishment)

Interesting fact: The book of Jeremiah contains various forms of *chasten* and *punish* twenty-six times in twenty-one verses. This frequency is more than any other book of the Bible and more than the entire New Testament combined. This should not be surprising for those familiar with the circumstances and message of Jeremiah's ministry.

Bible study tip: When studying Old Testament history, especially the times of the kings and prophets, a good Bible student identifies the kings associated with the ministries of various prophets and vice versa. This study provides additional context into the times and circumstances of any given period of time.

Sunday, Day 211—Church Day (no devotional)
Monday, Day 212—*The Motive of Chastening*
Tuesday, Day 213—*The Product of Chastening*
Wednesday, Day 214—Church Night (no devotional)
Thursday, Day 215—*The Proper Reaction to Chastening*
Friday, Day 216—*Proper Discipline in the Home*
Saturday, Day 217—*Proper Discipline in the Church*

Day 211: Church Day

*Psalm 38:1 O LORD, rebuke me not in thy wrath: **neither chasten me in thy hot displeasure**.*

Day 212: (Monday)
The Motive of Chastening

*Hebrews 12:6 For **whom the Lord loveth he chasteneth**, and scourgeth every son whom he receiveth.*

INTRODUCTORY THOUGHTS

One who has little understanding of chastening might suggest that God's chastening is an act born of hatred, but it actually represents an overflowing love from the heart of God. God expresses His motives for chastening His children in **Hebrews 12:6** when He says, *"For whom the Lord loveth he chasteneth."* Again in **Revelation 3:19** the Lord says, *"As many as I love, I rebuke and chasten."* This again displays a distinction between punishment and chastening. The source of punishment could be construed as anger, justice, or wrath, but the motive of true biblical chastening involves the purest form of love. This means that chastening does not merely benefit the one implementing the chastening, but takes place for the good of the one chastened.

Devotional Thoughts

- **(For children):** Would you want your parents to love or hate you? Love involves chastening *(Proverbs 13:24)*. You do not like it at the time, but you need it when you misbehave *(Proverbs 15:10)*. God and your parents would always rather see you do right *(Lamentations 3:33)*.
- **(For everyone):** If chastening is an act of love, how could you identify those in your life who have truly loved you? Who would you list as ones who have loved you the most when considering chastening?
- Has God ever chastened you? How does the truth that chastening is founded upon love change how you feel about anytime in the past when you were chastened? What does it suggest about your relationship with God?

Prayer Thoughts

- Thank God for loving you enough to chasten you.
- Ask the Lord to give you the proper attitude toward chastening.

SONG: *BE STILL, MY SOUL*

Day 213: (Tuesday)
The Product of Chastening

Hebrews 12:11 Now **no chastening for the present seemeth to be joyous, but grievous: nevertheless afterward it yieldeth the peaceable fruit of righteousness unto them which are exercised thereby.**

Introductory Thoughts

God designed and intended for biblical chastening to have righteousness as its intended outcome. Recipients of chastening may find the process grievous, but *"afterward it yieldeth the peaceable fruit of righteousness unto them which are exercised thereby."* The process may not be at all enjoyable or peaceable, yet the Bible affirms that the outcome is peace. A careful look at the word *chasten* provides this insight. The root word for *chasten* is the word *chaste*. The end goal for those being chastened is that they would become chaste. Chastening is intended to be a purification process that corrects the wrongs for which it was initially implemented. It always leaves the recipient that endures the chastening a stronger and purer person than before the process began.

DEVOTIONAL THOUGHTS
- **(For children)**: God wants us to have the right desires *(Proverbs 11:23)*. This is done through knowing and obeying His word *(Psalm 119:138; Psalm 19:8, 11)*. When we sin, God wants our hearts to get right with Him. This is accomplished through chastening *(Psalm 119:67, 71)*.
- **(For everyone)**: Have you ever experienced the chastening of the Lord for a particular sin? What was the outcome of the chastening? Did you end up closer to God as an end result?
- Do you think that anyone considers the process of chastening to be enjoyable? Would you consider the end result to be worth any troubles faced by the process?

PRAYER THOUGHTS
- Ask the Lord to give you a deeper understanding of chastening.
- Ask God to help you see His desired outcome of chastening.

SONG: *AFFLICTIONS, THOUGH THEY SEEM SEVERE*

Day 214: Church Night

Psalm 94:12 Blessed is the man whom thou chastenest, O LORD, and teachest him out of thy law;

Day 215: (Thursday)
The Proper Reaction to Chastening

Revelation 3:19 As many as I love, I rebuke and chasten: **be zealous therefore, and repent.**

INTRODUCTORY THOUGHTS

Even though God's motive and desired outcome of chastening both prove to be a blessing to believers, believers do not always react properly to the chastening hand of the Lord. Some respond to God's chastening by becoming bitter against the Lord, frustrated that they are reaping what they have sown. Others respond by becoming weary from the pressures of the process of chastening. Yet others might respond by running away from the things of God once they realize that God wants them to grow beyond their present level of Christianity. None of these are the proper reaction to chastening. The only proper response to chastening is given in **Revelation 3:19**: *"be zealous therefore, and repent."*

Devotional Thoughts

- **(For children):** Read *Isaiah 26:16*. Chastening helps us to turn back to the Lord and be sorry for our sin. Consider David's attitude. He admitted his sin *(Psalm 51:1-3)*; he did not want to do it again *(Psalm 51:10)*; he wanted to teach others not to sin *(Psalm 51:13)*.
- **(For everyone):** What happens if we have the wrong response to God's chastening? How could it actually yield additional measures of chastening?
- How do you initially respond to chastening? Do you find yourself offended that God would chasten you? How long does it take for you to decide to repent and conform to God's plan for your life?

Prayer Thoughts

- Ask God to help you respond properly to chastening.
- Ask the Lord to help you desire His will for your life.

SONG: *TAKE MY LIFE, AND LET IT BE*

Day 216: (Friday)
Proper Discipline in the Home

Proverbs 19:18 Chasten thy son while there is hope, *and let not thy soul spare for his crying.*

Introductory Thoughts

Far too often what is done in the home under the guise of chastening is far from God's scriptural pattern of discipline. This is nothing new. According to *Hebrews 12:10*, the Jewish fathers were guilty of chastening their children *"after their own pleasure."* Two major problems commonly surface in the discipline implemented in the home: (1) the reason for correction and (2) the motive in correction. According to God's pattern, parents should never discipline their children because of an annoyance but because of a direct violation of a known law. This is God's way and should be the consistent practice of godly parents. In addition to this, godly parents should follow God's pattern and chasten in love for the sake of the child.

Devotional Thoughts

- **(For children)**: In *Psalm 89:30-33*, God Himself tells us the proper reason for disciplining. It also reminds us that through it all, God loves us.
- **(For everyone):** Do you have any children? What drives you to correct them? Do you only offer chastening when they get on your nerves? Do you correct them because they upset you? Are these proper reasons?
- How could the balance in reasoning for chastening and motive in chastening solve the problems with child abuse or the absence of disciplining altogether?

Prayer Thoughts

- Ask God to strengthen your home with biblical principles.
- Thank the Lord for a godly home where love is prominent.

SONG: *O! TO BE LIKE THEE*

Day 217: (Saturday)
Proper Discipline in the Church

***Galatians 6:1** Brethren, if a man be overtaken in a fault, ye which are spiritual, restore such an one in the spirit of meekness; considering thyself, lest thou also be tempted.*

Introductory Thoughts

Church discipline has commonly taken place under one of two extremes. It is either nonexistent or overused. Church discipline, however, is intended to be one of God's methods of chastening. Before weak and unscriptural churches became so prevalent, those disciplined by one body of believers would not be readily accepted into another congregation while in a state of rebellion. Issues had to be settled and hearts made right. People had to repent and seek restoration. Discipline was implemented not only for the purity of the body, but also so that those who had gone astray might repent and find true restoration amongst the body. God used this chastening to purify saints and churches alike.

Devotional Thoughts

- **(For children):** Jesus laid down some rules regarding trouble in the church *(Matthew 18:15-17)*. The desire is that the one who is wrong will make things right. If he does not, church members may have to separate from him *(1 Corinthians 5:11-13; 2 Thessalonians 3:14)* but still love him *(2 Thessalonians 3:15)*.
- **(For everyone):** How does the world view church discipline? How do you view it? How can it be implemented scripturally with the correct motive of love and restoration?
- How could church discipline be used by the Lord as a means of chastening? How could people lose the understanding of chastening with the failure to implement church discipline?

Prayer Thoughts

- Ask the Lord to strengthen the leaders in your local body.
- Ask God to give you a biblical perspective of chastening.

SONG: *BRETHREN, WE HAVE MET TO WORSHIP*

Notes: ___

Notes:

Quotes from the next volume
(VOLUME 4, WEEK 31)
Subject: Government and Nations (con't)

Believers should be the most faithful and conscientious citizens in every country around the world.

A country's leaders are to condone righteousness and condemn evil.

It should never be the desire of any believer to stand against his own government. At the same time, each believer will, at some point, be confronted with the conflicting choice to obey God rather than to obey men's antiscriptural precepts.

32

Rebellion

Rebellion—found ninety-eight times in ninety-three verses

Variations: rebel, rebelled, rebellest, rebellion, rebellious, rebels

First usage: *Genesis 14:4* (rebelled)

Last usage: *Hosea 13:16* (rebelled)

Defined: stubbornness, obstinance, or resistance

Interesting fact: Scripture describes rebellion using various visual illustrations (i.e., a heart waxed gross, ears dull of hearing, a stiff neck, a hard heart, etc.). One association of special interest pertains to the Old Testament command found in **Deuteronomy 10:16** where the Bible says, *"Circumcise therefore the foreskin of your heart, and be no more stiffnecked."* The Jews obviously failed in this area causing them to miss the Messiah when Christ came down from heaven's glory. In fact, Stephen rebuked the Jews' failure when he said, *"Ye stiffnecked and uncircumcised in heart and ears, ye do always resist the Holy Ghost: as your fathers did, so do ye"* **(Acts 7:51).**

Bible study tip: When studying a book of the Bible, the student should integrate several steps to insure the desired, untainted, truthful outcome. First, the student should read the entire book of the Bible. Preferably, this should happen several times. Secondly, the student should attempt to determine the major divisions within the book. The divisions may simply match the chapter divisions, but frequently a division will include multiple chapters. At this point, it would be wise to create an outline of the book with the Roman numerals representing the major divisions found within the book. From here, the process can be repeated but focused within each major section of the book until the student has a breakdown of each individual verse within the book. This process must be done with all diligence. Bible study is work!

Sunday, Day 218—Church Day (no devotional)
Monday, Day 219—*A Rebel Refuses to Yield*
Tuesday, Day 220—*A Rebel Refuses to Hear*
Wednesday, Day 221—Church Night (no devotional)
Thursday, Day 222—*The Heart of a Rebel*
Friday, Day 223—*The Rebel's Guide*
Saturday, Day 224—*A Rebel Keeps His Distance*

Day 218: Church Day

*1 Samuel 15:23 For **rebellion is as the sin of witchcraft**, and stubbornness is as iniquity and idolatry. Because thou hast rejected the word of the LORD, he hath also rejected thee from being king.*

Day 219: (Monday)
A Rebel Refuses to Yield

*2 Chronicles 30:8 Now **be ye not stiffnecked**, as your fathers were, but **yield yourselves unto the LORD**, and enter into his sanctuary, which he hath sanctified for ever: and serve the LORD your God, that the fierceness of his wrath may turn away from you.*

☐ Completion Date Rebellion • 257

Introductory Thoughts

Rebellion thrives upon the self-will of any individual or group of individuals. It parallels stubbornness, hard-heartedness, and a stiff neck. The first use of *rebellion* in the Bible indicates that it is a refusal to submit to the will or authority of another (***Genesis 14:4***; see also ***2 Kings 18:7***). Sometimes, rebellion may be the refusal to *go* at the command of another ***(Deuteronomy 1:26)***, while at other times, it is the refusal to *stay **(Deuteronomy 1:43)***. The point is that rebellion is a refusal on the part of a person or group to submit and yield to the rule of another. It involves a conscious decision to cease from following, and though there may be times when resistance needs to be made against the world, *"God forbid that we should rebel against the LORD" **(Joshua 22:29)***.

Devotional Thoughts

- **(For children):** Moses and Aaron did not submit to God's authority when He told them to speak to the rock in order to bring forth water. God called this rebellion ***(Numbers 20:2-12, 23-24; Deuteronomy 32:48-52)***.
- **(For everyone):** How do you see rebellion? Is it an honourable attribute? Is it a trait with which you should be pleased? Is it an attribute that you recognize in your own heart?
- What is the first act of rebellion in the Bible that comes to mind? Who was the first one to demonstrate rebellion? What does this teach you about the nature and source of rebellion?

Prayer Thoughts

- Ask God to soften your hard heart.
- Ask the Lord to guard you from the sin of rebellion.

SONG: *OFT HAVE I TURNED MY EYES WITHIN*

Day 220: (Tuesday)
A Rebel Refuses to Hear

Deuteronomy 1:43 *So **I spake unto you; and ye would not hear, but rebelled** against the commandment of the LORD, and went presumptuously up into the hill.*

Introductory Thoughts

A sure sign of rebellion involves the rejection of God's word. Throughout scripture, the Lord associates rebellion with a willful decision on the part of an individual or people group to refuse to hear. In **Psalm 107:11** the Bible says, *"Because they rebelled against the words of God, and contemned the counsel of the most High."* In **Nehemiah 9:26** the scripture declares, *"Nevertheless they were disobedient, and rebelled against thee, and cast thy law behind their backs."* Those who make their necks stiff in rebellion will not incline their ears in order to receive instruction *(Jeremiah 17:23)*. They may accept the counsel of others but refuse the Lord's counsel *(Isaiah 30:1)*.

Devotional Thoughts

- **(For children)**: God wants children to obey their parents *(Colossians 3:20)*. When they refuse to do so, they are rebellious *(Deuteronomy 21:18-20)*. How well do you obey your parents? Would you be considered rebellious?
- **(For everyone)**: Will you listen to biblical counsel? How do you feel when others offer you scriptural advice? Do you choose rather to hear worldly counsel that better suits your desires?
- How did the Lord describe rebellious people in *Isaiah 30:9*? Does the description fit anyone you know? Does it fit you? What can you do in order to quell your rebellion?

Prayer Thoughts

- Ask the Lord to give you a desire to hear His words.
- Ask God to give you a respect for His commandments.

SONG: *HIS WAY WITH THEE*

Day 221: Church Night

Lamentations 1:18 The LORD is righteous; for I have rebelled against his commandment: *hear, I pray you, all people, and **behold my sorrow**: my virgins and my young men are gone into captivity.*

Day 222: (Thursday)
The Heart of a Rebel

Psalm 78:8 *And might not be as their fathers,* ***a stubborn and rebellious generation;*** *a generation that set not their heart aright, and whose spirit was not stedfast with God.*

INTRODUCTORY THOUGHTS

As it is with all sin, rebellion originates within the heart. Long before it manifests itself in the individual's actions, it finds life by taking root within his heart. The Lord described a rebellious generation by saying that they were *"a generation that set not their heart aright, and whose spirit was not stedfast with God."* A man with a wicked heart and the wrong spirit cannot enjoy sweet fellowship with the Lord. As rebellion takes root in his heart, the rebellion pushes out the desires for prayer and for God's word. Humility is crowded out because of pride and self-will to the extent that a man justifies, perhaps even with scripture, his rebellious spirit. His once soft heart becomes hardened because of the deceitfulness of sin.

DEVOTIONAL THOUGHTS

- **(For children):** Satan was the first one recorded in scripture to rebel against God. His rebellion started in his heart *(Isaiah 14:12-14)*. This is true of the sin committed by Ananias and Sapphira. It too started in their hearts *(Acts 5:3)* as did the sin of Judas *(John 13:2)*. Guard your heart *(Psalm 119:10-11)*.
- **(For everyone):** How does a rebellious heart affect those around you? How does it affect you? How can it begin to destroy the joy and peace that the Lord wants you and others to enjoy?
- How can you catch rebellion in its early stages? What indicators can you watch for to suggest that rebellion might be taking root within your heart?

PRAYER THOUGHTS

- Ask the Lord to examine your heart.
- Ask God to protect you from rebellion.

SONG: *NOTHING BETWEEN*

Day 223: (Friday)
The Rebel's Guide

Isaiah 65:2 *I have spread out my hands all the day unto* **a rebellious people, which walketh** *in a way that was not good,* ***after their own thoughts;***

Introductory Thoughts

Men get into trouble when they begin to think too highly of their own thoughts. If they are not careful, these opinions will become the driving force in their decision making. This will mean that the word of God finds itself in competition for the seat of authority. The sad truth is that men often fail to notice within themselves this substitution of authorities. While their mouths may falsely testify of a loyal submission to the scriptures, their actions testify that their opinions are instead leading the way. The Devil works subtly because he knows how to gradually lead men astray by keeping them from noticing any abrupt changes within their hearts and outward deeds. By the time rebellion is detected, the Devil has a stronghold only broken by prayer and heartfelt submission to God.

Devotional Thoughts

- **(For children):** King Saul knew what God wanted him to do, but he only partially obeyed *(1 Samuel 15:3, 7-9)*. Yet, he still failed to see what was wrong with his actions *(1 Samuel 15:13-15, 20)*. He was greatly fooled *(1 Samuel 15:10-11, 18-19, 22-23)*.
- **(For everyone):** What leads your emotion and decision making? What gives you joy or frustration? What moves you to the point of making a decision? What is driving your mind and heart?
- Have you ever heard someone suggest that you should merely follow your heart? How can that be wicked counsel that is contrary to the word of God?

Prayer Thoughts

- Ask the Lord to help you hide His word in your heart.
- Ask God to give you a proper perspective on your own thoughts.

SONG: *HE LEADETH ME*

Day 224: (Saturday)
A Rebel Keeps His Distance

Isaiah 46:12 *Hearken unto me,* ***ye stouthearted, that*** *are* ***far from righteousness****:*

Introductory Thoughts

Rebels are sometimes known as loners. Today's scripture says that this trait can be attributed to their desire to keep their distance from righteousness. Many who would be identified by these terms do not disassociate from sin or sinners. Instead, they disassociate from truth and righteousness. Righteous thoughts and words have been known to melt the hard heart. They penetrate the rocky soil and begin to break down pride and rebellion. In order for a rebel to remain in his rebellion, he must keep a distance between himself and the truth. The very concepts of righteousness and rebellion refuse to coexist. Hence the battle rages: as the Lord works to draw man's attention to righteousness, the Devil fights to keep man's distance from it.

Devotional Thoughts

- **(For children):** The children of Israel kept refusing to hear the truth ***(Jeremiah 7:23-29)***. Many people today are refusing to do the same ***(2 Timothy 4:2-4)***.
- **(For everyone):** Why does the Devil work hard to keep you blind to the true condition of your heart? What can begin to happen when you get a glimpse of the wickedness of your heart?
- How does righteousness and truth change your heart? What happens as you begin to distance yourself from these things? What happens to your heart (see ***Isaiah 46:12***)?

Prayer Thoughts

- Thank the Lord for bringing these things to your attention.
- Ask the Lord to show you the condition of your heart.

SONG: *NEAR TO THE HEART OF GOD*

Notes:

Quotes from the next volume

(VOLUME 4, WEEK 32)

Subject: Rest

Man must realize that life is more closely associated to a marathon than to a sprint. A man's failure to take time away from the pressures of life will eventually take time away from his sum total of years.

There is no doubt the Sabbath was a sign between the Lord and Israel *(Exodus 31:13, 17)*, but it also demonstrates a principle that man needs a period set aside to rest.

Man is like the ground. Every time he does something that produces fruit, he loses part of himself. He must have time to receive from the Lord what he has given to others.

33

Rebellion (con't)

Rebellion—found twenty-three times in twenty verses in the book of Ezekiel

Variations: rebel, rebelled, rebellest, rebellion, rebellious, rebels

Interesting fact: God created man to have dominion over the animal kingdom; however, the Bible depicts the animal kingdom as much more consistent than man in the area of obedience. The opening lines of the book of Isaiah contrast the obedience of man to that of the animal kingdom. Concerning men, the Lord said, *"I have nourished and brought up children, and they have rebelled against me" (Isaiah 1:2).* The Lord contrasted this rebuke with the following concerning the animal kingdom, *"The ox knoweth his owner, and the ass his master's crib" (Isaiah 1:3).*

Bible study tip: In certain situations, the Bible depicts current or historical events to teach present truths. For instance, some Galilaeans reminded the Lord of some fellow Galilaeans *"whose blood Pilate had mingled with their sacrifices" (Luke 13:1).* The Lord used this event to teach of the need of all men to repent *(Luke 13:2-3).* He then reminded His listeners of eighteen people who died when *"the tower in Si-*

*loam fell, and slew them" **(Luke 13:4)**.* Once again, the Lord reminded the audience concerning the need for all men to repent. In such cases, the Bible student may not possess all the details of the current event, but the point of the teaching can be plainly established. While searching for some deep, dark, historical secret, do not miss the obvious teachings which simply state the truth concerning a particular event.

Sunday, Day 225—Church Day (no devotional)
Monday, Day 226—*The Nature of Rebellion*
Tuesday, Day 227—*A Stiff Neck*
Wednesday, Day 228—Church Night (no devotional)
Thursday, Day 229—*Turning the Shoulder*
Friday, Day 230—*God's Dealings with Rebels*
Saturday, Day 231—*Rebels Dwell in a Dry Land*

Day 225: Church Day

Daniel 9:5 We *have sinned, and have committed iniquity, and have done wickedly, and* **have rebelled, even by departing from thy precepts and from thy judgments:**

9 *To the Lord our God belong mercies and forgivenesses, though we have rebelled against him;*

Day 226: (Monday)
The Nature of Rebellion

1 Samuel 15:23 *For rebellion is as the sin of witchcraft, and stubbornness is as iniquity and idolatry. Because thou hast rejected the word of the LORD, he hath also rejected thee from being king.*

Introductory Thoughts

Man's opinion concerning the sinfulness of sin very rarely reflects God's holy, perfect, and righteous declarations. This is because man does not think like God. The Lord expressed these sentiments in *Isaiah 55:8-9* when He said, *"For my thoughts are not your thoughts, neither are your ways my ways, . . . For as the heavens are higher than the earth, so are my ways higher than your ways, and my thoughts than your thoughts."* Even a cursory study of rebellion verifies these truths as a man generally thinks of it more lightly than he ought. Man describes rebellion as strong willed or independent; however, God provides an accurate description as He states that *"rebellion is as the sin of witchcraft, and stubbornness is as iniquity and idolatry."* Because God likens rebellion to witchcraft, the Old Testament punishment for rebellion was likewise death **(Deuteronomy 21:18-23)**. There can be no doubt as to the seriousness of this sin from God's perspective.

Devotional Thoughts

- **(For children):** King Saul knew what would happen if he rebelled against God **(1 Samuel 12:13-15)**. Yet, he rebelled several times **(1 Samuel 13:9, 13-14; 1 Samuel 15:18-19)**. In fact, his death was a direct result of his rebellion **(1 Chronicles 10:13-14)**.
- **(For everyone):** What is your opinion of rebellion? How does your opinion compare with God's opinion? How will a faulty opinion on your part hinder any meaningful fellowship with the Lord?
- Do you sense any rebellion in your own heart? When did this rebellion first show up? What needs to be done on your part to yield your rebellious actions to the Lord?

Prayer Thoughts

- Ask the Lord to identify any rebellion in your heart.
- Ask the Lord to help you adopt His views on rebellion.

SONG: *NOTHING BETWEEN*

Day 227: (Tuesday)
A Stiff Neck

Psalm 75:5 *Lift not up your horn on high:* **speak not with a stiff neck.**

Introductory Thoughts

Rebellion is identified in a variety of ways, but the Lord often associates it to someone with a stiff neck. Society should find this concept easily grasped. A stiff neck impedes the head from bowing. Moses directly associated the stiff neck with rebellion when he said, *"For I know thy rebellion, and thy stiff neck" (Deuteronomy 31:27)*. Like Moses, the Lord identified the rebellion of the children of Israel when He stated that they were *"a stiffnecked people" (Exodus 32:9)*. Isaiah likewise attested to this truth by stating that rebellious people had a neck of iron sinew and a brow of brass *(Isaiah 48:4)*. These descriptive terms demonstrate that rebellion is exemplified by an individual who refuses to bow and allow the mind to be changed. He has an unyielding spirit.

Devotional Thoughts

- **(For children):** God told Ezekiel how the children of Israel felt toward Him *(Ezekiel 2:3; Ezekiel 3:7)*. They rebelled against God, His prophets, and even God's Son. Stephen referred to them as *"stiffnecked" (Acts 7:51-60)*.
- **(For everyone):** Have you ever been described as stubborn, obstinate, stiffnecked, or hardheaded? Did you take it as something for which you should be proud? How should you take such comments when they accurately depict your spirit?
- Are you willing to allow the Lord to control and direct your will? Are you willing to submit yourself to God's plan for your life and future? Are you willing to submit to godly influences as commanded by the Lord?

Prayer Thoughts

- Ask the Lord to give you a neck willing to bow to Him.
- Ask God to help you see your rebellion as He sees it.

SONG: *WHAT OPPOSITES I FEEL WITHIN!*

Day 228: Church Night

*Isaiah 65:2 I have spread out my hands all the day unto **a rebellious people**, **which walketh** in a way that was not good, **after their own thoughts**;*

☐ Completion Date   Rebellion (con't) • 267

Day 229: (Thursday)
Turning the Shoulder

Zechariah 7:11 **But they refused to hearken,** *and* **pulled away the shoulder,** *and* **stopped their ears,** *that they should not hear.*

INTRODUCTORY THOUGHTS

Rebellion is a willing conscious decision to refuse the instruction of another. The Lord describes this in **Zechariah 7:11** when He said, *"they refused to hearken and pulled away the shoulder, and stopped their ears, that they should not hear."* This is a powerful illustration and picture! It almost seems like the Lord has a hand on the shoulder of the rebel but when faced with the Lord's instruction, a rebel pulls away from the Lord's gentle grasp. As he pulls away, the rebel turns his back and closes his ears to the Lord's instruction. The Lord affirms this in **Jeremiah 32:33** when He said, *"they have turned unto me the back, and not the face: though I taught them, rising up early and teaching them, yet they have not hearkened to receive instruction."*

DEVOTIONAL THOUGHTS

- **(For children):** Through the prophet Ahijah, God made His instructions clear to Jeroboam *(1 Kings 11:29-38)*. However, Jeroboam made a conscious decision to refuse to hearken *(1 Kings 12:26-30)*. He definitely turned his back to the Lord *(1 Kings 14:7-10a)*.
- **(For everyone):** Try to picture the illustration presented for rebellion. Demonstrating the actions would help. How would you feel if someone pulled away his or her shoulder while you were trying to give him or her instructions? How does your rebellion offend the Lord?
- How did the Lord Jesus demonstrate submission to His Father's will *(Isaiah 50:5)*? How could you demonstrate that same type of submission?

PRAYER THOUGHTS

- Ask the Lord to give you the heart and mind of His Son.
- Ask God to help you show Him your face rather than your back.

SONG: *COME, THOU FOUNT OF EVERY BLESSING*

Day 230: (Friday)
God's Dealings with Rebels

***Joshua 22:18** But that ye must turn away this day from following the LORD? and it will be, seeing **ye rebel to day against the LORD**, that **to morrow he will be wroth with the whole congregation of Israel**.*

INTRODUCTORY THOUGHTS

Sin can never be flippantly disregarded. If the Lord is just, and He is, He must mete out consequences for rebellion. The biblical descriptions of the Lord's reaction to rebellion varies from *"he will be wroth"* **(Joshua 22:18)** to *"then shall the hand of the LORD be against you"* **(1 Samuel 12:15)** to *"ye shall be devoured with the sword"* **(Isaiah 1:20)** to *"I will come up into the midst of thee in a moment, and consume thee"* **(Exodus 33:5)** to *"I will purge out from among you the rebels"* **(Ezekiel 20:38)** to *"I will even send a curse upon you, and I will curse your blessings"* **(Malachi 2:2)**. Though there are variations in the response, the constant truth remains that the Lord hates rebellion and responds to the rebellion with judgment.

DEVOTIONAL THOUGHTS

- **(For children):** God loves His children and wants to bless them, but He will not let them get by with rebellion *(Psalm 81:10-16)*. He longed for His people (Israel) to do right, but they chose rebellion *(2 Chronicles 36:15-17)*.
- **(For everyone):** How should parents respond to rebellious children? How should employers respond to rebellious employees? How should the law of the land respond to rebels? How should the Lord respond?
- Have you rebelled against the Lord? Has He responded with chastening in order to get your attention? Have you yielded to His chastening? What does it mean if there is no chastening from the Lord?

PRAYER THOUGHTS

- Ask God to give you a submissive will.
- Ask the Lord to help you respond when He chastens.

SONG: *COME, YE DISCONSOLATE*

Day 231: (Saturday)
Rebels Dwell in a Dry Land

Psalm 68:6 *God setteth the solitary in families: he bringeth out those which are bound with chains: but **the rebellious dwell in a dry land**.*

INTRODUCTORY THOUGHTS

Rebels will not and cannot enjoy the breadth of God's intended blessings. For those harmed by the consequences of sin, God desires to make things right. The Bible says that *"he bringeth out those which are bound with chains."* God delivers those taken captive by the wicked. For this reason, the Bible says that He will be *"a father of the fatherless, and a judge of the widows" (Psalm 68:5)*. Yet, He also withholds blessings from those who rebel against His will. Rebels will instead *"dwell in a dry land"* bereaved of the blessings of God. Though this was no doubt intended as the literal withholding of rain, it bears a spiritual truth that rebels will miss out on the richness of what God has for them. The Lord wants men to know His joy and His peace; however, rebellion offers nothing but a dearth of God's blessings.

DEVOTIONAL THOUGHTS

- **(For children):** *Jeremiah 17:5-8* tells us the difference in the way of life between those who rebel against God (*"heart departeth from the Lord"*) and those who do not. Also read ***Deuteronomy 11:11-17***.
- **(For everyone):** Are you in the midst of a spiritual drought? Do you find yourself blaming others for the dry land in which you dwell? Is it possible that the drought has resulted from the rebellion within your heart?
- What does the Lord want from you? Have you been obedient to His known will for your life? Has rebellion caused you to miss out on some blessings?

PRAYER THOUGHTS

- Thank the Lord for showing you any rebellion within your heart.
- Ask God to help you enjoy His blessings.

SONG: *JESUS, I MY CROSS HAVE TAKEN*

Notes: _____

Quotes from the next volume

(VOLUME 4, WEEK 33)

Subject: Rest (con't)

Life will present difficult situations. The only viable solution will, at times, involve taking a step back and regrouping mentally, emotionally, and spiritually.

Most Christians know the commandment of Christ given to the apostles to go *"into all the world, and preach the gospel to every creature"* **(Mark 16:15)**, but far too few recognize the same Lord commanded these same apostles to separate themselves *"into a desert place, and rest a while"* **(Mark 6:31)**. It is better to obediently rest than to prematurely burn out in the service of God.

34

Relationships

Relationships—The studies to follow focus particularly upon relationships prior to marriage as well as those within and outside of the marriage bond. This week's study focuses upon premarital relations.

Interesting fact: God's word always strikes the perfect balance when it references the physical relations between a man and a woman. In doing so, it safeguards the purity of the children's minds. Adults reading the Bible all know what God meant when He said, *"Adam knew Eve his wife; and she conceived" (Genesis 4:1)*. However, this statement hardly even piques a child's innocent curiosity. For those who might attempt to find fault with the first example as somehow unclear, God gives a more explicit passage yet still retains the spirit of purity. The book of Judges says, *"they found . . . four hundred virgins, that had known no man by lying with any male" (Judges 21:12)*. Clearly, these four hundred virgins had not known a man because they had never lain with man.

Bible study tip: Be careful not to define a Bible word simply based upon its usage within a single context. There frequently exists broader or more distinct meanings used within other contexts in scripture. Failure to properly understand a Bible word in one context will hinder one's understanding of a verse in other contexts. The word *virgin* serves as a good case in point.

Sunday, Day 232—Church Day (no devotional)
Monday, Day 233—*Whoso Findeth a Wife*
Tuesday, Day 234—*Seeking Wise Counsel*
Wednesday, Day 235—Church Night (no devotional)
Thursday, Day 236—*Preparations for Marriage*
Friday, Day 237—*A Call for Purity*
Saturday, Day 238—*The Sins of the Parents*

Day 232: Church Day

Ruth 2:9 Let thine eyes be on the field that they do reap, and go thou after them: **have I not charged the young men that they shall not touch thee?** *and when thou art athirst, go unto the vessels, and drink of that which the young men have drawn.*

Day 233: (Monday)
Whoso Findeth a Wife

Proverbs 18:22 Whoso findeth a wife findeth a good thing, and obtaineth favour of the LORD.

INTRODUCTORY THOUGHTS

God made man with the natural desire for companionship. Similar to all of God's other creation; the world, the flesh, and the Devil have corrupted the method by which this desire is consummated. God created Adam as a single man. As time elapsed, it became obvious that Adam did not need to be alone but needed a wife. Although the details do vary from situation to situation, the principles of God's provisions for companionship for Adam provide superior guidelines for someone seeking the same relationship today. Adam found a wife when the Lord brought Eve to him and not the other way around. Adam too did not go searching for a wife, but God brought her to him. Though times have changed, God can and will do the same today for those who faithfully love and serve Him.

☐ Completion Date Relationships • 273

DEVOTIONAL THOUGHTS
- **(For children):** God made Adam a wife that would be a help meet for him *(Genesis 2:18)*. Above all things, a companion should love the Lord *(Psalm 119:63)*. Since God knows hearts, it is better to let Him do the choosing of a spouse *(Proverbs 19:14b)*.
- **(For everyone):** How does the world suggest one should find a companion? What would be some wise rules for finding a spouse? What are some details about God's provision for Adam that would assist you?
- How could it be dangerous to get ahead of the Lord in finding a spouse? Upon what should your decisions be based? Upon what basis do most people choose a husband or wife?

PRAYER THOUGHTS
- Ask God to guide your children as they look for the Lord's will.
- Ask the Lord for strength to withstand the world's assaults.

SONG: *TRUSTING JESUS*

Day 234: (Tuesday)
Seeking Wise Counsel

Judges 14:1 And **Samson went down to Timnath, and saw a woman in Timnath of the daughters of the Philistines.**

2 And **he came up, and told his father and his mother,** *and said, I have seen a woman in Timnath of the daughters of the Philistines:* **now therefore get her for me to wife.**

3 Then **his father and his mother said unto him, Is there never a woman among the daughters of thy brethren, or among all my people, that thou goest to take a wife of the uncircumcised Philistines?** *And Samson said unto his father, Get her for me; for she pleaseth me well.*

4 But his father and his mother knew not that it was of the LORD, that he sought an occasion against the Philistines: for at that time the Philistines had dominion over Israel.

274 • Relationships ☐ Completion Date

Introductory Thoughts

The godly choice of whom to marry likely will never again be as obvious as it was for Adam and Eve. Yet, the wrong choice can and will usually bring disastrous outcomes along with lifelong consequences. Wise counsel to avoid pitfalls related to bad choices is vitally important! Samson's choice was ultimately of the Lord, but not because it was wise. His parents knew that his decision was fleshly and attempted to redirect him. Esau rebelliously sought a wife that would never meet his parents' approval *(Genesis 28:6-9)*. Throughout the Old Testament, parents were involved in the process of choosing the right spouse for their children. It may not be a direct command from God, but it remains a wise principle to follow. Parents are not always right, but the Lord is pleased to use them in this decision-making process.

Devotional Thoughts

- **(For children):** Ruth chose to live with Naomi because she wanted to serve the true God *(Ruth 1:15-16)*. God led Ruth to work in the right field. Ruth listened to the wise counsel of her mother-in-law *(Ruth 2:19-23; Ruth 3:5-6; Proverbs 19:20)*; this resulted in her becoming the great-grandmother of king David *(Ruth 4:17)*.
- **(For everyone):** Who brought Eve to Adam? Who was involved in the selecting of a wife for Isaac *(Genesis 24:1-3, 50)*? Why is it dangerous to make the decision without counsel and without God?
- Some have taken this principle and morphed it into some type of spiritual command. What are some scenarios where parents might not be able to be a help? Who could offer you wise counsel in their stead?

Prayer Thoughts

- Ask God to work in the lives of those who are not yet married.
- Ask God to help those who have not made wise choices.

SONG: *THE FOUR RULERS*

Day 235: Church Night

***Genesis 20:6** And **God said** unto him in a dream, Yea, I know that thou didst this in the integrity of thy heart; for **I also withheld thee from sinning against me: therefore suffered I thee not to touch her**.*

☐ Completion Date

Day 236: (Thursday)
Preparations for Marriage

*Proverbs 16:1 **The preparations of the heart in man**, and the answer of the tongue, **is from the LORD**.*

Introductory Thoughts

Like other callings upon a person's life, God prepares men and women for marriage. Obviously, God prepares the heart, but He also prepares other areas in order to provide for a strong home. When God created Adam, He could have immediately created Eve, but He chose to allow Adam to experience the sense of being alone. Perhaps there are other reasons, but God may have thought it wise to prepare Adam for marriage. He needed to experience life without Eve. Adam needed to come to the place where he desired companionship. He needed to be alone before he could truly appreciate a wife. In addition to the preparation of Adam's heart, the Lord gave him a job, a means by which he could provide for Eve *(Genesis 2:8-9, 15)*. All of these preparations were necessary for a strong marriage relationship.

Devotional Thoughts

- **(For children):** Children who are lazy and do not consider the hard work done daily by their parents are often overwhelmed when they have a home and children of their own. Develop good work habits without complaining *(Proverbs 6:6-11; Proverbs 31:27b; Ecclesiastes 9:10a; Hebrews 6:12a; Philippians 2:14)*.
- **(For everyone):** Read *Titus 2:3-5*. What are some areas in which a young lady should be prepared prior to marriage? How can she learn the things she needs to learn in order to be prepared for becoming a spouse?
- Read *Titus 2:6-8* and *1 Timothy 5:8*. What are some areas in which a young man needs preparation before he is ready to be responsible for a wife and children?

Prayer Thoughts

- Ask the Lord to give wisdom to those considering marriage.
- Ask God to prepare your children for a strong godly marriage.

SONG: *YOUTH THAT PRIZE GOD'S PRECIOUS TRUTH*

Day 237: (Friday)
A Call for Purity

1 Corinthians 7:1 *Now concerning the things whereof ye wrote unto me:* **It is good for a man not to touch a woman.**

INTRODUCTORY THOUGHTS

Modern society is increasingly mocking purity, yet God is pleased with those who endeavour to keep themselves pure before marriage. Increasing temptations combined with the declining standards concerning courting have made purity a rarity rather than the norm. Regardless of this trend, young people with a deep and abiding love for the Lord will continually strive to overcome these obstacles and remain pure. Those who have failed in the past will renew their commitment to the Lord seeking to prevent further regrets. This must be accomplished with a firm resolve. A young person must determine that he or she is going to respect the commandments of God and the other individual with whom he or she is courting. Beyond this, each young person must determine to build fences of protection to keep from entering into tempting situations. The Devil does not need much room to rob a youth of his or her purity *(Ephesians 4:27)*.

DEVOTIONAL THOUGHTS

- **(For children):** God wants us to live right *(1 Thessalonians 4:7)*. The Devil does not *(1 Peter 5:8)*. God is greater than the Devil *(1 John 4:4)* and will help you overcome any desire to do evil *(1 Corinthians 10:13; 2 Peter 2:9a)*.
- **(For everyone):** Read *1 Corinthians 7:1* and *1 Thessalonians 5:22*. What are some rules that a young person could establish to help protect his or her purity before marriage?
- What is the greatest area of vulnerability for a young man? What about for a young lady? How can this knowledge help a young person protect his or her purity?

PRAYER THOUGHTS

- Ask the Lord to protect the purity of your young family members.
- Ask God to raise the standard of courting in your home.

SONG: *NEARER, STILL NEARER*

☐ Completion Date

Day 238: (Saturday)
The Sins of the Parents

Genesis 26:6 And Isaac dwelt in Gerar:

7 And **the men of the place asked him of his wife; and he said, She is my sister: for he feared** *to say, She is my wife; lest, said he, the men of the place should kill me for Rebekah; because she was fair to look upon.*

INTRODUCTORY THOUGHTS

No believer should knowingly marry an unbeliever *(2 Corinthians 6:14)*. Additionally, the unmarried should look for other strengths and weaknesses in a prospective spouse before agreeing to marriage. Oftentimes, these strengths and weaknesses can be seen by interaction with the other's parents. Isaac lied about Rebekah *(Genesis 26:6-7)* just as his father Abraham lied about Sarah *(Genesis 12:10-13; Genesis 20:1-2)*. Solomon's weakness for women *(1 Kings 11:1)* was first witnessed in his father David *(2 Samuel 11:1-4)*. Rachel learned deception *(Genesis 31:32-35)* by watching her father act deceptively *(Genesis 29:25)*. A careful observation of parents can reveal prospective problems in a future spouse.

DEVOTIONAL THOUGHTS

- **(For children):** Jehoshaphat, king of Judah, loved the Lord *(2 Chronicles 17:3-4)* but helped the wicked king of Israel *(2 Chronicles 19:1-3)*. This association caused his son Jehoram to pick up evil ways and he married the wicked king's daughter *(2 Chronicles 21:5-6)*. Jehoram's son Ahaziah also did wrong *(2 Chronicles 22:1-4)*.
- **(For everyone):** How do most young people learn how to handle conflicts within the home? How do young men learn the right or wrong way to treat a lady? How would a young lady learn to react to her future husband?
- How could you interact with a person's family without making it seem as though you are scrutinizing them?

PRAYER THOUGHTS

- Ask God for wisdom when making decisions that will impact your entire future.

- Ask the Lord to give you a scriptural foundation for courting and the willpower to succeed.

SONG: *HE LEADETH ME*

Notes: _____

_____

_____

_____

_____

_____

_____

_____

_____

Quotes from the next volume

(VOLUME 4, WEEK 34)

Subject: Religion

In spite of his religious clout, the apostle Paul was lost and on his way to hell until he trusted Jesus Christ as Saviour *(Philippians 3:7-11)*. He considered his former actions as service to the Lord which he later likened to dung.

Unfortunately, far too many people have forsaken the simplicity which is in Christ and have instead pursued the complexity and labour of religion *(2 Corinthians 11:3)*.

While it is true that Christianity is based upon a personal relationship with Jesus Christ, the Bible is also clear that there is such a thing as *"pure"* religion. Thus most religion is man-made with the only exception being the purest form of worship directed solely at the preeminence of Christ.

35

Relationships (con't)

Relationships—The studies to follow focus particularly upon relationships prior to marriage as well as those within and outside of the marriage bond. This week's study focuses upon the marriage relationship.

Interesting fact: Many sermons have been preached along with many songs sung about a land called *Beulah*. Though the name for most Christians is quite familiar, the definition and meaning of *Beulah* is lesser known. According to **Isaiah 62:4**, the land of Israel shall be called *Beulah* because it will be married. According to **Revelation 21:9-10**, the holy Jerusalem descending from heaven will be called *"the Lamb's wife."*

Bible study tip: Some of Paul's epistles were written while Paul was being held as a prisoner in Rome. In order to identify which epistles were written while he was imprisoned, the Bible student should hone in on words such as *"prisoner" (Ephesians 3:1; Ephesians 4:1)* and *"bonds" (Ephesians 6:20)*.

Sunday, Day 239—Church Day (no devotional)
Monday, Day 240—*He Made Them Male and Female*
Tuesday, Day 241—*The Equal Yoke*
Wednesday, Day 242—Church Night (no devotional)

Thursday, Day 243—*What Is Marriage?*
Friday, Day 244—*The Purpose of Marriage*
Saturday, Day 245—*A Privilege of Marriage*

Day 239: Church Day

1 Timothy 5:14 I will therefore that the younger women marry, bear children, guide the house, **give none occasion to the adversary to speak reproachfully**.

Day 240: (Monday)
He Made Them Male and Female

Matthew 19:3 The Pharisees also came unto him, tempting him, and saying unto him, Is it lawful for a man to put away his wife for every cause?

4 And he answered and said unto them, Have ye not read, that he which made them **at the beginning made them male and female**,

5 And said, For this cause shall a man leave father and mother, and shall cleave to his wife: and they twain shall be one flesh?

INTRODUCTORY THOUGHTS

God instituted marriage and He alone has the right to establish the rightful candidates to join together in this or any other union. Man has no God-given right to interfere with the precepts of God. Everything in creation declares that marriage always includes only a relationship between one man and one woman. Additionally, the marriage bounds are not subject to popular vote of society nor subject to modification by any court or law of the land. Its conditions are set by the highest law and the highest court. God could have presented Adam with another man, but He did not. In God's eyes, marriage is a specific relationship fulfilled only between one man and one woman *(Genesis 2:21-23)*, and any deviation of this is unseemly and an abomination to God *(Leviticus 18:22; Leviticus 20:13; Romans 1:26-27)*.

DEVOTIONAL THOUGHTS

- **(For children):** When Paul was instructing married couples, he referred to them as a husband and wife *(1 Corinthians 7:10, 11b)*. Ob-

viously, a husband is a man and a wife is a woman. For example, Elkanah was called a man and a husband *(1 Samuel 1:21-22)*. Hannah was called a wife and a woman *(1 Samuel 1: 2a, 23)*.
- **(For everyone):** What are some ways in which creation plainly declares that marriage was made to only exist between a man and a woman? How does the ability to reproduce further authenticate and validate the same truth?
- What are some reasons that it is imperative for a society to have the scriptural viewpoint on the proper candidates for marriage? In what ways could the wrong view spell the society's demise?

Prayer Thoughts
- Ask God to protect your family from unscriptural views.
- Ask the Lord to send your children godly spouses.

SONG: *HOW CLOSELY JOINED ARE MAN AND WIFE*

Day 241: (Tuesday)
The Equal Yoke

2 Corinthians 6:14 Be ye not unequally yoked together with unbelievers: for what fellowship hath righteousness with unrighteousness? and what communion hath light with darkness?

Introductory Thoughts

Scripture plainly reveals that God repeatedly calls for His people to separate from the world. This separation extends to every aspect of life, especially including the marriage bond. Why? Because God knows the very real danger that unbelievers pose to believers by drawing them away from Him *(Deuteronomy 7:3-4; Judges 3:6-7; 1 Kings 11:2)*. This is why God specifically instructed His people in both the Old and New Testament to marry among themselves (Jew with Jew and Christian with Christian). The nation of Israel was forbidden to yoke up with the surrounding nations because Israel would adopt heathen practices and the worship of false gods *(Exodus 34:15-16)*. Though God's commands for the New Testament believer are often different from His plan for the Jew, in this aspect they remain constant and unchangeable.

282 • Relationships (con't)

Devotional Thoughts

- **(For children):** Do you love God, the things of God, and coming to His house? Ask Him to find you a spouse that feels the same as you. If you do not, your heart could be turned away from God *(Amos 3:3; 2 Peter 3:17).* Consider Paul's advice to widows *(1 Corinthians 7:39).*
- **(For everyone):** What are some scriptural examples of God's people intermarrying with the heathen? Did the unbeliever or heathen turn the heart of the believer away from God and what is right?
- What are some practical reasons that believers should never yoke up with nonbelievers in marriage? How could marriage lead to future troubles?

Prayer Thoughts

- Ask God for wisdom in making choices for marriage.
- Ask the Lord to protect future generations through godly homes.

SONG: *GOD, GIVE US CHRISTIAN HOMES!*

Day 242: Church Night

1 Timothy 4:1 Now the Spirit speaketh expressly, that **in the latter times some shall depart from the faith***, giving heed to seducing spirits, and doctrines of devils;*

3 **Forbidding to marry***, and commanding to abstain from meats, which God hath created to be received with thanksgiving of them which believe and know the truth.*

Day 243: (Thursday)
What Is Marriage?

Genesis 2:21 And the LORD God caused a deep sleep to fall upon Adam, and he slept: and he took one of his ribs, and closed up the flesh instead thereof;

22 And the rib, which **the LORD God** *had taken from man,* **made** *he* **a woman, and brought her unto the man.**

☐ Completion Date   Relationships (con't) • 283

*23 And Adam said, **This is now bone of my bones, and flesh of my flesh**: she shall be called Woman, because she was taken out of Man.*

*24 **Therefore shall a man leave his father and his mother, and shall cleave unto his wife: and they shall be one flesh.***

INTRODUCTORY THOUGHTS

Marriage involves a relationship between a man and a woman, but what constitutes a scriptural marriage? Scripturally speaking, it is not merely *"flesh joining flesh."* This is plain in that a man could marry a wife only to find that she had been unfaithful with another man to whom she was not married **(Deuteronomy 24:1; Matthew 5:32)**. It is also clear that Shechem defiled Dinah, but then asked if she could become his wife **(Genesis 34:1-4)**. The woman at the well had an improper relationship with a man, but the Lord declared that that particular man was not her husband **(John 4:16-18)**. Instead, marriage occurs when God joins a man and a woman **(Genesis 2:21-24; Mark 10:9)**, and it is often established by a ceremony with vows given to each other **(Matthew 22:1-13; John 2:1-2)**.

DEVOTIONAL THOUGHTS

- **(For children)**: Marriage is one of the most serious matters. God brings a man and woman together and in His eyes, they become one. He expects this bond to last for a lifetime. It is a command, not a request **(Matthew 19:6)**. Abraham and Sarah had troubles and trials but stayed together until Sarah died at the age of 127.
- **(For everyone)**: Why is it important that we have a proper understanding of what marriage is? How can an unscriptural view of marriage lead to gross immorality?
- With certain aspects of relationship available only for those who are married, why does it make sense that the world would try to corrupt the means of establishing a marriage?

PRAYER THOUGHTS

- Ask the Lord to give you a biblical view of marriage.
- Ask God to help your home have a godly respect for marriage.

SONG: *A CHRISTIAN HOME*

Day 244: (Friday)
The Purpose of Marriage

*Psalm 34:3 O **magnify** the LORD with me, **and** let us **exalt** his name **together**.*

INTRODUCTORY THOUGHTS

Marriage is a lifelong invitation to serve the Lord together and strengthen one another in that service. God instituted marriage so that man would not have to be alone. Every groom was to enter into marriage for the purpose of glorifying God with his spouse. The context of **Psalm 34** does not directly refer to marriage, but verse 3 provides an amazing invitation that should be presented to every couple entering into the marriage relationship. A young man should ask a young lady to marry him because he believes that they can better magnify the Lord as a couple rather than individually. If the Lord wills, it is an invitation to bear children and train them up in such a way that the next generation would likewise desire to magnify the Lord.

DEVOTIONAL THOUGHTS

- **(For children):** Zacharias and Elisabeth had a marriage that glorified God *(Luke 1:5-6)*. Likewise, their son John (the Baptist) also glorified God *(Luke 1:13-17)*.
- **(For everyone):** What are some ways in which two believers unified in marriage can better glorify the Lord than a single believer? How can they strengthen each other during tough times?
- What should a married couple do to ensure that they magnify the Lord? How can they reach other couples for the Lord? How can they work to ensure the holiness of future generations?

PRAYER THOUGHTS

- Ask the Lord to help your home magnify Him.
- Ask God to help your children have homes that glorify Him.

SONG: *BLESS, O MY SOUL, THE LIVING GOD*

Day 245: (Saturday)
A Privilege of Marriage

1 Corinthians 7:1 Now concerning the things whereof ye wrote unto me: It is good for a man not to touch a woman.

*2 Nevertheless, **to avoid fornication, let every man have his own wife, and let every woman have her own husband.***

*3 **Let the husband render unto the wife due benevolence: and likewise also the wife unto the husband.***

*4 **The wife hath not power of her own body, but the husband: and likewise also the husband hath not power of his own body, but the wife.***

*5 **Defraud ye not one the other, except it be with consent for a time,** that ye may give yourselves to fasting and prayer; **and come together again, that Satan tempt you not for your incontinency.***

6 But I speak this by permission, and not of commandment.

7 For I would that all men were even as I myself. But every man hath his proper gift of God, one after this manner, and another after that.

8 I say therefore to the unmarried and widows, It is good for them if they abide even as I.

9 But if they cannot contain, let them marry: for it is better to marry than to burn.

Introductory Thoughts

It is natural for a man to be attracted to a woman and for a woman to find a man attractive. In fact, in the proper context, this desire is established and even nurtured by the Lord. Yet, this desire is never to be acted upon outside of the marriage bounds *(Hebrews 13:4)*. For this reason, the Bible sets certain parameters. For instance, the Bible says that a man should not *"touch a woman" (1 Corinthians 7:1)*. The Lord gave this privilege only to those who are joined together in marriage. In marriage, neither the husband nor the wife has power over his or her own body *(1 Corinthians 7:4)*. In fact, the only time this privilege is to be withheld from the spouse is for the sake of fasting and prayer *(1 Corinthians 7:5)*. Even this spiritual duty only lasts temporarily so that Satan's temptation does not overcome the husband or his wife.

Devotional Thoughts

- **(For children):** Mrs. Potiphar had a husband, but she wanted Joseph too. Read Joseph's godly answer to her *(Genesis 39:9)*. When David took a wife not belonging to him, God was angry *(2 Samuel 12:9-10)* and God has not changed.
- **(For everyone):** Why is it important for people to refrain from acting upon physical attractions until joined in marriage? How does this make marriage even more precious?
- What kind of temptations exist when a husband and wife refrain from intimacy for long periods of time? Would it be fair to say that long periods lacking intimacy are unscriptural *(1 Corinthians 7:5)*?

Prayer Thoughts

- Ask God to protect our children from a loss of purity.
- Ask the Lord to strengthen your relationship with your spouse.

SONG: *TRUST AND OBEY*

Notes: _____

_____

_____

_____

_____

Quotes from the next volume

(VOLUME 4, WEEK 35)

Subject: Respect

Though there are times where God respects some while rejecting others, His acceptance and rejection is never a baseless respect. This teaching opposes the doctrines of Calvinism.

Mankind has made many varying attempts in an effort to gain God's attention. Most of these things are vain, self-serving, and prideful at best.

36
Relationships (con't)

Relationships—The studies to follow focus particularly upon relationships prior to marriage as well as those within and outside of the marriage bond. This week's study focuses upon those elements which tend to sever the family unit.

Interesting fact: As has already been stated, the land of Israel will be identified as *Beulah* because it will be married *(Isaiah 62:4)*. The holy Jerusalem that will descend will not only be called *"the Lamb's wife" (Revelation 21:9-10)* but is also identified as *"the mother of us all" (Galatians 4:26)*. When the new Jerusalem descends, it will do so *"prepared as a bride adorned for her husband" (Revelation 21:2)*.

Bible study tip: God integrates earthly and understandable illustrations within His word to teach or foreshadow heavenly truths. For instance, the earthly tabernacle and temple pictures the heavenly tabernacle and temple. The husband and wife relationship pictures Christ's love for His church. The birth of a child illustrates the new birth experienced by all those who trust Christ as Saviour. When these methods are used, the association will be identified which alerts the reader into the necessity of recognizing the heavenly truth being taught.

Sunday, Day 246—Church Day (no devotional)
Monday, Day 247—*Trouble in the Home*
Tuesday, Day 248—*He Hateth Putting Away*
Wednesday, Day 249—Church Night (no devotional)
Thursday, Day 250—*The Hardness of Your Hearts*
Friday, Day 251—*Grounds for Divorce*
Saturday, Day 252—*The Fatherless and Widows*

Day 246: Church Day

1 Corinthians 7:10 And unto the married I command, yet not I, but the Lord, **Let not the wife depart from her husband:**

11 But and if she depart, let her remain unmarried, or be reconciled to her husband: and **let not the husband put away his wife.**

12 But to the rest speak I, not the Lord: **If any brother hath a wife that believeth not, and she be pleased to dwell with him, let him not put her away.**

13 And **the woman which hath an husband that believeth not, and if he be pleased to dwell with her, let her not leave him.**

14 For **the unbelieving husband is sanctified by the wife, and the unbelieving wife is sanctified by the husband: else were your children unclean; but now are they holy.**

15 But **if the unbelieving depart, let him depart. A brother or a sister is not under bondage in such cases:** *but God hath called us to peace.*

16 For what knowest thou, O wife, whether thou shalt save thy husband? or how knowest thou, O man, whether thou shalt save thy wife?

Day 247: (Monday)
Trouble in the Home

Proverbs 11:17 The merciful man doeth good to his own soul: but **he that is cruel troubleth his own flesh.**

29 **He that troubleth his own house shall inherit the wind:** *and the fool shall be servant to the wise of heart.*

☐ Completion Date　　　　　Relationships (con't) • 289

Introductory Thoughts

Even the best of homes experience times when trouble arises. Unfortunately, few homes seem to possess the willingness to endure those difficulties which arise. Though divorce is often viewed as a solution to resolve marital and family problems, it generally further complicates an already unstable situation. It is the Devil and not God who convinces couples that divorce could solve the problems created by sin or life's inherent difficulties. Every home faces troublous times, but those homes built upon a love for the Lord seek to work through the trouble with their ultimate objective of glorifying the Lord. Rarely today do couples determine to endure the difficulties presented in the early years of marriage in order to find the joys of growing old together. These relationships lack the character to patiently wait as beauties of old age arise from the battles of youth.

Devotional Thoughts

- **(For children)**: Every marriage will experience troubles *(1 Corinthians 7:28c)*; however, there is no trouble that cannot be worked out *(Ephesians 4:32)*. God wants a husband and wife to stay together so that they may rejoice in old age *(Proverbs 5:18b; Ecclesiastes 9:9a)*.
- **(For everyone)**: Are you married? If so, how long have you been married? Is your marriage stronger today than it was at the beginning? What are some blessings you would not have experienced had you decided to divorce rather than work through your troubles?
- What are some troubles you presently deal with in your home? Does the Devil try to convince you that divorce is the solution?

Prayer Thoughts

- Ask the Lord to protect your home from divorce.
- Ask God to give you the character to endure troubles.

SONG: *GRACE GREATER THAN OUR SIN*

Day 248: (Tuesday)
He Hateth Putting Away

Malachi 2:16 **For the LORD, the God of Israel, saith that he hateth putting away:** *for one covereth violence with his garment, saith the LORD of hosts: therefore take heed to your spirit, that ye deal not treacherously.*

INTRODUCTORY THOUGHTS

God tells us in His word that He never intended for a marriage to end in divorce. He desires for one man and one woman to remain together until death parts the two asunder. Divorce would be nonexistent apart from sin **(Mark 10:5)**. Just as God hates sin, He also hates the results of sin. Instead of recognizing God's true feelings for divorce, men often seek to justify their sinful choices suggesting that God understands and would not want them to remain in an unhappy environment. As sin increases, men's opinions concerning divorce continue to drift away from God. Years ago, communities, families, and churches frowned upon the act of divorce; however, today divorce has become accepted as the norm rather than the exception. Unfortunately, divorce is not only accepted in the world but readily accepted in the pew and the pulpit.

DEVOTIONAL THOUGHTS

- **(For children):** Ruth's mind was made up to never leave her mother-in-law **(Ruth 1:16-17)**. How much more should a husband and wife have this type of commitment (whom God has brought together and made one). Read His command in **1 Corinthians 7: 10, 11c**.
- **(For everyone):** What is God's viewpoint of divorce? What is your viewpoint of divorce? Why is it imperative that your viewpoint match God's viewpoint?
- What is the perception of your home when it comes to divorce? What about the perception of your church? How can faulty perceptions lead you to make wrong choices?

PRAYER THOUGHTS

- Ask the Lord to help you adopt His view of divorce.
- Ask God to strengthen your home.

SONG: *CHRIST LIVETH IN ME*

Day 249: Church Night

1 Corinthians 7:27 Art thou bound unto a wife? seek not to be loosed. Art thou loosed from a wife? seek not a wife.

Day 250: (Thursday)
The Hardness of Your Hearts

Matthew 19:3 The Pharisees also came unto him, tempting him, and saying unto him, **Is it lawful for a man to put away his wife for every cause?**

4 And he answered and said unto them, Have ye not read, that he which made them at the beginning made them male and female,

5 And said, For this cause shall a man leave father and mother, and shall cleave to his wife: and they twain shall be one flesh?

6 Wherefore they are no more twain, but one flesh. **What therefore God hath joined together, let not man put asunder.**

7 They say unto him, **Why did Moses then command to give a writing of divorcement, and to put her away?**

8 He saith unto them, **Moses because of the hardness of your hearts suffered you to put away your wives: but from the beginning it was not so.**

INTRODUCTORY THOUGHTS

Because of the hardness of man's heart, God permitted man to seek a divorce. The Pharisees, who generally sought to broaden the law's reach and its application, sought to expand the justification for a divorce. The Lord never condoned this type of perversion of truth but quickly told the Pharisees that God never intended for marriage to have an escape clause when a man simply grew weary or discontented. God introduced the bill of divorcement because of the hardness of men's hearts. Even then, the Lord indicated very limited grounds for a biblical divorce. Divorce was never intended to be an option for the masses, and even in those cases where a bill of divorcement was justified or allowed, the Lord still preferred reconciliation between the husband and wife.

Devotional Thoughts

- **(For children):** The Pharisees were known for strictly carrying out the law. They knew the answers to their own questions. Jesus said, *"Have ye not read?"* When we stubbornly refuse to turn from wrongdoing in spite of warnings, our hearts will become hardened *(Hebrews 3:12-13)*.
- **(For everyone):** Why did the Lord introduce the bill of divorcement? What was God's original intent in marriage? Why do men always seek justification to violate God's intention?
- What should your mindset be when entering into marriage? What steps should you take prior to marriage to ensure a healthy and holy marriage?

Prayer Thoughts

- Thank God for the godly homes and ask Him to preserve them.
- Ask the Lord to help you understand the reason for divorce.

SONG: *TAKE MY LIFE, AND LET IT BE*

Day 251: (Friday)
Grounds for Divorce

Matthew 19:9 And I say unto you, **Whosoever shall put away his wife, except it be for fornication, and shall marry another, committeth adultery:** *and whoso marrieth her which is put away doth commit adultery.*

Introductory Thoughts

The world justifies an almost unlimited range of reasons for divorce, but the Lord is much more narrow-minded than today's promiscuous society. Society reduced it strictness concerning divorce and now the populace accepts no-fault divorces generally citing incompatibility as the cause. The Lord only offered one just cause for divorce in *Matthew 19:9*. An excellent cross reference *(Deuteronomy 24:1)* indicates that the fornication mentioned may have been directed more toward an uncleanness found within the woman that took place prior to marriage. One might argue that the Lord broadened this scope when speaking of the unbelieving spouse leaving the believer, but even there the Lord said to the believing husband, *"let him not put her away"* *(1 Corinthians 7:12)* and to the believing wife, *"let her not leave him"* **(1 Corinthians 7:13).**

Devotional Thoughts

- **(For children):** Abigail was a godly woman married to a wicked husband **(1 Samuel 25:3, 17c).** She remained with Nabal until his death **(1 Samuel 25:38).** She then became David's wife **(1 Samuel 25:39-42).**
- **(For everyone):** What does God's narrow viewpoint concerning divorce suggest about how highly He values the marriage relationship? Why is it important that we adopt His respect for the sanctity of marriage?
- Have you been divorced or know someone who has been divorced? Can God use those who have been divorced? Give some examples of God graciously using those with troubled pasts.

Prayer Thoughts

- Ask the Lord to build strong homes within your church.
- Thank the Lord for placing such a high value on marriage.

SONG: *BEWARE LEST THOU FORGET THE LORD*

Day 252: (Saturday)
The Fatherless and Widows

Psalm 68:5 A father of the fatherless, and a judge of the widows, is God in his holy habitation.

Introductory Thoughts

Divorce is not the only tragedy that can directly split a home. In fact, the separation caused by death often impacts the home similar to the act of divorce. Throughout scripture, the Lord promises to minister to and defend those whose homes are torn apart because of death's sting. Though this separation is not always directly caused by specific sin, all death results as a consequence of the entry of sin into the world. As such, the Lord shows Himself strong to those who feel its impact most. Any time a home is severed there are difficulties, but the difficulties of losing a husband and father require special attention from the Lord and He is glad to offer His strength to those directly affected. The God of the Bible is the God of the widow and the fatherless, and He never forsakes His own.

Devotional Thoughts

- **(For children):** ***Psalm 146:9*** says that the Lord *"relieveth the fatherless and widow."* One example is the story of the widow and her two sons found in ***2 Kings 4:1-7***. Since the Bible says that God cares for the fatherless and the widow, how should you treat them?
- **(For everyone):** Look up some verses on the fatherless and widow. What are some ways in which the Lord plainly declared His loyalty to those who have lost loved ones to death?
- How can the loss of a loved one negatively affect a wife and children? How can the Lord take the loss and use it for an opportunity to show His faithfulness?

Prayer Thoughts

- Thank the Lord for His faithfulness.
- Ask the Lord to bless those who have lost loved ones.

SONG: *DOES JESUS CARE?*

Notes: _____

_____

_____

_____

Quotes from the next volume

(VOLUME 4, WEEK 36)

Subject: Respect (con't)

Respect in the Bible refers to looking at two different things and preferring one over the other. If there is anything in this world that is worthy of man's respect, it is the written word of God.

In a self-centered world, it is hard to imagine what it would be like to find a people who esteemed *"other better than themselves"* ***(Philippians 2:3)***, but that is exactly what God expects from Christians.

37

Reputation

Reputation—found seven times in seven verses

Variations: reputation, reputed

First usage: *Job 18:3* (reputed)

Last usage: *Philippians 2:29* (reputation)

Defined: the manner in which someone is esteemed or valued in the eyes of another

Interesting fact: It has been said that a good reputation takes a lifetime to build but only a moment to destroy. It is not the great things that trip up the man but frequently the little things. According to *Ecclesiastes 10:1*, something as simple and common as dead flies can cause an otherwise delightful smell of the apothecary to become a stinking savour. In like manner, a *little* foolish behaviour pollutes a man's otherwise spotless reputation.

Bible study tip: Approach the scripture open-mindedly. Preconceived notions frequently may be correct, but when they are not correct, they too can serve as the obstruction to your understanding of a passage. Simply because a particular interpretation has become popular and generally accepted does not make it correct or accurate. Consider **Psalm 127:1**—to what type of house does the psalm refer? Based upon **Psalm 127:3-5**, we assume that it refers to a man's family. However, the subtitle says, "A Song of degrees for Solomon." Solomon built the temple for the Lord. Is it possible **Psalm 127:1** could instead be referring to the temple **(1 Kings 8:27)**? Perhaps our preconceived notion is accurate, but an open mind invites actual Bible study to determine the veracity of any teaching.

Sunday, Day 253—Church Day (no devotional)
Monday, Day 254—*A Good Name*
Tuesday, Day 255—*The Day of One's Death*
Wednesday, Day 256—Church Night (no devotional)
Thursday, Day 257—*The Cornerstone of a Good Reputation*
Friday, Day 258—*Behaviour Affects Your Reputation*
Saturday, Day 259—*Favour in the Sight of God and Man*

Day 253: Church Day

Acts 16:1 Then came he to Derbe and Lystra: and, behold, a certain disciple was there, named **Timotheus**, *the son of a certain woman, which was a Jewess, and believed; but his father was a Greek:*
2 Which **was well reported of by the brethren that were at Lystra and Iconium.**

Day 254: (Monday)
A Good Name

Proverbs 22:1 **A good name is rather to be chosen than great riches**, *and loving favour rather than silver and gold.*

INTRODUCTORY THOUGHTS

In scripture, a man's name frequently refers to his reputation. The wise man values a good name far above the accumulated wealth of the entire world. Its value is priceless. A good name is what others think of a man resulting from his conduct. Unfortunately, many people throughout history have willingly sabotaged their good name in order to get gain and earthly pleasure. Yet, those who truly believe and trust the word of God know that *"A good name is rather to be chosen than great riches."* With this in mind, the believer should reflect upon the long-term effects every decision brings upon his reputation. Reaping immediate gratification takes a back seat to the prolonged benefits of having a good name among other believers, the unsaved, and especially the Lord.

Devotional Thoughts

- **(For children):** Mary of Bethany had a reputation of loving the Lord *(Luke 10:38-42; John 12:1-8; Mark 14:9)*. Timothy had a good name among his fellow Christians *(Acts 16:1-2; Philippians 2:19-22)*. What is your reputation?
- **(For everyone):** Have you ever heard old-timers talk about a business or individual having "a good name"? What did they mean when they paid this compliment?
- What is your reputation among family, or friends, or brothers and sisters in Christ, or the lost? How has that reputation come to be what it is?

Prayer Thoughts

- Ask God to show you the value of a good name.
- Ask the Lord to give you wisdom in protecting your name.

SONG: *TAKE TIME TO BE HOLY*

Day 255: (Tuesday)
The Day of One's Death

Ecclesiastes 7:1 A good name is better than precious ointment; and the day of death than the day of one's birth.

Introductory Thoughts

As is often the case, men's opinions and those of God are at opposite ends of the spectrum. For instance, man emphasizes celebrating the day of one's birth and mourns the day of one's death. Scripture points out that the day of one's death is far better than the day of one's birth. Why? The day of one's death comes with very few questions concerning the individual. The person has lived his life and left behind a reputation, good or bad. However, when a child enters into this world, he does so with numerous uncertainties. What kind of person will he be? Will he love and serve the Lord, or will he live wickedly? Only a life fully lived answers these questions. Each day's work contributes to a man's reputation so that death leaves few questions.

Devotional Thoughts

- **(For children):** When Judas and Paul were born into this world, people did not know what they would accomplish in their lives. Yet, the end of their lives told how they would be remembered *(Matthew 27:3-5; 2 Timothy 4:6-7).*
- **(For everyone):** What do you envision will be said of you when you leave this earth in death? What is your reputation? What have you done to ensure that you have left a godly mark upon those you have influenced?
- What is known of an individual who dies that cannot yet be known of one who was just born into this world? How does this confirm that the day of death is better than the day of birth?

Prayer Thoughts

- Ask the Lord to help you leave behind a godly reputation.
- Ask God to help you clear up the uncertainties of birth.

SONG: *DEATH ENDS OUR MORTAL STRIFE*

Day 256: Church Night

Acts 10:22 And they said, **Cornelius the centurion, a just man, and one that feareth God, and of good report among all the nation of the Jews,** *was warned from God by an holy angel to send for thee into his house, and to hear words of thee.*

Day 257: (Thursday)
The Cornerstone of a Good Reputation

Hebrews 11:1 Now **faith** *is the substance of things hoped for, the evidence of things not seen.*

2 For **by it the elders obtained a good report.**

☐ Completion Date   Reputation • 299

INTRODUCTORY THOUGHTS

Undoubtedly, there are many personal traits that serve as the building blocks for a good reputation. Yet, the scripture plainly identifies one particular trait that serves as the cornerstone of a good reputation: Faith! Hebrews chapter 11, commonly known as the "Hall of Faith," chronicles how the saints of old developed good reputations *by* and *through* faith. Though these men and women performed great works, the works were accomplished through faith. The Bible plainly declares that it was by faith that *"the elders obtained a good report"* **(Hebrews 11:1-2)**. To reemphasize this truth, the Lord repeated this thought in **Hebrews 11:39** when He said, *"And these all, having obtained a good report through faith."*

DEVOTIONAL THOUGHTS

- **(For children):** Barnabas lived a life of faith *(Acts 11:24)*. He helped the early church *(Acts 4:36-37)*, urged people to do right, taught them, and could be trusted *(Acts 11:22-30)*. He also gave a second chance to Christians who failed *(Acts 15:36-40)*.
- **(For everyone):** How could faith give the elders a good report among other believers? How do you feel about those you know who are faithless or unbelieving? How does their conduct harm their reputation?
- Do you know someone who lives a life of faith? What is your opinion of that person? How should you live your life? How would that change your reputation?

PRAYER THOUGHTS

- Ask God to help you see the tie between faith and the right reputation.
- Ask the Lord to give you strong faith.

SONG: *FAITH IS THE VICTORY*

Day 258: (Friday)
Behaviour Affects Your Reputation

***1 Samuel 18:30** Then the princes of the Philistines went forth: and it came to pass, after they went forth, that **David behaved himself** more **wisely** than all the servants of Saul; so that **his name was much set by**.*

300 • Reputation ☐ Completion Date

INTRODUCTORY THOUGHTS

For the most part, David's reputation is one to be admired. That reputation as a servant of God and of Saul was established by his pattern of godly behaviour. According to scripture, David's *"name was much set by."* Why? Because he *"behaved himself more wisely than all the servants of Saul."* The way in which David conducted himself even during times of extreme adversity caused the people of God to speak of him often and he became elevated in their minds and hearts. David moved ahead of Saul in popularity not by eloquent speeches of self-aggrandizement, but merely because he allowed God to use his good behaviour to gain a godly reputation among the people. In similar fashion, men today are still not going to develop good reputations apart from the right behaviour.

DEVOTIONAL THOUGHTS

- **(For children):** Read what David wrote in ***Psalm 101:2a***. When living in the land of the Philistines, king Achish had nothing but praise for David *(1 Samuel 29:3)*. When the apostles needed helpers, read what kind of reputation the chosen men had to exhibit *(Acts 6:3-5)*.
- **(For everyone):** What is your behaviour among believers? What is your behaviour among nonbelievers? How has this formed your reputation? What kind of reputation have you formed?
- What kind of things did David do early in his life in order to develop a good reputation? What must you do if you would like to have a good reputation?

PRAYER THOUGHTS

- Ask God to show you the reputation your behaviour will likely develop.
- Thank God for those in your life who have given you the right example.

SONG: *JESUS CALLS US*

Day 259: (Saturday)
Favour in the Sight of God and Man

*Proverbs 3:1 My son, **forget not my law; but let thine heart keep my commandments**:*

2 For **length of days, and long life, and peace, shall they add to thee.**

3 **Let not mercy and truth forsake thee**: *bind them about thy neck; write them upon the table of thine heart:*

4 **So shalt thou find favour and good understanding in the sight of God and man.**

INTRODUCTORY THOUGHTS

Men not only develop reputations among other men, but they also develop a reputation with the Lord. A wise individual seeks *"favour and good understanding in the sight of God and man."* Fortunately, the path to favour in the sight of God follows the same course as that of finding favour in the sight of the right kind of men. According to **Proverbs 3:1-3**, these elements include remembrance of God's law, keeping the commandments, and forsaking not mercy and truth. Before dismissing the importance of this dual favour amongst both God and man, consider that the scriptures inform us that the Lord Jesus increased in wisdom leading to an increase in *"favour with God and man."*

DEVOTIONAL THOUGHTS

- **(For children):** Samuel grew in favour with God and man *(1 Samuel 2:11, 26)*, as did Daniel *(Daniel 1:8-9; Daniel 6:3)*, as did Joseph *(Genesis 39:3-4, 21-23)*. Consider **Romans 14:17-18**.
- **(For everyone):** Who are some others in scripture that found good favour in the sight of God and man? How did their reputations help them find favour?
- Why is it important to have a good reputation with the Lord and amongst the right kind of people? How much is your reputation based upon your own efforts?

PRAYER THOUGHTS

- Ask the Lord to help you find favour in His sight.
- Ask God to show you His path to a good reputation.

SONG: *O! TO BE LIKE THEE*

Notes:

Quotes from the next volume

(VOLUME 4, WEEK 37)

Subject: Salutations

A man's salutation is the initial window to the condition of his heart.

Paul's salutation was so important that though he did not personally pen all of his epistles, he informed us that he personally penned his salutation *(2 Thessalonians 3:17)*.

38

Reputation (con't)

Reputation—Of the seven occurrences in scripture, Philippians chapter 2 contains two of them *(Philippians 2:7, 29)*.

Variations: reputation, reputed

Last usage in the Old Testament: *Daniel 4:35* (reputed)

First usage in the New Testament: *Acts 5:34* (reputation)

Interesting fact: Prior to the Lord's incarnation, Jesus was **reputed** as *"the Word" (John 1:1)* in heaven. As the Word, He *"was with God and . . . was God."* Yet, when He came to this earth, He *"made himself of no reputation, and took upon him the form of a servant, and was made in the likeness of men" (Philippians 2:7)*, condescending *"a little lower than the angels" (Hebrews 2:9)*. Why did He do all this? For *"all the inhabitants of the earth"* who *"are reputed as nothing" (Daniel 4:35)*. Now, the redeemed of the earth (those truly saved) can claim the **reputation** of *"sons of God" (1 John 3:2)*.

Bible study tip: Timothy was the bishop or pastor of the church of the Ephesians (*1 Timothy 1:3* along with the postscript found at the end of Second Timothy). Titus was the bishop or pastor of the church of the Cretians (*Titus 1:5* along with the postscript found at the end of the book of Titus). As such, Paul's epistles to these two pastors are identified as the Pastoral Epistles and contain the qualifications along with the job descriptions of the pastor.

Sunday, Day 260—Church Day (no devotional)
Monday, Day 261—*Your Reputation Precedes You*
Tuesday, Day 262—*From Murder to Meekness*
Wednesday, Day 263—Church Night (no devotional)
Thursday, Day 264—*Well Reported Of*
Friday, Day 265—*A Reputation Worthy of Thanks*
Saturday, Day 266—*A Good Report Yields Opportunity*

Day 260: Church Day

Ecclesiastes 10:1 Dead flies cause the ointment of the apothecary to send forth a stinking savour: so doth a little folly him that is in reputation for wisdom **and** *honour.*

Day 261: (Monday)
Your Reputation Precedes You

Acts 9:13 Then Ananias answered, Lord, **I have heard by many of this man, how much evil he hath done to thy saints at Jerusalem**:
14 And here he hath authority from the chief priests to bind all that call on thy name.

Introductory Thoughts

Saul chose to persecute the church of God **(Galatians 1:13)** which caused great hesitancy on the part of believers to accept Saul after he was converted to Christ. When the Lord spoke to Ananias, Ananias reminded the Lord of Saul's past endeavours as well as Saul's "present mission." The Lord had to reassure Ananias that all was well, and that Saul (changed to Paul) was a chosen vessel to be used of God. When Paul began preaching Christ, many were amazed because they knew Paul as *"he that destroyed them which called on this name"* **(Acts 9:21)**. When Paul *"was come to Jerusalem, he assayed to join himself to the disciples: but they were all afraid of him, and believed not that he was a disciple"* **(Acts 9:26)**.

☐ Completion Date

Some sinners dig such a mighty deep pit for themselves that only the grace of God and the wisdom of the believers can overcome.

Devotional Thoughts

- **(For children):** Even as a child, you have a reputation *(Proverbs 20:11)*. Are friends glad to have you visit with them in their homes or do they dread to see you coming? How do you act in Sunday School; before, during, and after church; at the store, etc?
- **(For everyone):** Why was Ananias hesitant about going to Paul? Why were the disciples hesitant about accepting Paul into their fellowship and number? How can your actions cause others to be hesitant in accepting or rejecting you?
- Paul was converted in Acts chapter 9, but it took years for his reputation to catch up to the new man. What can we learn from Paul's struggles about the importance of maintaining a good reputation at all times?

Prayer Thoughts

- Ask the Lord to show you the importance of each action that you take.
- Ask God to give you patience as you seek to fix and repair your tainted reputation.

SONG: *AND CAN IT BE THAT I SHOULD GAIN?*

Day 262: (Tuesday)
From Murder to Meekness

Exodus 2:14 And he said, **Who made thee a prince and a judge over us? intendest thou to kill me, as thou killedst the Egyptian?** *And Moses feared, and said, Surely this thing is known.*

Introductory Thoughts

The Bible has many examples of reputations that were changed. For instance, Moses grew up in Egypt, specifically in the house of Pharaoh. One day, when he was a grown man, he witnessed an Egyptian smiting a Jew. Moses killed the Egyptian in order to protect his kinsman. Bad news travels fast and Moses immediately developed a reputation as a short-tempered killer. He learned of this when he attempted to intervene during a dispute between two Hebrews. After the Pharaoh found out

Moses' identity, Moses ran for his life and spent the next forty years in hiding. Eventually, the Lord spoke to Moses and called him to lead the Israelites out of Egypt and into a land of promise. Moses failed to lead the people into Canaan, but he succeeded in changing his tarnished reputation into something that God commended *(Numbers 12:3)*.

Devotional Thoughts

- **(For children):** On Paul's first missionary journey, John Mark left the work *(Acts 13:13)*. To Paul, he had the reputation of being a "quitter" *(Acts 15:36-40)*. Mark proved himself and Paul later commended him for his good reputation *(Colossians 4:7-11; Philemon 24; 2 Timothy 4:11)*.
- **(For everyone):** Moses was forty years old when he left Egypt as a killer and eighty years old when he returned as Israel's saviour. In the least, how long did it take Moses to change his reputation? What does this teach you about the importance of time and patience especially once we have made a mess of things?
- What is your reputation? Is there anything you would like to change? What are you willing to do to redeem your reputation?

Prayer Thoughts

- Thank the Lord for the opportunity to change your reputation.
- Ask God for the diligence to change what needs to be changed.

SONG: *AMAZING GRACE!*

Day 263: Church Night

Luke 6:44 **For every tree is known by his own fruit.** *For of thorns men do not gather figs, nor of a bramble bush gather they grapes.*

Day 264: (Thursday)
Well Reported Of

Acts 16:1 Then came he to Derbe and Lystra: and, behold, a certain disciple was there, named **Timotheus,** *the son of a certain woman, which was a Jewess, and believed; but his father was a Greek:*

2 Which **was well reported of by the brethren** *that were at Lystra and Iconium.*

☐ Completion Date	Reputation (con't) • 307

Introductory Thoughts

The brethren have become notorious about speaking of one another, not always in the best light. Frequently, the individual's reputation who is the subject of the conversation dictates the tone of the conversation. We have several examples of the brethren speaking of Timothy. Thankfully, each instance involved a report of praise. If someone chose to speak evil of Timothy, the conversation would have had to revolve around some sort of baseless accusation. According to the Bible's testimony of Timothy, he had a wonderful reputation among believers at Lystra and Iconium. Paul likewise gave a good report of Timothy when he said, *"I have no man likeminded, who will naturally care for your state. . . . But ye know the proof of him, that as a son with the father, he hath served with me in the gospel"* **(Philippians 2:20-22)**. Every Christian should live in such a way that any evil report would be baseless and rejected by those who know you best.

Devotional Thoughts

- **(For children):** Many people in the Bible had a good reputation. Consider Ruth **(Ruth 2:11-12; Ruth 3:11)**; Timothy's mother and grandmother **(2 Timothy 1:5; 2 Timothy 3:15)**; Demetrius **(3 John 12)**; Cornelius **(Acts 10:2, 22)**.
- **(For everyone):** What were the keys to Timothy's development of a good reputation? How could those keys be instrumental in your own development of a good reputation?
- Can you dictate everything that people are going to say about you? Can you dictate any of the things that people will say about you? How can this dual understanding change your life?

Prayer Thoughts

- Ask God to give you a reputation like Timothy.
- Ask the Lord to give you the wisdom to maintain a good report.

SONG: *SAVED, SAVED!*

Day 265: (Friday)
A Reputation Worthy of Thanks

***Romans 1:8** First, I thank my God through Jesus Christ for you all, that your faith is spoken of throughout the whole world.*

Introductory Thoughts

No doubt Paul spoke to the Lord about Hymenaeus and Alexander and their wickedness *(1 Timothy 1:20; 2 Timothy 4:14),* but he most likely expended his strength thanking God for believers like those in Rome *(Romans 1:8).* All believers should thank God for those whose reputations have been carefully maintained. Throughout the world, people spoke of the faith of those in Rome. The Bible tells us that news of their obedience spread abroad unto all men *(Romans 16:19).* Although Paul would commend them for their godly reputations, he knew who ultimately deserved the thanks. In like manner, believers today should put forth more strength thanking God for good reputations.

Devotional Thoughts

- (**For children**): Read why Paul was thankful for Philemon *(Philemon 4-7);* for the saints in the church at Colosse *(Colossians 1:1-4).* Name someone who lives for the Lord and for whom you are especially thankful.
- (**For everyone**): When is the last time you thanked God for the good reputations of certain believers? Do you spend too much time complaining about the carnal saints and too little time thanking God for those who bear a good testimony?
- Do you have a good reputation? How did you ultimately gain that reputation? Have you thanked God for it?

Prayer Thoughts

- Thank God for the godly reputations of those you know.
- Ask God to protect these believers.

SONG: *COUNT YOUR BLESSINGS*

Day 266: (Saturday)
A Good Report Yields Opportunity

Acts 6:1 And in those days, when the number of the disciples was multiplied, there arose a murmuring of the Grecians against the Hebrews, because their widows were neglected in the daily ministration.

2 Then the twelve called the multitude of the disciples unto them, and said, It is not reason that we should leave the word of God, and serve tables.

3 Wherefore, brethren, **look ye out among you seven men of honest report, full of the Holy Ghost and wisdom,** *whom we may appoint over this business.*

Introductory Thoughts

With the need so great, Christians frequently wonder why they are not used more in the Lord's service and work. They fail to realize that their reputations have limited many of their opportunities. Until their reputations are repaired, their opportunities will remain hindered. In the early church, a problem came to the attention of the apostles when the *"widows were neglected in the daily ministration" (Acts 6:1)*. As the apostles gave counsel for a solution, they suggested that the believers look out among them *"seven men of honest report, full of the Holy Ghost and wisdom" (Acts 6:3)*. Why was it so important to consider the reputations of those men who were potential candidates? The apostles knew that the reputation of man hinders or helps in the service of the Lord.

Devotional Thoughts

- **(For children):** David kept sheep for his father. He had an excellent reputation. Even one of king Saul's servants knew his stellar reputation. When Saul needed someone to play a harp, David was offered the opportunity and later became Saul's armourbearer *(1 Samuel 16:17-22)*.
- **(For everyone):** God can overcome someone's reputation, but men require more time. Why is it important to have a good reputation among the saved and among the lost?

- What are some other areas of service in which the Lord demanded a good reputation as a qualification for service? What does this suggest about our reputations?

PRAYER THOUGHTS
- Ask the Lord to give you a good report and opportunity to serve.
- Thank God for the light He has given in His word.

SONG: *HOLD FAST TILL I COME*

Notes: _____

Quotes from the next volume

(VOLUME 4, WEEK 38)

Subject: Sin

When man avoids the words of God, he avoids his only hope for knowing what sin is and how it affects him both now and in eternity.

The word of God is truth *(John 17:17)*. As such, it does not always paint man in a positive light but, rather, always portrays him accurately.

The Lord knows man's foolishness *(Psalm 69:5)*; He can search it out though it is hidden in the very depths of man's heart *(Psalm 44:20-21)*.

39

Sacrifices

Sacrifices—found 339 times in 312 verses

Variations: sacrifice, sacrificed, sacrificedst, sacrifices, sacrificeth, sacrificing

First usage: *Genesis 31:54* (sacrifice)

Last usage: *Revelation 2:20* (sacrificed)

Defined: to surrender something, give it up, or suffer it to be lost

Interesting fact: Many Bible students have noted a close association between the New Testament book of *Hebrews* and the Old Testament book of *Leviticus*. This association is heightened when considering the present subject of *sacrifice*. Each of these books, Hebrews in the New Testament and Leviticus in the Old Testament, references the word *sacrifice* and its variations more than any of their counterparts within their particular testaments.

Bible study tip: When studying the Old Testament sacrifices, be sure not to neglect the literal interpretation of scripture. While there is no doubt many, if not all, of the sacrifices which foreshadowed Christ, the study should first give consideration to the actual and literal details of each sacrifice. Once these truths are firmly settled, then, and only then, should the Bible student seek to comprehend how the sacrifices typified the Lord Jesus Christ.

Sunday, Day 267—Church Day (no devotional)
Monday, Day 268—*Christ, Sacrificed for Us*
Tuesday, Day 269—*To Him Shall Ye Do Sacrifice*
Wednesday, Day 270—Church Night (no devotional)
Thursday, Day 271—*God Makes the Rules*
Friday, Day 272—*God Does Not Need Your Sacrifices*
Saturday, Day 273—*With Such Sacrifices God Is Pleased*

Day 267: Church Day

***Psalm 4:5** Offer the sacrifices of righteousness, and put your trust in the LORD.*

Day 268: (Monday)
Christ, Sacrifices for Us

***1 Corinthians 5:7** Purge out therefore the old leaven, that ye may be a new lump, as ye are unleavened. For even **Christ our passover is sacrificed for us**:*

INTRODUCTORY THOUGHTS

God demands righteousness, and when man fails to meet His standards, He calls for the shedding of blood for the remission of sins **(Hebrews 9:22)**. Throughout the Old Testament, sacrifices majored on the blood of animals, but these animal sacrifices could never take away sins **(Hebrews 10:4)**. God, in mercy, sent His Son to give *"himself for us an offering and a sacrifice to God for a sweetsmelling savour"* **(Ephesians 5:2)**. Unlike the Old Testament sacrifices, the Lord Jesus was a single onetime sacrifice that offered forgiveness of sin for all and to all. In shedding His blood, the Lord Jesus Christ became man's sacrifice, and man need look no further than the shed blood of Christ for the means by which God is satisfied.

Devotional Thoughts

- **(For children):** When a person performs some type of sacrifice, he gives up something so that others can be helped in some manner. Our greatest example of a sacrifice is when Christ gave up His life so that we could live forever in heaven *(John 3:16; I Corinthians 15:3-4; 2 Corinthians 5:21; 1 Peter 3:18)*.
- **(For everyone):** How is the life, death, and resurrection of Christ best described as a sacrifice? How does His sacrifice for our salvation cancel the need for any other sacrifices?
- To what extent did Christ's sacrifice of Himself for our sins cost Him? What was the nature of His heart in offering Himself for us?

Prayer Thoughts

- Thank God for the sacrifice of His Son.
- Ask God to give you a heart of thanksgiving for His sacrifice.

SONG: *ALAS! AND DID MY SAVIOUR BLEED?*

Day 269: (Tuesday)
To Him Shall Ye Do Sacrifice

*2 Kings 17:36 But **the LORD**, who brought you up out of the land of Egypt with great power and a stretched out arm, him shall ye fear, and him shall ye worship, and **to him shall ye do sacrifice**.*

Introductory Thoughts

The scriptures plainly and repeatedly state that Christ gave Himself as man's complete and only sacrifice. Yet, the New Testament proclaims that because of salvation, the believer can offer spiritual sacrifices to God *(1 Peter 2:5)*. Before a believer can determine the complete nature of these sacrifices, he must first recognize that any such sacrifices must be made to God only. The Lord declared His jealous nature in the Old Testament when He said, *"He that sacrificeth unto any god, save unto the LORD only, he shall be utterly destroyed" (**Exodus 22:20**)*. Though much has changed, God still demands that man's sacrifices be presented to Him and Him alone.

Devotional Thoughts

- **(For children):** God alone deserves our sacrifice *(Isaiah 42:8)*. Consider what these men did when they realized who the true God was: fishermen *(Jonah 1:15-16)*; Naaman *(2 Kings 5:15-17)*.
- **(For everyone):** What gods competed with the one true God as the recipients of men's sacrifices? What are some things (gods) to which modern societies might offer sacrifices, spiritual or otherwise?
- Why is it so crucial that we learn to whom we should offer our sacrifices? How does this dictate the nature and purity of our sacrifices?

Prayer Thoughts

- Ask the Lord to show you the rivals for receiving your sacrifices.
- Ask God to help all your sacrifices to be made unto Him alone.

SONG: *TO GOD BE THE GLORY*

Day 270: Church Night

Psalm 54:6 I will freely sacrifice unto thee: I will praise thy name, O LORD; for it is good.

Day 271: (Thursday)
God Makes the Rules

Joshua 22:29 God forbid that we should rebel against the LORD, and turn this day from following the LORD, to build an altar for burnt offerings, for meat offerings, or for sacrifices, beside the altar of the LORD our God that is before his tabernacle.

Introductory Thoughts

Since God is the rightful recipient of man's sacrifices, then, by necessity, He is the only One who can rightfully provide the rules for the administration of the sacrifices. In the Old Testament, God established rules about the place *(Joshua 22:29)* and purity *(Malachi 1:8, 14)* of man's sacrifices. Men who violated these rules, choosing rather to adopt their own rules of sacrifice and worship, often suffered harsh consequences, including death. The sacrifice of Christ for sin has changed many details of God's demands for sacrifice; it has not, however, changed the fact that man must do things God's way. God's rules for sacrifice whether performed in the past, present, or future are to be dictated by scripture.

DEVOTIONAL THOUGHTS

- **(For children):** We should sacrifice to God, but before we do, God wants something else from us first *(Proverbs 23:26a)*. Consider these passages: *1 Samuel 15:22; Jeremiah 6:19-20*. The Macedonians first gave their hearts to the Lord and then honoured Him with their giving *(2 Corinthians 8:1-5)*.
- **(For everyone):** God desired pure sacrifices in the Old Testament. How could that same truth be applied to every New Testament believer? What is the nature of your sacrifices to God?
- What are some rules by which the New Testament believer should offer sacrifices to God? What are some sacrifices that you can offer to Him today?

PRAYER THOUGHTS

- Ask the Lord to show you His rules for sacrifice.
- Ask God to help you submit to His plan rather than your own.

SONG: *FAITHFUL IS HE THAT PROMISES*

Day 272: (Friday)
God Does Not Need Your Sacrifices

Isaiah 1:11 To what purpose is the multitude of your sacrifices unto me? saith the LORD: **I am full of the burnt offerings of rams, and the fat of fed beasts; and I delight not in the blood of bullocks, or of lambs, or of he goats.**

INTRODUCTORY THOUGHTS

God desires the sacrifices of men because they demonstrate the love men have for Him. Yet, in reality, man's sacrifices do not fulfil any need that God inherently has. The Lord made this clear to the Old Testament saints when He said, *"I am full of the burnt offerings" (Isaiah 1:11)*. In another place He told them, *"If I were hungry, I would not tell thee: for the world is mine, and the fulness thereof" (Psalm 50:12)*. The New Testament believer offers sacrifices of praise and thanksgiving *(Hebrews 13:15)*, and these sacrifices please God, but these sacrifices do not improve God in any way. With or without the sacrifices of men, God continues to be who He is.

DEVOTIONAL THOUGHTS
- **(For children):** Paul made it clear in his sermon to the Athenians from Mars' Hill that since God is the creator, He needs nothing from us *(Acts 17:24-25)*.
- **(For everyone):** Think of some sacrifices that New Testament believers can offer to the Lord. Consider each one, and discuss why God has no need of that sacrifice.
- Why would men give God sacrifices that He does not need? What opportunities do these sacrifices provide for men? How can you declare your genuine love for God through sacrifice?

PRAYER THOUGHTS
- Thank God for the opportunity to show Him your love.
- Ask the Lord to show you just how great He truly is.

SONG: *GREAT IS THY FAITHFULNESS*

Day 273: (Saturday)
With Such Sacrifices God Is Pleased

Hebrews 13:16 **But to do good and to communicate forget not: for with such sacrifices God is well pleased.**

INTRODUCTORY THOUGHTS

The word of God makes things perfectly clear that God does not need anything from man. Yet, we see that God finds great delight in receiving those sacrifices from His creation. The apostle Paul plainly declared this truth to the Philippian believers when he said that their sacrifice was *"an odour of a sweet smell, a sacrifice acceptable, wellpleasing to God"* **(Philippians 4:18)**. He rehearsed the same truth to Hebrew believers when he said, *"But to do good and to communicate forget not: for with such sacrifices God is well pleased"* **(Hebrews 13:16)**. The sacrifices of men demonstrate a will that chooses to give something to God. Why? Because love constrains them to do so.

☐ Completion Date   Sacrifices • 317

Devotional Thoughts

- **(For children):** Sacrificing to God includes praise and thanksgiving *(Hebrews 13:15; Psalm 107:21-22)*. Look around the room. Can you thank God for at least ten things He has given you? Can you praise Him with a song *(Psalm 69:30)* like David did?
- **(For everyone):** How does it make you feel to know that you can please God with your sacrifices? How should this knowledge compel you to look for opportunities to give God that which He desires?
- What kind of sacrifices do you offer unto the Lord on a daily basis? Do those sacrifices please God? Do those sacrifices demonstrate your love for Him?

Prayer Thoughts

- Thank God for the opportunity to please Him.
- Ask the Lord to find your sacrifices acceptable and wellpleasing.

SONG: *I WILL SING THE WONDROUS STORY*

Notes: _____

Sacrifices

☐ Completion Date

Notes: _____

Quotes from the next volume

(VOLUME 4, WEEK 39)
Subject: Sin (con't)

Sin is not something that man does by accident. It is something that man allows or willingly does based upon an unwillingness to stop the act before it becomes sin.

At its root, no one thing is sinful in and of itself, but almost all things can and will become sinful when misused.

40

Sacrifices (con't)

Sacrifices—found 298 times in 272 Old Testament verses and forty-one times in forty New Testament verses

Variations: sacrifice, sacrificed, sacrificedst, sacrifices, sacrificeth, sacrificing

Last usage in the Old Testament: *Malachi 1:14* (sacrificeth)

First usage in the New Testament: *Matthew 9:13* (sacrifice)

Interesting fact: Many of the Old Testament burnt offerings most likely produced an unpleasant and unbearable smell for those who were within a reasonable distance of the sacrifice as it was offered. The unpleasantness was a constant reminder of sin and its dire consequences. However, the descriptive phrase implemented in such sacrifices describes the Lord's perspective on the matter by saying that it was a *"sweet savour"* **(Leviticus 1:9, 13, 17)** unto the Lord. Sacrifices made with the right heart reminded man of his sinfulness and its consequences. Interestingly, these same sacrifices reminded the Lord of the beauty of man's faithful obedience to His statutes.

Bible study tip: It can be quite difficult to distinguish between names and titles in the Bible. This is especially true concerning those who are new to the Bible or just beginning faithful Bible study. Though there are numerous examples of titles that could be perceived as names, the clearest and simplest one to distinguish is the title *Pharaoh*. After all, it is quite clear that the Pharaoh who dealt with Moses **(Exodus 6:29)** is not the Pharaoh with whom Solomon made affinity **(1 Kings 3:1)**.

Sunday, Day 274—Church Day (no devotional)
Monday, Day 275—*He Shall Cause the Sacrifice to Cease*
Tuesday, Day 276—*Motive Means Everything*
Wednesday, Day 277—Church Night (no devotional)
Thursday, Day 278—*Companions of Sacrifice*
Friday, Day 279—*Offering Up Spiritual Sacrifices*
Saturday, Day 280—*Let Us Offer Sacrifices Continually*

Day 274: Church Day

Psalm 116:17 I will offer to thee the sacrifice of thanksgiving, and will call upon the name of the LORD.

Day 275: (Monday)
He Shall Cause the Sacrifice to Cease

Daniel 9:27 And he shall confirm the covenant with many for one week: and in the midst of the week **he shall cause the sacrifice and the oblation to cease**, *and for the overspreading of abominations he shall make it desolate, even until the consummation, and that determined shall be poured upon the desolate.*

INTRODUCTORY THOUGHTS

The Devil despises any praise offered toward God. Men who sacrifice to God demonstrate their valuation of Him. For this reason, the Devil longs to eliminate godly sacrifices. **Daniel 9:27** references a future time known as Daniel's seventieth week when the Devil will cause the reinstituted Jewish animal sacrifices to cease. In the present age, God has clearly shown that He has no desire for man to sacrifice animals. Instead, believers offer spiritual sacrifices to God thus demonstrating their praise and declaring their love for God. Just as the Devil will one day seek to end the physical sacrifices given to the Lord by the Jewish people, he presently works hard to keep New Testament believers from offering the spiritual sacrifices of praise to God.

Devotional Thoughts

- **(For children):** The Devil has always wanted to be God *(Isaiah 14:12-14)*. While Jesus was on earth, the Devil tried to get Jesus to worship him in place of God. Jesus refused and answered the Devil with a Bible verse *(Matthew 4:8-10)*.
- **(For everyone):** Why does the Devil hate for God to receive praise? What efforts does he put forth in your life to keep you from praising God through spiritual sacrifices?
- Do you love God? What do you do in order to demonstrate your love for Him? What kind of a battle do you face when you seek to offer spiritual sacrifices unto the Lord?

Prayer Thoughts

- Ask God to help you thwart the efforts to stop your sacrifices.
- Thank God for giving you reasons to offer spiritual sacrifices.

SONG: *AM I A SOLDIER OF THE CROSS?*

Day 276: (Tuesday)
Motive Means Everything

*Proverbs 21:27 **The sacrifice of the wicked is abomination**: how much more, when **he bringeth it with a wicked mind**?*

Introductory Thoughts

The Lord loves to receive sacrifices from men. Yet, it is important to recognize that the Lord looks beyond the actual sacrifices and into the heart of those making the offerings. What He sees in the heart is far more important to Him than the actual sacrifice itself. This is because a man may offer the right sacrifices but does so from a heart of ungodliness. God does not approve of such sacrifices. There were individuals who lived in the days of animal sacrifices who brought sacrifices as prescribed by the law but did so with improper motives. The Lord said of these sacrifices that to Him, these sacrifices were an abomination. Though the nature of sacrifices has changed, the fact remains that men can, and do, offer sacrifices of praise or thanksgiving outwardly all the while their hearts are far from God *(Matthew 15:8)*.

DEVOTIONAL THOUGHTS

- **(For children)**: Some believers in the early church sacrificed by selling lands or houses and bringing the money to the apostles to help others. Barnabas, Ananias, and Sapphira were among them. Read ***Acts 4:36-37*** and ***Acts 5:1-11***. Whose heart was right with God?
- **(For everyone)**: Do you know anyone who speaks highly of the Lord or publickly gives God thanks but refuses to draw near to the Lord in his or her heart?
- Do you give the Lord praise with your lips? Do you do so to impress others? Do you do so to deceive others into believing your walk with the Lord is more than it truly is?

PRAYER THOUGHTS

- Ask God to purify your motives in sacrifice.
- Ask the Lord to enlighten you as to your motives.

SONG: *CLEANSE ME*

Day 277: Church Night

Romans 12:1 *I beseech you therefore, brethren, by the mercies of God, that ye* **present your bodies a living sacrifice, holy, acceptable unto God, which is your reasonable service***.*

Day 278: (Thursday)
Companions of Sacrifice

Nehemiah 12:43 *Also that day* **they offered great sacrifices, and rejoiced**: *for God had made them rejoice with great joy:* **the wives also and the children rejoiced**: *so that* **the joy of Jerusalem was heard even afar off***.*

☐ Completion Date   Sacrifices (con't) • 323

INTRODUCTORY THOUGHTS

Any man desiring to know the motive of his sacrifices should consider the companions of his sacrifices. If a man offers a sacrifice followed by sorrow or regret, his motive was surely wrong. For instance, some people answer the call to give financially in a time of need. They sacrifice, but frustration accompanies their sacrifice because of the loss of money. This reaction should not and will not accompany godly sacrifice given with godly motives. One who sacrifices to the Lord from a godly motive will find joy and peace accompanying his sacrifice. When God works in an individual's heart, encouraging a sacrifice, the heart rejoices at the opportunity to be obedient and declare one's love for a holy God.

DEVOTIONAL THOUGHTS

- **(For children)**: The apostles were willing to sacrifice their own comfort and lives to do what God wanted them to do—preach the gospel. They did this with joy even under difficult circumstances. Read ***Acts 5:38-42; Acts 16:22-25; Acts 20:22-24***.
- **(For everyone)**: What accompanies your sacrifices unto the Lord? What follows when you witness for the Lord? What follows when you give financially to a need?
- Do you have joy in your heart as you serve the Lord? Do you have peace knowing you are giving the Lord the sacrifices He deserves?

PRAYER THOUGHTS

- Ask the Lord to give you joy in sacrificing unto Him.
- Ask God to help your sacrifices to bring joy to others as well.

SONG: *STEPPING IN THE LIGHT*

Day 279: (Friday)
Offering Up Spiritual Sacrifices

*1 Peter 2:5 Ye also, as lively stones, **are built up a spiritual house, an holy priesthood, to offer up spiritual sacrifices**, acceptable to God by Jesus Christ.*

Sacrifices (con't)

INTRODUCTORY THOUGHTS

God no longer expects His people to bring animal sacrifices to a temple made with hands. The Lord Jesus Christ sacrificed Himself for man, and in doing so, became the ultimate sacrifice, once and for all. To bring an animal to any religious facility in the present age would be directly disobedient to the clear teachings of the New Testament. Yet, the Lord still desires to receive sacrifices from men. The sacrifices today consist of believers presenting their bodies to the Lord *(Romans 12:1)* and giving thanks to Him with their lips *(Hebrews 13:15)*. In **Hebrews 13:16** the Bible also says *"to do good and to communicate . . . for with such sacrifices God is well pleased."*

DEVOTIONAL THOUGHTS

- **(For children):** Offering thanksgiving to God is called a sacrifice *(Psalm 116:17)*. We have many things for which to thank Him *(Psalm 68:19)*. Many forget to thank Him *(Luke 17:12-18)*. We can always praise Him for giving us His word *(Psalm 56:10)*.
- **(For everyone):** What is to be the nature of sacrifices given by New Testament believers *(1 Peter 2:5)*? What are some sacrifices that would qualify *(Hebrews 13:15; Jeremiah 33:11; Psalm 51:17)*?
- Do you offer spiritual sacrifices unto the Lord? Do you give Him your heart, your body, your life, your praise, and your thanks? What do such sacrifices suggest to the Lord?

PRAYER THOUGHTS

- Thank the Lord for the opportunity to give something to Him.
- Ask God to help you give Him proper sacrifices.

SONG: *WE GATHER TOGETHER*

Day 280: (Saturday)
Let Us Offer Sacrifices Continually

*Hebrews 13:15 By him therefore **let us offer the sacrifice of praise to God continually**, that is, the fruit of our lips giving thanks to his name.*

☐ Completion Date   Sacrifices (con't) • 325

Introductory Thoughts

In the Old Testament, sacrifices were often scheduled. The sacrifice might be a sacrifice that was offered once in a year, or one that was offered as a result of some specific sin. Regardless, most often the sacrifices were based upon a schedule given by the Lord. It would appear that no such schedule is given for the New Testament believer. Instead **Hebrews 13:15** suggests that believers ought to *"offer the sacrifice of praise to God continually."* There is no need to wait until any certain day to come around next week, next month, or even next year. Every day the believer has reason to open his mouth in praise to God. Every day he has reason to give God thanks for all that He has done and is doing.

Devotional Thoughts

- **(For children):** David was a man after God's own heart. He knew God deserved his praise continually. Read **Psalm 34:1; Psalm 35:28; Psalm 70:4**. What can you praise God for right now?
- **(For everyone):** How often do you praise God? How often do you thank Him for what He has done for you? Do you wait until there are others around or do you offer Him sacrifices on a daily basis, even in the privacy of your own home?
- Has God been good to you? What has He done for you? Have you taken time to thank and praise Him?

Prayer Thoughts

- Thank God for being so good to you.
- Ask God to help you sacrifice unto Him continually.

SONG: *THANKS TO GOD*

Notes: _____
_____
_____
_____
_____
_____

Notes:

Quotes from the next volume
(VOLUME 4, WEEK 40)
Subject: Sin (con't)

Sin brings consequences. Though the blood of Christ cleanseth from all sin *(1 John 1:7)*, some things cannot merely be undone.

When a man gets right with the Lord, he should likewise look for opportunities to make things right with his fellow man.

41

Salvation

Salvation—found 523 times in 500 verses; However, some of these occurrences will refer to physical deliverance; and other Bible words are often implemented for the purpose of describing the spiritual birth of which these lessons speak.

Variations: salvation, save, saved, savest, saveth, saving

Defined: In a basic sense, the word *salvation* means deliverance which can be physical or spiritual depending upon the context.

Interesting fact: The Bible plainly teaches a completed or finished salvation *(1 Peter 1:18-19; 1 Corinthians 1:18; Ephesians 2:5, 8; 2 Timothy 1:9; Titus 3:5)*; however, it also promises a future salvation *(Romans 5:9-10; Romans 13:11; 1 Thessalonians 5:9)*. The reconciliation of the seeming conflict becomes clear as the Bible student considers that man is a three-part being. The man who has trusted Christ as Saviour has a quickened spirit *(Ephesians 2:1, 5)*, a redeemed soul *(Hebrews 10:39)*, but awaits the redemption of his body *(Romans 8:23)*.

Bible study tip: Salvation is truly a complex study. As such, it is unwise to pull one verse from its intended context in order to prove or disprove any doctrinal position. Such actions have caused many problems especially concerning things like the involvement or exclusion of repentance in salvation. Be sure to consider all verses possible when studying such a complex and frequently disputed subject like salvation. This study takes many hours and involves a considerable amount of work **(2 Timothy 2:15)**. Carefully considering the context adds another element of difficulty, and the Bible student must ensure that he is dealing with the spiritual birth as opposed to any physical deliverance.

Sunday, Day 281—Church Day (no devotional)
Monday, Day 282—*What Is Salvation?*
Tuesday, Day 283—*The Fall of Man*
Wednesday, Day 284—Church Night (no devotional)
Thursday, Day 285—*Man's Need for Salvation*
Friday, Day 286—*God's Offer to Man*
Saturday, Day 287—*What Must I Do to Be Saved?*

Day 281: Church Day

*1 Peter 1:23 Being **born again**, not of corruptible seed, but **of incorruptible, by the word of God**, which liveth and abideth for ever.*

Day 282: (Monday)
What Is Salvation?

Genesis 49:18 I have waited for thy salvation, O LORD.

INTRODUCTORY THOUGHTS

As already discussed, the word *salvation* is used throughout the word of God, but depending upon the context, the intended meaning varies. Failure to understand the different usages has led many to espouse some of the most egregious false doctrines. It is important to understand that the foundational meaning of the word *salvation* refers to *deliverance*. The vast majority of occurrences in the word of God actually refer to physical deliverance rather than a soul's salvation. The word *salvation* can often

☐ Completion Date   Salvation • 329

be found within the context to describe the time when someone received deliverance from a specific trial or a threatening enemy. The most common usage today among believers relates to spiritual deliverance offered through the finished work of Jesus Christ.

Devotional Thoughts

- **(For children):** God saves us from many physical dangers daily (***Psalm 71:15***; i.e., accidents, falls, wrecks, germs). But sin is a heart problem and separates us from God ***(Mark 7:21-23; Isaiah 59:2)***. Jesus came to save us from sin ***(Matthew 1:21)***.
- **(For everyone):** Read *Exodus 14:13* and *1 Chronicles 16:35*. What is the meaning of the word *salvation* in each passage? Did this salvation have anything to do with Christ's death, burial and resurrection?
- According to *1 Corinthians 15:1-2,* people are saved by believing the gospel. The gospel is defined in *1 Corinthians 15:3-4*. Is this salvation more than physical deliverance?

Prayer Thoughts

- Thank God for His offer of salvation.
- Ask the Lord to teach you more about His salvation.

SONG: *HE IS ABLE TO DELIVER THEE*

Day 283: (Tuesday)
The Fall of Man

*Genesis 3:6 And when **the woman saw that the tree was good for food, and** that it was pleasant to the eyes, and a tree to be desired to make one wise, she took of the fruit thereof, and **did eat, and gave also unto her husband with her; and he did eat**.*

*7 And **the eyes of them both were opened, and they knew that they were naked;** and **they sewed fig leaves together, and made themselves aprons**.*

*8 And **they heard the voice of the LORD God** walking in the garden in the cool of the day: and **Adam and his wife hid themselves from the presence of the LORD God** amongst the trees of the garden.*

Introductory Thoughts

God created man without sin. In his infancy, man had no knowledge of evil but knew only the joys of fellowship with God. The first man had a perfect environment, a perfect spouse, and an uncorrupted mind. He had little in the way of commandments as God only gave one *"thou shalt not" **(Genesis 2:16-17)***. Of all the things man could have done within the will of God, man chose to violate God's one restriction by partaking of the tree of the knowledge of good and evil. Immediately man's eyes were opened to good and evil, and he died spiritually just as God had promised. In order to rescue man, God sacrificed an animal, providing coats of skin to cover man's nakedness, and removed him from the garden.

Devotional Thoughts

- **(For children):** Adam and Eve chose to disobey God. Obedience is a proof of love. Read what Jesus said we would do if we loved Him ***(John 14:15, 23)***. When we disobey our parents ***(Colossians 3:20)***, we are not showing love to them or the Lord.
- **(For everyone):** Why did God place a tree in the garden that could potentially break the fellowship between man and Himself? What would the option to sin prove had man instead chosen to do right?
- How did God offer salvation to Adam and Eve? What did He do for them? What did He do to keep them from doing further damage?

Prayer Thoughts

- Ask God to show you how the sin of Adam and Eve affects you.
- Thank God for His care for mankind.

SONG: *CHRIST RECEIVETH SINFUL MEN*

Day 284: Church Night

Titus 3:4 But after that the kindness and love of God our Saviour toward man appeared,

5 **Not by works of righteousness which we have done, but according to his mercy he saved us***, by the washing of regeneration, and renewing of the Holy Ghost;*

6 Which he shed on us abundantly through Jesus Christ our Saviour;

Day 285: (Thursday)
Man's Need for Salvation

*1 Corinthians 15:22 For as **in Adam all die**, even so in Christ shall all be made alive.*

INTRODUCTORY THOUGHTS

When Adam transgressed, he affected and infected all that would come after him. When God created man, He did so after His own likeness *(Genesis 1:26; Genesis 5:1)*, but when Adam bore a son after the fall, the Bible says that Adam *"begat a son in his own likeness" (Genesis 5:3)*. Adam's sin came with dire consequences experienced by all. All those born of Adam's seed bear Adam's image *(1 Corinthians 15:47-49)* and the Bible points out that *"in Adam all die" (1 Corinthians 15:22)*. At the same time, no man faces the eternal judgment of God for bearing Adam's image, but he does so based upon his own practice of sin and refusal to accept God's free gift of salvation through His Son, Jesus Christ.

DEVOTIONAL THOUGHTS

- **(For children):** The Bible is very plain that man needs to be saved. The answer to the question in *Proverbs 20:9* is no one. Read also *Romans 5:12; Romans 5:19; Romans 3:23; Romans 6:23*. What do you learn from these verses?
- **(For everyone):** What evidence exists that Adam's sin has affected you? What naturally lies within you that did not originally exist within Adam?
- How have you added to the problem by personally choosing to sin? Have you tried to blame Adam and Eve rather than realizing you would face God's judgment based upon your own sin?

PRAYER THOUGHTS

- Ask the Lord to begin working in your heart if you are not saved.
- Thank God for considering man's great need for salvation.

SONG: *LOOK AND LIVE*

Day 286: (Friday)
God's Offer to Man

John 3:16 **For God so loved the world, that he gave his only begotten Son, that whosoever believeth in him should not perish, but have everlasting life.**

17 **For God sent not his Son into the world to condemn the world; but that the world through him might be saved.**

INTRODUCTORY THOUGHTS

Man made himself the enemy of God when he chose sin *(Romans 5:10)*, but God had no desire to remain man's enemy so He provided the ultimate solution. Instead of returning man's hatred, the Bible says that *"God commendeth his love toward us, in that, while we were yet sinners, Christ died for us" (Romans 5:8)*. The Lord knew man could never justly find salvation through his own merits and works *(Titus 3:5)*. God knew man could never be reconciled on his own. Rather than simply allow countless multitudes to go to hell without hope, the Lord determined to provide Himself as the sacrifice for man's sin. Man would not be dependent upon his own faulty righteousness, but on the righteousness of the spotless Lamb of God *(1 Peter 1:18-20)*.

DEVOTIONAL THOUGHTS

- **(For children):** Jesus had no sin *(1 John 3:5)*. He loved us and died for our sins *(Revelation 1:5)*. He offers you the greatest trade of all time *(2 Corinthians 5:21)*. He is the only way to be saved *(John 14:6; Acts 4:12)*.
- **(For everyone):** Why did man require the sacrifice of God's Son? What moved God to send His Son? What must man do to be reconciled to the God he offended by choosing to sin?
- How would the world be different had God refused to give His Son? How would your life be different had God not sent His Son for you?

PRAYER THOUGHTS

- Ask God to help you realize your need if you are not saved.
- Thank God for His offer of salvation through His Son.

SONG: *THE LIGHT OF THE WORLD IS JESUS*

☐ Completion Date   Salvation • 333

Day 287: (Saturday)
What Must I Do to Be Saved?

Acts 16:25 And at midnight Paul and Silas prayed, and sang praises unto God: and the prisoners heard them.

26 And suddenly there was a great earthquake, so that the foundations of the prison were shaken: and immediately all the doors were opened, and every one's bands were loosed.

*27 And **the keeper of the prison awaking out of his sleep, and seeing the prison doors open, he drew out his sword, and would have killed himself, supposing that the prisoners had been fled**.*

*28 But **Paul cried with a loud voice, saying, Do thyself no harm: for we are all here.***

*29 Then **he called for a light, and sprang in, and came trembling, and fell down before Paul and Silas**,*

*30 And **brought them out, and said, Sirs, what must I do to be saved?***

*31 And **they said, Believe on the Lord Jesus Christ**, and thou shalt be saved, and thy house.*

INTRODUCTORY THOUGHTS

Man has corrupted the simplicity of salvation. Some say entrance to heaven is based upon following some set of creeds, joining a church, being baptized, or expressing some heartless prayer. Others have suggested that God will put each man's good works in a balance with his bad works, and so long as the good outweighs the bad, man will find entrance into heaven. Still others suggest there is any number of ways to gain entrance into heaven. How can man possibly wade his way through the confusion and be certain that heaven will be his future destination? To a great extent, this was the question that the Philippian jailor posed to the apostle Paul. Paul boldly answered, *"Believe on the Lord Jesus Christ, and thou shalt be saved, and thy house."* Paul told the jailor the truth and then prophesied that the family would follow his lead in salvation.

DEVOTIONAL THOUGHTS

- **(For children):** Cornelius needed to be saved *(Acts 10:1-6; Acts 11:13-14)*. Peter told him the only way was by believing in the Lord Jesus Christ *(Acts 10:36, 38-43)*.

- **(For everyone):** Read *John 3:36; Acts 8:37; Acts 13:38-39;* and *Romans 10:9-10, 13*. What does God say that a man must do in order to be saved?
- What are you trusting for your salvation? Do you remember a time when you realized that you had sinned against a holy God and were unable to work your way to heaven? Did you call upon the name of the Lord for salvation?

PRAYER THOUGHTS

- If you have not, call upon the Lord for salvation.
- If you are saved, thank God for His salvation.

SONG: *ONCE FOR ALL*

Notes: _____

_____

_____

_____

_____

_____

Quotes from the next volume

(VOLUME 4, WEEK 41)

Subject: Sin (con't)

Sin cripples a man in every way. It hides God's face *(Isaiah 59:2)* and withholds good things from man that he would otherwise enjoy *(Jeremiah 5:25)*.

Failure on man's part to confess his sins is to forfeit God's mercy *(Proverbs 28:13)*.

Man's natural reaction is almost always likened to that of Cain when he said, *"My punishment is greater than I can bear"* *(Genesis 4:13)*.

42

Salvation (con't)

Salvation—found 351 times in 337 Old Testament verses and 172 times in 163 New Testament verses; However, some of these occurrences will refer to physical deliverance; and other Bible words are often implemented for the purpose of describing the spiritual birth of which these lessons speak.

Variations: salvation, save, saved, savest, saveth, saving

Interesting fact: Though the details of the New Testament began with the first words of the gospel of Matthew, the New Testament was of no force until the death of the testator—Jesus Christ *(Hebrews 9:16-17)*. Yet, when Jesus died, He did so for the redemption of all transgressions including those that were under the first testament *(Hebrews 9:15)*. Legally, men who knew the Lord had to go to the holding place called Abraham's bosom *(Luke 16:22)*, or paradise *(Luke 23:43)*, until after the death, burial, and resurrection of Christ. At that point, paradise was delivered into the presence of the Father in the third heaven *(2 Corinthians 12:4)*. During this resurrection, the Bible says that many of the saints appeared in Jerusalem.

Bible study tip: It is not always easy to identify those who knew the Lord in the Old Testament. However, there are various phrases that help to determine the truth of the matter. For instance, Hebrews chapter 11 chronicles the life of faithful Old Testament saints, but one phrase in particular stands out—*"These all died in faith"* **(Hebrews 11:13)**. It is also likely that some hint exists in the various phrases closely associated with a man being *"gathered unto his people"* at his death **(Numbers 20:24)**. This took place *"until Shiloh"* came, and the Bible says that unto Him was *"the gathering of the people"* **(Genesis 49:10)**.

Sunday, Day 288—Church Day (no devotional)
Monday, Day 289—*The Active Ingredients of Salvation*
Tuesday, Day 290—*The Change of Salvation*
Wednesday, Day 291—Church Night (no devotional)
Thursday, Day 292—*The Present Benefits of Salvation*
Friday, Day 293—*The Eternal Benefits of Salvation*
Saturday, Day 294—*The Responsibility of Salvation*

Day 288: Church Day

Acts 4:12 Neither is there salvation in any other: for there is none other name under heaven given among men, whereby we must be saved.

Day 289: (Monday)
The Active Ingredients of Salvation

*Romans 8:28 And we know that **all things work together for good** to them that love God, to them who are the called according to his purpose.*

INTRODUCTORY THOUGHTS

The working of God is quite often misunderstood due to its complexities. God often uses multiple things and allows them to work together to accomplish His will. He does this in the life of one who has been saved but also does this to bring about that person's salvation. Just like medications offer active ingredients to cure a physical sickness, the Lord has several active ingredients to cure spiritual sickness. Without man's faith *(Romans 10:9)* and repentance *(Acts 20:21)*, Christ's faith *(Galatians 2:16)*, God's grace *(Ephesians 2:5, 8)*, His mercy *(Titus 3:5)*, His word *(1 Peter 1:23)*, Christ's blood *(Hebrews 9:11-14)*, and the Lord's name *(Acts 4:12)*, salvation would be inadequate. Anything presently identified as the gospel that excludes any of the above is a false gospel.

DEVOTIONAL THOUGHTS

- **(For children):** Look under the hood of a car. All the parts work together to enable us to move from one location to another. Salvation is a onetime event which assures us of heaven. Salvation has many parts that we cannot see but each of those parts works together. For instance, we believe and repent and God does the rest.
- **(For everyone):** Have you ever trusted Christ as Saviour? How did each of the active ingredients listed above work together to bring about your new birth?
- Salvation is simple for the sinner, but the Lord's working is quite complex. When is the last time you thought to thank God for the individual pieces that worked together to lead to your salvation?

PRAYER THOUGHTS

- Thank God for working to bring about your salvation.
- Ask the Lord to give a deeper understanding of salvation.

SONG: *REDEEMED (CROSBY)*

Day 290: (Tuesday)
The Change of Salvation

*2 Corinthians 5:17 Therefore **if any man be in Christ, he is a new creature**: old things are passed away; behold, all things are become new.*

INTRODUCTORY THOUGHTS

Man does not change in order to be saved, but true salvation always brings about an evident change in the life of the new believer. Perhaps the change is less noticeable in some new believers and more noticeable in others; however, no change means no salvation. The change is not always an immediate outward change because it involves a change of the inward nature. A person who trusts Christ for salvation becomes a new creature *(Galatians 6:15)*. It might be best to consider how this could be likened to a dog *(Matthew 15:26-27)* becoming a sheep *(John 10:16)*. A *new man* now dwells within the new Christian to help combat and defeat the old sinful nature *(Ephesians 4:22-24)*. Salvation is not merely the turning over of a new leaf; it is a new birth *(John 3:3)* where one is passed from spiritual death to spiritual life *(John 5:24)*.

Devotional Thoughts

- **(For children):** The Bible tells of people who changed after they met the Lord. A wicked woman became a witness *(John 4:15-26, 28-29)*. Saul the persecutor of Christians became Paul the persecuted Christian *(Acts 9:1-2; Acts 21:13)*. Zacchaeus became a cheerful giver *(Luke 19:8)*.
- **(For everyone):** Have you been born again by the grace of God? What can you point to in your life as obvious changes that occurred since you believed on the Lord?
- Are you concerned about your salvation? Are you willing to examine yourself *(2 Corinthians 13:5)*? Read *The First Epistle General of John*. Do you find these proofs of salvation in your life?

Prayer Thoughts

- Ask God to give you light concerning your salvation.
- Ask God to continue to change you for His glory.

SONG: *AMAZING GRACE!*

Day 291: Church Night

Acts 20:21 Testifying both to the Jews, and also to the Greeks, repentance toward God, and faith toward our Lord Jesus Christ.

Day 292: (Thursday)
The Present Benefits of Salvation

Galatians 5:22 But the fruit of the Spirit is love, joy, peace, longsuffering, gentleness, goodness, faith,

*23 **Meekness, temperance: against such there is no law.***

*24 **And they that are Christ's have crucified the flesh with the affections and lusts.***

INTRODUCTORY THOUGHTS

Christians sometimes focus most upon the benefits believers will enjoy after this life is over, yet the benefits of salvation enjoyed in this present life are just as grand as those yet in the future. Perhaps the lack of focus on present benefits has caused some individuals to put off their salvation. Thus it is important to emphasize that salvation changes a person's present circumstances just as much as it will his future. Salvation does not change a man's surroundings; it changes the man. When it does, it brings things like love, joy, and peace to the individual. The very things that the average lost person expresses as his greatest needs can only be found through a present, personal relationship with the Lord Jesus Christ.

DEVOTIONAL THOUGHTS

- **(For children):** A present benefit of salvation is seen in God's promises to the saints. A few of these are He never leaves us *(**Romans 8:35-39**)*, answered prayer *(**Jeremiah 33:3; 1 John 5:14-15**)*, needs supplied *(**Philippians 4:19**)*, and help in times of trouble *(**Psalm 46:1**)*.
- **(For everyone):** How has your life changed since you trusted Christ as Saviour? How has love, joy, and peace increased? What are some other notable benefits you are presently enjoying?
- Write down some great things that have happened in your life since the day you were born again. How many of these things might not have occurred had you not trusted Christ?

PRAYER THOUGHTS

- Thank the Lord for His benefits *(**Psalm 68:19**)*.
- Ask the Lord to continually remind you of His benefits.

SONG: *JOY UNSPEAKABLE*

Day 293: (Friday)
The Eternal Benefits of Salvation

***John 14:1** Let not your heart be troubled: ye believe in God, believe also in me.*

2 In my Father's house are many mansions: if it were not so, I would have told you. I go to prepare a place for you.

*3 And **if I go and prepare a place for you, I will come again, and receive you unto myself;** that where I am, there ye may be also.*

INTRODUCTORY THOUGHTS

When a lost man leaves this world, he finds himself in the midst of the inconceivable judgment of hell *(Luke 16:19-31)*. Yet, when a saved person leaves this world, he finds himself in the glorious presence of the Lord *(2 Corinthians 5:8)* and in the midst of inconceivable joys *(Psalm 16:11)*. Most Christians have heard about the many mansions in the Father's house *(John 14:2)*, but the Bible also speaks of the absence of tears, death, sorrow, and pain because *"the former things are passed away" (Revelation 21:4)*. Not only is eternal life going to be great for the believer because of the absence of these things, but even more so because of the presence of the One who died so that believers might have that life.

DEVOTIONAL THOUGHTS

- **(For children):** God promises eternal life to those who believe, and God cannot lie *(Titus 1:2; 1 John 2:25; 1 John 5:11-13)*. We will be with Him forever *(1 Thessalonians 4:16-17)*, and we will never sin again *(1 Corinthians 15:51-53; Philippians 3:21; 1 John 3:2)*.
- **(For everyone):** What are you most looking forward to about heaven? What are some other benefits not mentioned above that you are longing to enjoy?
- Do you have some loved ones already with the Lord? Do you look forward to meeting some of the characters you read about in God's word? Are you looking forward to worshipping the Lord without any sin to hinder you?

PRAYER THOUGHTS

- Thank the Lord for the life you will enjoy in eternity.
- If lost, ask the Lord to save you so you can enjoy these benefits.

SONG: *O THAT WILL BE GLORY*

☐ Completion Date

Day 294: (Saturday)
The Responsibility of Salvation

2 Corinthians 5:18 *And all things are of **God**, who hath reconciled us to himself by Jesus Christ, and **hath given to us the ministry of reconciliation**;*

INTRODUCTORY THOUGHTS

Man is not saved by works; however, through the new birth, he is *"created in Christ Jesus unto" **(Ephesians 2:10)*** and should be *"zealous of" **(Titus 2:14)*** good works. The Lord could easily save a man and immediately take him to heaven, but He chooses to leave man here on this earth to do a work for Him. Though the Lord's work on this earth is made up of many details, it always includes *"the ministry of reconciliation" **(2 Corinthians 5:18)***. Similar to the responsibility to tell others about a known cure for a dreaded disease, every Christian has the responsibility to express to others their knowledge of the cure for the coming judgment of God and how to be reconciled to God.

DEVOTIONAL THOUGHTS

- **(For children):** God is not willing that any should perish ***(2 Peter 3:9)***. Salvation comes by hearing and believing the word of God ***(Romans 10:17)***. Some will never read the Bible and we must tell them the good news ***(Mark 16:15; Acts 1:8)***.
- **(For everyone):** How did the apostle Paul work to fulfil his calling to tell others about Christ? What resources did he use to help him in this endeavour?
- Who have you told about the death, burial, and resurrection of Christ? When is the last time you told somebody about Christ? Are you ashamed of the gospel of Christ ***(Romans 1:16)***?

PRAYER THOUGHTS

- Ask God to give you boldness to witness.
- Ask the Lord to give you His burden for lost souls.

SONG: *HE WAS NOT WILLING*

Notes:

Quotes from the next volume
(VOLUME 4, WEEK 42)
Subject: Stealing

Long before sin manifests itself to the eyes of others, sin develops, plots, schemes, and finalizes its dastardly deeds within the heart of the guilty.

As a sin of selfishness, stealing does not care for the well-being of those whom it victimizes.

A man who gets right with the Lord should naturally look for ways to restore that which he has stolen *(Luke 19:1-10)*.

43
Sobriety

Sobriety—found seventeen times in seventeen verses

Variations: sober, soberly, soberness, sobriety

First usage: *Acts 26:25* (soberness)

Last usage: *1 Peter 5:8* (sober)

Defined: of a sound or serious mind or the absence of being overcome by emotions, alcohol, or other outside influences

Interesting fact: The qualifications of the bishop are given in *1 Timothy 3:1-7* and *Titus 1:6-9*. The separate lists of qualifications demonstrate some uniqueness but also share some overlap. One of these common qualifications is *sobriety (1 Timothy 3:3; Titus 1:8)*. Sobriety in the ministry is of the utmost importance. For this reason, Paul admonished Timothy to let no man despise his youth. Instead, Timothy was to endeavour in every facet of his life to be an example to other believers.

Bible study tip: In order to fully understand biblical terminology, word connections are crucial to formulate. These connections can be easily classified as comparisons or contrasts. In the case of sobriety, the Bible student should create two different word association columns with the variations above (sober, soberly, soberness, and sobriety) in the middle of the two columns. On one side (left), identify all the words associated with your study in a *comparative* way. On the other side (right), identify all the words associated in a *contrasting* manner. Write those things closest to the middle if the word more closely associates to the word study. The less something associates with the word study, the farther away it should be from the middle (where the words of study are listed). Ultimately, the Bible student should end up with a rather clear concept and a more concise biblical definition.

Sunday, Day 295—Church Day (no devotional)
Monday, Day 296—*What Is Sobriety?*
Tuesday, Day 297—*The Expectation of Sobriety*
Wednesday, Day 298—Church Night (no devotional)
Thursday, Day 299—*Salvation Teaches Sobriety*
Friday, Day 300—*The Last Days Demand Sobriety*
Saturday, Day 301—*Sobriety Protects from the Enemy*

Day 295: Church Day

*1 Peter 1:13 Wherefore **gird up the loins of your mind, be sober**, and hope to the end for the grace that is to be brought unto you at the revelation of Jesus Christ;*

Day 296: (Monday)
What Is Sobriety?

*2 Corinthians 5:13 For **whether we be beside ourselves**, it is to God: **or whether we be sober**, it is for your cause.*

INTRODUCTORY THOUGHTS

Most people unfortunately limit the meaning of sobriety to the absence of alcohol, but scripturally speaking, the meaning involves a much broader scope. Sobriety is the opposite of being beside oneself *(2 Cor-*

☐ Completion Date Sobriety • 345

inthians 5:13) or mad *(Acts 26:25)* and is akin to being alert *(1 Thessalonians 5:6)*. The word *sober* is used in conjunction with the words *grave (1 Timothy 3:11; Titus 2:2)* and *temperate (Titus 1:8; Titus 2:2)* indicating that it is accomplished when one is in control, down to earth, and finds the proper balance in his thoughts and actions. One who is sober is humble *(Romans 12:3)*, not drunken *(1 Thessalonians 5:7-8)*, and well aware of the circumstances surrounding him at all times *(1 Thessalonians 5:6, 8; 1 Peter 5:8)*.

Devotional Thoughts
- **(For children):** No matter what we are doing, God should be in our thoughts. Situations will come up in which we need to pay attention to doing the correct thing *(2 Corinthians 10:5b; Exodus 23:13a)*. How could you be sober when playing with a selfish child; with a sibling who wants to keep playing when you are told it is bedtime?
- **(For everyone):** Why is it important to understand that sobriety is broader than the mere absence of alcohol? Is it possible for someone who has never had any alcohol to have a problem with sobriety?
- How would you define sobriety? Do you consider yourself to be a sober individual? In what areas of life do you find that the Devil attacks your sobriety?

Prayer Thoughts
- Ask the Lord to help you find sobriety in every aspect of life.
- Ask God to teach you scriptural sobriety.

SONG: *TAKE TIME TO BE HOLY*

Day 297: (Tuesday)
The Expectation of Sobriety

Titus 2:1 But speak thou the things which become sound doctrine:

*2 **That the aged men be sober**, grave, temperate, sound in faith, in charity, in patience.*

3 The aged women likewise, that they be in behaviour as becometh holiness, not false accusers, not given to much wine, teachers of good things;

*4 **That they may teach the young women to be sober**, to love their husbands, to love their children,*

5 To be discreet, chaste, keepers at home, good, obedient to their own husbands, that the word of God be not blasphemed.

*6 **Young men likewise exhort to be sober minded.***

INTRODUCTORY THOUGHTS

Sobriety is not some special and unique requirement expected from an elite group of believers, but rather it serves as the expectation of the Lord for all who have called upon His name in salvation. Certainly God expects sobriety from the leaders in the New Testament church *(1 Timothy 3:2, 11; Titus 1:8)*, but He also expects it from the women *(1 Timothy 2:9)*, the aged men *(Titus 2:2)*, the young women *(Titus 2:4)*, and the young men *(Titus 2:6)*. No group is exempt! If this were not enough, the apostle Paul made an open appeal for sobriety to all believers collectively *(1 Thessalonians 5:6, 8; Titus 2:12)*. Simon Peter seemed a bit more adamant when he demanded sobriety from his audience *(1 Peter 4:7; 1 Peter 5:8)*.

DEVOTIONAL THOUGHTS

- **(For children):** In their youth, the thought lives of Samuel and Timothy were focused upon the Lord *(1 Samuel 2:11b, 18, 26; 2 Timothy 3:15)*. As a boy, Jesus thought soberly *(Luke 2:49)*. How can you be sober at home, at church, and even at the store?
- **(For everyone):** Why is sobriety important for young men? Why would it be important for young women? Why is sobriety crucial for the aged men? What about the older ladies?
- What specific issues are you currently facing that would be greatly enhanced by your possession of sobriety? What troubles could come if you fail to be sober in mind and in deed?

PRAYER THOUGHTS

- Ask God to impress upon your heart that He requires sobriety.
- Ask the Lord to show you the benefits of sobriety.

SONG: *OUR BEST*

Day 298: Church Night

*1 Thessalonians 5:8 But **let us, who are of the day, be sober**, putting on the breastplate of faith and love; and for an helmet, the hope of salvation.*

Day 299: (Thursday)
Salvation Teaches Sobriety

*Titus 2:11 **For the grace of God that bringeth salvation hath appeared to all men**,*
*12 **Teaching us that**, denying ungodliness and worldly lusts, **we should live soberly**, righteously, and godly, in this present world;*

INTRODUCTORY THOUGHTS

The Lord, in His omniscience, has provided man with everything he needs through salvation and the grace that brings salvation. One might ask, "How does salvation teach sobriety?" A proper understanding of grace and salvation reminds man that he is completely inadequate in and of himself. Apart from the Lord's intervention, man would be on a slippery slope towards the pits of hell. In his very best state, man's righteous acts are no better than filthy rags *(Isaiah 64:6)*. When a man meditates upon his salvation and the grace of God that gave him salvation, he avoids the snare of pride. He knows full well who he is and what God had to do to make him fit for heaven. He knows he owes the Lord a great debt and determines to be alert in his daily walk.

DEVOTIONAL THOUGHTS

- **(For children):** God used the apostle Paul in a mighty way. Yet, he never forgot what God did for him *(**1 Timothy 1:12-15; 2 Corinthians 10:17**)*. We may not do the wicked things Paul did as he persecuted Christians, but without salvation we are all headed to the same place *(**Romans 3:23; Romans 6:23**)*.
- **(For everyone):** What was your life like when the Lord saved you? Were you deserving of God's grace and mercy? How often do you reflect upon God's goodness for saving you from an eternity in hell?
- What happens when people become convinced that they are good enough for salvation and a home in heaven? How does this pride thwart sobriety?

Prayer Thoughts
- Thank the Lord for saving a wretch like you.
- Ask God to remind you where and how He found you.

SONG: *SONG OF THE SOLDIER*

Day 300: (Friday)
The Last Days Demand Sobriety

1 Peter 4:7 **But the end of all things is at hand: be ye therefore sober,** *and watch unto prayer.*

Introductory Thoughts

As time winds down, the need for sobriety increases. Temptations are seemingly escalating from every angle and source. Even if sin did not have the ability to lure away a believer, busyness and hobbies tug at his heart to steal away one's time and strength. The Devil labours to keep the believer from working while it is day *(John 9:4)* knowing that a sober believer gets much more accomplished for the Lord. While men are spiritually asleep *(Matthew 13:25)*, the enemy has free reign to disrupt and destroy the lives of others. The apostle Paul saw this dilemma and warned *"that, knowing the time, that now it is high time to awake out of sleep: for now is our salvation nearer than when we believed"* **(Romans 13:11)**.

Devotional Thoughts

- **(For children):** The last days are wicked and dangerous *(2 Timothy 3:1)*. What does God want us to do? Realize time is short *(1 Corinthians 7:29a)* and continue working for Him *(2 Timothy 3:13-14a; Ephesians 5:15-16)*.
- **(For everyone):** What are some things the Devil has done in the last days to keep men asleep or preoccupied? How many of these things would be considered vain or empty?
- What is the focus of your home? Does this focus confirm or deny the presence of sobriety? What is the focus of your church? Does this focus suggest a people who know that time is short?

PRAYER THOUGHTS
- Ask the Lord to remind you that time is short.
- Ask God to help you refuse to sleep or be sidetracked.

SONG: *BACK TO BETHEL*

Day 301: (Saturday)
Sobriety Protects from the Enemy

1 Peter 5:8 Be sober, be vigilant; **because your adversary the devil,** *as a roaring lion,* **walketh about, seeking whom he may devour***:*

INTRODUCTORY THOUGHTS

A sleeping enemy is generally easiest to overcome. The Devil is no stronger today than he was in the early days of the church, yet he seemingly works with a much greater success rate in these last days. Something has changed and it is not the Devil, or the Lord, so it must be believers. Men have lost their sobriety. They seem so busy playing games, sleeping, or murmuring to notice that the enemy is on the prowl. This lack of sobriety has caused great harm. Fewer souls are being saved, believers have little to no desire to live holy, and even fewer know enough Bible to keep from being deceived. Believers cannot fight the Devil while sleeping or distracted. A good fight requires sobriety!

DEVOTIONAL THOUGHTS

- **(For children):** Read *Judges 7:2-7*. God decreased Gideon's army so that only God could get the glory when Israel defeated the Midianites. Yet, we should pay attention to the type of men God chose—those chosen were watchful and sober.
- **(For everyone):** When would you think would be the best time to attempt to break into a house? Why would you choose such circumstances? How is this like the Devil's efforts in destroying you?
- Are you sleeping on the Lord? Are you preoccupied by things that really do not count for anything in eternity? Are you willing to repent, wake up, and serve the Lord with the type of sobriety that glorifies God?

PRAYER THOUGHTS
- Ask God to help you see your present condition.
- Ask the Lord to help you live soberly for Him.

SONG: *WHO IS ON THE LORD'S SIDE?*

Notes:

Quotes from the next volume

(VOLUME 4, WEEK 43)

Subject: Stealing (con't)

A saved man, though previously a thief, will labour so that he may have to give to others. Only the power of the gospel can take a thief and make him charitable. What an amazing transformation!

It is a life-threatening matter when a man steals glory belonging only to the Lord and accepts it for himself ***(Acts 12:21-23)***.

44
Sobriety (con't)

Sobriety—found nine of the seventeen times in the pastoral epistles

Variations: sober, soberly, soberness, sobriety

Interesting fact: Man is supposed to *"think soberly" (**Romans 12:3**)*, *"be sober minded" (**Titus 2:6**)*, and *"gird up the loins of"* his *"mind"* and *"be sober" (**1 Peter 1:13**)*. The mind is the central area of necessity concerning sobriety being the source of every action of man.

Bible study tip: When studying any particular passage, two rather subtil temptations seem to plague Bible students. Two of these temptations can be summarized as follows: *"Never read the past into the present,"* and *"Never read the future into the present."* By way of illustration, the Bible student should never simply assume that an Old Testament doctrine applies to a passage containing New Testament teachings. Likewise, the student should never assume New Testament doctrines were understood by those actually living during the Old Testament days. Additionally, these truths apply within the testaments along with the books of the Bible.

Sunday, Day 302—Church Day (no devotional)
Monday, Day 303—*Gird Up the Loins of Your Mind*
Tuesday, Day 304—*We Should Live Soberly*
Wednesday, Day 305—Church Night (no devotional)
Thursday, Day 306—*Sobriety and Gravity*
Friday, Day 307—*Let Us Watch and Be Sober*
Saturday, Day 308—*Be Sober and Watch unto Prayer*

Day 302: Church Day

*1 Timothy 3:2 **A bishop then must be** blameless, the husband of one wife, vigilant, **sober**, of good behaviour, given to hospitality, apt to teach;*

Day 303: (Monday)
Gird Up the Loins of Your Mind

*1 Peter 1:13 Wherefore **gird up the loins of your mind, be sober**, and hope to the end for the grace that is to be brought unto you at the revelation of Jesus Christ;*

INTRODUCTORY THOUGHTS

A man's thoughts serve as the foundation for his actions. If a man fails to be sober minded, he will likely fail to behave soberly. The Bible likens a sober mind to one that has girded loins. When a man would gird his loins, he would tie off his garments in such a way to assist him during work or when he was running. A man's mind is best prepared to work properly when it is girded up with sobriety. This sobriety keeps a man humble by keeping him from thinking *"of himself more highly than he ought to think"* **(Romans 12:3)**. Pride hinders a man's ability to work for the Lord, but sobriety girds up the mind with humility. It is very important for this sobriety to begin taking root in one's youth **(Titus 2:6)**.

DEVOTIONAL THOUGHTS

- **(For children):** When David faced the giant, he had already girded up the loins of his mind. He thought seriously about what he was going to do by reflecting upon what he had done in the past. Equally important or more important was his giving to God all the credit and glory *(1*

Samuel 17:32-37, 45-47). We, too, must realize that we need God to fight and win our battles *(James 4:10; 1 Peter 5:6)*.
- **(For everyone):** What kind of attacks does the Devil launch against your mind? How could these attacks be overcome if your mind were girded up with sobriety?
- What are some ways in which sobriety helps your mind to function better for the glory of God? What pitfalls does sobriety help you avoid?

Prayer Thoughts
- Ask the Lord to teach you how to gird up your mind.
- Ask the Lord to keep you from the snares of Satan.

SONG: *FOLLOW ON*

Day 304: (Tuesday)
We Should Live Soberly

Titus 2:12 Teaching us that, denying ungodliness and worldly lusts, we should live soberly, righteously, and godly, in this present world;

Introductory Thoughts

Sobriety is much more than simply a way of thinking; it is the scriptural approach to Christian living. The grace of God, through the Holy Ghost *(John 16:13)*, teaches the believer the proper approach to living the Christian life. Grace teaches separation by stating that believers should deny *"ungodliness and worldly lusts."* Yet, grace does not stop there. It also teaches a threefold approach to living life: *"soberly, righteously, and godly."* Not only must a believer have a sober mind, he must also approach every aspect of his life with sobriety. He should pray with sobriety. He should read the scriptures with sobriety. He should witness with sobriety. Any contrary thing will cause the believer to suffer great loss.

Devotional Thoughts
- **(For children):** *Proverbs 23:7* says that as a man *"thinketh in his heart, so is he."* The best way to live soberly is to keep your thoughts on God's word and upon other associated things *(Psalm 1:1-3; Psalm 19:14; Psalm 119:59; Philippians 4:8)*.

- **(For everyone):** Why is it important to approach every aspect of life with sobriety? How can sobriety help your Bible study and prayer life? How can sobriety assist you in witnessing to others?
- How does sobriety, or the lack of sobriety, affect a believer's ability to live righteously and godly in this present world? Can a person live righteously and godly without living soberly?

PRAYER THOUGHTS
- Thank the Lord for teaching you to live soberly.
- Ask God to remind you that life is to be approached soberly.

SONG: *STAND LIKE THE BRAVE*

Day 305: Church Night

1 Peter 5:8 **Be sober,** *be vigilant;* **because your adversary the devil,** *as a roaring lion,* **walketh about, seeking whom he may devour**:

Day 306: (Thursday)
Sobriety and Gravity

Romans 12:3 For **I say**, *through the grace given unto me,* **to every man** *that is among you, not to think of himself more highly than he ought to think; but* **to think soberly**, *according as God hath dealt to every man the measure of faith.*

INTRODUCTORY THOUGHTS

Sobriety helps the believer *"not to think of himself more highly than he ought to think."* In other words, it keeps him grounded rather than haughty. Pride is one of the greatest destructive forces in the world. Pride led to the fall of Satan and will likewise destroy the believer's walk with the Lord along with his testimony before others. Sobriety is a companion to gravity *(1 Timothy 3:11; Titus 2:2)* and causes a believer to perceive himself as he really is. The Devil fell when he began to think more highly of himself *(Isaiah 14:12-14)*. In his heart, he thought to exalt his throne and be like the most High. If the believer is not sober, he too can begin to think thoughts of pride. Just as it was with Satan, this pride will be his downfall.

☐ Completion Date

DEVOTIONAL THOUGHTS

- **(For children):** What can you do well: sing, play an instrument, draw, color, memorize scripture? God wants us to seriously consider and contemplate the things we can do well so that we do not become prideful. Learn early to give all credit to the Lord *(1 Corinthians 4:7; Galatians 6:14)*.
- **(For everyone):** How does the law of gravity physically keep men grounded on the earth? How does sobriety and gravity keep men spiritually grounded?
- Do you think more highly of yourself than you ought to think? Does God have to humble you, or do you willingly humble yourself?

PRAYER THOUGHTS

- Ask God to help you embrace humility and sound thinking.
- Thank God for reminding you of who you truly are.

SONG: *I NEED THEE EVERY HOUR*

Day 307: (Friday)
Let Us Watch and Be Sober

1 Thessalonians 5:6 Therefore ***let us not sleep****, as do others;* ***but let us watch and be sober****.*

INTRODUCTORY THOUGHTS

In the last days, believers must remain alert. There is no time for sleeping. For it is while believers sleep that the enemy works most effectively. Even the Lord Jesus acknowledged the great need of the day when He said, *"I must work the works of him that sent me, while it is day: the night cometh, when no man can work" **(John 9:4)***. Just as it was in the days of Gideon *(Judges 7:5-7)*, the Lord wants soldiers who are fully aware of their surroundings. A sober minded believer keeps his eyes open, knowing he has an enemy that is on the prowl and ready to devour *(1 Peter 5:8)*. The sober minded believer also knows that one lapse in judgment can cause immense damage during the spiritual battle. Sobriety keeps every reality in the forefront of the mind.

Devotional Thoughts
- **(For children):** The Devil can attack our minds (tempting us to do wrong or think wrong) or attack us through others. No matter what, we are to be good soldiers, keeping our minds on what God wants us to do *(2 Timothy 2:3-4)*.
- **(For everyone):** What are some ways in which sobriety would be a necessity during a physical war or skirmish? How could you be harmed by fellowsoldiers who were not sober?
- How does sobriety help the believer in his spiritual warfare *(1 Thessalonians 5:8)*? How does it keep him safe when the enemy attacks *(1 Peter 5:8)*?

Prayer Thoughts
- Thank the Lord for offering help in the spiritual battle.
- Ask the Lord to constantly remind you to be watchful.

SONG: *AM I A SOLDIER OF THE CROSS?*

Day 308: (Saturday)
Be Sober and Watch unto Prayer

1 Peter 4:7 **But** ***the end of all things is at hand: be ye therefore sober, and watch unto prayer.***

Introductory Thoughts

Many of those in the world perceive prayer as a crutch or a tool that shows weakness. Yet, the saint of God knows prayer to be one of the most powerful weapons during times of war. As the Lord Jesus prepared to face the mob that would soon arrest Him, He spent His remaining time in earnest prayer *(Matthew 26:36-46)*. It was during this time that He taught the disciples saying, *"Watch and pray, that ye enter not into temptation: the spirit indeed is willing, but the flesh is weak"* *(Matthew 26:41)*. Prayer does not distract the believer from the battle at hand; rather, it strengthens him and aids him during even the fiercest parts of the battle. Prayer reminds the believer of who he is, who his enemy is, and it reminds him of the power of his God.

☐ Completion Date

Devotional Thoughts

- **(For children):** Nothing is too hard for the Lord *(Jeremiah 32:17)*. The God who created all things can help us with any situation. Thank God that He wants us to be sober and talk to Him *(1 Chronicles 16:11; Luke 18:1; Colossians 4:2; 1 Thessalonians 5:17).*
- **(For everyone):** How do you perceive prayer? Is it a tool for the weak that yields additional weakness, or is it a powerful resource available to those who are in the midst of a spiritual battle?
- What are some instances when you can recall that sobriety mixed with prayer helped you through some difficulties? How did these two things work together to bring you victory?

Prayer Thoughts

- Thank God for the privilege of prayer.
- Ask the Lord to strengthen your prayer life.

SONG: *STAND UP, STAND UP FOR JESUS*

Notes:

Notes:

Quotes from the next volume
(VOLUME 4, WEEK 44)
Subject: Strength

The people of God are typically the underdogs during times of battle. The enemy is most often stronger, wiser, and more desirous of gaining victory at any cost.

Change brings about much uncertainty and fear. As such, it must be met and handled with strength.

Man is not promised an endless supply of strength; rather, God promises to provide the necessary grace and strength for the present trials.

45

Stewardship

Stewardship—found twenty times in eighteen verses

Variations: steward, stewards, stewardship

First usage: *Genesis 15:2* (steward)

Last usage: *1 Peter 4:10* (stewards)

Defined: the oversight of another man's substance or possessions

Interesting fact: Many people focus upon the qualifications of the bishop but fail to note the association of this man's work to his stewardship. The Bible states that the bishop is to *"be blameless, as the steward of God" (Titus 1:7)*. In fact, every qualification that follows verse seven describes the qualifications one would seek from the man entrusted as a steward. It only stands to reason that God would also say that *"if a man know not how to rule his own house, how shall he take care of the church of God?" (1 Timothy 3:5)*.

Bible study tip: Some Bible studies prove resourceful in unlocking additional keys to understanding other Bible studies. Every Bible student should study the chronology and details of Paul's missionary journeys recorded in the book of Acts. An adequate grasp of these journeys enhances one's understanding of each of Paul's epistles.

Sunday, Day 309—Church Day (no devotional)
Monday, Day 310—*What Is a Stewardship?*
Tuesday, Day 311—*The Requirement for Stewardship*
Wednesday, Day 312—Church Night (no devotional)
Thursday, Day 313—*An Unjust Steward*
Friday, Day 314—*The Responsibility of the Steward*
Saturday, Day 315—*The Steward's Account*

Day 309: Church Day

1 Peter 4:10 As every man hath received the gift, even so minister the same one to another, as **good stewards of the manifold grace of God**.

Day 310: (Monday)
What Is a Stewardship?

1 Chronicles 28:1 And David assembled all the princes of Israel, the princes of the tribes, and the captains of the companies that ministered to the king by course, and the captains over the thousands, and captains over the hundreds, and **the stewards over all the substance and possession of the king**, and of his sons, with the officers, and with the mighty men, and with all the valiant men, unto Jerusalem.

INTRODUCTORY THOUGHTS

Basically, a steward is one who oversees someone else's possessions. The scripture shows stewards overseeing the substance and possession of the king *(1 Chronicles 28:1)* or administering the oversight of labourers within a vineyard *(Matthew 20:8)*. The life of a steward was devoted to his master's needs, wants, and demands. The job description was broad and comprehensive. Eliezer, Abraham's steward *(Genesis 15:2)*, ruled over all that Abraham had *(Genesis 24:2)* but also went forth to find a wife for Abraham's son Isaac *(Genesis 24:9)*. The master's needs became the responsibilities of the steward. Simply put, the steward was responsible for what the master had placed under his care and supervision.

☐ Completion Date

Devotional Thoughts

- **(For children):** Potiphar placed Joseph over all his possessions *(Genesis 39:4-6)*. Joseph ended up in prison as a result of a lie told about him. He again became a steward while imprisoned *(Genesis 39:20-23)*. Eventually, he became a steward for Pharaoh over the land of Egypt *(Genesis 41:40-47)*.
- **(For everyone):** Look up the word *steward* in scripture. What are some of the responsibilities given to stewards? What can you learn from the work of a steward that might assist you in understanding how to become a better Christian?
- In what ways can stewardships parallel that of being a Christian? What responsibilities do you have that would be similar to that of a steward?

Prayer Thoughts

- Ask the Lord to teach you how to be a good steward.
- Ask God to help you to be faithful in your stewardship for Him.

SONG: *AS A VOLUNTEER*

Day 311: (Tuesday)
The Requirement for Stewardship

1 Corinthians 4:2** Moreover **it is required in stewards, that a man be found faithful.

Introductory Thoughts

Stewardship requires one predominant trait, that being faithfulness. People are gifted with many assorted skill sets requiring varying degrees of expertise. Yet, stewardship demands only a single element—faithfulness. The master of the house can teach his steward how to think ahead or how to deal with problems and even problem people, but the master cannot teach faithfulness. A wise master knows that his greatest need in a steward is faithfulness *(Luke 12:42)*. In like manner, believers, as stewards of God, may be inadequately qualified for every needed task, but the importance of faithfulness must never be underestimated. No man can be a good steward if he lacks faithfulness

Devotional Thoughts

- **(For children):** The following people had different positions because they were faithful: Moses over Israel *(Numbers 12:7)*; Nehemiah's treasurers *(Nehemiah 13:13)*; Daniel—first president of the empire *(Daniel 6:1-4)*; Timothy—preacher and teacher *(Philippians 2:19-23; 2 Timothy 2:2)*. Can the Lord count you faithful?
- **(For everyone):** The apostle Paul considered himself to be a steward of God *(1 Corinthians 4:1; 1 Corinthians 9:17; 1 Thessalonians 2:4)*. What qualification did he say caused the Lord to put him into the ministry *(1 Timothy 1:12)*?
- What are some weaknesses that could stop you from serving God? How could these weaknesses be overcome by faithfulness?

Prayer Thoughts

- Thank God for the opportunity to be a steward.
- Ask the Lord to teach you the importance of faithfulness.

SONG: *HIS WAY WITH THEE*

Day 312: Church Night

1 Corinthians 4:1 Let a man so account of us, as of the ministers of Christ, and stewards of the mysteries of God.

Day 313: (Thursday)
An Unjust Steward

*Luke 16:1 And he said also unto his disciples, **There was a certain rich man, which had a steward; and the same was accused unto him that he had wasted his goods.***

*2 And **he called him, and said unto him, How is it that I hear this of thee? give an account of thy stewardship;** for thou mayest be no longer steward.*

*3 Then **the steward said within himself, What shall I do?** for my lord taketh away from me the stewardship: I cannot dig; to beg I am ashamed.*

*4 **I am resolved what to do, that, when I am put out of the stewardship, they may receive me into their houses.***

5 So he called every one of his lord's debtors unto him, and said unto the first, How much owest thou unto my lord?

6 And he said, An hundred measures of oil. And he said unto him, Take thy bill, and sit down quickly, and write fifty.

7 Then said he to another, And how much owest thou? And he said, An hundred measures of wheat. And he said unto him, Take thy bill, and write fourscore.

8 And **the lord commended the unjust steward, because he had done wisely:** *for the children of this world are in their generation wiser than the children of light.*

9 And I say unto you, Make to yourselves friends of the mammon of unrighteousness; that, when ye fail, they may receive you into everlasting habitations.

10 He that is faithful in that which is least is faithful also in much: and he that is unjust in the least is unjust also in much.

11 If therefore ye have not been faithful in the unrighteous mammon, who will commit to your trust the true riches?

12 And if ye have not been faithful in that which is another man's, who shall give you that which is your own?

Introductory Thoughts

A steward has the responsibility for properly caring for the possessions of another. In this capacity, he does not determine what is proper or improper; rather, the master of the house sets the standards of care for his possessions. In the parable beginning in **Luke 16:1**, a certain rich man (the master of the house) accused his steward of wasting his goods. The steward was told to give an account of his stewardship knowing that his irresponsible actions could soon end his stewardship. The Bible identifies the steward as *"unjust"* because of his unfaithfulness with the possessions of the master. The steward was not unjust because he lacked skill, but because he was not faithful.

Devotional Thoughts

- **(For children):** Joash, king of Judah, gave orders to the priests and Levites to collect money to repair the temple. These men were unfaithful and had to be rebuked by the king. He took their responsibility away from them and devised a new plan **(2 Chronicles 24:4-10)**.

- **(For everyone):** One day every believer is going to be called upon to give an account of his stewardship. What kind of a steward have you been? Have you taken care of the things that God has placed within the scope of your supervision?
- The unjust steward did not lack wisdom *(Luke 16:8)*. How was his wisdom overshadowed by his lack of faithfulness?

PRAYER THOUGHTS

- Ask the Lord to remind you that you will soon give an account of your stewardship.
- Ask God to help you to be a faithful and submissive steward.

SONG: *TAKE MY LIFE, AND LET IT BE*

Day 314: (Friday)
The Responsibility of the Steward

Luke 19:13 And he called his ten servants, and delivered them ten pounds, and said unto them, **Occupy till I come.**

INTRODUCTORY THOUGHTS

    A steward is a man entrusted with a certain responsibility. He may have a greater or lesser area of oversight, but he always has something placed under his care of great importance to the master. If he is to care for money, he is to do so faithfully and to the best of his ability. If he is to care for fields or houses, he is to do likewise. Whether the master of the house is present or absent, the steward is to do as he has been commissioned by the one who owns that for which he is a steward. Stewardship is a great privilege. It is an honourable thing for any man to be considered worthy of the task, but at the same time, it is a position of great responsibility and one that must be done with great sobriety.

DEVOTIONAL THOUGHTS

- **(For children):** Jerusalem is important to God *(Psalm 87:2-3)*. Nehemiah loved the city too and was sad when the Babylonians left it in ruins *(Nehemiah 1:3-4)*. After Nehemiah rebuilt the walls, read why he placed Hananiah in charge of the gates *(Nehemiah 7:1-3)*.

- **(For everyone):** Are you a steward of God *(1 Corinthians 4:1)*? What has He presently placed under your care? Are you fulfilling your responsibilities as God's steward?
- What happens when you fail to do what God has given you to do? How does this hurt others? How does it hurt the work of the Lord?

Prayer Thoughts
- Ask God to remind you that He is the Master.
- Ask the Lord to show you the things He has placed in your care.

SONG: *WHERE HE LEADS I'LL FOLLOW*

Day 315: (Saturday)
The Steward's Account

Romans 14:12 **So then every one of us shall give account of himself to God.**

Introductory Thoughts

Every believer will stand before the Lord Jesus Christ to give an account for his stewardship while living upon this earth. Perhaps no one understood this quite like the apostle Paul. He was the apostle of the Gentiles *(Romans 11:13)* and had a special calling as a steward *"of the mysteries of God" (1 Corinthians 4:1)*. He spoke often about the fact that the gospel had been put in his trust *(1 Thessalonians 2:4; 1 Timothy 1:11; Titus 1:3)*. The apostle Paul feared what would happen if he failed to fulfil his stewardship *(1 Corinthians 9:16-17)* because he knew a time of accounting faced all believers including himself. Though Paul's calling was special, the fact that he would give an account was not unique to him only.

Devotional Thoughts
- **(For children):** God sees and examines all that we do *(Psalm 11:4; Psalm 33:13-15; Jeremiah 32:19)*. We will give an account to Him *(Matthew 12:36; 2 Corinthians 5:10)*. The Bible warns us to be good stewards *(Luke 12:42-43; 1 John 2:28)*.
- **(For everyone):** How are your responsibilities different from Paul's? How are some of your responsibilities similar to those of the apostle Paul? How are you fulfilling your responsibilities?

- What do you know about the time when you will give an account to the Lord? How should this knowledge cause you to be more faithful in your stewardship?

PRAYER THOUGHTS
- Ask God to constantly remind you of the account to be given.
- Thank God for the privilege of serving Him.

SONG: *TRIUMPH BY AND BY*

Notes: _____

Quotes from the next volume

(VOLUME 4, WEEK 45)

Subject: Strength (con't)

At times, the Lord strengthens the hands of His enemies in order to bring about His desired plan in the lives of His own people.

The Lord looks for opportunities *"to shew himself strong in the behalf of them whose heart is perfect toward him"* **(2 Chronicles 16:9)**.

46

Stewardship (con't)

Stewardship—found six times in six Old Testament verses and fourteen times in twelve New Testament verses

Variations: steward, stewards, stewardship

Last usage in the Old Testament: *1 Chronicles 28:1* (stewards)

First usage in the New Testament: *Matthew 20:8* (steward)

Interesting fact: Luke chapter 16 includes seven references to stewardship, more than any other book of the Bible. Within that chapter, we learn of a wise but unjust steward. The recommendation of the Lord at the end of the parable was to *"make to yourselves friends of the mammon of unrighteousness"* **(Luke 16:9)**.

Bible study tip: In order to achieve the most complete Bible study, one must identify associated Bible words. For instance, a complete study of the word *stewardship* would include considering words like *minister*, *ministry*, and *dispensation*. This may take more time but insures a more complete context to your study.

Sunday, Day 316—Church Day (no devotional)
Monday, Day 317—*The Steward Owns Nothing*
Tuesday, Day 318—*Committed unto Your Trust*
Wednesday, Day 319—Church Night (no devotional)
Thursday, Day 320—*The Character of a Steward*
Friday, Day 321—*The Desire to Please*
Saturday, Day 322—*The Steward's Reward*

Day 316: Church Day

*1 Corinthians 4:2 Moreover **it is required in stewards, that a man be found faithful**.*

Day 317: (Monday)
The Steward Owns Nothing

*1 Chronicles 28:1 And David assembled all the princes of Israel, the princes of the tribes, and the captains of the companies that ministered to the king by course, and the captains over the thousands, and captains over the hundreds, and **the stewards over all the substance and possession of the king**, and of his sons, with the officers, and with the mighty men, and with all the valiant men, unto Jerusalem.*

INTRODUCTORY THOUGHTS

The steward is not distinguished for his own possessions but, rather, for the care of another's possessions. This is true of the life and ministry of every believer. He has been purchased by the blood of Christ and claims nothing as his own. If he has a family, his family is a blessing from God still belonging to God. If he has any ministries, they too belong to God. Even his own spirit, soul, and body belong to the Lord and not to himself **(1 Corinthians 6:20)**. Understanding these truths makes a steward prosper in his walk with the Lord and in his service to the Lord. He recognizes and accepts that life is not all about him. He knows that every aspect of life should revolve around caring for each of the possessions of his heavenly Master.

☐ Completion Date Stewardship (con't) • 369

Devotional Thoughts

- **(For children):** *John 1:3* tells us God made everything. It all belongs to Him. This includes the world and the people *(Psalm 24:1)*, all animals and birds *(Psalm 50:10-11)*, all money *(Haggai 2:8)*, and even you *(Ezekiel 18:4; Romans 14:8)*. Take care of those things He has put in your possession or under your control.
- **(For everyone):** Do you have a family? Do you have children? To whom did they belong before they were yours? Whose will they be long after this world ceases to exist? Whose are they now? How should this change your dealings with them?
- What do you have that does not belong to God? How should that change the way you use the things placed under your care?

Prayer Thoughts

- Ask the Lord to remind you that everything belongs to Him.
- Thank God for trusting you to care for His possessions.

SONG: *SINCE YE ARE NOT YOUR OWN*

Day 318: (Tuesday)
Committed unto Your Trust

Colossians 1:25 Whereof I am made a minister, according to **the dispensation of God which is given to me** *for you, to fulfil the word of God;*

Introductory Thoughts

The relationship between the master and his stewards is one built upon trust. The master places his possessions into the hands of a steward. He will be reluctant to do this unless that man has proven himself trustworthy. The apostle Paul found no shame in claiming to be a faithful steward of God *(1 Corinthians 4:1)*. As such, he understood the principle that the ministry was placed under his care because God had entrusted it to him *(1 Corinthians 9:17; Colossians 1:25; 1 Thessalonians 2:4; 1 Timothy 1:11; Titus 1:3)*. This fact affected everything the apostle said and did. This truth constantly reminded him that he did not live for himself, and that one day he must give an account for his stewardship.

Devotional Thoughts

- **(For children):** God called Samuel to judge His people. When the people asked for a king instead to judge them, Samuel's description of his service *(1 Samuel 12:1-5)* along with his advice to the people (which he followed throughout his ministry) *(1 Samuel 12:20b)* proved he could be trusted.
- **(For everyone):** What has God entrusted into your care? Do you treat your family, or ministry, or work as though it belongs to the Lord? How would things change if you did?
- How could this truth be considered a blessing? How could this truth be considered a curse? What is the proper balance that a believer should seek?

Prayer Thoughts

- Ask the Lord to help you walk worthy of your calling.
- Ask God to help you to be faithful with His possessions.

SONG: *A CHARGE TO KEEP I HAVE*

Day 319: Church Night

Romans 14:12 So then **every one of us shall give account of himself to God.**

Day 320: (Thursday)
The Character of a Steward

Titus 1:7 For a bishop must be blameless, as **the steward of God**; *not selfwilled, not soon angry, not given to wine, no striker, not given to filthy lucre;*

Introductory Thoughts

Every trustworthy steward must possess a high level of moral character. This is demonstrated in the qualifications of a bishop. As a steward of God, he must not be self-willed. He must recognize that his life and his possessions are not his own. In addition to this, he must not be easily distracted, overcome by anger, wine, fightings, or money. Each of these issues affects the individual's ability to think and rationally behave. As a steward, a man must dedicate himself to a high level of character

☐ Completion Date Stewardship (con't) • 371

and morality. After all, the definition of the steward means that he has been entrusted not with his own work or possessions but with those of his master. As stewards of God, believers must not allow themselves to become distracted from the task at hand, always properly caring for the things of God.

DEVOTIONAL THOUGHTS

- **(For children):** Noah's testimony remained proper and true in the midst of a godless world. While he was building the ark, he preached to the people to get right with God. He remained true to God and subsequently saved his family from the impending doom **(Genesis 6:5-9; Genesis 7:1-7).**
- **(For everyone):** What if you were hiring someone to care for your most prized possessions? What kind of traits would be most important to you? What would be the most important things to consider before offering to hire the individual?
- What are some character flaws you have that might hinder you as a steward of God? What should you do to fix those and make them right?

PRAYER THOUGHTS

- Ask the Lord to prepare you to be a better steward for Him.
- Ask God to show you any areas in which you need to repent.

SONG: *TAKE TIME TO BE HOLY*

Day 321: (Friday)
The Desire to Please

*1 Thessalonians 2:4 But as **we were allowed of God to be put in trust with the gospel**, even so **we speak**; not **as pleasing** men, but **God**, which trieth our hearts.*

INTRODUCTORY THOUGHTS

A good steward is recognized for his strong desire to please his master. For this reason, he does not expend the majority of his time and energy toward pleasing other stewards. He recognizes his first responsibility as accountability toward his master. So long as he pleases his master, all other issues will adequately fall into their rightful place. So it is with the steward of God. It is not that he lacks any desire to please others, but this desire pales in comparison to his desire to please the Lord. Simply put, he does not allow others to conflict with his primary responsibility of pleasing his Master. Unfortunately, this issue has become one of the most significant hindrances facing modern Christianity—the inordinate desire men have to please one another rather than the One that matters most.

Devotional Thoughts

- **(For children):** Jesus always pleased His heavenly Father *(John 8:29)*. Enoch too had a testimony of pleasing God *(Hebrews 11:5)*. It is our Christian duty to do the same *(1 Thessalonians 4:1)*. As children, learn how to please God by learning obedience toward your parents *(Colossians 3:20)*.
- **(For everyone):** Is it unhealthy for children to desire to please their parents while they are young? Should they eventually come to a place where they do the right thing for other reasons? How is this like Christianity?
- Do you desire to please God? How will your desire to please Him also please the right kind of people?

Prayer Thoughts

- Ask the Lord to strengthen your desire to please Him.
- Ask God to give you a deeper love for Him.

SONG: *OUR BEST*

Day 322: (Saturday)
The Steward's Reward

*1 Corinthians 9:17 For **if I do this thing willingly, I have a reward**: but if against my will, a dispensation of the gospel is committed unto me.*

Introductory Thoughts

Learning how to be the right kind of steward can seem difficult, but never without reward. The Lord Jesus taught and explained His parables of stewardship. In these teachings, He presented the faithful steward receiving his reward at the time of accounting for his stewardship. The

☐ Completion Date

apostle Paul confessed this truth in *1 Corinthians 9:17* when he said, *"if I do this thing willingly, I have a reward."* Paul knew God had a special calling upon his life and also knew he would stand before God to give account for his service. In like manner, each believer will one day stand before the Master (Jesus Christ) to give an account of his stewardship. Those who have served as good stewards will receive reward, while those who failed to do so will suffer loss *(1 Corinthians 3:11-15)*.

Devotional Thoughts

- **(For children):** How do you feel when dad or mom says, *"Good job"?* God has a work for every believer to do and it will not go unnoticed *(2 Chronicles 15:7; 1 Corinthians 15:58; Revelation 22:12)*. What do you think it would be like after your life's work is finished to hear Him say, *"Well done" (Matthew 25:23a)*?
- **(For everyone):** Have you faithfully served in your stewardship for the Lord? Are there areas you would go back and change at this point? How would you like to finish?
- Do you desire to please the Lord? Do you want to receive rewards from Him at the Judgment Seat of Christ? What would have to change in order to receive those rewards?

Prayer Thoughts

- Ask God to help you finish your stewardship well.
- Ask God to remind you that a day of accounting is coming.

SONG: *WE'LL WORK TILL JESUS COMES*

Notes: _____

Notes:

Quotes from the next volume

(VOLUME 4, WEEK 46)

Subject: Strength (con't)

Sorrow has its benefits. For instance, God uses the right type of sorrow to lead men to repentance *(2 Corinthians 7:9-11)*. Yet, it is in the joy of the LORD that saints specifically find strength.

Strength is not tested or demonstrated during times of ease. Rather, it is in times of adversity that one finds out just how strong he is (or how weak he has become).

47

Temptation

Temptation—found seventy-three times in sixty-four verses

Variations: tempt, temptation, temptations, tempted, tempter, tempteth, tempting

First usage: *Genesis 22:1* (tempt)

Last usage: *Revelation 3:10* (temptation)

Defined: a time of trial or testing

Interesting fact: *James 1:13* contains the words *tempted* or *tempteth* four times. *1 Corinthians 10:13* contains the words *temptation* or *tempted* three times. These two verses alone offer a vast doctrinal treatise on the source of, commonality of, and help available during times of temptation.

Bible study tip: At times, the Lord uses figures of speech to reinforce an associated truth. For example, Paul desired that those requiring *"circumcision"* of the believers of Galatia *(Galatians 5:2, 11)* would be *"cut off"* *(Galatians 5:12)*. In the same chapter, Paul expressed fear that the people would *"bite and devour one another,"* and in doing so, they might consume one another *(Galatians 5:15)*.

376 • Temptation

Sunday, Day 323—Church Day (no devotional)
Monday, Day 324—*Temptations Are Not the Same*
Tuesday, Day 325—*The Authors of Temptation*
Wednesday, Day 326—Church Night (no devotional)
Thursday, Day 327—*Every Man Is Tempted When . . .*
Friday, Day 328—*Avoiding Temptation*
Saturday, Day 329—*Candidates for Temptation*

Day 323: Church Day

***Acts 20:19** Serving the Lord with all humility of mind, and with many tears, and **temptations**, which befell me by the lying in wait of the Jews:*

Day 324: (Monday)
Temptations Are Not the Same

***Genesis 22:1** And it came to pass after these things, that **God did tempt Abraham**, and said unto him, Abraham: and he said, Behold, here I am.*

INTRODUCTORY THOUGHTS

When a believer considers the Bible's use of *"temptation,"* he most often associates its usage to something sinful. Though this may be the scripture's most common usage of the word, context must always be the determining factor. God undeniably tempted Abraham, yet the temptation was not meant to bring about sin. The temptation served as a test of Abraham's faith. Basically, temptation functions as a means to try one's faith. ***James 1:2-3*** clearly offers the connection as it incorporates the words *"temptations"* and *"trying"* interchangeably. The author, the purpose, and the circumstances surrounding temptations will vary, but the underlying premise remains constant. Each believer must learn how to discern the specifics when tempted.

DEVOTIONAL THOUGHTS

- **(For children):** *Psalm 11:5* says, *"The Lord trieth the righteous."* Job knew he was being tried as he had done nothing worthy of losing all his possessions, his health, and most of his family ***(Job 1:1; Job 23:10)***.

As Job was tried, God revealed Job's character to Satan. Satan hoped Job would sin, but he refused to do so *(Job 1:11, 22; Job 2:5, 9-10)*.
- **(For everyone):** Why is it important for believers to study the various details of temptation? How could this study help believers find victory during any times of temptation?
- Have you ever been tempted? What was the source of the temptation? Were you able to get victory over the temptation, or did you fall into sin? What could you have done differently?

Prayer Thoughts
- Ask God to teach you about scriptural temptation.
- Ask the Lord to give you wisdom when tempted.

SONG: *CLEANSE ME*

Day 325: (Tuesday)
The Authors of Temptation

Matthew 4:1 Then was Jesus led up of the Spirit into the wilderness to be tempted of the devil.

2 And when he had fasted forty days and forty nights, he was afterward an hungred.

*3 And when **the tempter came to him**, he said, If thou be the Son of God, command that these stones be made bread.*

Introductory Thoughts

Discerning the difference between the workings of God and the mischief of Satan sometimes serves as a difficult task for believers. Although the Devil is called the tempter in **Matthew 4:3** and **1 Thessalonians 3:5**, the Bible also shows that God uses temptation to try a man **(Genesis 22:1)**. Other than the association to instigating temptation, God and Satan have no other common ground in this matter. The Devil's motive and method of temptation is simply wicked. On the other hand, the Lord tempts only for the sake of trying one's faith to bring about a righteous outcome. Do not discount the fact that God never tempted anyone with evil **(James 1:13)**.

Devotional Thoughts

- **(For children):** Consider the story of Joseph. His faith and obedience were tested by God *(Psalm 105:16-21)*. Yet, Satan always tempts people to do evil. Consider Judas *(John 13:2)* and Ananias and Sapphira *(Acts 5:3)*.
- **(For everyone):** Why is it important to be able to discern whether the instigator of your temptation is the Lord or the Devil? How can this affect your response to the temptation?
- What foundational distinctions can be found in the temptations of God and the temptations of Satan? How do these specific distinctions reflect the character of God versus Satan?

Prayer Thoughts

- Ask the Lord to give you discernment in times of temptation.
- Ask God to show you the desire of your enemy to destroy.

SONG: *FELLOW SOLDIER, WHERE'S THINE ARMOUR?*

Day 326: Church Night

*1 Thessalonians 3:5 **For this cause, when I could no longer forbear, I sent to know your faith, lest by some means the tempter have tempted you,** and our labour be in vain.*

Day 327: (Thursday)
Every Man Is Tempted When . . .

*James 1:13 **Let no man say when he is tempted, I am tempted of God**: for God cannot be tempted with evil, neither tempteth he any man:*

*14 But **every man is tempted, when he is drawn away of his own lust, and enticed**.*

15 Then when lust hath conceived, it bringeth forth sin: and sin, when it is finished, bringeth forth death.

Introductory Thoughts

The context of today's passage confirms that it involves the temptation to do evil. This shows that the author of the temptation is not God, nor can it ever be Him in this context. The death of the one being tempted is the end result. This is why it is so very important for every believer to achieve a scriptural understanding of the source of his temptation. According to **James 1:14**, *"every man is tempted, when he is drawn away of his own lust, and enticed."* The first step of any temptation is a drawing away. If a man refuses to be drawn away, he simply cannot be tempted to do wrong. If a man allows himself to be drawn away, the Devil's next step involves enticement. It is often at this point that the Devil captures his prey leading him into sin.

Devotional Thoughts
- (**For children**): Eve did not know that the serpent was the Devil, but she did know God's command. She allowed herself to be drawn away from the truth and enticed by the Devil **(Genesis 3:1-6, 13; 2 Corinthians 11:3)**. Compare **Genesis 3:6** with **1 John 2:16**.
- (**For everyone**): What does it mean to be drawn away? What does it mean to be enticed? At what point does a temptation become sin? How can this understanding help to ensure the believer's ability to get victory?
- What kind of things does the Devil use to draw you away from walking with the Lord? What can you do to make sure that you do not fall prey to his devices?

Prayer Thoughts
- Ask the Lord to guard you from the attacks of Satan.
- Ask God to help you walk circumspectly in this world.

SONG: *YIELD NOT TO TEMPTATION*

Day 328: (Friday)
Avoiding Temptation

Matthew 26:41 Watch and pray, that ye enter not into temptation: the spirit indeed is willing, but the flesh is weak.

Introductory Thoughts

Every believer battling temptation faces an inward struggle. A part of him (his spirit) wants to do right and to please the Lord, while another part of him (his flesh) loves sin and self more than the Saviour. If this struggle goes unchecked, the flesh will certainly win every time. Man's spirit requires reinforcements in order to win this battle. According to *Matthew 26:41*, two of these resources include watchfulness and prayer. It is imperative for each believer to implement both, for one without the other leaves a person with certain vulnerabilities when temptations arise. Watchfulness demonstrates the saint's personal responsibility, while prayer demonstrates his need for God's intervention.

Devotional Thoughts

- **(For children):** We constantly have a battle going on inside us *(Galatians 5:17)*. Satan would love for us to do wrong *(Ephesians 6:11-12)*. We need to watch and pray to ensure the victory *(Ephesians 6:18; Colossians 4:2)*.
- **(For everyone):** What are some examples from scripture showing people who fell into temptation because they refused to watch and pray? How can you learn from their failures?
- How do watchfulness and prayer work together in delivering the saint from temptations? In what ways is one weakened with the absence of the other?

Prayer Thoughts

- Ask God to keep you watchful and in prayer.
- Thank God for the privilege and strength of prayer.

SONG: *I ASKED THE LORD THAT I MIGHT GROW*

Day 329: (Saturday)
Candidates for Temptation

1 Timothy 6:9 **But they that will be rich fall into temptation and a snare,** *and into many foolish and hurtful lusts, which drown men in destruction and perdition.*

Introductory Thoughts

Every individual to a certain degree is a prime target for temptation. Yet, because of personal choices and circumstances, some people are a far greater target than others. According to scripture, ungodly fellowship

☐ Completion Date   Temptation • 381

(Exodus 23:33; Exodus 34:12; Proverbs 22:24-26), riches *(Deuteronomy 7:25; 1 Timothy 6:9)*, and broken vows *(Proverbs 20:25)* are a few of the things that weaken the believer's ability to endure temptation. Some of these are blatantly sinful while others can be innocent. Each believer needs to diligently seek the Lord regardless of whether or not any of these things are present in his life. However, the presence of these things only works to heighten a man's temptations.

Devotional Thoughts
- **(For children):** How did the desire to be rich cause the following men to sin: Achan *(Joshua 7:11, 21)*; Gehazi *(2 Kings 5:20-27)*; Judas *(Matthew 26:14-16)*? Wrong companions caused God's people to serve other gods *(Psalm 106:34-36; 1 Kings 11:4, 9-10)*.
- **(For everyone):** What things exist in your life that might cause you to become prone to temptations? Do any of these things need to be removed, or do you consider them necessary evils?
- How many temptations could you have avoided if you would have simply removed things from your life that made you an easier target for temptation?

Prayer Thoughts
- Ask the Lord to help you inspect your life for dangers.
- Thank God for protecting you from many troubles.

SONG: *TRUSTING JESUS*

Notes: _____
_____
_____
_____
_____
_____
_____
_____

Notes:

Quotes from the next volume

(VOLUME 4, WEEK 47)

Subject: Toleration

Christians more scripturally knowledgeable should never mock or disdain any weaker believer, nor should they seek to allow themselves to be a stumblingstone toward others.

There are issues in which not all believers will necessarily agree. At times, these things are doctrinal issues forcing them to be addressed. At other times, the disagreements may revolve around issues where the scriptures are silent. In such cases, believers should be even more gracious with others.

48
Temptation (con't)

Temptation—found seventeen times in sixteen Old Testament verses and fifty-six times in forty-eight New Testament verses

Variations: tempt, temptation, temptations, tempted, tempter, tempteth, tempting

Last usage in the Old Testament: *Malachi 3:15* (tempt)

First usage in the New Testament: *Matthew 4:1* (tempted)

Interesting fact: The Lord Jesus Christ serves as our *"great high priest" (Hebrews 4:14)*. Surprisingly, the fact that the Lord Jesus was tempted in His earthly ministry uniquely qualifies Him to serve in this capacity. According to **Hebrews 2:17**, *"it behoved him [Christ] to be made like unto his brethren, that he might be a merciful and faithful high priest in things pertaining to God."* In the same context, the Bible sets forth, *"in that he himself hath suffered being tempted, he is able to succor them that are tempted" (**Hebrews 2:18**)*. Why is Christ so uniquely qualified? He *"was in all points tempted like as we are, yet without sin" (**Hebrews 4:15**)*.

Bible study tip: We often describe travel northward as going *up* and southbound travel as going *down*. However, the scriptures sometime incorporate the words *up* and *down* to describe elevation changes. One such example found in **Acts 25:6-7** shows the apostle Paul being moved to Caesarea where he was met with *"Jews which came **down** from Jerusalem."* Yet, Caesarea is located northwest of Jerusalem so directionally they would not have come *down* from Jerusalem to Caesarea, but up. This expression only makes sense when considering land elevations. Be sure to allow the context of the passage to define the intent of the terms as to whether the terminology relates to **direction** or to **elevation**. The Acts chapter 25 example refers to the latter.

Sunday, Day 330—Church Day (no devotional)
Monday, Day 331—*A Tempted Saviour*
Tuesday, Day 332—*Temptations Are Common*
Wednesday, Day 333—Church Night (no devotional)
Thursday, Day 334—*Temptations Are Escapable*
Friday, Day 335—*The Joy of Temptations*
Saturday, Day 336—*The Hour of Temptation*

Day 330: Church Day

Deuteronomy 6:16 Ye shall not tempt the LORD your God, as ye tempted him in Massah.

Day 331: (Monday)
A Tempted Saviour

*Hebrews 4:15 For we have not **an high priest** which cannot be touched with the feeling of our infirmities; but was **in all points** tempted like as we are, yet without sin.*

Introductory Thoughts

Man has no greater high priest than the Lord Jesus Christ for the Lord knows what man endures. Like man, He was tempted in all points. In a basic sense, man's temptations involve three distinct facets: *"the lust of the flesh, and the lust of the eyes, and the pride of life"* **(1 John 2:16)**.

☐ Completion Date Temptation (con't) • 385

During the Lord's earthly ministry, He faced and conquered temptation in each area *(Matthew 4:1-11)*. As such, the Lord is *"touched with the feeling of our infirmities" (Hebrews 4:15)*. He knows what it is like to face the temptation to depart from the will of God. He knows what it is like to be tempted to sin against the Heavenly Father. Yet, He differs from man in that His temptation was without the knowledge of sin, for He was victorious in all points.

DEVOTIONAL THOUGHTS

- **(For children):** Even through His trial and crucifixion, Jesus was tempted *(Luke 22:63-65; Matthew 27:34, 39-42)*. Yet, He never sinned *(Luke 23:33-34; 1 Peter 2:21-23)*. Knowing the word of God can help us be more like Him during our times of temptation *(Psalm 119:11)*.
- **(For everyone):** Study the record of the temptation of Christ. Match His temptation with the three areas in which man can also be tempted. What was the Lord's weapon of choice in obtaining victory over temptation? How can you use the same weapon to withstand temptation today?
- Job longed for a daysman *"that might lay his hand upon"* both God and man *(Job 9:33)*. How was this answered in Christ?

PRAYER THOUGHTS

- Thank the Lord for enduring temptation.
- Ask God to help you handle temptation as the Saviour did.

SONG: *WHAT A FRIEND WE HAVE IN JESUS*

Day 332: (Tuesday)
Temptations Are Common

1 Corinthians 10:13 There hath no temptation taken you but such as is common to man: but God is faithful, who will not suffer you to be tempted above that ye are able; but will with the temptation also make a way to escape, that ye may be able to bear it.

INTRODUCTORY THOUGHTS

Throughout history, man has battled the idea that he is the only one who has had to endure temptation with a desire to do right *(1 Kings 19:13-14)*. This lie was conceived by the father of lies *(John 8:44)* with the intent of convincing the believer into thinking that no one understands his difficulty. Though it is true that one man's specific temptations may differ from that of another man, the basic premise is true: *"There hath no temptation taken you but such as is common to man"* **(1 Corinthians 10:13)**. In Elijah's day, there were 7,000 others (probably referring to only those in Israel) who experienced temptations similar to those experienced by Elijah **(1 Kings 19:18)**.

Devotional Thoughts

- **(For children):** The Bible says that *"there is no new thing under the sun" (Ecclesiastes 1:9)*. Whatever situation you face, somewhere, someone has experienced a problem similar to yours. Read what Peter said in **1 Peter 5:8-9**.
- **(For everyone):** What temptations do you face? How are your temptations like those of your brothers and sisters in Christ? How can you work together to gain victory when tempted?
- How does it benefit the Devil when the believer assumes that he is the only one battling a specific temptation? What does the Bible teach about strength in numbers *(Ecclesiastes 4:9-10)*?

Prayer Thoughts

- Ask God to give you others with whom you can fight temptation.
- Ask the Lord to remind you that you are not alone.

SONG: *I NEED THEE EVERY HOUR*

Day 333: Church Night

Matthew 26:41 Watch and pray, that ye enter not into temptation: the spirit indeed is willing, but the flesh is weak.

Day 334: (Thursday)
Temptations Are Escapable

1 Corinthians 10:13 There hath no temptation taken you but such as is common to man: but **God** *is faithful, who* **will not suffer you to be tempted above that ye are able; but will with the temptation also make a way to escape***, that ye may be able to bear it.*

Introductory Thoughts

Man never sins without willingly doing so. Unfortunately, man's vocabulary infers that sin is simply an uncontrollable accident or unfortunate mistake. Yet, in reality, we choose to sin. This is extremely obvious when one considers that the Lord promises *"a way to escape"* during every temptation. It is not that the Lord offers a way to avoid temptation altogether, but He offers help that man *"may be able to bear it* [the temptation]." Man can never point his finger toward God in an attempt to assign some level of guilt for man's sins. God always makes a way for man to righteously endure and conquer every type of temptation known to man. The failure to escape from any temptation is not for lack of opportunity to do so.

Devotional Thoughts

- **(For children):** To have victory over temptation, we must believe God can help during every time of need **(Hebrews 2:18; 2 Peter 2:9)**. He tells us to pray **(Hebrews 4:16)**, use His word **(Ephesians 6:11, 17)**, resist **(James 4:7)**, and flee **(1 Corinthians 10:14; 1 Timothy 6:10-11; 2 Timothy 2:22)**.
- **(For everyone):** What are your besetting sins? When is the last time you chose to fall prey to one of those sins? Looking back, can you remember God's way to escape? Why do you think you choose to ignore that way to escape?
- How did Jesus Christ escape temptation when dealing with the Devil? How could you escape through the same means?

Prayer Thoughts

- Thank God for offering you victory when tempted.
- Ask God for power to take the way of escape when tempted.

SONG: *JESUS! WHAT A FRIEND FOR SINNERS*

Day 335: (Friday)
The Joy of Temptations

James 1:2 *My brethren,* **count it all joy when ye fall into divers temptations;**

3 *Knowing this, that the trying of your faith worketh patience.*

Temptation (con't) ☐ Completion Date

INTRODUCTORY THOUGHTS

The average believer might never consider the word *joy* as an appropriate term to associate with temptations. The reason for this perplexity has to do with the fact that far too many believers fail to experience the God-intended victory when tempted. Temptations put a man's faith on trial. When his faith stands the test, he learns patience. Therefore, he sees temptation as a means by which he can grow in the Lord and experience added virtues such as patience. It is not that he finds joy within the temptation itself, but that God can and will use that temptation to make him *"perfect and entire, wanting nothing" (James 1:4)*. Believers who fight through and obtain victory find joy in knowing that their faith pleases God *(Hebrews 11:6)*.

DEVOTIONAL THOUGHTS

- **(For children)**: When we think of **Romans 8:28**, we can have joy in hard times. The Lord found joy in His temptations *(Hebrews 12:2)*. Paul had many temptations *(2 Corinthians 11:23b-28)*. Consider his attitude *(Acts 20:24; 2 Timothy 4:7)*.
- **(For everyone)**: Have you ever found joy in the midst of temptations? What moved you to this joy? How has God used your temptations to draw you closer to Himself?
- How is the joy of temptation *(James 1:2)* different from the *"pleasures of sin" (Hebrews 11:25)*? Which one is enduring and righteous? Which one is most often sought by men?

PRAYER THOUGHTS

- Ask God to help you rejoice in the victories over temptation.
- Thank the Lord for helping you during difficult times.

SONG: *YIELD NOT TO TEMPTATION*

Day 336: (Saturday)
The Hour of Temptation

*Revelation 3:10 Because thou hast kept the word of my patience, **I** also will keep thee from the hour of temptation, which shall come upon all the world, to try them that dwell upon the earth.*

☐ Completion Date Temptation (con't) • 389

Introductory Thoughts

Temptation is commonly linked to the trying of one's faith, but *"the hour of temptation"* is not the typical temptation experienced by the believer. In fact, the Lord promised to *"keep"* the church *"from the hour of temptation."* So what is this temptation to which the Lord speaks? First of all, it is connected to a specific time as indicated by the use of the word *hour*. Secondly, this temptation is one that is yet future as demonstrated by the phrase, *"shall come."* Lastly, it is a temptation designed to *"come upon all the world, to try them that dwell upon the earth."* This temptation is known as Daniel's Seventieth Week and refers to a temptation for the unsaved Jews and Gentiles during that terrible future time.

Devotional Thoughts

- **(For children):** Daniel's Seventieth Week will bring severe testing and suffering upon the world. Jesus described this time to His disciples *(Matthew 24:3-13)*. John also described it in **Revelation 6:9-17**. This event is yet future. If you are saved now, you will not go through this time *(1 Thessalonians 4:13-18; 1 Thessalonians 5:9)*.
- **(For everyone):** God offers man a way to escape in every temptation. How is God's offer to escape *"the hour of temptation"* different from His offer of escape in the temptations faced today by believers?
- God promised to *"keep"* the church *"from the hour of temptation."* Why is the church exempt from this temptation *(Jeremiah 30:7)*? What have you done to escape?

Prayer Thoughts

- Thank God for keeping the church from the hour of temptation.
- Ask God to work in the hearts of your lost loved ones.

SONG: *BELOVED, NOW ARE WE*

Notes: _____

_____

_____

_____

_____

_____

Notes: _____

_____
_____
_____
_____
_____
_____
_____
_____
_____
_____
_____
_____
_____
_____
_____
_____
_____

Quotes from the next volume

(VOLUME 4, WEEK 48)

Subject: Truth

The God of the Bible is a God of truth.

If God is *"a God of truth"* **(Deuteronomy 32:4)**, it makes sense that the words proceeding forth from His mouth would reflect and demonstrate the same nature as their author.

Because of God's mercy, mankind has access to His truth.

49

Tradition

Tradition—found thirteen times in thirteen verses, all in the New Testament

Variations: tradition, traditions

First usage: *Matthew 15:2* (tradition)

Last usage: *1 Peter 1:18* (tradition)

Defined: a belief or practice handed down from one generation to the next

Interesting fact: Though we do not know all the traditions that consumed the Jews during the earthly ministry of Christ, we are informed that they included the washing of hands before eating bread *(Mark 7:2-5)* and the washing of cups, pots, brasen vessels, and tables *(Mark 7:4, 8)*. Sadly, the Lord additionally reproved the Jews concerning the *"many other such like things ye do" (Mark 7:8)*.

Bible study tip: In Bible study as well as in life, many things are neutral (neither righteous nor sinful) in and of themselves. Yet, things like traditions and religion are almost always identified by conservative Christianity as referring to something evil. However, scripture testifies that there exists traditions which should be cause for believers to beware *(Colossians 2:8)* and other traditions which believers should firmly hold *(2 Thessalonians 2:15)*.

Sunday, Day 337—Church Day (no devotional)
Monday, Day 338—*What Is a Tradition?*
Tuesday, Day 339—*When Tradition and Scripture Conflict*
Wednesday, Day 340—Church Night (no devotional)
Thursday, Day 341—*Commandments That Turn*
Friday, Day 342—*Whose Tradition Is It?*
Saturday, Day 343—*Hold the Tradition*

Day 337: Church Day

Romans 16:17 *Now I beseech you, brethren,* **mark them which cause divisions and offences contrary to the doctrine which ye have learned;** *and avoid them.*

Day 338: (Monday)
What Is a Tradition?

2 Thessalonians 2:15 Therefore, brethren, stand fast, and **hold the traditions which ye have been taught,** *whether by word, or our epistle.*

INTRODUCTORY THOUGHTS

It is difficult to find one who has a scriptural balance concerning tradition. Some see every so-called tradition as a direct violation of scripture, while others see traditions as equal to or superior to scripture. Scripturally speaking, both views are fundamentally flawed. In a basic sense, traditions are anything that men *"have been taught"* *(2 Thessalonians 2:15)*. It involves a teaching that has been *"delivered"* *(Mark 7:13)* and *"received"* *(2 Thessalonians 3:6; 1 Peter 1:18)*. At times, tradition is scripture or, in the least, scriptural *(2 Thessalonians 2:15; 2 Thessalonians 3:6)*, while at other times, tradition is ungodly and makes *"the word of God of none effect"* *(Mark 7:13)*.

☐ Completion Date	Tradition • 393

Devotional Thoughts
- **(For children):** God does not tell the New Testament church believers to celebrate holidays. These days are traditions which man can choose to celebrate in a good way or in a bad way. How do you celebrate holidays? Do you do so to the glory of God or for personal gain?
- **(For everyone):** What are some traditions you hold dear? Are those traditions scriptural or, at least, complimentary to the scripture? Do you hold any traditions that cannot be supported by scripture or perhaps are even unscriptural?
- Name an unscriptural tradition. Do you know someone who holds this tradition? How could you help them know the truth?

Prayer Thoughts
- Ask God to teach you scriptural traditions.
- Ask the Lord to help you consider the nature of your traditions.

SONG: *THE BIBLE IS THE TEST OF ALL*

Day 339: (Tuesday)
When Tradition and Scripture Conflict

*Mark 7:8 For **laying aside the commandment of God, ye hold the tradition of men**, as the washing of pots and cups: and many other such like things ye do.*

*9 And he said unto them, **Full well ye reject the commandment of God, that ye may keep your own tradition.***

Introductory Thoughts

Many of man's traditions are in direct opposition to scripture. God's servants who have pledged allegiance to the scripture cannot in good conscience accept these unscriptural traditions. During the earthly ministry of the Lord Jesus, the religious leaders laid aside *(Mark 7:8)* or rejected *(Mark 7:9)* the commandment of God in order to hold *(Mark 7:8)* or keep *(Mark 7:9)* the tradition of men. By doing so, the Lord said they made *"the word of God of none effect" (Mark 7:13).* One who loves the Lord examines every tradition through the lens of scripture to ensure that it does not oppose scripture. He does not accept the commandments of men knowing that God is the source of ultimate truth.

Devotional Thoughts

- **(For children):** Some men teach that Jesus' mother Mary should be prayed to and worshipped. What does the Bible say *(1 Timothy 2:5)*? Mary needed Jesus to be her Saviour too *(Luke 1:46-47)*. God's word is always true *(Psalm 119:160a)*. Believe it over men's words.
- **(For everyone):** Do you allow your doctrines to be tested against the truths of scripture? Is it possible you have accepted the teachings of men as authoritative despite the fact that they are unscriptural?
- What or who is your authority for truth? Have you ever had to change or adjust your doctrine in order to be more scriptural? If not, is it possible that you have an improper authority?

Prayer Thoughts

- Ask the Lord to give you the proper authority for truth.
- Ask God to perfect your doctrine.

SONG: *THE OLD BOOK AND THE OLD FAITH*

Day 340: Church Night

*2 Thessalonians 3:6 Now we command you, brethren, in the name of our Lord Jesus Christ, that ye **withdraw yourselves from every brother that walketh disorderly, and not after the tradition which he received of us**.*

Day 341: (Thursday)
Commandments That Turn

*Titus 1:14 Not giving heed to Jewish fables, and **commandments of men, that turn from the truth**.*

Introductory Thoughts

The commandments of men posed great risk to the early church. So much so, the apostle Paul encouraged Titus to warn his flock against accepting extra-biblical teachings. These *"fables"* and *"commandments"* turned people from the truth. Perhaps in the beginning one might be able to accept both, but eventually the acceptance of one demands the rejection of the other. Titus was charged with the responsibility of ensuring that the saints of God made the right choice. Like in the days of old,

☐ Completion Date

God has given the church faithful men charged with warning the saints about accepting fables that turn believers from the truth.

DEVOTIONAL THOUGHTS

- **(For children):** Paul gave Timothy a warning about the commandments or teachings of men *(1 Timothy 4:1-5; 2 Timothy 4:4)*. He instructed Timothy what to do about these things *(1 Timothy 4:6-7; 2 Timothy 4:2)*.
- **(For everyone):** Name some unscriptural traditions that men have accepted as truth. How have these traditions actually worked to turn these same men from the truth of God's word?
- What was Titus to do with those who might teach or accept men's traditions as the commandments of God *(Titus 1:13)*? What might happen if Titus fulfilled his responsibility?

PRAYER THOUGHTS

- Ask the Lord to protect you from error.
- Ask God to help you *"be sound in the faith."*

SONG: *GLORIOUS BIBLE*

Day 342: (Friday)
Whose Tradition Is It?

*Mark 7:3 For the Pharisees, and all the Jews, except they wash their hands oft, eat not, holding **the tradition of the elders**.*

4 And when they come from the market, except they wash, they eat not. And many other things there be, which they have received to hold, as the washing of cups, and pots, brasen vessels, and of tables.

*5 Then the Pharisees and scribes asked him, Why walk not thy disciples according to **the tradition of the elders**, but eat bread with unwashen hands?*

6 He answered and said unto them, Well hath Esaias prophesied of you hypocrites, as it is written, This people honoureth me with their lips, but their heart is far from me.

*7 Howbeit in vain do they worship me, teaching for doctrines **the commandments of men**.*

*8 For laying aside the commandment of God, ye hold **the tradition of men**, as the washing of pots and cups: and many other such like things ye do.*

*9 And he said unto them, Full well ye reject the commandment of God, that ye may keep **your own tradition**.*

10 For Moses said, Honour thy father and thy mother; and, Whoso curseth father or mother, let him die the death:

11 But ye say, If a man shall say to his father or mother, It is Corban, that is to say, a gift, by whatsoever thou mightest be profited by me; he shall be free.

12 And ye suffer him no more to do ought for his father or his mother;

*13 Making the word of God of none effect through **your tradition**, which ye have delivered: and many such like things do ye.*

INTRODUCTORY THOUGHTS

Sometimes a deep chasm exists between the doctrines, traditions, and commandments of men and those that are God-ordained. Perhaps no passage better identifies this contrast than Mark chapter 7. The religious leaders of Christ's day held *"the tradition of the elders" **(Mark 7:3, 5)**, "the tradition of men" **(Mark 7:8)**,* and their own *"tradition" **(Mark 7:9, 13)**.* In doing so, they rejected *"the commandment of God" **(Mark 7:9)**.* This clearly displays the critical importance of identifying whose traditions one willingly receives and accepts. If traditions are truly of the Lord, they are to be accepted and implemented into the believer's life *(2 **Thessalonians 2:15)**.* Yet, those man-made, unscriptural traditions are to be rejected altogether.

DEVOTIONAL THOUGHTS

- **(For children):** There are no works involved in salvation. We are saved by believing *(**Ephesians 2:8-9)**.* Any other plan is based upon the tradition of men *(**1 Peter 1:18-19; Colossians 2:20-22)**.* Consider Paul's testimony *(**Galatians 1:13-16)**.*
- **(For everyone):** How can one determine whose traditions he accepts or rejects? Where can one find traditions that be of God? What should he do once he finds those traditions?

- Upon whose traditions do you stand? Have you fallen prey to the exaltation of the traditions of men? What can you do in order to turn and follow only the traditions of the Lord?

PRAYER THOUGHTS
- Ask God for wisdom.
- Ask the Lord to show you whose traditions you hold dear.

SONG: *THE BIBLE STANDS*

Day 343: (Saturday)
Hold the Tradition

2 Thessalonians 2:15 Therefore, brethren, stand fast, and **hold the traditions which ye have been taught, whether by word, or our epistle***.*

INTRODUCTORY THOUGHTS

The previous generation has handed down to the present generation some wonderful traditions. Those most precious are directly found in scripture while others are closely associated with scriptural principles. Paul admonished believers at Thessalonica to *"hold"* these types of traditions. Likewise, believers today should diligently continue in godly traditions. Those that are directly taken from scripture are a given, but there are others that are also important. No Bible verse specifically states believers should attend a midweek worship service, but it is certainly a scriptural tradition *(Hebrews 10:25)*. In like manner, no Bible verse indicates that the early church held Sunday School, yet it is a very scriptural tradition *(2 Timothy 2:15)*.

DEVOTIONAL THOUGHTS
- **(For children):** Read *1 Corinthians 11:23-26*. Even though the Bible does not say how often we take the Lord's Supper, it was a tradition Paul *"received"* from God and *"delivered"* to the Corinthians which they were supposed to follow. We should maintain such traditions.
- **(For everyone):** What are some traditions you hold dear that can be found in scripture? What are some scriptural traditions you hold that might not be specifically commanded in scripture?

- What determines whether or not a tradition crosses the line into the realm of unscriptural? How can one protect himself from believing such traditions?

Prayer Thoughts
- Thank the Lord for scriptural traditions.
- Ask God for strength to hold the right traditions.

SONG: *I AM RESOLVED*

Notes: _____

Quotes from the next volume

(VOLUME 4, WEEK 49)

Subject: Truth (con't)

If man rejects the initial ray of truth from the Lord, the Lord is not bound to give any additional light.

A nation should rather choose to find themselves without food and water than to endure a famine of truth.

Initially, men might think that truth binds men, but a man enlightened by the truth knows nothing could be farther from the truth.

50

Tradition (con't)

Tradition—found eight times in the Gospels, four times in Paul's epistles, and one time in Peter's first epistle

Variations: tradition, traditions

Interesting fact: Traditions are deviations from the truth (slight or otherwise). In answering Peter's question about the apostle John's future, Jesus said, *"If I will that he tarry till I come, what is that to thee?" (John 21:22)*. From those words, men spread the tradition *"that that disciple* [John] *should not die" (John 21:23)*. Far too many of today's most prominent religious traditions originate from a misrepresented Bible truth.

Bible study tip: Unless specifically stated, one should never assume an Old Testament saint understood a truth yet to be revealed (either later within the Old Testament or in the pages of the New Testament). However, the Bible student should always view the Old Testament through a New Testament lens. This is especially true in passages where the New Testament adds details or clarity concerning an Old Testament person, place, or event.

400 • Tradition (con't) ☐ Completion Date

Sunday, Day 344—Church Day (no devotional)
Monday, Day 345—*Making the Word of God of None Effect*
Tuesday, Day 346—*Zealous of the Traditions*
Wednesday, Day 347—Church Night (no devotional)
Thursday, Day 348—*Spoiled Through Traditions*
Friday, Day 349—*Vain Conversation Received by Tradition*
Saturday, Day 350—*Separation Because of Tradition*

Day 344: Church Day

Mark 7:9 And he said unto them, **Full well ye reject the commandment of God, that ye may keep your own tradition.**

Day 345: (Monday)
Making the Word of God of None Effect

Mark 7:13 **Making the word of God of none effect through your tradition,** *which ye have delivered: and many such like things do ye.*

INTRODUCTORY THOUGHTS

One of the most important issues that every believer must face involves the question of ultimate authority. The Pharisees abused their God-given authority by *"laying aside the commandment of God"* and replacing it with *"the tradition of men"* **(Mark 7:8)**. They simply transgressed *"the commandment of God"* in order to obey and follow their tradition **(Matthew 15:3)**. Through these unwise actions, they plainly declared that the traditions of men were their ultimate authority rather than God and His word. As a result, the Lord Jesus said they made the word of God of none effect. This same truth applies today. When a man accepts men's traditions as superior to the scripture, he makes scripture ineffective for God's intended purposes. The Bible must be believed in order for it to be effectual **(1 Thessalonians 2:13)**.

DEVOTIONAL THOUGHTS

- **(For children):** Tradition places three wise men at the manger scene. The Bible never specifies how many wise men came but simply mentions three gifts. When the wise men reached Bethlehem, Jesus was

a child living in a house *(Matthew 2:1-2, 9-11)*. Will you believe the Bible over any tradition?
- **(For everyone):** What are some beliefs that you hold dear? What is your authority for holding onto those beliefs? Are any of those unscriptural? If so, will you accept the traditions of men over the scripture?
- What are some common beliefs that people hold that are unscriptural? Where did those doctrines originate? Is there any scripture that plainly shows those doctrines unscriptural?

PRAYER THOUGHTS
- Ask God to help you maintain the proper authority.
- Ask the Lord to show you any unscriptural views you have.

SONG: *THE OLD BOOK AND THE OLD FAITH*

Day 346: (Tuesday)
Zealous of the Traditions

Galatians 1:14 *And profited in the Jews' religion above many my equals in mine own nation, being more exceedingly **zealous of the traditions of my fathers**.*

INTRODUCTORY THOUGHTS

Many people are quite zealous of following the traditions of men. For instance, the apostle Paul was so exceedingly zealous of the traditions of his fathers that he *"persecuted this way unto the death, binding and delivering into prisons both men and women"* **(Acts 22:4)**. This same act has been true throughout church history. History reveals that many saints of God were severely punished and even put to death for rejecting unscriptural traditions such as infant baptism. In some cases, babies were ripped from the arms of their mothers and cast into lakes and rivers. Others were tossed into arenas with lions for rejecting traditions choosing to hold up scripture. Why? Because men are zealous of their traditions and will persecute to keep their ways intact!

Devotional Thoughts

- **(For children):** God's chosen people were zealous of their traditions of keeping the law and refused to believe Jesus was their Messiah *(John 1:11; Romans 10:1-4)*. Their zeal caused them to want to kill Jesus *(John 5:15-18)*.
- **(For everyone):** Why are people so zealous over traditions even when these traditions lack any scriptural foundation? What are some examples you know of someone persecuted or martyred for accepting the scripture rather than the traditions of men?
- What are some of the most prominent unscriptural traditions for which men have been persecuted? Where do you stand concerning these traditions?

Prayer Thoughts

- Ask God to give you boldness to stand for His word.
- Ask the Lord to help you to be faithful unto death.

SONG: *STANDING ON THE PROMISES*

Day 347: Church Night

*2 Thessalonians 2:15 Therefore, brethren, stand fast, and **hold the traditions which ye have been taught, whether by word, or our epistle**.*

Day 348: (Thursday)
Spoiled Through Traditions

*Colossians 2:8 Beware lest any man **spoil you** through philosophy and vain deceit, **after the tradition of men**, after the rudiments of the world, and not after Christ.*

Introductory Thoughts

Tradition robs men of the blessings only derived from one's obedience to the truth. The word *spoil* is a term used during wartime meaning that one side in a battle breaks forth into the territory of the other side and takes their valuable possessions. According to scripture, philosophies and deceit based upon the traditions of men rob the saint of God of the benefits offered by merely accepting the truths of the word of God.

☐ Completion Date Tradition (con't) • 403

The price of spoiling is high. For the lost, they can be spoiled of their eternal life by accepting the traditions (false gospels) and philosophies (evolution) of men. For the saved, they can lose some eternal rewards by the acceptance of traditions contrary to the plain truths of scripture.

Devotional Thoughts

- **(For children):** Jesus Christ is the only way to heaven *(John 14:6; 1 Corinthians 15:1-4)*. The Galatians were fooled by those who said Christ was not sufficient because they needed to keep the law too. Paul told them this was not true *(Galatians 3:1, 10-13; Galatians 2:16, 20-21)*.
- **(For everyone):** What are some ways in which you could be spoiled by accepting the traditions of men? What can you do to insure this does not happen?
- Name some people in scripture who were spoiled by the traditions of men. Did those men or women ever recover what had been taken from them?

Prayer Thoughts

- Ask the Lord to protect you from the spoiling of man's tradition.
- Ask God for wisdom in the area of traditions.

SONG: *LOYALTY TO CHRIST*

Day 349: (Friday)
Vain Conversation Received by Tradition

1 Peter 1:18 Forasmuch as ye know that ye were not redeemed with corruptible things, as silver and gold, from your **vain conversation received by tradition from your fathers***;*

Introductory Thoughts

The traditions of men produce lives lived in vain. According to scripture, the word *conversation* means much more than merely words being spoken from one person to another. The context shows that the word refers to the way in which a person lives his life *(2 Corinthians 1:12; 1 Peter 3:1)*. As such, those who build their lives upon the traditions of men may work very hard and be even deemed faithful. Yet, this life is all for naught because their lives are built upon vanity. Sadly, some of the most faithful followers of religion are those who are promoting the traditions of men from which they will gain no eternal benefits. The only conversation that proves fruitful in eternity is the one built upon the commandments of God.

DEVOTIONAL THOUGHTS
- **(For children):** Many teach that we get to heaven by doing good works. The only *"work"* that one does is to believe *(John 6:28-29; 1 John 3:23a)*. Good works follow faith; they do not precede it *(Ephesians 2:8-10; Titus 3:5-8)*. If one does not believe first, works will be worthless *(Matthew 7:21-23)*.
- **(For everyone):** How can a life based upon tradition be a life of vanity? How can it contain a lot of activity but be less fruitful? What can you do to make sure that your life counts in eternity?
- What are some things that people do in the name of religion that will leave them without reward? How will some people work their whole lives only to end up in hell?

PRAYER THOUGHTS
- Ask the Lord to help your life count for something.
- Thank the Lord for giving you His word by which you can live.

SONG: *LITTLE IS MUCH WHEN GOD IS IN IT*

Day 350: (Saturday)
Separation Because of Tradition

*2 Thessalonians 3:6 Now we command you, brethren, in the name of our Lord Jesus Christ, that ye **withdraw yourselves from every brother that walketh** disorderly, and **not after the tradition which he received of us**.*

INTRODUCTORY THOUGHTS

Scriptural traditions are worthy of the believer's allegiance and should move him to break fellowship with those who refuse to adhere to those biblical traditions. The apostle Paul spoke of traditions that the believers in Thessalonica had received from him. These traditions were good and were to be maintained by the believers *(2 Thessalonians 2:15)*. In fact, these traditions were so important that the people of God were to *"withdraw"* themselves from those (including *"every brother"*) who walked disorderly (in disobedience to the traditions). No doubt, these traditions were the very ones which Paul made known in his epistles.

Devotional Thoughts

- **(For children):** The Bible is very clear that we separate from those (saved or lost) who go against the scriptures which we have been taught. Some examples are **Romans 16:17; 1 Corinthians 5:11; Ephesians 5:11; 1 Timothy 6:3-5; 2 Timothy 3:1-5; 2 John 1:7, 9-10.**
- **(For everyone):** In a day when everyone suggests compromise in order to get along, what should the Bible-loving Christian do to stay true to the word of God?
- For what should you be willing to separate? From whom should you be willing to separate? What is your scriptural authority for your thoughts?

Prayer Thoughts

- Ask the Lord to help you be willing to separate when needed.
- Ask God to put a hedge about your fellow believers.

SONG: *THY TESTIMONY'S MY DELIGHT*

Notes:

406 • Tradition (con't) ☐ Completion Date

Notes:

Quotes from the next volume
(VOLUME 4, WEEK 50)
Subject: Truth (con't)

Truth and love can and must coexist in ths that would hinder his ability to fight spiritual battles.

51

Violence

Violence—found seventy-seven times in seventy-five verses

Variations: violence, violent, violently

First usage: *Genesis 6:11* (violence)

Last usage: *Revelation 18:21* (violence)

Defined: physical force inflicting injury

Interesting fact: In all of Paul's epistles, the word *violence* (and its various forms) only occurs one time **(Hebrews 11:34)**. In that passage, the reference is to the troubles endured by faithful saints in days past. Interestingly, James, Peter, John, and Jude never used the word in their epistles. This notable absence of the word *violence* should underscore two great distinguishing features in New Testament Christianity: (1) the nature of our warfare should be primarily focused upon the spiritual, and (2) the Lord wants us to be at peace with one another.

Bible study tip: Some books of the Bible contain dialog exchanged between several people. In such cases, it is very important to note (as much as possible) when the speaker changes from one person to the next. If possible, make notations to draw your attention to the speaker change so that you do not assign the words to the wrong speaker. The book of Job is a prime example. One important factor of note is that the Lord scolded Job's friends saying, *"ye have not spoken of me the thing which is right, like my servant Job"* **(Job 42:8)**.

Sunday, Day 351—Church Day (no devotional)
Monday, Day 352—*The Earth Was Filled with Violence*
Tuesday, Day 353—*Violence Covereth Their Mouths*
Wednesday, Day 354—Church Night (no devotional)
Thursday, Day 355—*The Rich Men Are Full of Violence*
Friday, Day 356—*They Covet and Take by Violence*
Saturday, Day 357—*Do Violence to No Man*

Day 351: Church Day

Proverbs 16:29 A violent man enticeth his neighbour, and leadeth him into the way **that is** *not good.*

Day 352: (Monday)
The Earth Was Filled with Violence

Genesis 6:11 The earth also was corrupt before God, and **the earth was filled with violence**.

12 And God looked upon the earth, and, behold, it was corrupt; for all flesh had corrupted his way upon the earth.

13 And God said unto Noah, **The end of all flesh is come before me; for the earth is filled with violence through them**; *and, behold, I will destroy them with the earth.*

INTRODUCTORY THOUGHTS

The days preceding the flood were evil in many ways, but they were specifically identified as days filled with violence. In fact, the LORD specifically told Noah, *"The end of all flesh is come before me; for the earth is filled with violence through them; and, behold, I will destroy them with the earth."* In Ezekiel's day, the scriptures declare, *"the land is full of bloody* crimes, and the city is full of violence" *(Ezekiel 7:23)*. The presence of excessive violence expresses much concerning the nature of any time (past or present). Although the Lord promised not to destroy the earth again with a flood, worldwide violence moves the Lord to bring judgment.

DEVOTIONAL THOUGHTS

- **(For children)**: Violence refers to an act of physical force with the intent to injure another. Cain was violent when he killed Abel *(Genesis 4:8)*. Herod showed that he was violent when he ordered his men to slay children *(Matthew 2:16)*. The Ninevites were a violent people, but repented in hopes that God would not destroy them *(Jonah 3:4-10)*.
- **(For everyone)**: What is the present level of violence upon the earth? Would it be safe to say that the earth is becoming more filled with violence every year? How will this fact one day move the Lord to judge?
- Many acts of violence are illegal while some have become legal forms of entertainment. What are some violent forms of entertainment? How does this show the wickedness of our generation?

PRAYER THOUGHTS

- Ask the Lord to show you His view of violence.
- Ask God to help you avoid the world's love for violence.

SONG: *WHOLLY THINE (HAWKS)*

Day 353: (Tuesday)
Violence Covereth Their Mouths

Proverbs 10:6 Blessings are upon the head of the just: but **violence covereth the mouth of the wicked.**
11 The mouth of a righteous man is a well of life: but **violence covereth the mouth of the wicked.**

INTRODUCTORY THOUGHTS

The focus of people's speech generally revolves around things they find most important. This is why the Bible says, *"The mouth of a righteous man is a well of life."* How is that so? Because righteous things are important to him; they tend to dominate much of his conversation and focus. To the contrary, the wicked enjoy violence and tend to focus upon it, sometimes even unintentionally. They stir up controversy in the hopes that it yields the violence they crave. They view violent material in order to analyze the various aspects of violence ever needing new forms to entertain. It tends to dominate their discussions whether amongst friends or strangers. They pay money to view various events containing violence and leave disappointed if the violence does not reach their level of satisfaction. As a generation becomes enamored by violence, it consumes their thought life and their speech.

Devotional Thoughts

- **(For children):** Haman wanted the Jews destroyed, spoke lies against them, and was willing to pay money to have them destroyed *(Esther 3:8-9; Proverbs 24:2)*. He even spoke of his desire for violence with his family *(Esther 5:11-14)*. The Bible offers a clear description of a violent man *(Romans 3:13-18)*.
- **(For everyone):** How much of your speech is marked by violence? Do you love to see violence in the news or in your forms of entertainment? Do you speak of it often?
- What topics do you find easiest when holding conversation with those you do not know? What things do you focus upon to find common ground with those whom you first meet? How much of your time is given to speaking of violence?

Prayer Thoughts

- Ask God to help keep your conversation in check.
- Ask the Lord to help you speak of righteousness.

SONG: *HIS WAY WITH THEE*

Day 354: Church Night

*Jonah 3:8 But **let man** and beast be covered with sackcloth, and **cry mightily unto God: yea, let them turn every one from his evil way, and from the violence that** is in their hands.*

Day 355: (Thursday)
The Rich Men Are Full of Violence

*Micah 6:12 For **the rich men thereof are full of violence**, and the inhabitants thereof have spoken lies, and their tongue is deceitful in their mouth.*

INTRODUCTORY THOUGHTS

The world would have us believe that riches belong to those of greatest sophistication while poverty tends to induce violence. However, the truth testifies otherwise. In *Micah 6:12*, the Bible speaks of a time when the rich were *"full of violence."* In like manner, Amos spoke of those who would *"store up violence and robbery in their palaces" (Amos 3:10)*. Asaph spoke of *"the prosperity of the wicked" (Psalm 73:3)* and that *"violence covereth them as a garment" (Psalm 73:6)*. Riches do not remove a man's desire for violence. In fact, riches often promote a man's hunger for it. Many have suggested that poverty lies at the root of much of the violence in the world; however, the scriptures teach otherwise.

DEVOTIONAL THOUGHTS

- **(For children):** Hezekiah had shown the Babylonians all his treasures *(Isaiah 39:1-7)*. Later when king Nebuchadnezzar had a desire to gain more power, land, and riches, he used violence to take what he wanted *(Daniel 5:18-19; 2 Chronicles 36:16-20)*.
- **(For everyone):** What are some ways in which the rich are more susceptible to violence in our day? What are some events where riches give men greater access to violence?
- Do you know of anyone who seems to get worked up in the presence of violence? What about you? Do you find yourself frequently paying to see or take part in violence?

PRAYER THOUGHTS

- Ask the Lord to keep you from violence.
- Ask God for wisdom to see the baseness of violence.

SONG: *LET NOT MY LIFE IN SIN BE PASSED*

Day 356: (Friday)
They Covet and Take by Violence

***Micah 2:2** And **they covet fields, and take them by violence; and houses, and take them away**: so they oppress a man and his house, even a man and his heritage.*

INTRODUCTORY THOUGHTS

Covetousness has often moved men to violence that they might not have otherwise been inclined to do. For instance, wicked king Ahab had a strong desire to obtain a vineyard belonging to Naboth *(1 Kings 21:1-4)*. When Naboth refused to sell the vineyard, Ahab returned to his house to mourn. When Jezebel saw her husband's grief, she created a plan to take the vineyard by force *(1 Kings 21:5-16)*. This principle is not limited to Ahab and Jezebel but has unfortunately been the historical motive for many acts of violence. When men cannot fulfil the lusts of their flesh in a righteous manner, they simply resort to other means which often includes violence.

DEVOTIONAL THOUGHTS

- **(For children):** In the story of the good Samaritan, the man who was travelling was a victim of violence by covetous men *(Luke 10:30)*. The book of Job speaks of the covetousness of the wicked *(Job 20:19; Job 24:2-4)*. Yet, Ephesians tells us how to get what we desire *(Ephesians 4:28)*.
- **(For everyone):** Have you seen or read in the news about any acts of violence done in order to gain someone else's possessions? How is that similar to what was done by Ahab and Jezebel?
- What are some things for which you long (i.e., material goods, emotional needs, physical needs)? What would you be willing to do in order to obtain those things?

PRAYER THOUGHTS

- Ask God to help you to learn to be content with what He has given you.
- Ask the Lord to help you see the wickedness of violence.

SONG: *HE LEADETH ME*

Day 357: (Saturday)
Do Violence to No Man

Luke 3:14 And the soldiers likewise demanded of him, saying, And what shall we do? And he said unto them, ***Do violence to no man****, neither accuse any falsely; and be content with your wages.*

Introductory Thoughts

When asked about the requirements for baptism, John the Baptist gave several suggestions including, *"Do violence to no man."* It can be argued that John was not simply giving baptismal requirements but simply attempting to draw attention to the wickedness of those seeking his baptism. Regardless, we know that John admonished the people to cease from violence. The Bible makes obvious exceptions during times of war or in the exacting of righteous judgment. However, as a rule, God calls the righteous to live peaceably with others and avoid violence **(Romans 12:18)**. Christians are further admonished against finding any pleasure in those who do such things **(Romans 1:29, 32)**.

Devotional Thoughts

- **(For children):** Out of jealousy, Saul tried to kill David. When David could have killed Saul, he did not, but tried to make peace **(1 Samuel 24:8-12; 16-18; 1 Samuel 26:7-11, 15-21)**. The Lord is not for violence **(Jeremiah 22:3)** but for peace **(Psalm 34:14; Matthew 5:9)**.
- **(For everyone):** How do you handle conflict? Do you resort to a violent response? Do you lift your hand in violence in order to resolve your problems, or do you know how to use your speech to make peace?
- What are some times when violence is within the boundaries of righteousness? Why is it so important to learn how to distinguish between these times and the unrighteous acts of violence?

Prayer Thoughts

- Ask the Lord to help you resolve problems without violence.
- Ask God to give you a compassion for others.

SONG: *WHO LAUGHS AT SIN*

☐ Completion Date

Notes:

Quotes from the next volume

(VOLUME 4, WEEK 51)

Subject: Witchcraft

Believers ought to reject astrology (i.e., horoscopes) and any other unscriptural use of the signs in the heavens.

In the eyes of man, witchcraft has grown more acceptable with each passing year, but God has not wavered on His opinion of these matters.

52

Violence (con't)

Violence—found sixty-five times in sixty-four Old Testament verses and only twelve times in eleven verses in the New Testament

Variations: violence, violent, violently

Last usage in the Old Testament: *Malachi 2:16* (violence)

First usage in the New Testament: *Matthew 8:32* (violently)

Interesting fact: The last mention of the word *violence* refers to the Lord's destruction of *"that great city Babylon" (Revelation 18:21)*. The Bible refers to this city as *"drunken with the blood of the saints, and with the blood of the martyrs of Jesus" (Revelation 17:6)*. This city and religion has continually filled the earth with violence but will one day reap what she has sown.

Bible study tip: The Bible is a patriarchal book. As such, people groups are often identified by merely adding the suffix *ite(s)* to the father's name; for example, the children of Israel are known as Israelites *(Joshua 13:6)*. In some cases, this is slightly varied; for instance, the descendants of Benjamin are called Benjamites *(Judges 20:35-36)*. The patriarchal association is important from the standpoint of word formation and identity. However, it can also help identify the spiritual condition of a people group's origin and even their present condition.

Sunday, Day 358—Church Day (no devotional)
Monday, Day 359—*The Most High Regardeth*
Tuesday, Day 360—*The Soul That Loveth Violence*
Wednesday, Day 361—Church Night (no devotional)
Thursday, Day 362—*Thou Savest Me from Violence*
Friday, Day 363—*Evil Shall Hunt the Violent Man*
Saturday, Day 364—*When Violence Is No More*

Day 358: Church Day

***Psalm 86:14** O God, the proud are risen against me, and **the assemblies of violent men have sought after my soul; and have not set thee before them**.*

Day 359: (Monday)
The Most High Regardeth

***Ecclesiastes 5:8** If thou seest the oppression of the poor, and **violent perverting of judgment and justice in a province, marvel not at the matter: for he that is higher than the highest regardeth**; and there be higher than they.*

INTRODUCTORY THOUGHTS

The world is increasingly becoming more filled with violence. At times, it may seem like judgment and justice are silent while the wicked continue to thrive. Throughout the years, this has caused many to question the Lord's existence or, in the least, His presence and love. The seeming absence of God during these violent times is nothing more than proof He is longsuffering with mankind. King Solomon suggested the same when he said, *"If thou seest . . . violent perverting of judgment and justice in a province, marvel not at the matter: for he that is higher than the highest regardeth; and there be higher than they."* It was likewise Solomon who said, *"The eyes of the LORD are in every place, beholding the evil and the good" (Proverbs 15:3).* God's longsuffering does not indicate indifference or apathy.

Devotional Thoughts

- **(For children):** The Lord is conscious of all that is going on *(Psalm 11:4; Jeremiah 17:10; Jeremiah 23:24).* He knew He was going to destroy the earth during Noah's day, yet He delayed for 120 years while Noah preached to the people *(Genesis 6:3; 1 Peter 3:20; 2 Peter 2:5).*
- **(For everyone):** Why is it so important for the saints of God to know that God is paying attention to all the wrong that is going on in the world? How does this bring comfort to those that are saved?
- What does the Bible say happens when God holds back on immediate judgment *(Ecclesiastes 8:11)*? Why would God continue to refrain from judgment if people tend to respond with a rebellious attitude?

Prayer Thoughts

- Thank God for regarding the evil that takes place in the world.
- Thank the Lord for being longsuffering.

SONG: *LEANING ON THE EVERLASTING ARMS*

Day 360: (Tuesday)
The Soul That Loveth Violence

Psalm 11:5 The LORD trieth the righteous: **but the wicked and him that loveth violence his soul hateth.**

Introductory Thoughts

It may appear at times as though the wicked have all the advantage over the righteous, but it is important to note that the LORD has never lost His control of this world. The Bible says of God that His soul hateth *"him that loveth violence."* Yet, *"The LORD trieth the righteous"* and often accomplishes this through the wickedness of the wicked. According to the psalms, the wicked *"bend their bow, they make ready their arrow upon the string, that they may privily shoot at the upright in heart" (Psalm 11:2)*, and the Lord allows this to happen. Why? Because He wants to reveal the hearts of those who claim to fear Him. In the end, the Lord will take care of His own but will *"rain snares, fire and brimstone, and an horrible tempest"* upon the wicked *(Psalm 11:6).*

418 • Violence (con't) ☐ Completion Date

DEVOTIONAL THOUGHTS
- **(For children)**: *Psalm 37:1* tells us not to fret or worry because of those who do evil. They will not have a happy ending *(Psalm 9:17a; Psalm 37:10, 12, 14-15; Proverbs 24:19-20)*. God wants them to repent *(2 Peter 3:9)*. We should want them to be saved also.
- **(For everyone)**: Saved people ought to be a peaceable people. Have you trusted Christ as your Saviour? If so, are you enjoying the fruit of the Spirit which includes *"peace" (Galatians 5:22)*?
- Would you rather face temporary trials or eternal wrath? If you are saved, you will have times of difficulty but will be rewarded in the end. How should this truth help you fight on for the Lord?

PRAYER THOUGHTS
- Thank God for the future you have in His Son.
- Ask the Lord to give you a heart for those who love violence.

SONG: *GOD WILL TAKE CARE OF YOU*

Day 361: Church Night

Psalm 72:14 He shall redeem their soul from deceit and violence: and precious shall their blood be in his sight.

Day 362: (Thursday)
Thou Savest Me from Violence

2 Samuel 22:3 The God of my rock; in him will I trust: he is my shield, and the horn of my salvation, my high tower, and my refuge, my saviour; **thou savest me from violence.**

INTRODUCTORY THOUGHTS

As violence escalates, the dependence of the saints upon the Lord for safety becomes increasingly apparent. David serves as a wonderful demonstration of this truth. Seemingly, he constantly found himself threatened by violent men. Shortly after the Lord's deliverance from the hands of Saul, David wrote a song in which he praised the Lord for saving him from violence *(2 Samuel 22:3)*. Not only was safety from violence the subject of David's songs, but it was also the theme of his prayers

(Psalm 140:1-4). David understood the inevitable presence of violence but also understood that his safety was of the Lord.

Devotional Thoughts

- **(For children):** Pharaoh said the children of Israel could leave Egypt, but then he changed his mind *(Exodus 14:5-10)*. God saved His people in a miraculous way *(Exodus 14:13-16, 21-28)*. Moses sang a song of deliverance *(Exodus 15:1-13)*.
- **(For everyone):** What are some examples from the life of David where God saved him from violence? How can you learn from these examples? How can this give you increased confidence in God's protection?
- How many times has God protected you from violence? Is it possible that there are times when God kept you safe when you did not even know that you were in the path of violence?

Prayer Thoughts

- Thank the Lord for keeping you safe from violence.
- Ask God to continue to protect you from violence.

SONG: *HE IS ABLE TO DELIVER THEE*

Day 363: (Friday)
Evil Shall Hunt the Violent Man

Psalm 140:11 Let not an evil speaker be established in the earth: ***evil shall hunt the violent man to overthrow him.***

Introductory Thoughts

David prayed that the Lord would watch over his safety but also prayed that the Lord would hinder the efforts of the wicked. He asked God to refuse to grant the desires of the wicked and return their mischief upon their own heads. Within this context, he also prayed that the evil conceived by the wicked might *"hunt the violent man to overthrow him."* He spoke of a similar theme when he sang of the wicked, *"His mischief shall return upon his own head, and his violent dealing shall come down upon his own pate" (Psalm 7:16)* or crown of his head. David knew the reward eventually yielded by violence was the return of violence upon the offender.

Devotional Thoughts

- **(For children):** Read what the Bible has to say about the wicked *(Proverbs 11:5b; Proverbs 26:27)*. Consider the following examples: Adoni-bezek *(Judges 1:5-7)*; Ahab *(1 Kings 21:19; 1 Kings 22:34-35, 38)*; Haman *(Esther 5:14; Esther 7:10)*.
- **(For everyone):** Have you ever heard the statement, "What goes around, comes around"? How is that similar to *"whatsoever a man soweth, that shall he also reap" (Galatians 6:7)*? How is the principle confirmed in the issue of violence?
- Have you been violent with others? How could this bring violence into your own life? What should you do to stop the cycle?

Prayer Thoughts

- Ask God to forgive you for times of violence.
- Ask the Lord to help you apologize if you have wronged others.

SONG: *TURN YOUR EYES UPON JESUS*

Day 364: (Saturday)
When Violence Is No More

Isaiah 60:18 Violence shall no more be heard in thy land, wasting nor destruction within thy borders; but thou shalt call thy walls Salvation, and thy gates Praise.

Introductory Thoughts

Though violence rages today, the saint of God can find great comfort in knowing that violence is only a temporary attribute of living. There is coming a day when violence will no longer find place amongst mankind. Isaiah relayed this truth to his people when he stated that there would come a time when *"Violence shall no more be heard in thy land, wasting nor destruction within thy borders; but thou shalt call thy walls Salvation, and thy gates Praise."* Although the conditions and timing may vary for the Jews and the church of God, the reality of a future void of violence remains constant. One day, hopefully soon, each believer will find himself in the presence of the very God who will cause all violence to cease.

☐ Completion Date   Violence (con't) • 421

Devotional Thoughts

- **(For children):** One day saved people will forever be with the Lord *(1 Thessalonians 4:16-17)*. *Isaiah 9:6* calls the Lord the Prince of Peace. We will have real fulness of joy *(Psalm 16:11)*. There will be no violence *(Revelation 21:3-4)*.
- **(For everyone):** Has your life been filled with violence? Have you lost loved ones because of war or some other act that included violence? Do you look forward to a time when violence is no more?
- How is the truth that violence is temporary a blessing for the Jewish people? How is it a blessing for the church of God? What have both had in common in their histories?

Prayer Thoughts

- Thank the Lord that violence is temporary.
- Ask the Lord to keep you safe until the violence passes.

SONG: *OUR GOD, OUR HELP*

Notes: _____

Notes:

Quotes from the next volume
(VOLUME 4, WEEK 52)
Subject: Witchcraft (con't)

God and Satan are always at odds because Satan refuses to submit. In like manner, there are always two spirits at work: the Holy Ghost and a satanic or false spirit.

The world cares not for the ultimate consequences of polluting the minds and hearts of the masses, so long as they find temporal profit in doing so.

When the *"name of the Lord Jesus"* is truly magnified *(Acts 19:17)*, everything contrary to Him either becomes insignificant or obviously wicked.

Scripture Index

Genesis 1:26. 331	Genesis 4:8. . . . . 82, 109, 409
Genesis 1:29. . . . . 26, 28	Genesis 4:9. 82
Genesis 2:8. 275	Genesis 4:10. . . . . 76, 82
Genesis 2:9. 275	Genesis 4:11. 82
Genesis 2:15. . . . . 194, 275	Genesis 4:12. 82
Genesis 2:16. 330	Genesis 4:13. . . . . 239, 241, 334
Genesis 2:17. . . . . 3, 98, 330	Genesis 5:1. 331
Genesis 2:18. . . . . 197, 201, 273	Genesis 5:3. 331
Genesis 2:19. 197	Genesis 5:12. 9
Genesis 2:20. 197	Genesis 5:29. 59
Genesis 2:21. . . . . 197, 280, 282, 283	Genesis 6:3. . . . . 75, 417
Genesis 2:22. . . . . 197, 280, 282, 283	Genesis 6:5. 371
Genesis 2:23. . . . . 280, 283	Genesis 6:6. 371
Genesis 2:24. . . . . 189, 283	Genesis 6:7. 371
Genesis 2:25. 189	Genesis 6:8. 371
Genesis 3:1. . . . . 164, 379	Genesis 6:9. 371
Genesis 3:2. . . . . 164, 379	Genesis 6:11. . . . . 407, 408
Genesis 3:3. . . . . 164, 379	Genesis 6:12. 408
Genesis 3:4. . . . . 107, 164, 379	Genesis 6:13. 408
Genesis 3:5. . . . . 164, 379	Genesis 7:1. . . . . 182, 371
Genesis 3:6. . 35, 164, 189, 216, 329, 379	Genesis 7:2. 371
Genesis 3:7. . . . . 217, 329	Genesis 7:3. 371
Genesis 3:8. . . . . 217, 235, 329	Genesis 7:4. 371
Genesis 3:9. . . . . 163, 222	Genesis 7:5. . . . . 195, 371
Genesis 3:10. 222	Genesis 7:6. 371
Genesis 3:11. 222	Genesis 7:7. . . . . 195, 371
Genesis 3:12. 222	Genesis 8:1. 226
Genesis 3:13. . . . . 223, 379	Genesis 8:2. 226
Genesis 3:14. 223	Genesis 8:3. 227
Genesis 3:16. . . . . 98, 191, 194, 202	Genesis 8:4. 227
Genesis 3:17. . . . . 98, 194	Genesis 8:5. 227
Genesis 3:18. . . . . 98, 194	Genesis 8:6. 227
Genesis 3:19. . . . . 3, 98, 194	Genesis 8:7. 227
Genesis 4:1. . . . . 82, 271	Genesis 8:8. 227
Genesis 4:2. 82	Genesis 8:9. 227
Genesis 4:3. . . . . 82, 109	Genesis 8:10. 227
Genesis 4:4. . . . . 82, 109	Genesis 8:11. 227
Genesis 4:5. . . . . 82, 109	Genesis 8:12. 227
Genesis 4:6. . . . . 82, 109	Genesis 8:13. 227
Genesis 4:7. . . . . 82, 109	Genesis 8:14. 227

Genesis 8:21	7
Genesis 9:21	46
Genesis 9:22	46
Genesis 9:23	46
Genesis 9:24	46
Genesis 9:25	46
Genesis 12:10	277
Genesis 12:11	277
Genesis 12:12	277
Genesis 12:13	277
Genesis 13:5	76, 228
Genesis 13:6	76, 228
Genesis 13:7	76, 228
Genesis 13:8	77
Genesis 13:9	77
Genesis 14:4	255, 257
Genesis 14:5	33
Genesis 15:2	359, 360
Genesis 15:19	33
Genesis 15:20	33
Genesis 15:21	33
Genesis 16:1	224
Genesis 16:2	224
Genesis 16:3	224
Genesis 16:4	224
Genesis 16:5	224
Genesis 16:6	224
Genesis 18:1	65
Genesis 18:2	29, 65
Genesis 18:3	65
Genesis 18:4	65
Genesis 18:5	65
Genesis 18:8	29
Genesis 18:11	2
Genesis 18:18	191
Genesis 18:19	191
Genesis 18:22	29
Genesis 18:33	231
Genesis 19:3	182
Genesis 19:31	46
Genesis 19:32	46
Genesis 19:33	46
Genesis 19:34	46
Genesis 19:35	46
Genesis 19:36	46
Genesis 20:1	277
Genesis 20:2	277
Genesis 20:6	274
Genesis 21:16	200
Genesis 22:1	375, 376, 377
Genesis 23:1	53
Genesis 23:2	53
Genesis 24:1	274
Genesis 24:2	274, 360
Genesis 24:3	274
Genesis 24:9	360
Genesis 24:50	274
Genesis 24:67	60, 61
Genesis 25:8	52
Genesis 25:22	185
Genesis 25:23	185
Genesis 25:24	185
Genesis 25:25	185
Genesis 25:26	185
Genesis 25:29	34
Genesis 25:30	34
Genesis 25:31	34
Genesis 25:32	34
Genesis 25:33	34
Genesis 25:34	34
Genesis 26:6	277
Genesis 26:7	277
Genesis 26:12	99, 109
Genesis 26:13	99, 109
Genesis 26:14	99, 109
Genesis 26:15	109
Genesis 26:16	109
Genesis 26:17	109
Genesis 27:41	80
Genesis 27:42	80
Genesis 27:43	80
Genesis 27:44	80
Genesis 27:45	80
Genesis 28:6	274
Genesis 28:7	274
Genesis 28:8	274
Genesis 28:9	274
Genesis 29:7	196
Genesis 29:8	196
Genesis 29:9	196
Genesis 29:10	196
Genesis 29:25	277
Genesis 30:1	99
Genesis 31:32	277
Genesis 31:33	277
Genesis 31:34	277
Genesis 31:35	277
Genesis 31:54	311

Genesis 32:11 81	Genesis 50:21 . . . . 101, 230
Genesis 33:1. 195	Exodus 2:3 199
Genesis 33:2. 195	Exodus 2:14. 305
Genesis 33:3. 195	Exodus 2:16. 196
Genesis 33:4. . . . . 81, 195	Exodus 2:17. 196
Genesis 33:5. 195	Exodus 2:18. 196
Genesis 33:6. 195	Exodus 2:19. 196
Genesis 33:7. 195	Exodus 3:10. 94
Genesis 34:1. 283	Exodus 3:14. 84
Genesis 34:2. 283	Exodus 3:21. 221
Genesis 34:3. 283	Exodus 3:22. 221
Genesis 34:4. 283	Exodus 6:29. 320
Genesis 35:18 52	Exodus 7:7. 11
Genesis 35:29 9	Exodus 14:5. 419
Genesis 37:11 101	Exodus 14:6. 419
Genesis 37:18 101	Exodus 14:7. 419
Genesis 37:20 101	Exodus 14:8. 419
Genesis 37:26 101	Exodus 14:9. 419
Genesis 37:27 101	Exodus 14:10. 419
Genesis 37:35 59	Exodus 14:13. . . . . 329, 419
Genesis 39:3. 301	Exodus 14:14. 419
Genesis 39:4. . . . . 301, 361	Exodus 14:15. 419
Genesis 39:5. 361	Exodus 14:16. 419
Genesis 39:6. 361	Exodus 14:21. 419
Genesis 39:9. 286	Exodus 14:22. 419
Genesis 39:20 361	Exodus 14:23. 419
Genesis 39:21 . . . . 301, 361	Exodus 14:24. 419
Genesis 39:22 . . . . 301, 361	Exodus 14:25. 419
Genesis 39:23 . . . . 301, 361	Exodus 14:26. 419
Genesis 41:40 361	Exodus 14:27. 419
Genesis 41:41 361	Exodus 14:28. 419
Genesis 41:42 361	Exodus 15:1. 419
Genesis 41:43 361	Exodus 15:2. 419
Genesis 41:44 361	Exodus 15:3. 419
Genesis 41:45 361	Exodus 15:4. 419
Genesis 41:46 361	Exodus 15:5. 419
Genesis 41:47 361	Exodus 15:6. 419
Genesis 42:36 49	Exodus 15:7. 419
Genesis 43:16 27	Exodus 15:8. 419
Genesis 45:16 7	Exodus 15:9. 419
Genesis 45:17 7	Exodus 15:10. 419
Genesis 45:18 7	Exodus 15:11. 419
Genesis 48:10 2	Exodus 15:12. 419
Genesis 49:10 336	Exodus 15:13. 419
Genesis 49:17 43	Exodus 16:14. 35
Genesis 49:18 328	Exodus 16:15. 35
Genesis 50:3. 54	Exodus 16:16. 35
Genesis 50:10 49	Exodus 16:17. 35
Genesis 50:20 230	

Exodus 16:18	35
Exodus 16:19	35
Exodus 16:20	35
Exodus 17:1	92
Exodus 17:7	91
Exodus 20:1	157
Exodus 20:2	157
Exodus 20:3	157
Exodus 20:4	157
Exodus 20:5	157
Exodus 20:12	165
Exodus 20:15	102
Exodus 21:22	81, 86
Exodus 21:23	81, 86
Exodus 21:24	81, 86
Exodus 21:25	81, 86
Exodus 22:20	313
Exodus 23:13	158, 345
Exodus 23:33	381
Exodus 25:22	235
Exodus 31:13	262
Exodus 31:17	262
Exodus 32:1	223
Exodus 32:2	223
Exodus 32:3	223
Exodus 32:4	223
Exodus 32:5	223
Exodus 32:6	31, 223
Exodus 32:7	31, 223
Exodus 32:8	31, 223
Exodus 32:9	266
Exodus 32:19	31
Exodus 32:20	31
Exodus 32:21	223
Exodus 32:22	223
Exodus 32:23	223
Exodus 32:24	223
Exodus 32:26	31
Exodus 32:27	31
Exodus 32:28	31
Exodus 33:5	268
Exodus 34:12	381
Exodus 34:13	158
Exodus 34:14	158
Exodus 34:15	281
Exodus 34:16	281
Exodus 36:5	151
Leviticus 1:9	319
Leviticus 1:13	319
Leviticus 1:17	319
Leviticus 11:1	28
Leviticus 11:2	28
Leviticus 11:3	28
Leviticus 11:4	28
Leviticus 11:5	28
Leviticus 11:6	28
Leviticus 11:7	28
Leviticus 11:8	28
Leviticus 11:9	28
Leviticus 11:10	28
Leviticus 11:11	28
Leviticus 11:12	28
Leviticus 11:13	28
Leviticus 11:14	28
Leviticus 11:15	28
Leviticus 11:16	28
Leviticus 11:17	28
Leviticus 11:18	28
Leviticus 11:19	28
Leviticus 11:20	28
Leviticus 11:21	28
Leviticus 11:22	28
Leviticus 11:23	28
Leviticus 17:7	115
Leviticus 17:11	105
Leviticus 18:22	280
Leviticus 18:23	67
Leviticus 20:13	280
Leviticus 26:24	240, 241
Leviticus 26:28	240, 241
Numbers 6:2	42
Numbers 6:3	42
Numbers 8:24	14
Numbers 8:25	14
Numbers 11:4	34, 219
Numbers 11:5	34, 219
Numbers 11:6	34
Numbers 12:2	94
Numbers 12:3	306
Numbers 12:4	95
Numbers 12:5	95
Numbers 12:6	95
Numbers 12:7	95, 155, 362
Numbers 12:8	95
Numbers 12:9	95
Numbers 12:10	95

Numbers 12:11	95
Numbers 12:12	95
Numbers 12:13	95
Numbers 12:14	95
Numbers 12:15	95
Numbers 16:23	225
Numbers 16:24	225
Numbers 16:25	225
Numbers 16:26	225
Numbers 16:27	225
Numbers 20:2	257
Numbers 20:3	257
Numbers 20:4	257
Numbers 20:5	257
Numbers 20:6	257
Numbers 20:7	257
Numbers 20:8	257
Numbers 20:9	257
Numbers 20:10	257
Numbers 20:11	257
Numbers 20:12	257
Numbers 20:13	91
Numbers 20:23	257
Numbers 20:24	91, 257, 336
Numbers 20:29	54
Numbers 21:4	221
Numbers 21:5	221
Numbers 21:6	221
Numbers 21:7	221
Numbers 21:8	221
Numbers 21:9	221
Numbers 27:14	91, 92
Numbers 27:20	164, 165
Numbers 35:33	172
Deuteronomy 1:26	257
Deuteronomy 1:43	257
Deuteronomy 2:5	181
Deuteronomy 6:16	384
Deuteronomy 7:3	281
Deuteronomy 7:4	281
Deuteronomy 7:25	381
Deuteronomy 8:5	242, 243
Deuteronomy 8:15	19
Deuteronomy 8:16	19
Deuteronomy 10:16	255
Deuteronomy 11:11	269
Deuteronomy 11:12	17, 269
Deuteronomy 11:13	269
Deuteronomy 11:14	269
Deuteronomy 11:15	269
Deuteronomy 11:16	269
Deuteronomy 11:17	269
Deuteronomy 15:5	17
Deuteronomy 15:14	147
Deuteronomy 21:18	258, 265
Deuteronomy 21:19	258, 265
Deuteronomy 21:20	31, 258, 265
Deuteronomy 21:21	265
Deuteronomy 21:22	265
Deuteronomy 21:23	265
Deuteronomy 24:1	283, 292
Deuteronomy 29:5	19
Deuteronomy 31:27	266
Deuteronomy 32:4	390
Deuteronomy 32:7	6
Deuteronomy 32:48	257
Deuteronomy 32:49	257
Deuteronomy 32:50	257
Deuteronomy 32:51	257
Deuteronomy 32:52	257
Deuteronomy 33:8	91
Deuteronomy 34:7	11
Deuteronomy 34:8	54
Joshua 1:16	166
Joshua 1:17	166
Joshua 1:18	166
Joshua 6:18	217
Joshua 7:11	217, 381
Joshua 7:19	217
Joshua 7:20	217
Joshua 7:21	217, 381
Joshua 7:22	217
Joshua 13:6	415
Joshua 14:6	10
Joshua 14:7	11
Joshua 14:8	11
Joshua 14:9	11
Joshua 14:10	11
Joshua 14:11	11
Joshua 14:12	11
Joshua 17:13	11
Joshua 22:18	268
Joshua 22:29	257, 314
Judges 1:5	420
Judges 1:6	420

Judges 1:7	420
Judges 3:6	281
Judges 3:7	281
Judges 7:2	349
Judges 7:3	349
Judges 7:4	349
Judges 7:5	349, 355
Judges 7:6	349, 355
Judges 7:7	349, 355
Judges 13:8	193
Judges 14:1	273
Judges 14:2	273
Judges 14:3	273
Judges 14:4	273
Judges 19:5	27
Judges 20:35	415
Judges 20:36	415
Judges 21:12	271
Ruth 1:8	233
Ruth 1:9	233
Ruth 1:10	233
Ruth 1:11	233
Ruth 1:12	233
Ruth 1:13	233
Ruth 1:14	179, 233
Ruth 1:15	179, 233, 274
Ruth 1:16	179, 233, 274, 290
Ruth 1:17	179, 233, 290
Ruth 1:18	233
Ruth 2:8	61
Ruth 2:9	61, 272
Ruth 2:10	61
Ruth 2:11	61, 307
Ruth 2:12	61, 307
Ruth 2:13	61
Ruth 2:14	61
Ruth 2:19	274
Ruth 2:20	274
Ruth 2:21	274
Ruth 2:22	274
Ruth 2:23	274
Ruth 3:5	274
Ruth 3:6	274
Ruth 3:11	307
Ruth 4:15	6
Ruth 4:17	274
1 Samuel 1:2	103
1 Samuel 1:3	103
1 Samuel 1:4	103
1 Samuel 1:5	103
1 Samuel 1:6	21, 103
1 Samuel 1:7	38, 103
1 Samuel 1:8	103
1 Samuel 1:9	103
1 Samuel 1:10	103
1 Samuel 1:11	103
1 Samuel 1:12	103
1 Samuel 1:13	103
1 Samuel 1:14	103
1 Samuel 1:15	103
1 Samuel 1:16	103
1 Samuel 1:17	103
1 Samuel 1:18	103
1 Samuel 1:19	103
1 Samuel 1:20	103
1 Samuel 1:21	281
1 Samuel 1:22	281
1 Samuel 2:11	301, 346
1 Samuel 2:18	346
1 Samuel 2:19	200
1 Samuel 2:22	13
1 Samuel 2:26	7, 207, 301, 346
1 Samuel 2:27	13
1 Samuel 2:28	13
1 Samuel 2:29	13
1 Samuel 3:13	13
1 Samuel 4:8	76
1 Samuel 12:1	7, 370
1 Samuel 12:2	7, 370
1 Samuel 12:3	7, 370
1 Samuel 12:4	7, 370
1 Samuel 12:5	370
1 Samuel 12:13	265
1 Samuel 12:14	265
1 Samuel 12:15	265, 268
1 Samuel 12:20	370
1 Samuel 13:8	224
1 Samuel 13:9	224, 265
1 Samuel 13:10	224
1 Samuel 13:11	224
1 Samuel 13:12	224
1 Samuel 13:13	224, 265
1 Samuel 13:14	224, 265
1 Samuel 14:5	179
1 Samuel 14:6	179
1 Samuel 14:7	179

1 Samuel 14:8 179	1 Samuel 19:6 235
1 Samuel 14:9 179	1 Samuel 19:7 235
1 Samuel 14:10 179	1 Samuel 20:31 177
1 Samuel 14:11 179	1 Samuel 20:32 . . . . 72, 177
1 Samuel 14:12 179	1 Samuel 20:33 . . . . 72, 177
1 Samuel 14:13 179	1 Samuel 20:34 . . . . 72, 177
1 Samuel 14:14 179	1 Samuel 22:3 6
1 Samuel 15:3 260	1 Samuel 22:4 6
1 Samuel 15:7 260	1 Samuel 23:15 177
1 Samuel 15:8 260	1 Samuel 23:16 177
1 Samuel 15:9 260	1 Samuel 23:17 177
1 Samuel 15:10 260	1 Samuel 23:18 177
1 Samuel 15:11 260	1 Samuel 24:1 167
1 Samuel 15:13 260	1 Samuel 24:2 167
1 Samuel 15:14 260	1 Samuel 24:3 167
1 Samuel 15:15 260	1 Samuel 24:4 167
1 Samuel 15:18 . . . . 260, 265	1 Samuel 24:5 167
1 Samuel 15:19 . . . . 260, 265	1 Samuel 24:6 167
1 Samuel 15:20 260	1 Samuel 24:7 167
1 Samuel 15:22 . . . . 260, 315	1 Samuel 24:8 . . . . 167, 413
1 Samuel 15:23 . . . . 256, 260, 264	1 Samuel 24:9 . . . . 167, 413
1 Samuel 16:17 309	1 Samuel 24:10 . . . . 167, 413
1 Samuel 16:18 309	1 Samuel 24:11 . . . . 167, 413
1 Samuel 16:19 309	1 Samuel 24:12 . . . . 168, 413
1 Samuel 16:20 309	1 Samuel 24:13 168
1 Samuel 16:21 . . . . 93, 309	1 Samuel 24:16 413
1 Samuel 16:22 . . . . 93, 309	1 Samuel 24:17 413
1 Samuel 17:32 352	1 Samuel 24:18 413
1 Samuel 17:33 . . . . 12, 352	1 Samuel 25 79
1 Samuel 17:34 352	1 Samuel 25:1 46
1 Samuel 17:35 352	1 Samuel 25:2 . . . . 46, 175
1 Samuel 17:36 352	1 Samuel 25:3 . . . . 46, 175, 293
1 Samuel 17:37 352	1 Samuel 25:4 . . . . 46, 175
1 Samuel 17:42 12	1 Samuel 25:5 . . . . 46, 175
1 Samuel 17:45 352	1 Samuel 25:6 . . . . 46, 175
1 Samuel 17:46 352	1 Samuel 25:7 . . . . 46, 175
1 Samuel 17:47 352	1 Samuel 25:8 . . . . 46, 175
1 Samuel 18:1 93	1 Samuel 25:9 . . . . 46, 175
1 Samuel 18:2 93	1 Samuel 25:10 . . . . 46, 175
1 Samuel 18:5 72	1 Samuel 25:11 . . . . 46, 175
1 Samuel 18:6 72	1 Samuel 25:12 . . . . 46, 175
1 Samuel 18:7 72	1 Samuel 25:13 . . . . 46, 175
1 Samuel 18:8 . . . . 72, 93	1 Samuel 25:14 . . . . 46, 175
1 Samuel 18:9 . . . . 72, 93	1 Samuel 25:15 . . . . 46, 175
1 Samuel 18:30 299	1 Samuel 25:16 . . . . 46, 175
1 Samuel 19:2 235	1 Samuel 25:17 . . . . 46, 175, 293
1 Samuel 19:3 235	1 Samuel 25:18 175
1 Samuel 19:4 . . . . 72, 177, 235	1 Samuel 25:19 175
1 Samuel 19:5 . . . . 72, 235	1 Samuel 25:20 175

Reference	Pages
1 Samuel 25:21	175
1 Samuel 25:22	175
1 Samuel 25:23	175, 201
1 Samuel 25:24	175, 201
1 Samuel 25:25	175, 201
1 Samuel 25:26	175, 201
1 Samuel 25:27	175, 201
1 Samuel 25:28	175, 201
1 Samuel 25:29	175, 201
1 Samuel 25:30	175, 201
1 Samuel 25:31	175, 201
1 Samuel 25:32	175, 201
1 Samuel 25:33	175, 201
1 Samuel 25:34	175
1 Samuel 25:35	175
1 Samuel 25:36	46, 175
1 Samuel 25:37	46, 175
1 Samuel 25:38	175, 293
1 Samuel 25:39	293
1 Samuel 25:40	293
1 Samuel 25:41	293
1 Samuel 25:42	293
1 Samuel 26:7	413
1 Samuel 26:8	413
1 Samuel 26:9	413
1 Samuel 26:10	413
1 Samuel 26:11	413
1 Samuel 26:15	413
1 Samuel 26:16	413
1 Samuel 26:17	413
1 Samuel 26:18	413
1 Samuel 26:19	413
1 Samuel 26:20	413
1 Samuel 26:21	413
1 Samuel 28:18	38
1 Samuel 28:19	38
1 Samuel 28:20	38
1 Samuel 28:21	38
1 Samuel 28:22	38
1 Samuel 28:23	38
1 Samuel 29:3	300
1 Samuel 30:6	157
1 Samuel 31:1	224
1 Samuel 31:2	224
1 Samuel 31:6	224
2 Samuel 1:17	54
2 Samuel 1:18	54
2 Samuel 1:19	54
2 Samuel 1:23	55
2 Samuel 1:24	55
2 Samuel 1:25	55
2 Samuel 7:14	243
2 Samuel 11:1	277
2 Samuel 11:2	277
2 Samuel 11:3	277
2 Samuel 11:4	277
2 Samuel 11:6	169
2 Samuel 11:7	169
2 Samuel 11:8	169
2 Samuel 11:9	169
2 Samuel 11:10	169
2 Samuel 11:11	169
2 Samuel 11:12	169
2 Samuel 11:13	169
2 Samuel 12:1	142
2 Samuel 12:2	142
2 Samuel 12:3	142
2 Samuel 12:4	142
2 Samuel 12:5	142
2 Samuel 12:6	142
2 Samuel 12:7	142
2 Samuel 12:9	286
2 Samuel 12:10	286
2 Samuel 12:15	50, 193
2 Samuel 12:16	38, 50, 193
2 Samuel 12:17	38, 50
2 Samuel 13:37	234
2 Samuel 13:38	234
2 Samuel 13:39	234
2 Samuel 14:1	234
2 Samuel 14:21	234
2 Samuel 14:22	234
2 Samuel 14:23	234
2 Samuel 14:24	234
2 Samuel 14:28	234
2 Samuel 15:1	136
2 Samuel 15:2	136
2 Samuel 15:3	136
2 Samuel 15:4	136
2 Samuel 15:5	136
2 Samuel 15:6	136
2 Samuel 15:7	136
2 Samuel 15:8	136
2 Samuel 15:9	136
2 Samuel 15:10	136
2 Samuel 15:11	136
2 Samuel 15:12	136

2 Samuel 15:13 176	1 Kings 3:26. 199
2 Samuel 15:14 176	1 Kings 8:27. 296
2 Samuel 15:15 176	1 Kings 11:1 277
2 Samuel 15:19 170	1 Kings 11:2 281
2 Samuel 15:20 170	1 Kings 11:4 . . . . 7, 187, 381
2 Samuel 15:21 170	1 Kings 11:5 187
2 Samuel 15:31 174	1 Kings 11:6 187
2 Samuel 15:32 174	1 Kings 11:7 187
2 Samuel 15:33 174	1 Kings 11:8 187
2 Samuel 15:34 174	1 Kings 11:9 . . . . 187, 381
2 Samuel 15:35 174	1 Kings 11:10 381
2 Samuel 15:36 174	1 Kings 11:29 267
2 Samuel 15:37 174	1 Kings 11:30 267
2 Samuel 17:1 174	1 Kings 11:31 267
2 Samuel 17:2 174	1 Kings 11:32 267
2 Samuel 17:3 174	1 Kings 11:33 267
2 Samuel 17:4 174	1 Kings 11:34 267
2 Samuel 17:15 174	1 Kings 11:35 267
2 Samuel 17:16 174	1 Kings 11:36 267
2 Samuel 17:27 177	1 Kings 11:37 267
2 Samuel 17:28 177	1 Kings 11:38 267
2 Samuel 17:29 177	1 Kings 12:1 78
2 Samuel 18:1 175	1 Kings 12:2 78
2 Samuel 18:2 175	1 Kings 12:3 78
2 Samuel 18:3 175	1 Kings 12:4 78
2 Samuel 18:4 176	1 Kings 12:5 78
2 Samuel 18:33 53	1 Kings 12:6 78
2 Samuel 19:31 177	1 Kings 12:7 78
2 Samuel 19:32 . . . . 1, 177	1 Kings 12:8 78
2 Samuel 19:33 177	1 Kings 12:9 78
2 Samuel 19:34 . . . . 2, 177	1 Kings 12:10 78
2 Samuel 19:35 . . . . 2, 177	1 Kings 12:11 78
2 Samuel 19:36 177	1 Kings 12:12 78
2 Samuel 19:37 177	1 Kings 12:13 78
2 Samuel 19:38 177	1 Kings 12:14 78
2 Samuel 21:15 176	1 Kings 12:15 78
2 Samuel 21:16 176	1 Kings 12:16 78
2 Samuel 21:17 176	1 Kings 12:26 267
2 Samuel 22:3 418	1 Kings 12:27 267
2 Samuel 22:16 181	1 Kings 12:28 267
2 Samuel 23:13 178	1 Kings 12:29 267
2 Samuel 23:14 178	1 Kings 12:30 267
2 Samuel 23:15 178	1 Kings 13:7 69
2 Samuel 23:16 178	1 Kings 13:8 69
2 Samuel 23:17 178	1 Kings 13:9 69
	1 Kings 13:10 69
1 Kings 1:1 2	1 Kings 13:15 69
1 Kings 3:1 320	1 Kings 13:16 69
1 Kings 3:12 187	1 Kings 13:17 69

1 Kings 13:18. 69	1 Kings 19:14. . . . . 173, 385
1 Kings 13:19. 69	1 Kings 19:15. 173
1 Kings 13:20. 69	1 Kings 19:16. 173
1 Kings 13:21. 69	1 Kings 19:17. 173
1 Kings 13:22. 69	1 Kings 19:18. . . . . 173, 386
1 Kings 13:23. 69	1 Kings 21:1. 412
1 Kings 13:24. 69	1 Kings 21:2. 412
1 Kings 13:25. 69	1 Kings 21:3. 412
1 Kings 13:26. 69	1 Kings 21:4. 412
1 Kings 14:7. 267	1 Kings 21:5. 412
1 Kings 14:8. 267	1 Kings 21:6. 412
1 Kings 14:9. 267	1 Kings 21:7. 412
1 Kings 14:10. 267	1 Kings 21:8. . . . . 88, 412
1 Kings 15:11. 226	1 Kings 21:9. . . . . 88, 412
1 Kings 15:13. 226	1 Kings 21:10. . . . . 88, 412
1 Kings 17:6. 28	1 Kings 21:11. . . . . 88, 412
1 Kings 17:8. 226	1 Kings 21:12. . . . . 88, 412
1 Kings 17:9. 226	1 Kings 21:13. . . . . 88, 412
1 Kings 17:10. 226	1 Kings 21:14. 412
1 Kings 17:11. 226	1 Kings 21:15. 412
1 Kings 17:12. 226	1 Kings 21:16. 412
1 Kings 17:13. 226	1 Kings 21:19. 420
1 Kings 17:14. 226	1 Kings 22:34. 420
1 Kings 17:15. 226	1 Kings 22:35. 420
1 Kings 17:16. 226	1 Kings 22:38. 420
1 Kings 18:12. 14	
1 Kings 18:25. 158	2 Kings 2:23. 211
1 Kings 18:26. 158	2 Kings 4:1. 294
1 Kings 18:27. 158	2 Kings 4:2. 294
1 Kings 18:28. 158	2 Kings 4:3. 294
1 Kings 18:29. 158	2 Kings 4:4. 294
1 Kings 18:30. 158	2 Kings 4:5. 294
1 Kings 18:31. 158	2 Kings 4:6. 294
1 Kings 18:32. 158	2 Kings 4:7. 294
1 Kings 18:33. 158	2 Kings 4:18. 200
1 Kings 18:34. 158	2 Kings 4:19. 200
1 Kings 18:35. 158	2 Kings 4:20. 200
1 Kings 18:36. 158	2 Kings 4:21. 200
1 Kings 18:37. 158	2 Kings 4:22. 200
1 Kings 18:38. 158	2 Kings 5:1. 210
1 Kings 18:39. 158	2 Kings 5:2. 210
1 Kings 19:5. 28	2 Kings 5:3. 210
1 Kings 19:6. 28	2 Kings 5:4. 210
1 Kings 19:7. 28	2 Kings 5:5. 210
1 Kings 19:8. 28	2 Kings 5:6. 210
1 Kings 19:10. 173	2 Kings 5:7. 210
1 Kings 19:11. 173	2 Kings 5:8. 210
1 Kings 19:12. 173	2 Kings 5:9. 210
1 Kings 19:13. . . . . 173, 385	2 Kings 5:10. 210

2 Kings 5:11 210
2 Kings 5:12 210
2 Kings 5:13 210
2 Kings 5:14 210
2 Kings 5:15 .... 210, 314
2 Kings 5:16 .... 210, 314
2 Kings 5:17 .... 210, 314
2 Kings 5:18 210
2 Kings 5:19 210
2 Kings 5:20 381
2 Kings 5:21 381
2 Kings 5:22 381
2 Kings 5:23 381
2 Kings 5:24 381
2 Kings 5:25 381
2 Kings 5:26 381
2 Kings 5:27 381
2 Kings 6:8 73
2 Kings 6:9 73
2 Kings 6:10 73
2 Kings 6:11 73
2 Kings 6:12 73
2 Kings 6:13 73
2 Kings 6:14 73
2 Kings 6:18 73
2 Kings 6:19 73
2 Kings 6:25 36
2 Kings 6:28 36
2 Kings 6:29 36
2 Kings 14:10 183
2 Kings 17:36 313
2 Kings 18:4 222
2 Kings 18:7 257
2 Kings 19:9 218
2 Kings 19:10 218
2 Kings 19:11 218
2 Kings 19:12 218
2 Kings 19:13 218
2 Kings 19:14 .... 22, 218
2 Kings 19:15 .... 22, 218
2 Kings 19:16 .... 22, 218
2 Kings 19:17 .... 22, 218
2 Kings 19:18 .... 22, 218
2 Kings 19:19 .... 22, 218
2 Kings 19:35 22

1 Chronicles 10:13 265
1 Chronicles 10:14 265
1 Chronicles 11:15 171

1 Chronicles 11:16 171
1 Chronicles 11:17 171
1 Chronicles 11:18 171
1 Chronicles 11:19 171
1 Chronicles 16:11 357
1 Chronicles 16:35 329
1 Chronicles 23:1 9
1 Chronicles 28:1 .... 360, 367, 368
1 Chronicles 29:19 193
1 Chronicles 29:28 9

2 Chronicles 13:12 183
2 Chronicles 15:7 .... 180, 373
2 Chronicles 16:9 366
2 Chronicles 17:3 277
2 Chronicles 17:4 277
2 Chronicles 19:1 277
2 Chronicles 19:2 277
2 Chronicles 19:3 277
2 Chronicles 21:5 277
2 Chronicles 21:6 277
2 Chronicles 22:1 277
2 Chronicles 22:2 277
2 Chronicles 22:3 277
2 Chronicles 22:4 277
2 Chronicles 24:4 363
2 Chronicles 24:5 363
2 Chronicles 24:6 363
2 Chronicles 24:7 363
2 Chronicles 24:8 363
2 Chronicles 24:9 363
2 Chronicles 24:10 363
2 Chronicles 24:15 9
2 Chronicles 30:8 256
2 Chronicles 34:3 14
2 Chronicles 35:21 .... 182, 184
2 Chronicles 35:22 .... 182, 184
2 Chronicles 35:23 .... 182, 184
2 Chronicles 35:24 .... 56, 182, 184
2 Chronicles 35:25 56
2 Chronicles 36:15 268
2 Chronicles 36:16 .... 268, 411
2 Chronicles 36:17 .... 268, 411
2 Chronicles 36:18 411
2 Chronicles 36:19 411
2 Chronicles 36:20 411

Ezra 7:10 120
Ezra 8:21 209

Ezra 9:7	67
Ezra 9:13	242
Nehemiah 1:3	364
Nehemiah 1:4	364
Nehemiah 7:1	364
Nehemiah 7:2	364
Nehemiah 7:3	364
Nehemiah 9:26	258
Nehemiah 12:43	322
Nehemiah 13:13	362
Esther 1:10	46
Esther 1:11	46
Esther 1:12	46
Esther 1:20	200
Esther 2:1	46
Esther 2:5	209
Esther 2:6	209
Esther 2:7	209
Esther 2:20	209
Esther 2:21	163, 166, 179
Esther 2:22	163, 166, 179
Esther 2:23	163, 166, 179
Esther 3:1	78, 133
Esther 3:2	78, 133
Esther 3:3	78
Esther 3:4	78
Esther 3:5	78
Esther 3:6	78
Esther 3:8	410
Esther 3:9	410
Esther 4:7	209
Esther 4:8	209
Esther 4:16	209
Esther 5:11	133, 410
Esther 5:12	133, 410
Esther 5:13	133, 410
Esther 5:14	410, 420
Esther 6:1	163, 180
Esther 6:2	163, 180
Esther 6:3	163, 180
Esther 6:4	163, 180
Esther 6:5	163, 180
Esther 6:6	163, 180
Esther 6:7	163, 180
Esther 6:8	163, 180
Esther 6:9	163, 180
Esther 6:10	163, 180
Esther 6:11	163, 180
Esther 7:1	163
Esther 7:2	163
Esther 7:3	163
Esther 7:4	163
Esther 7:5	163
Esther 7:6	163
Esther 7:7	163
Esther 7:8	163
Esther 7:9	163
Esther 7:10	133, 163, 420
Esther 8:1	163
Esther 8:2	163
Job 1:1	376
Job 1:5	193
Job 1:11	377
Job 1:20	50, 228
Job 1:21	50, 228
Job 1:22	228, 377
Job 2:5	377
Job 2:9	193, 228, 377
Job 2:10	228, 377
Job 4:2	234
Job 5:2	100
Job 5:17	245
Job 8:13	131, 132, 140
Job 9:33	385
Job 14:1	214
Job 18:3	295
Job 19:18	211
Job 20:5	131, 133
Job 20:19	412
Job 23:10	376
Job 23:12	28
Job 24:2	412
Job 24:3	412
Job 24:4	412
Job 27:8	140
Job 28:28	13
Job 29:2	39
Job 29:4	14
Job 29:5	39
Job 29:15	65
Job 29:16	65
Job 30:25	65
Job 32:6	13
Job 32:7	13
Job 32:9	2, 13

Job 33:4 63	Psalm 37:7 23
Job 38:39 25	Psalm 37:10 418
Job 42:8 408	Psalm 37:12 418
Job 42:17 9	Psalm 37:14 418
	Psalm 37:15 418
Psalm 1:1 353	Psalm 37:23 4
Psalm 1:2 353	Psalm 37:25 6
Psalm 1:3 353	Psalm 37:28 157
Psalm 3:1 20	Psalm 38:1 248
Psalm 3:4 20	Psalm 41:13 205
Psalm 3:5 20	Psalm 44:15 67
Psalm 3:6 20	Psalm 44:20 310
Psalm 4:4 233	Psalm 44:21 310
Psalm 4:5 312	Psalm 46:1 339
Psalm 7:16 419	Psalm 50:10 369
Psalm 8:5 165	Psalm 50:11 369
Psalm 9:17 418	Psalm 50:12 . . . . 18, 315
Psalm 11:2 417	Psalm 50:17 128
Psalm 11:4 . . . . 365, 417	Psalm 51:1 251
Psalm 11:5 . . . . 376, 417	Psalm 51:2 251
Psalm 11:6 417	Psalm 51:3 251
Psalm 12:1 156	Psalm 51:6 236
Psalm 16:11 . . . . 134, 340, 421	Psalm 51:10 251
Psalm 19:8 250	Psalm 51:13 251
Psalm 19:11 250	Psalm 51:17 324
Psalm 19:14 353	Psalm 54:6 314
Psalm 23:4 62	Psalm 56:10 324
Psalm 24:1 369	Psalm 68:5 . . . . 269, 293
Psalm 31:19 104	Psalm 68:6 269
Psalm 33:6 63	Psalm 68:19 . . . . 154, 324, 339
Psalm 33:7 63	Psalm 69:4 79
Psalm 33:8 63	Psalm 69:5 310
Psalm 33:9 63	Psalm 69:30 317
Psalm 33:13 365	Psalm 70:2 73
Psalm 33:14 365	Psalm 70:4 325
Psalm 33:15 365	Psalm 71:1 70
Psalm 34:1 325	Psalm 71:5 14
Psalm 34:3 284	Psalm 71:9 4
Psalm 34:4 20	Psalm 71:15 329
Psalm 34:11 207	Psalm 71:18 . . . . 3, 4
Psalm 34:14 413	Psalm 72:14 418
Psalm 34:15 236	Psalm 73:3 . . . . 102, 411
Psalm 35:1 72	Psalm 73:4 102
Psalm 35:2 72	Psalm 73:5 102
Psalm 35:3 72	Psalm 73:6 411
Psalm 35:4 . . . . 72, 73	Psalm 75:5 265
Psalm 35:26 73	Psalm 77:2 59
Psalm 35:28 325	Psalm 77:6 . . . . 232, 233
Psalm 37:1 . . . . 22, 23, 418	Psalm 78:8 259

436 • Scripture Index

Reference	Pages
Psalm 81:10	268
Psalm 81:11	268
Psalm 81:12	268
Psalm 81:13	268
Psalm 81:14	268
Psalm 81:15	268
Psalm 81:16	268
Psalm 83:18	246
Psalm 86:14	416
Psalm 87:2	364
Psalm 87:3	364
Psalm 89:1	237
Psalm 89:30	252
Psalm 89:31	252
Psalm 89:32	252
Psalm 89:33	252
Psalm 90:10	1, 9
Psalm 90:12	10
Psalm 94:12	245, 250
Psalm 101:2	12, 300
Psalm 102	123
Psalm 102:1	38
Psalm 102:2	38
Psalm 102:3	38
Psalm 102:4	38
Psalm 105:16	378
Psalm 105:17	378
Psalm 105:18	378
Psalm 105:19	378
Psalm 105:20	378
Psalm 105:21	378
Psalm 106:32	91
Psalm 106:34	381
Psalm 106:35	381
Psalm 106:36	381
Psalm 107:11	258
Psalm 107:18	38
Psalm 107:21	317
Psalm 107:22	317
Psalm 109:3	79
Psalm 113:1	198
Psalm 113:9	198
Psalm 115:3	158
Psalm 115:4	158
Psalm 115:5	158
Psalm 115:6	158
Psalm 115:7	158
Psalm 115:8	158
Psalm 115:9	158
Psalm 116:17	320, 324
Psalm 119:10	259
Psalm 119:11	7, 259, 385
Psalm 119:59	353
Psalm 119:63	273
Psalm 119:67	245, 250
Psalm 119:71	250
Psalm 119:76	60
Psalm 119:138	250
Psalm 119:160	117, 394
Psalm 119:163	117
Psalm 127:1	20, 296
Psalm 127:3	296
Psalm 127:4	296
Psalm 127:5	296
Psalm 128:1	39, 192
Psalm 128:2	39, 192
Psalm 128:3	39, 189, 192
Psalm 128:4	39
Psalm 139:14	30
Psalm 139:23	145, 233
Psalm 139:24	145, 233
Psalm 140:1	419
Psalm 140:2	419
Psalm 140:3	419
Psalm 140:4	419
Psalm 140:11	419
Psalm 142:1	218
Psalm 142:2	218
Psalm 142:3	218
Psalm 142:4	218
Psalm 142:5	218
Psalm 142:6	218
Psalm 142:7	218
Psalm 145:18	236
Psalm 146:9	294
Psalm 147:9	26
Psalm 148:12	207
Psalm 148:13	207
Psalm 149:7	242
Proverbs 3:1	208, 300, 301
Proverbs 3:2	208, 301
Proverbs 3:3	208, 301
Proverbs 3:4	208, 301
Proverbs 3:9	150
Proverbs 3:10	150
Proverbs 3:11	240, 244
Proverbs 3:12	244

Proverbs 3:27. 79	Proverbs 16:26. . . . . 34, 36
Proverbs 3:28. 79	Proverbs 16:28. 88
Proverbs 3:29. 79	Proverbs 16:29. 408
Proverbs 3:30. . . . . 79, 91	Proverbs 16:31. . . . . 5, 13
Proverbs 3:31. 104	Proverbs 17:1. . . . . 84, 222
Proverbs 5:18. 289	Proverbs 17:11. 164
Proverbs 6:6. 275	Proverbs 17:14. . . . . 76, 83, 184
Proverbs 6:7. 275	Proverbs 17:19. 85
Proverbs 6:8. 275	Proverbs 17:22. 47
Proverbs 6:9. 275	Proverbs 18:1. . . . . 186, 187
Proverbs 6:10. 275	Proverbs 18:6. 186
Proverbs 6:11. 275	Proverbs 18:19. . . . . 80, 86
Proverbs 6:12. 105	Proverbs 18:22. 272
Proverbs 6:13. 105	Proverbs 19:3. 22
Proverbs 6:14. 105	Proverbs 19:13. . . . . 75, 203
Proverbs 6:15. 105	Proverbs 19:14. 273
Proverbs 6:16. 105	Proverbs 19:17. 150
Proverbs 6:17. 105	Proverbs 19:18. . . . . 243, 251
Proverbs 6:18. 105	Proverbs 19:20. 274
Proverbs 6:19. 105	Proverbs 20:1. 42
Proverbs 8:5. 125	Proverbs 20:3. . . . . 83, 95, 181, 185
Proverbs 8:13. 102	Proverbs 20:6. 158
Proverbs 8:17. 207	Proverbs 20:9. 331
Proverbs 9:4. 125	Proverbs 20:11. . . . . 206, 211, 305
Proverbs 9:13. 125	Proverbs 20:19. 181
Proverbs 10:6. 409	Proverbs 20:25. 381
Proverbs 10:11. 409	Proverbs 20:29. 5
Proverbs 10:12. 89	Proverbs 21:9. . . . . 76, 203
Proverbs 11:5. 420	Proverbs 21:19. 76
Proverbs 11:9. 134	Proverbs 21:27. 321
Proverbs 11:17. 288	Proverbs 22:1. . . . . 92, 146, 296
Proverbs 11:21. 242	Proverbs 22:9. 150
Proverbs 11:23. 250	Proverbs 22:10. . . . . 79, 92, 216
Proverbs 11:25. 149	Proverbs 22:15. 243
Proverbs 11:29. 288	Proverbs 22:24. 381
Proverbs 13:10. . . . . 75, 78, 86, 91	Proverbs 22:25. 381
Proverbs 13:24. . . . . 243, 249	Proverbs 22:26. 381
Proverbs 14:1. 198	Proverbs 23:1. . . . . 26, 37
Proverbs 14:15. 126	Proverbs 23:2. . . . . 26, 37
Proverbs 14:25. 126	Proverbs 23:3. 26
Proverbs 14:30. 105	Proverbs 23:7. 353
Proverbs 14:32. 57	Proverbs 23:13. 243
Proverbs 15:1. . . . . 186, 214	Proverbs 23:14. 243
Proverbs 15:3. 417	Proverbs 23:17. 101
Proverbs 15:10. 249	Proverbs 23:19. 31
Proverbs 15:17. 200	Proverbs 23:20. 31
Proverbs 15:18. . . . . 89, 225	Proverbs 23:21. 31
Proverbs 16:1. 275	Proverbs 23:22. 209
Proverbs 16:7. 221	Proverbs 23:26. 315

Proverbs 23:29. 44
Proverbs 23:30. 44
Proverbs 23:32. 42
Proverbs 23:35. 45
Proverbs 24:1. 100
Proverbs 24:2. 410
Proverbs 24:19. . . . . 23, 418
Proverbs 24:20. 418
Proverbs 24:21. . . . . 176, 181, 184
Proverbs 25:15. 186
Proverbs 25:16. 36
Proverbs 25:24. . . . . 76, 203
Proverbs 26:17. . . . . 83, 86, 181, 182, 185
Proverbs 26:20. . . . . 83, 86, 89
Proverbs 26:21. . . . . 83, 87, 89
Proverbs 26:27. 420
Proverbs 27:3. 108
Proverbs 27:4. . . . . 100, 108
Proverbs 27:15. . . . . 75, 91, 203
Proverbs 27:16. 203
Proverbs 28:13. . . . . 217, 334
Proverbs 28:25. 89
Proverbs 28:27. . . . . 148, 150
Proverbs 29:17. 208
Proverbs 29:25. 160
Proverbs 30:8. 35
Proverbs 30:9. 35
Proverbs 30:11. 208
Proverbs 30:17. 208
Proverbs 30:21. 203
Proverbs 30:23. 203
Proverbs 30:33. 91
Proverbs 31:1. 199
Proverbs 31:4. 46
Proverbs 31:5. 46
Proverbs 31:12. 201
Proverbs 31:13. 194
Proverbs 31:14. 194
Proverbs 31:15. . . . . 194, 199
Proverbs 31:16. . . . . 194, 198
Proverbs 31:17. 198
Proverbs 31:18. 198
Proverbs 31:19. 198
Proverbs 31:25. 198
Proverbs 31:26. . . . . 198, 199
Proverbs 31:27. . . . . 198, 275
Proverbs 31:28. 199

Ecclesiastes 1:9 386

Ecclesiastes 3:21 52
Ecclesiastes 4:9 386
Ecclesiastes 4:10 386
Ecclesiastes 4:13 13
Ecclesiastes 5:8 416
Ecclesiastes 5:18 31
Ecclesiastes 6:7 . . . . 28, 36
Ecclesiastes 7:1 . . . . 53, 297
Ecclesiastes 8:11 . . . . 103, 417
Ecclesiastes 9:9 289
Ecclesiastes 9:10 275
Ecclesiastes 10:1 . . . . 295, 304
Ecclesiastes 10:17 31
Ecclesiastes 11:9 15
Ecclesiastes 12:1 . . . . 4, 14, 206, 207
Ecclesiastes 12:7 . . . . 3, 52
Ecclesiastes 12:13 102
Ecclesiastes 12:14 . . . . 16, 102

Isaiah 1:2 263
Isaiah 1:3 263
Isaiah 1:11 315
Isaiah 1:20 268
Isaiah 3:5 210
Isaiah 5:11 45
Isaiah 5:22 46
Isaiah 5:23 46
Isaiah 6:8 143
Isaiah 8:21 22
Isaiah 9:6 421
Isaiah 10:12 242
Isaiah 11:6 25
Isaiah 11:7 25
Isaiah 13:11 242
Isaiah 14:12 . . . . 110, 259, 321, 354
Isaiah 14:13 . . . . 110, 259, 321, 354
Isaiah 14:14 . . . . 110, 259, 321, 354
Isaiah 14:15 110
Isaiah 24:21 242
Isaiah 26:16 251
Isaiah 26:21 242
Isaiah 27:1 242
Isaiah 28:7 46
Isaiah 29:8 25
Isaiah 30:1 258
Isaiah 30:9 258
Isaiah 32:1 149
Isaiah 32:3 149
Isaiah 32:4 149

Isaiah 32:5	148, 149
Isaiah 32:6	135, 148
Isaiah 32:7	148
Isaiah 32:8	148
Isaiah 33:14	139
Isaiah 39:1	411
Isaiah 39:2	411
Isaiah 39:3	411
Isaiah 39:4	411
Isaiah 39:5	411
Isaiah 39:6	411
Isaiah 39:7	411
Isaiah 41:13	237
Isaiah 42:8	314
Isaiah 44:6	158
Isaiah 46:4	4
Isaiah 46:9	183
Isaiah 46:10	183
Isaiah 46:12	261
Isaiah 48:4	266
Isaiah 49:15	199
Isaiah 50:5	267
Isaiah 51:12	63
Isaiah 51:13	63
Isaiah 53:1	173
Isaiah 55:8	264
Isaiah 55:9	264
Isaiah 56:12	45
Isaiah 59:2	329, 334
Isaiah 60:18	420
Isaiah 62:4	279, 287
Isaiah 64:6	347
Isaiah 65:2	260, 266
Isaiah 66:13	62, 199
Jeremiah 3:1	115
Jeremiah 3:25	68
Jeremiah 5:25	334
Jeremiah 5:31	128
Jeremiah 6:11	9
Jeremiah 6:19	315
Jeremiah 6:20	315
Jeremiah 7:19	67
Jeremiah 7:23	261
Jeremiah 7:24	261
Jeremiah 7:25	261
Jeremiah 7:26	261
Jeremiah 7:27	261
Jeremiah 7:28	261
Jeremiah 7:29	261
Jeremiah 9:17	54
Jeremiah 16:17	217
Jeremiah 17:5	269
Jeremiah 17:6	269
Jeremiah 17:7	269
Jeremiah 17:8	269
Jeremiah 17:9	233
Jeremiah 17:10	417
Jeremiah 17:23	258
Jeremiah 22:3	413
Jeremiah 22:18	49
Jeremiah 23:6	84
Jeremiah 23:23	15
Jeremiah 23:24	15, 417
Jeremiah 25:12	242
Jeremiah 29:13	71, 207
Jeremiah 29:14	71
Jeremiah 30:7	389
Jeremiah 31:15	59
Jeremiah 32:17	357
Jeremiah 32:19	365
Jeremiah 32:33	267
Jeremiah 33:3	236, 339
Jeremiah 33:11	324
Jeremiah 35:5	209
Jeremiah 35:6	209
Jeremiah 35:7	209
Jeremiah 35:8	209
Jeremiah 35:9	209
Jeremiah 35:10	209
Jeremiah 35:18	209
Jeremiah 35:19	209
Jeremiah 36:21	128, 216
Jeremiah 36:22	128, 216
Jeremiah 36:23	128, 216
Jeremiah 36:24	128, 216
Jeremiah 36:25	128, 216
Jeremiah 36:26	216
Jeremiah 42:5	155
Jeremiah 46:25	242
Lamentations 1:1	49
Lamentations 1:18	258
Lamentations 3:33	249
Ezekiel 2:3	266
Ezekiel 3:7	266
Ezekiel 7:23	409

Ezekiel 18:4	369
Ezekiel 20:38	268
Ezekiel 23:30	115
Ezekiel 28:14	110
Ezekiel 28:15	110
Ezekiel 35:11	107
Ezekiel 47:19	91
Ezekiel 48:28	91
Daniel 1:5	44
Daniel 1:8	37, 44, 301
Daniel 1:9	37, 301
Daniel 1:10	37
Daniel 1:11	37
Daniel 1:12	37
Daniel 1:13	37
Daniel 1:14	37
Daniel 1:15	37
Daniel 1:16	37
Daniel 1:17	37
Daniel 1:18	37, 235
Daniel 1:19	37, 235
Daniel 1:20	37, 235
Daniel 3:14	159
Daniel 3:15	159
Daniel 3:16	159
Daniel 3:17	159
Daniel 3:18	159
Daniel 3:19	159
Daniel 3:20	159
Daniel 3:21	159
Daniel 3:22	159
Daniel 3:23	159
Daniel 3:24	159
Daniel 3:25	159
Daniel 3:26	159
Daniel 3:27	159
Daniel 3:28	159
Daniel 3:29	159
Daniel 4:35	303
Daniel 5:18	411
Daniel 5:19	411
Daniel 6:1	362
Daniel 6:2	362
Daniel 6:3	301, 362
Daniel 6:4	362
Daniel 9:5	264
Daniel 9:7	67, 69
Daniel 9:8	69
Daniel 9:9	264
Daniel 9:25	173
Daniel 9:27	320
Hosea 4:11	44
Hosea 11:12	163
Hosea 12:2	242
Hosea 13:8	49
Hosea 13:16	255
Amos 3:3	282
Amos 3:10	411
Amos 3:12	25
Jonah 1:1	245
Jonah 1:2	245
Jonah 1:3	245
Jonah 1:15	314
Jonah 1:16	314
Jonah 1:17	245
Jonah 2:1	245
Jonah 2:2	245
Jonah 3:1	245
Jonah 3:2	245
Jonah 3:3	245
Jonah 3:4	409
Jonah 3:5	409
Jonah 3:6	409
Jonah 3:7	409
Jonah 3:8	409, 410
Jonah 3:9	409
Jonah 3:10	409
Micah 2:2	412
Micah 6:12	411
Micah 7:6	208
Nahum 1:2	146
Habakkuk 1:3	83
Habakkuk 2:15	41, 42
Haggai 2:8	369
Zechariah 7:11	267
Zechariah 8:4	4
Zechariah 13:7	160
Zechariah 14:1	232
Zechariah 14:19	247

Malachi 1:8	314
Malachi 1:14	314, 319
Malachi 2:2	268
Malachi 2:16	290, 415
Malachi 3:6	133
Malachi 3:10	150
Malachi 3:15	383
Matthew 1:6	170
Matthew 1:21	329
Matthew 2:1	401
Matthew 2:2	401
Matthew 2:9	401
Matthew 2:10	401
Matthew 2:11	401
Matthew 2:16	86, 110, 409
Matthew 2:23	42
Matthew 4:1	377, 383, 385
Matthew 4:2	377, 385
Matthew 4:3	377, 385
Matthew 4:4	385
Matthew 4:5	385
Matthew 4:6	385
Matthew 4:7	385
Matthew 4:8	321, 385
Matthew 4:9	321, 385
Matthew 4:10	321, 385
Matthew 4:11	385
Matthew 5:9	413
Matthew 5:32	283
Matthew 5:37	234
Matthew 6:2	132, 133, 139, 140, 141
Matthew 6:3	140
Matthew 6:4	140
Matthew 6:5	140, 141
Matthew 6:6	140
Matthew 6:7	140
Matthew 6:8	140, 218
Matthew 6:16	140, 141
Matthew 6:17	140
Matthew 6:18	140
Matthew 6:25	18
Matthew 6:26	26
Matthew 6:32	18
Matthew 6:34	4
Matthew 7:15	124, 140
Matthew 7:21	404
Matthew 7:22	404
Matthew 7:23	404
Matthew 8:5	52
Matthew 8:6	52
Matthew 8:7	52
Matthew 8:23	21
Matthew 8:24	21
Matthew 8:25	21
Matthew 8:26	21
Matthew 8:32	415
Matthew 9:12	47
Matthew 9:13	319
Matthew 9:36	143
Matthew 9:37	143
Matthew 9:38	143
Matthew 11:19	31
Matthew 12:19	83
Matthew 12:34	232
Matthew 12:36	365
Matthew 13:4	140
Matthew 13:19	140
Matthew 13:25	348
Matthew 15:2	391
Matthew 15:3	400
Matthew 15:4	165
Matthew 15:7	117, 134
Matthew 15:8	117, 134, 322
Matthew 15:9	117
Matthew 15:17	30
Matthew 15:18	30
Matthew 15:19	30
Matthew 15:26	338
Matthew 15:27	338
Matthew 15:36	27
Matthew 16:1	141
Matthew 16:2	141
Matthew 16:3	141
Matthew 16:21	70
Matthew 16:22	70
Matthew 16:23	70
Matthew 17:14	193
Matthew 17:15	193
Matthew 17:16	193
Matthew 17:17	193
Matthew 17:18	193
Matthew 18:6	206
Matthew 18:10	206
Matthew 18:14	206
Matthew 18:15	253
Matthew 18:16	253
Matthew 18:17	253

Matthew 19:3................ 280, 291
Matthew 19:4................ 280, 291
Matthew 19:5................ 280, 291
Matthew 19:6................ 283, 291
Matthew 19:7...................... 291
Matthew 19:8...................... 291
Matthew 19:9...................... 292
Matthew 19:14..................... 206
Matthew 20:8................ 360, 367
Matthew 21:15..................... 207
Matthew 22:1...................... 283
Matthew 22:2...................... 283
Matthew 22:3...................... 283
Matthew 22:4...................... 283
Matthew 22:5...................... 283
Matthew 22:6...................... 283
Matthew 22:7...................... 283
Matthew 22:8...................... 283
Matthew 22:9...................... 283
Matthew 22:10..................... 283
Matthew 22:11..................... 283
Matthew 22:12..................... 283
Matthew 22:13..................... 283
Matthew 22:18..................... 142
Matthew 23:5...................... 132
Matthew 23:15..................... 142
Matthew 23:23................ 143, 144
Matthew 23:24..................... 144
Matthew 23:27..................... 132
Matthew 23:28..................... 132
Matthew 24:3...................... 389
Matthew 24:4...................... 389
Matthew 24:5...................... 389
Matthew 24:6...................... 389
Matthew 24:7...................... 389
Matthew 24:8...................... 389
Matthew 24:9...................... 389
Matthew 24:10..................... 389
Matthew 24:11..................... 389
Matthew 24:12..................... 389
Matthew 24:13..................... 389
Matthew 24:45..................... 163
Matthew 24:51..................... 131
Matthew 25:23..................... 373
Matthew 25:46................ 239, 247
Matthew 26:14..................... 381
Matthew 26:15..................... 381
Matthew 26:16..................... 381
Matthew 26:31...................... 70
Matthew 26:32...................... 70
Matthew 26:33...................... 70
Matthew 26:34...................... 70
Matthew 26:35...................... 70
Matthew 26:36..................... 356
Matthew 26:37..................... 356
Matthew 26:38..................... 356
Matthew 26:39..................... 356
Matthew 26:40..................... 356
Matthew 26:41....... 356, 379, 380, 386
Matthew 26:42..................... 356
Matthew 26:43..................... 356
Matthew 26:44..................... 356
Matthew 26:45..................... 356
Matthew 26:46..................... 356
Matthew 26:53...................... 96
Matthew 26:62...................... 96
Matthew 26:63...................... 96
Matthew 27:3...................... 298
Matthew 27:4...................... 298
Matthew 27:5...................... 298
Matthew 27:12...................... 96
Matthew 27:13...................... 96
Matthew 27:14...................... 96
Matthew 27:18................ 107, 109
Matthew 27:34..................... 385
Matthew 27:39.................. 96, 385
Matthew 27:40.................. 96, 385
Matthew 27:41.................. 96, 385
Matthew 27:42.................. 96, 385
Matthew 27:43...................... 96
Matthew 27:44...................... 96
Matthew 27:62..................... 183
Matthew 27:63..................... 183
Matthew 27:64..................... 183
Matthew 27:65..................... 183
Matthew 27:66..................... 183
Matthew 28:1...................... 183
Matthew 28:2...................... 183
Matthew 28:3...................... 183
Matthew 28:4...................... 183
Matthew 28:5...................... 183
Matthew 28:6...................... 183

Mark 1:29......................... 160
Mark 1:30......................... 160
Mark 1:31......................... 160
Mark 1:32......................... 160
Mark 4:37......................... 160

Mark 4:38	160
Mark 4:39	160
Mark 4:40	160
Mark 4:41	160
Mark 6:31	270
Mark 6:34	215
Mark 6:35	160, 215
Mark 6:36	160, 215
Mark 6:37	160, 215, 216
Mark 6:38	160
Mark 6:39	160
Mark 6:40	160
Mark 6:41	160
Mark 6:42	160
Mark 6:43	160
Mark 6:44	160
Mark 7:1	118
Mark 7:2	118, 391
Mark 7:3	118, 391, 395, 396
Mark 7:4	118, 391, 395
Mark 7:5	118, 391, 395
Mark 7:6	118, 395
Mark 7:7	118, 395
Mark 7:8	118, 391, 393, 396, 400
Mark 7:9	118, 393, 396, 400
Mark 7:10	396
Mark 7:11	396
Mark 7:12	396
Mark 7:13	392, 393, 396, 400
Mark 7:21	100, 329
Mark 7:22	100, 329
Mark 7:23	100, 329
Mark 7:25	200
Mark 7:26	200
Mark 7:27	200
Mark 7:28	200
Mark 7:29	200
Mark 7:30	200
Mark 10:5	290
Mark 10:6	197
Mark 10:7	197
Mark 10:8	197
Mark 10:9	197, 283
Mark 10:43	85
Mark 10:44	85
Mark 10:45	85
Mark 12:41	151
Mark 12:42	151
Mark 12:43	151
Mark 12:44	151
Mark 14:9	297
Mark 14:27	160
Mark 14:29	160
Mark 14:30	160
Mark 14:31	160
Mark 16:1	196
Mark 16:2	196
Mark 16:3	196
Mark 16:15	270, 341
Luke 1:5	11, 284
Luke 1:6	11, 284
Luke 1:7	11
Luke 1:8	11
Luke 1:9	11
Luke 1:10	11
Luke 1:11	11
Luke 1:12	11
Luke 1:13	11, 245, 284
Luke 1:14	284
Luke 1:15	284
Luke 1:16	284
Luke 1:17	284
Luke 1:18	245
Luke 1:19	245
Luke 1:20	245
Luke 1:46	394
Luke 1:47	394
Luke 1:57	245
Luke 1:58	245
Luke 1:59	245
Luke 1:60	245
Luke 1:61	245
Luke 1:62	245
Luke 1:63	245
Luke 1:64	245
Luke 1:80	11
Luke 2:36	6
Luke 2:37	6
Luke 2:38	6
Luke 2:49	346
Luke 2:51	165, 208
Luke 2:52	16, 208
Luke 3:14	413
Luke 4:3	35
Luke 4:28	110
Luke 4:29	110
Luke 4:30	110

Luke 4:38 52	Luke 16:1 . . . . 362, 363
Luke 4:39 52	Luke 16:2 362
Luke 6:38 154	Luke 16:3 362
Luke 6:41 145	Luke 16:4 362
Luke 6:42 145	Luke 16:5 363
Luke 6:44 306	Luke 16:6 363
Luke 7:28 11	Luke 16:7 363
Luke 7:34 31	Luke 16:8 . . . . 363, 364
Luke 8:52 28	Luke 16:9 . . . . 363, 367
Luke 8:53 28	Luke 16:10 363
Luke 8:54 28	Luke 16:11 363
Luke 8:55 28	Luke 16:12 363
Luke 9:9 170	Luke 16:19 340
Luke 9:52 213	Luke 16:20 340
Luke 9:53 213	Luke 16:21 340
Luke 9:54 213	Luke 16:22 . . . . 335, 340
Luke 9:55 213	Luke 16:23 . . . . 52, 230, 340
Luke 9:56 213	Luke 16:24 340
Luke 10:30 412	Luke 16:25 340
Luke 10:38 297	Luke 16:26 340
Luke 10:39 297	Luke 16:27 340
Luke 10:40 297	Luke 16:28 340
Luke 10:41 . . . . 17, 18, 297	Luke 16:29 340
Luke 10:42 297	Luke 16:30 340
Luke 11:28 211	Luke 16:31 340
Luke 11:39 132	Luke 17:12 324
Luke 12:4 160	Luke 17:13 324
Luke 12:5 160	Luke 17:14 324
Luke 12:42 . . . . 361, 365	Luke 17:15 324
Luke 12:43 365	Luke 17:16 324
Luke 13:1 263	Luke 17:17 324
Luke 13:2 263	Luke 17:18 324
Luke 13:3 263	Luke 18:1 357
Luke 13:4 264	Luke 18:11 134
Luke 13:10 144	Luke 18:12 134
Luke 13:11 144	Luke 18:13 134
Luke 13:12 144	Luke 19:1 342
Luke 13:13 144	Luke 19:2 342
Luke 13:14 144	Luke 19:3 342
Luke 13:15 144	Luke 19:4 342
Luke 13:16 144	Luke 19:5 342
Luke 13:17 144	Luke 19:6 342
Luke 13:32 139	Luke 19:7 342
Luke 14:1 144	Luke 19:8 . . . . 338, 342
Luke 14:2 144	Luke 19:9 342
Luke 14:3 144	Luke 19:10 342
Luke 14:4 144	Luke 19:13 364
Luke 14:5 144	Luke 22:3 110
Luke 14:6 144	Luke 22:4 110

Luke 22:24	85
Luke 22:63	385
Luke 22:64	385
Luke 22:65	385
Luke 23:33	385
Luke 23:34	96, 385
Luke 23:39	241
Luke 23:40	241
Luke 23:41	241
Luke 23:43	335
Luke 24:29	28
Luke 24:30	28
Luke 24:36	29
Luke 24:37	29
Luke 24:38	29
Luke 24:39	29
Luke 24:40	29
Luke 24:41	29
Luke 24:42	29
Luke 24:43	29
John 1:1	303
John 1:3	18, 369
John 1:11	402
John 1:12	244
John 2:1	41, 283
John 2:2	41, 283
John 2:3	41
John 2:4	41
John 2:5	41
John 2:6	41
John 2:7	41
John 2:8	41
John 2:9	41
John 2:10	41
John 2:11	41
John 3:3	338
John 3:14	221
John 3:16	182, 313, 332
John 3:17	332
John 3:27	23, 112
John 3:36	334
John 4:15	338
John 4:16	283, 338
John 4:17	283, 338
John 4:18	283, 338
John 4:19	338
John 4:20	338
John 4:21	338
John 4:22	338
John 4:23	338
John 4:24	338
John 4:25	173, 338
John 4:26	338
John 4:28	338
John 4:29	338
John 4:46	52
John 4:47	52
John 5:15	402
John 5:16	402
John 5:17	402
John 5:18	402
John 5:24	338
John 6:9	209
John 6:11	27
John 6:26	36
John 6:28	404
John 6:29	404
John 8:29	372
John 8:44	385
John 9:4	348, 355
John 9:18	160
John 9:19	160
John 9:20	160
John 9:21	160
John 9:22	160
John 9:23	160
John 9:24	160
John 9:25	160
John 9:26	160
John 9:27	160
John 9:28	160
John 9:29	160
John 9:30	160
John 9:31	160
John 9:32	160
John 9:33	160
John 9:34	160
John 10:16	338
John 11:19	54
John 11:23	57
John 11:24	57
John 11:25	57
John 11:26	57
John 11:27	57
John 11:31	54
John 11:32	54
John 11:33	54

Reference	Pages
John 11:34	54
John 11:35	54
John 11:36	54
John 11:48	109
John 12:1	135, 297
John 12:2	135, 297
John 12:3	135, 297
John 12:4	135, 297
John 12:5	135, 297
John 12:6	135, 297
John 12:7	135, 297
John 12:8	135, 297
John 12:42	141
John 12:43	141
John 13:2	259, 378
John 13:13	85
John 13:14	85
John 13:15	85
John 13:16	85
John 13:17	85
John 13:30	155
John 14:1	340
John 14:2	340
John 14:3	340
John 14:6	116, 332, 403
John 14:15	330
John 14:16	63
John 14:17	63
John 14:23	330
John 14:26	62
John 14:27	19
John 15:24	79
John 15:25	79
John 16:13	353
John 16:33	214
John 17:17	116, 310
John 18:3	155
John 19:15	110, 216
John 19:16	110
John 19:26	7
John 19:27	7
John 21:22	399
John 21:23	399
Acts 1:8	230, 341
Acts 2:22	79
Acts 2:23	79
Acts 4:12	332, 336, 337
Acts 4:18	97
Acts 4:19	97
Acts 4:20	97
Acts 4:29	97
Acts 4:32	151, 231
Acts 4:34	151
Acts 4:36	299, 322
Acts 4:37	299, 322
Acts 5:1	322
Acts 5:2	322
Acts 5:3	63, 259, 322, 378
Acts 5:4	63, 322
Acts 5:5	322
Acts 5:6	322
Acts 5:7	322
Acts 5:8	322
Acts 5:9	322
Acts 5:10	322
Acts 5:11	322
Acts 5:18	237
Acts 5:19	237
Acts 5:20	237
Acts 5:21	237
Acts 5:27	97
Acts 5:28	97
Acts 5:29	97, 164, 202
Acts 5:34	183, 303
Acts 5:35	183
Acts 5:36	183
Acts 5:37	183
Acts 5:38	183, 323
Acts 5:39	183, 323
Acts 5:40	97, 323
Acts 5:41	97, 323
Acts 5:42	97, 323
Acts 6:1	219, 309
Acts 6:2	219, 309
Acts 6:3	219, 300, 309
Acts 6:4	219, 300
Acts 6:5	219, 300
Acts 7:23	11
Acts 7:25	94
Acts 7:51	255, 266
Acts 7:52	216, 266
Acts 7:53	266
Acts 7:54	128, 266
Acts 7:55	128, 266
Acts 7:56	128, 266
Acts 7:57	128, 170, 266
Acts 7:58	170, 266

Acts 7:59	170, 266
Acts 7:60	266
Acts 8:1	230
Acts 8:35	237
Acts 8:37	334
Acts 9:1	338
Acts 9:2	338
Acts 9:13	304
Acts 9:21	304
Acts 9:26	304
Acts 10:1	333
Acts 10:2	307, 333
Acts 10:3	333
Acts 10:4	333
Acts 10:5	333
Acts 10:6	333
Acts 10:22	298, 307
Acts 10:36	333
Acts 10:38	79, 333
Acts 10:39	110, 333
Acts 10:40	110, 333
Acts 10:41	110, 333
Acts 10:42	110, 333
Acts 10:43	333
Acts 11:13	333
Acts 11:14	333
Acts 11:22	299
Acts 11:23	299
Acts 11:24	299
Acts 11:25	299
Acts 11:26	299
Acts 11:27	299
Acts 11:28	299
Acts 11:29	299
Acts 11:30	299
Acts 12:1	170
Acts 12:2	170
Acts 12:21	350
Acts 12:22	350
Acts 12:23	350
Acts 13:1	93
Acts 13:2	93
Acts 13:3	93
Acts 13:4	93
Acts 13:13	306
Acts 13:36	14
Acts 13:38	334
Acts 13:39	334
Acts 13:42	110
Acts 13:43	110
Acts 13:44	110
Acts 13:45	110
Acts 13:50	89
Acts 14:1	89
Acts 14:2	89
Acts 14:5	89
Acts 14:6	89
Acts 14:7	89
Acts 14:19	89, 215
Acts 14:20	215
Acts 14:21	215
Acts 14:22	215
Acts 15:20	29
Acts 15:24	126
Acts 15:29	29
Acts 15:30	93
Acts 15:36	77, 92, 93, 299, 306
Acts 15:37	77, 92, 299, 306
Acts 15:38	77, 92, 299, 306
Acts 15:39	77, 83, 93, 299, 306
Acts 15:40	77, 93, 299, 306
Acts 15:41	77
Acts 16:1	192, 296, 297, 306
Acts 16:2	296, 297, 306
Acts 16:22	323
Acts 16:23	323
Acts 16:24	323
Acts 16:25	323, 333
Acts 16:26	333
Acts 16:27	333
Acts 16:28	333
Acts 16:29	333
Acts 16:30	333
Acts 16:31	333
Acts 16:32	237
Acts 17:1	111
Acts 17:2	111
Acts 17:3	111
Acts 17:4	111
Acts 17:5	111
Acts 17:6	111
Acts 17:7	111
Acts 17:8	111
Acts 17:9	111
Acts 17:10	124
Acts 17:11	124
Acts 17:24	316
Acts 17:25	316

Scripture Index

Acts 18:26 237
Acts 19:17 422
Acts 19:29 68
Acts 19:30 68
Acts 19:31 68
Acts 19:32 68
Acts 20:19 376
Acts 20:21 .... 337, 338
Acts 20:22 323
Acts 20:23 323
Acts 20:24 .... 323, 388
Acts 20:27 119
Acts 20:28 .... 119, 166
Acts 20:29 .... 119, 140
Acts 20:30 119
Acts 20:31 119
Acts 20:35 149
Acts 21:13 338
Acts 21:25 29
Acts 22:4 401
Acts 22:22 216
Acts 24:14 115
Acts 25:6 384
Acts 25:7 384
Acts 26:25 .... 343, 345
Acts 27:33 28
Acts 27:34 28
Acts 27:35 28
Acts 27:36 28
Acts 27:37 28
Acts 27:38 28

Romans 1:8 308
Romans 1:16 .... 237, 341
Romans 1:26 280
Romans 1:27 280
Romans 1:29 .... 107, 413
Romans 1:30 107
Romans 1:31 107
Romans 1:32 413
Romans 3:13 410
Romans 3:14 410
Romans 3:15 410
Romans 3:16 410
Romans 3:17 410
Romans 3:18 410
Romans 3:23 .... 331, 347
Romans 5:6 242
Romans 5:8 .... 242, 332
Romans 5:9 327
Romans 5:10 .... 242, 327, 332
Romans 5:12 331
Romans 5:19 331
Romans 6:12 45
Romans 6:22 45
Romans 6:23 .... 104, 216, 331, 347
Romans 8:9 63
Romans 8:23 327
Romans 8:28 .... 336, 388
Romans 8:35 339
Romans 8:36 339
Romans 8:37 339
Romans 8:38 339
Romans 8:39 339
Romans 10:1 402
Romans 10:2 402
Romans 10:3 .... 232, 402
Romans 10:4 402
Romans 10:9 .... 334, 337
Romans 10:10 334
Romans 10:13 .... 207, 334
Romans 10:16 173
Romans 10:17 341
Romans 11:2 173
Romans 11:13 365
Romans 12:1 .... 322, 324
Romans 12:3 .... 345, 351, 352, 354
Romans 12:6 150
Romans 12:7 150
Romans 12:8 150
Romans 12:15 .... 65, 112
Romans 12:17 137
Romans 12:18 413
Romans 13:1 166
Romans 13:2 166
Romans 13:11 .... 87, 327, 348
Romans 13:12 87
Romans 13:13 .... 87, 107
Romans 13:14 87
Romans 14:1 29
Romans 14:2 29
Romans 14:8 369
Romans 14:12 .... 16, 365, 370
Romans 14:14 29
Romans 14:17 .... 30, 301
Romans 14:18 301
Romans 14:21 47
Romans 15:1 65

Romans 15:4 63
Romans 15:20 97
Romans 15:25 149
Romans 15:26 149
Romans 15:30 97
Romans 16:17 . . . . 392, 405
Romans 16:18 . . . . 36, 125
Romans 16:19 . . . . 187, 308

1 Corinthians 1:18 327
1 Corinthians 3:1 . . . . 85, 113
1 Corinthians 3:2 . . . . 84, 85, 113
1 Corinthians 3:3 . . . . 84, 85, 113
1 Corinthians 3:4 . . . . 84, 85
1 Corinthians 3:11 373
1 Corinthians 3:12 373
1 Corinthians 3:13 373
1 Corinthians 3:14 373
1 Corinthians 3:15 373
1 Corinthians 3:16 44
1 Corinthians 3:17 44
1 Corinthians 3:19 136
1 Corinthians 4:1 . . . . 362, 365, 369
1 Corinthians 4:2 . . . . 361, 368
1 Corinthians 4:7 355
1 Corinthians 5:7 312
1 Corinthians 5:11 . . . . 33, 253, 405
1 Corinthians 5:12 253
1 Corinthians 5:13 253
1 Corinthians 6:20 368
1 Corinthians 7:1 . . . . 276, 285
1 Corinthians 7:2 285
1 Corinthians 7:3 285
1 Corinthians 7:4 285
1 Corinthians 7:5 . . . . 285, 286
1 Corinthians 7:6 285
1 Corinthians 7:7 285
1 Corinthians 7:8 285
1 Corinthians 7:9 285
1 Corinthians 7:10 . . . . 280, 288
1 Corinthians 7:11 . . . . 280, 288
1 Corinthians 7:12 . . . . 288, 292
1 Corinthians 7:13 . . . . 288, 293
1 Corinthians 7:14 288
1 Corinthians 7:15 288
1 Corinthians 7:16 288
1 Corinthians 7:27 291
1 Corinthians 7:28 289
1 Corinthians 7:29 348

1 Corinthians 7:39 282
1 Corinthians 9:16 365
1 Corinthians 9:17 . . 362, 365, 369, 372, 373
1 Corinthians 9:25 96
1 Corinthians 9:27 37
1 Corinthians 10:13 . . 276, 375, 385, 386
1 Corinthians 10:14 387
1 Corinthians 10:31 31
1 Corinthians 11:3 . . . . 190, 191
1 Corinthians 11:8 197
1 Corinthians 11:9 197
1 Corinthians 11:22 39
1 Corinthians 11:23 397
1 Corinthians 11:24 397
1 Corinthians 11:25 397
1 Corinthians 11:26 397
1 Corinthians 11:28 145
1 Corinthians 11:34 39
1 Corinthians 12:26 65
1 Corinthians 13:4 . . . . 112, 113
1 Corinthians 13:5 112
1 Corinthians 13:6 112
1 Corinthians 13:7 112
1 Corinthians 13:11 113
1 Corinthians 14:33 . . . . 70, 191
1 Corinthians 15:1 . . . . 329, 403
1 Corinthians 15:2 . . . . 329, 403
1 Corinthians 15:3 . . . . 313, 329, 403
1 Corinthians 15:4 . . . . 313, 329, 403
1 Corinthians 15:12 127
1 Corinthians 15:16 127
1 Corinthians 15:17 127
1 Corinthians 15:18 127
1 Corinthians 15:19 127
1 Corinthians 15:22 331
1 Corinthians 15:47 331
1 Corinthians 15:48 331
1 Corinthians 15:49 331
1 Corinthians 15:51 . . . . 3, 57, 340
1 Corinthians 15:52 . . . . 3, 57, 340
1 Corinthians 15:53 . . . . 3, 340
1 Corinthians 15:57 57
1 Corinthians 15:58 373
1 Corinthians 16:1 149
1 Corinthians 16:2 149
1 Corinthians 16:3 . . . . 147, 149
1 Corinthians 16:4 149

2 Corinthians 1:3 61	Galatians 1:14 .... 396, 401
2 Corinthians 1:4 .... 60, 61	Galatians 1:15 396
2 Corinthians 1:12 403	Galatians 1:16 396
2 Corinthians 5:8 .... 52, 230, 340	Galatians 2:16 .... 337, 403
2 Corinthians 5:10 365	Galatians 2:20 403
2 Corinthians 5:13 344	Galatians 2:21 403
2 Corinthians 5:17 337	Galatians 3:1 .... 121, 403
2 Corinthians 5:18 341	Galatians 3:2 121
2 Corinthians 5:20 236	Galatians 3:3 121
2 Corinthians 5:21 .... 313, 332	Galatians 3:10 403
2 Corinthians 6:14 .... 277, 281	Galatians 3:11 403
2 Corinthians 7:9 374	Galatians 3:12 403
2 Corinthians 7:10 374	Galatians 3:13 403
2 Corinthians 7:11 .... 17, 20, 374	Galatians 4:4 9
2 Corinthians 8:1 .... 151, 315	Galatians 4:26 287
2 Corinthians 8:2 .... 147, 151, 315	Galatians 5:2 375
2 Corinthians 8:3 .... 151, 315	Galatians 5:11 375
2 Corinthians 8:4 .... 151, 315	Galatians 5:12 375
2 Corinthians 8:5 315	Galatians 5:15 375
2 Corinthians 9:6 152	Galatians 5:17 380
2 Corinthians 9:7 152	Galatians 5:19 107
2 Corinthians 9:8 152	Galatians 5:20 107
2 Corinthians 9:9 152	Galatians 5:21 107
2 Corinthians 9:10 152	Galatians 5:22 .... 338, 418
2 Corinthians 9:11 152	Galatians 5:23 339
2 Corinthians 9:12 152	Galatians 5:24 339
2 Corinthians 9:13 .... 147, 152	Galatians 5:26 .... 23, 110
2 Corinthians 9:14 152	Galatians 6:1 252
2 Corinthians 9:15 152	Galatians 6:2 65
2 Corinthians 10:5 345	Galatians 6:6 231
2 Corinthians 10:17 347	Galatians 6:7 420
2 Corinthians 11:3 .... 278, 379	Galatians 6:14 355
2 Corinthians 11:13 124	Galatians 6:15 338
2 Corinthians 11:14 124	
2 Corinthians 11:15 124	Ephesians 1:6 66
2 Corinthians 11:23 .... 162, 388	Ephesians 2:1 327
2 Corinthians 11:24 .... 162, 388	Ephesians 2:5 .... 327, 337
2 Corinthians 11:25 .... 162, 388	Ephesians 2:8 .... 121, 327, 337, 396, 404
2 Corinthians 11:26 .... 162, 388	Ephesians 2:9 .... 121, 396, 404
2 Corinthians 11:27 .... 37, 162, 388	Ephesians 2:10 .... 341, 404
2 Corinthians 11:28 .... 162, 388	Ephesians 3:1 279
2 Corinthians 12:4 335	Ephesians 3:20 19
2 Corinthians 12:20 107	Ephesians 4:1 279
2 Corinthians 13:5 .... 145, 338	Ephesians 4:14 119
	Ephesians 4:22 338
Galatians 1:1 189	Ephesians 4:23 338
Galatians 1:8 69	Ephesians 4:24 338
Galatians 1:10 141	Ephesians 4:27 276
Galatians 1:13 .... 304, 396	Ephesians 4:28 412

Ephesians 4:32. . . . . 137, 289
Ephesians 5:2. 312
Ephesians 5:3. 113
Ephesians 5:11. 405
Ephesians 5:15. 348
Ephesians 5:16. 348
Ephesians 5:18. 43
Ephesians 5:20. 27
Ephesians 5:22. . . . . 191, 201
Ephesians 5:23. . . . . 191, 201
Ephesians 5:24. 202
Ephesians 5:25. . . . . 195, 202
Ephesians 5:33. 201
Ephesians 6:1. . . . . 165, 191, 208
Ephesians 6:2. . . . . 165, 208
Ephesians 6:4. . . . . 192, 205
Ephesians 6:8. 180
Ephesians 6:11. . . . . 380, 387
Ephesians 6:12. 380
Ephesians 6:17. 387
Ephesians 6:18. 380
Ephesians 6:20. 279

Philippians 1:3. 153
Philippians 1:12 230
Philippians 1:13 230
Philippians 1:14 230
Philippians 1:21 53
Philippians 1:23 53
Philippians 2:1. 94
Philippians 2:2. 94
Philippians 2:3. . . . . 94, 294
Philippians 2:4. 94
Philippians 2:5. 94
Philippians 2:6. 94
Philippians 2:7. . . . . 94, 303
Philippians 2:8. 94
Philippians 2:14 275
Philippians 2:19 . . . . 171, 297, 362
Philippians 2:20 . . . . . 171, 297, 307, 362
Philippians 2:21 . . . . . 171, 297, 307, 362
Philippians 2:22 . . . . . 171, 297, 307, 362
Philippians 2:23 362
Philippians 2:29 . . . . 295, 303
Philippians 3:7. 278
Philippians 3:8. 278
Philippians 3:9. 278
Philippians 3:10 278
Philippians 3:11 278

Philippians 3:18 35
Philippians 3:19 35
Philippians 3:21 340
Philippians 4:2. 87
Philippians 4:6. . . . . 4, 17, 18, 19, 52
Philippians 4:7. . . . . 19, 52
Philippians 4:8. 353
Philippians 4:14 231
Philippians 4:15 . . . . 153, 231
Philippians 4:16 153
Philippians 4:17 153
Philippians 4:18 316
Philippians 4:19 . . . . 4, 339

Colossians 1:1 308
Colossians 1:2 308
Colossians 1:3 308
Colossians 1:4 308
Colossians 1:25 369
Colossians 2:8 . . . . 121, 392, 402
Colossians 2:20 396
Colossians 2:21 396
Colossians 2:22 396
Colossians 3:8 232
Colossians 3:9 126
Colossians 3:14 112
Colossians 3:17 16
Colossians 3:18 190
Colossians 3:19 . . . . 190, 203
Colossians 3:20 . . 190, 209, 258, 330, 372
Colossians 3:21 190
Colossians 3:22 . . . . 132, 190
Colossians 3:23 132
Colossians 4:2 . . . . 357, 380
Colossians 4:7 306
Colossians 4:8 306
Colossians 4:9 306
Colossians 4:10 306
Colossians 4:11 306

1 Thessalonians 2:4. . . 362, 365, 369, 371
1 Thessalonians 2:13. 400
1 Thessalonians 3:5. . . . . 377, 378
1 Thessalonians 4:1. 372
1 Thessalonians 4:7. 276
1 Thessalonians 4:13. . . . . 54, 56, 389
1 Thessalonians 4:14. . . . . 57, 389
1 Thessalonians 4:15. . . . . 57, 389
1 Thessalonians 4:16. . . 57, 340, 389, 421

1 Thessalonians 4:17...57, 340, 389, 421
1 Thessalonians 4:18............57, 389
1 Thessalonians 5:6.......345, 346, 355
1 Thessalonians 5:7................345
1 Thessalonians 5:8...345, 346, 347, 356
1 Thessalonians 5:9............327, 389
1 Thessalonians 5:11.................64
1 Thessalonians 5:12.................64
1 Thessalonians 5:13.................65
1 Thessalonians 5:14.................65
1 Thessalonians 5:15.................65
1 Thessalonians 5:17...........236, 357
1 Thessalonians 5:22............47, 276
1 Thessalonians 5:23.................52

2 Thessalonians 1:7................242
2 Thessalonians 1:8................242
2 Thessalonians 1:9...........239, 242
2 Thessalonians 2:15. 392, 396, 397, 402, 404
2 Thessalonians 2:17................59
2 Thessalonians 3:6........392, 394, 404
2 Thessalonians 3:7.................12
2 Thessalonians 3:10...............147
2 Thessalonians 3:14...............253
2 Thessalonians 3:15...............253
2 Thessalonians 3:17...............302

1 Timothy 1:3.....................303
1 Timothy 1:11...............365, 369
1 Timothy 1:12...............347, 362
1 Timothy 1:13....................347
1 Timothy 1:14....................347
1 Timothy 1:15....................347
1 Timothy 1:20....................308
1 Timothy 2:1......................58
1 Timothy 2:2......................58
1 Timothy 2:4.....................207
1 Timothy 2:5.....................394
1 Timothy 2:9.....................346
1 Timothy 2:12....................196
1 Timothy 2:13....................196
1 Timothy 2:14....................196
1 Timothy 3:1.....................343
1 Timothy 3:2............343, 346, 352
1 Timothy 3:3.....................343
1 Timothy 3:4.....................343
1 Timothy 3:5...............343, 359
1 Timothy 3:6.....................343
1 Timothy 3:7.....................343
1 Timothy 3:11..........345, 346, 354
1 Timothy 4:1 29, 115, 118, 128, 282, 395
1 Timothy 4:2..............29, 118, 395
1 Timothy 4:3.........29, 118, 282, 395
1 Timothy 4:4............26, 28, 29, 395
1 Timothy 4:5.....................395
1 Timothy 4:6................129, 395
1 Timothy 4:7.....................395
1 Timothy 4:12.....................12
1 Timothy 5:8...............194, 275
1 Timothy 5:10....................199
1 Timothy 5:14..............199, 280
1 Timothy 5:23.....................47
1 Timothy 6:1.....................123
1 Timothy 6:3.....................405
1 Timothy 6:4.....................405
1 Timothy 6:5.....................405
1 Timothy 6:9................380, 381
1 Timothy 6:10....................387
1 Timothy 6:11....................387
1 Timothy 6:17.....................15
1 Timothy 6:18....................231

2 Timothy 1:5.......120, 192, 200, 307
2 Timothy 1:9.....................327
2 Timothy 1:13....................120
2 Timothy 1:16....................171
2 Timothy 1:17....................171
2 Timothy 1:18....................171
2 Timothy 2:2................14, 362
2 Timothy 2:3.....................356
2 Timothy 2:4.....................356
2 Timothy 2:15......119, 214, 328, 397
2 Timothy 2:17....................127
2 Timothy 2:18....................127
2 Timothy 2:22.................7, 387
2 Timothy 3:1........67, 211, 348, 405
2 Timothy 3:2............67, 211, 405
2 Timothy 3:3................67, 405
2 Timothy 3:4................67, 405
2 Timothy 3:5................67, 405
2 Timothy 3:12....................162
2 Timothy 3:13..........115, 124, 348
2 Timothy 3:14..........120, 124, 348
2 Timothy 3:15 .. 14, 120, 192, 200, 307, 346
2 Timothy 3:16..........117, 120, 240
2 Timothy 4:1......................14

Scripture Index

2 Timothy 4:2 . . . . 14, 128, 261, 395
2 Timothy 4:3 . . . . 14, 127, 261
2 Timothy 4:4 . . . . 14, 261, 395
2 Timothy 4:5 14
2 Timothy 4:6 . . . . 14, 162, 170, 298
2 Timothy 4:7 . . . . 14, 162, 298, 388
2 Timothy 4:8 14
2 Timothy 4:11 306
2 Timothy 4:14 308
2 Timothy 4:16 157
2 Timothy 4:17 157

Titus 1:2 . . . . 117, 150, 340
Titus 1:3 . . . . 365, 369
Titus 1:5 303
Titus 1:6 343
Titus 1:7 . . . . 343, 359, 370
Titus 1:8 . . . . 343, 345, 346
Titus 1:9 . . . . 120, 343
Titus 1:11 126
Titus 1:13 395
Titus 1:14 394
Titus 2:1 . . . . 6, 345
Titus 2:2 . . . . 6, 345, 346, 354
Titus 2:3 . . . . 6, 275, 345
Titus 2:4 . . . . 6, 200, 275, 346
Titus 2:5 . . . . 6, 123, 199, 202, 275
Titus 2:6 . . . . 6, 275, 346, 351, 352
Titus 2:7 . . . . 6, 12, 275
Titus 2:8 . . . . 6, 275
Titus 2:9 6
Titus 2:10 6
Titus 2:11 . . . . 6, 347
Titus 2:12 . . . . 346, 347, 353
Titus 2:14 341
Titus 3:1 168
Titus 3:2 168
Titus 3:3 113
Titus 3:4 330
Titus 3:5 . . . . 327, 330, 332, 337, 404
Titus 3:6 . . . . 330, 404
Titus 3:7 404
Titus 3:8 . . . . 97, 404
Titus 3:9 . . . . 75, 97, 98
Titus 3:10 116
Titus 3:11 116

Philemon 6 236
Philemon 9 12
Philemon 24 306

Hebrews 2:9 303
Hebrews 2:17 383
Hebrews 2:18 . . . . 383, 387
Hebrews 3:12 292
Hebrews 3:13 292
Hebrews 4:8 173
Hebrews 4:14 383
Hebrews 4:15 . . . . 383, 384, 385
Hebrews 4:16 387
Hebrews 5:14 243
Hebrews 6:10 . . . . 150, 180
Hebrews 6:12 275
Hebrews 9:11 337
Hebrews 9:12 337
Hebrews 9:13 337
Hebrews 9:14 337
Hebrews 9:15 335
Hebrews 9:16 335
Hebrews 9:17 335
Hebrews 9:22 312
Hebrews 10:4 312
Hebrews 10:25 397
Hebrews 10:29 239
Hebrews 10:39 327
Hebrews 11:1 . . . . 298, 299
Hebrews 11:2 . . . . 298, 299
Hebrews 11:5 372
Hebrews 11:6 388
Hebrews 11:13 336
Hebrews 11:25 388
Hebrews 11:32 161
Hebrews 11:33 161
Hebrews 11:34 . . . . 161, 407
Hebrews 11:35 161
Hebrews 11:36 161
Hebrews 11:37 161
Hebrews 11:38 161
Hebrews 11:39 299
Hebrews 12:2 388
Hebrews 12:6 . . . . 243, 244, 248
Hebrews 12:7 . . . . 243, 244
Hebrews 12:8 . . . . 243, 244
Hebrews 12:10 . . . . 245, 251
Hebrews 12:11 249
Hebrews 12:17 17
Hebrews 13:4 285
Hebrews 13:5 . . . . 4, 23, 112, 156, 174

Hebrews 13:6 160
Hebrews 13:7 166
Hebrews 13:9 119
Hebrews 13:15 . . . . . 6, 315, 317, 324, 325
Hebrews 13:16 . . . . 231, 316, 324
Hebrews 13:17 58

James 1:2 . . . . 376, 387, 388
James 1:3 . . . . 376, 387
James 1:4 388
James 1:5 . . . . 136, 147, 153
James 1:13 . . . . 41, 375, 377, 378
James 1:14 . . . . 378, 379
James 1:15 378
James 1:17 . . . . 23, 61, 112
James 1:22 208
James 3:13 95
James 3:14 95
James 3:15 . . . . 95, 186
James 3:16 . . . . 67, 71, 75, 95
James 3:17 . . . . 136, 187
James 4:5 113
James 4:7 387
James 4:10 353
James 5:11 228

1 Peter 1:6 220
1 Peter 1:13 . . . . 344, 351, 352
1 Peter 1:18   327, 332, 391, 392, 396, 403
1 Peter 1:19 . . . . 327, 332, 396
1 Peter 1:20 332
1 Peter 1:23 . . . . 328, 337
1 Peter 2:1 . . . . 99, 102, 131, 132, 144
1 Peter 2:2 . . . . 102, 113, 144, 243
1 Peter 2:3 144
1 Peter 2:5 . . . . 313, 323, 324
1 Peter 2:13 168
1 Peter 2:14 168
1 Peter 2:17 166
1 Peter 2:18 168
1 Peter 2:21 . . . . 96, 385
1 Peter 2:22 . . . . 96, 385
1 Peter 2:23 . . . . 96, 385
1 Peter 3:1 . . . . 202, 403
1 Peter 3:2 202
1 Peter 3:3 202
1 Peter 3:4 . . . . 202, 203
1 Peter 3:6 201
1 Peter 3:7 195

1 Peter 3:18 313
1 Peter 3:20 417
1 Peter 4:7 . . . . 346, 348, 356
1 Peter 4:8 112
1 Peter 4:10 . . . . 359, 360
1 Peter 4:12 . . . . 184, 214
1 Peter 4:13 184
1 Peter 4:14 184
1 Peter 4:15 184
1 Peter 4:16 184
1 Peter 5:6 353
1 Peter 5:7 . . . . 17, 19, 20, 207, 218
1 Peter 5:8 . . 22, 276, 343, 345, 346, 349,
    354, 355, 356, 386
1 Peter 5:9 386

2 Peter 1:5 112
2 Peter 1:6 112
2 Peter 1:7 112
2 Peter 1:21 117
2 Peter 2:1 . . . . 115, 129
2 Peter 2:2 129
2 Peter 2:5 417
2 Peter 2:9 . . . . 239, 276, 387
2 Peter 3:9 . . . . 71, 156, 341, 418
2 Peter 3:15 129
2 Peter 3:16 . . . . 47, 129
2 Peter 3:17 . . . . 129, 282
2 Peter 3:18 129

1 John 1:7. 326
1 John 1:8. 30
1 John 1:9. 30
1 John 1:10. 30
1 John 2:16. . . . . 379, 384
1 John 2:25. 340
1 John 2:26. 115
1 John 2:28. 365
1 John 3:2. . . . . 243, 303, 340
1 John 3:5. 332
1 John 3:11. 109
1 John 3:12. 109
1 John 3:23. 404
1 John 4:4. 276
1 John 5:7. 63
1 John 5:11. . . . . 71, 340
1 John 5:12. . . . . 71, 340
1 John 5:13. . . . . 71, 340
1 John 5:14. 339

Scripture Index

1 John 5:15 339

2 John 7 405
2 John 9 405
2 John 10 405

3 John 1 12
3 John 12 307

Revelation 1:5 332
Revelation 1:9 230
Revelation 1:10 232
Revelation 1:19 230
Revelation 2:10 158
Revelation 2:20 311
Revelation 3:10 . . . . 375, 388
Revelation 3:14 155
Revelation 3:19 . 239, 244, 245, 248, 250, 251
Revelation 4:11 197
Revelation 6:9 389
Revelation 6:10 389
Revelation 6:11 389
Revelation 6:12 389
Revelation 6:13 389
Revelation 6:14 389
Revelation 6:15 389
Revelation 6:16 389
Revelation 6:17 389
Revelation 17:5 84
Revelation 17:6 415
Revelation 18:21 . . . . 407, 415
Revelation 19:9 40
Revelation 19:11 155
Revelation 21:2 287
Revelation 21:3 421
Revelation 21:4 . . . . 340, 421
Revelation 21:5 155
Revelation 21:7 242
Revelation 21:8 242
Revelation 21:9 . . . . 279, 287
Revelation 21:10 . . . . 279, 287
Revelation 22:6 155
Revelation 22:12 373